Barcode in the back cover

# THE JAPANESE ECONOMY

*Also by Victor Argy*

AUSTRALIAN MACROECONOMIC POLICY IN A CHANGING
  WORLD ENVIRONMENT
CHOICE OF EXCHANGE RATE REGIME-CHALLENGE FOR
  SMALLER COUNTRIES *(edited with Paul De Grauwe)*
INFLATION AND UNEMPLOYMENT: Theory, Experience
  and Policy Making *(edited with John Neville)*
INTERNATIONAL MACROECONOMICS
THE POSTWAR INTERNATIONAL MONEY CRISIS

*Also by Leslie Stein*

ECONOMIC REALITIES IN POOR COUNTRIES
THE GROWTH OF EAST AFRICAN EXPORTS AND THEIR
  EFFECT ON ECONOMIC DEVELOPMENT
TRADE AND STRUCTURAL CHANGE

# The Japanese Economy

Victor Argy
*Macquarie University, Sydney*

and

Leslie Stein
*Macquarie University, Sydney*

NEW YORK UNIVERSITY PRESS
Washington Square, New York

© Renate Argy and Leslie Stein 1997

First published in the U.S.A. in 1997 by
NEW YORK UNIVERSITY PRESS
Washington Square
New York, N.Y. 10003

This book is printed on paper suitable for recycling and
made from fully managed and sustained forest sources.

Library of Congress Cataloging-in-Publication Data
Argy, Victor E.
The Japanese economy / by Victor Argy and Leslie Stein.
p.   cm.
Includes bibliographical references and index.
ISBN 0–8147–0659–2
1. Japan—Economic conditions—1989–   2. Industrial policy—Japan.
3. Japan—Foreign economic relations.   I. Stein, Leslie.
II. Title.
HC462.95.A724   1996
330.952'04—dc20                          96–21387
                                         CIP

Printed in Great Britain

To our wives Renate and Clara, with love and appreciation

# Contents

# List of Tables

# List of Figures

# Glossary

*Amakudari*: Descent from heaven, process of coopting retired civil servants

*Ansei*: Peace or quiet and rest

*Barakumin*: An inferior caste whose members are associated with dealings in meat and leather

*Dai-ten-ho*: Large retail store law

*Daimyō*: Feudal lord

*Edo period*: 1603–1867

*Gensaki*: Second-hand bond market

*Itai-Itai disease*: Cadmium poisoning (ouch ouch disease)

*Juko*: Cram college for entry into high school

*Kanban*: Production coupon or just in time production method

*Keidanren*: Federation of Economic Organizations

*Keiretsu*: An inter-firm alliance

*Keiretsuka*: Vertical activity in distribution

*Meiji period*: 1868–1911

*Minamata disease*: Organic mercury poisoning

*Nikkeiran*: Federation of industrial employers

*Nokyo*: Agricultural cooperative organization

*Norinchukin Bank*: Agricultural bank

*Rengo*: Trade union federation

*Ringi-sei*: Group decision making

*Ronin*: Masterless samurai

*Samurai*: Warrior class

*Sarakin*: Shark loans

*Sensei*: teacher/professor/doctor

*Shinkin Bank*: Bank based on credit cooperatives

*Shintoism*: National religion of Japan

*Shōgun*: Ruler

*Shukko*: Practice of shunting off personnel to a subsidiary

*Shunto*: Annual spring wage offensive

*Sogo Bank*: Bank serving small scale enterprise

*Sogo Byoin*: General hospital

*Sogo-Shosha*: Large trading company

*Sokaiya*: Company meeting gangsters

*Yobiko*: Cram college for entry into university

*Zaibatsu*: Pre-second world war industrial and finance grouping
*Zenchu*: Central union of Nokyo
*Zenro-ren*: Pro-communist trade union body
*Zoku*: Senior politician specializing in affairs of a particular sector

# Preface

In this book we have endeavoured to provide a broad account of the nature of the Japanese economy. We have set out to cover just about every major aspect, including industrial policy, the Japanese firm, agriculture, social services, and so on, so that the reader may gain an insight into and understanding of the workings of the Japanese economy in its entirety. Each topic is discussed in the context of its development and change throughout the entire postwar period, although contemporary events are by no means ignored. We have placed much emphasis in laying out the nature of Japan's various economic institutions and have attached some weight to social, political and other factors. We have tried to approach matters objectively and dispassionately. With the book intended to be used as a primer, we have not presented the reader with a tendentious monograph underlaid with our own hypotheses. Such a work may best be read after the ABC of the Japanese economy is first learnt. It is mainly for the latter purpose that this book has been written.

Our efforts have been directed towards catering for the needs of tertiary students. In our own university, we have successfully used the manuscript as the basis for lectures in both our second and third year undergraduate courses concerned with the Japanese economy. Student responses have been most gratifying and positive feedback has been incorporated into the text.

We also anticipate that this book will appeal to the general educated reader. In that light, we have avoided, where possible, the use of abstruse economic terminology and mathematics. Where economic concepts are utilized, they have generally been clarified.

My late colleague and dear friend Victor Argy and I set out to write this book at the beginning of 1992. In July 1993 Victor Argy suddenly passed away; from that time I continued to work on the manuscript alone. This does not mean that I had become the sole author. Far from it. Victor had in fact conceived the idea of the book in the first place and had managed to draft a number of chapters before his untimely death. We had spent countless hours together discussing the work and as I put the book together I not only had recourse to Victor's notes but his voice kept ringing in my head. Our joint efforts have persisted and this book is truly the fruit of a full partnership.

Numerous people have provided assistance in various stages of the book's preparation. Among those are Renate Argy (Victor's widow) who at the very time of her bereavement made sure that all of Victor's documents were transferred to me. Professor Mitsuaki Okabe had carefully read and commented on the chapter on industrial policy, as did Mr Louis Haddad. I had also received beneficial advice when presenting segments of the book at staff seminars at the University of Sydney, the Australian National University and at a seminar of the Institute for Monetary and Economic Studies of the Bank of Japan. The Bank of Japan invited me to Tokyo for a three-month period as part of its visiting scholars programme. It was there that I researched on and drafted the chapter on Japanese foreign investment. I am also grateful to Toyota Finance Ltd (Australia) for a scholarship to investigate structural change in Japan.

My family have been very supportive. My wife, Clara and my son Mark volunteered to proofread various chapters, while my daughter Karen and son-in-law Craig were used as sounding boards over weekly dinners. Finally, I would like to thank Ms Debbie Jeffery for her competent and careful secretarial assistance and Mrs Jane Oldroyd for doing the graphics.

LESLIE STEIN
Macquarie University
Sydney, Australia

# Part I

# The Macroeconomy

# 1 Macro Foundations of the Japanese Economy

## INTRODUCTION

This chapter scans some of the highlights of Japan's modern economic history. It does not purport to be anything other than a brief synopsis, for its major objective is simply to draw to the reader's attention, the obvious fact, that the groundwork for current economic activity is embedded in the past. The narrative relating to the prewar era in particular, represents more of a list of landmark events than an attempt to provide a fully coherent account of the earlier stages of Japan's economic development.

As a means of providing a broad backdrop to the way in which the economy had progressed, the chapter begins with a short socio-political history. We then proceed to assess economic developments within the Edo period (1603–1867) and during the Meiji restoration (1868–1912). Thereafter, we touch on the First World War, the interwar period and finally, we move on to postwar trends.

## JAPAN'S SOCIO-POLITICAL HISTORY IN A NUTSHELL

In very early days, in fact as far back as the fifth century, most of Japan was governed by the imperial family but between the fifteenth and seventeenth centuries, the country was racked by a succession of civil wars. These conflicts were eventually subdued with the victory in 1600 of Tokugawa Ieyasu, who soon designated himself shōgun, unified the country and enforced a general peace. The Tokugawa family ruled for some 250 years and for most of that time, Japan was effectively isolated from the rest of the world. Within the sixteenth century, Europeans had partially entered Japan and began proselytizing the Japanese. However, the Japanese authorities soon adopted a hostile stance against both the missionaries and their converts and by 1640 almost all foreigners were expelled.

The period of dominance of the Tokugawa family is known as the

Edo period by virtue of the fact that the shōgun resided in Edo (now Tokyo). Formally, the shōgun's power was derived from the Emperor, who dwelled in Kyoto, but in practice, the Emperor's role was merely symbolic.

The Tokugawa Shogunate had direct control of about a quarter of the land. The rest was divided into 270 domains each headed by a daimyō who in turn remained subordinate to each successive shōgun. As one of the many ruses employed to preserve his authority, the shōgun insisted that some members of each daimyō family stayed in Edo where essentially they served as hostages.

The Tokugawa reign was a feudalistic one in which the population was divided into four distinct categories, which, in order of importance were: the samurai or warrior class (this group included the daimyō and the run of the mill soldier); the peasantry; the artisans and the merchants. Rules governing the social behaviour of each class which related to mode of dress and public bearing were enforced. However, although the merchants were ranked as the lowest order, many were wealthy and lent money to the daimyōs, which meant that their actual status did not always strictly conform to their formal one.

By the nineteenth century the Tokugawa regime had came under increasing pressures: domestic challenges; economic difficulties and continuing concerns over great power intrusions and intentions. A succession of Western ships (Russian, British and American) called into Japan ostensibly to obtain supplies. The authorities sought to discourage such visits but in 1853 matters finally came to a head, when with a show of strength, four American ships under Commodore Perry appeared in Tokyo Bay demanding commercial access to Japan's economy. After some initial vacillation, Japan acceded to the American requests by signing a treaty in 1854 opening up the ports of Shimoda and Hakodate to American ships. Similar agreements were then reached with the British, Dutch and Russians.

To a large extent, the sudden appearance of Western powers capable of dictating terms to an emasculated Japan, helped to galvanize forces into action which sought the demise of the Tokugawa regime and its replacement by a more enlightened one capable of ushering Japan into the twentieth century. After a brief struggle, the regime collapsed and the Emperor was notionally restored to power in 1868 by the inauguration of the Meiji regime. However, as before, real power was vested elsewhere, this time in a coalition of lower rung samurai, public officials, the more prosperous farmers and petty traders, all of whom took upon themselves the destiny of modernizing Japan. With most of the leadership consisting of 'the more able and independent members of the former ruling class', [Lockwood 1954:11] the Meiji Restoration was clearly not in the mould of a traditional middle class revolt against feudalism.

Where the new regime parted from the old was in its adoption of Western practices, both economic and social. Impressed with and envious of Western achievements, the government dispatched hoards of students abroad to investigate and assimilate western science and technology as well as alternative political institutions and methods of economic management. In addition, scores of foreign experts were brought into Japan to provide advice, oversee new projects and impart their ideas to aspiring Japanese technicians, managers and public officials ever eager to acquire new knowledge.

Although some of the new rulers' reforms accorded with Western liberal values, they were almost all motivated by a desire to industrialize Japan so that it would have the military capability to ensure its independence. Their slogan was 'a rich country and a strong army'. By the late nineteenth century conscripts issued with modern weaponry began undergoing intensive training.

The first major confrontation with a foreign power occurred in 1894 when Japan went to war with China over the control of Korea. With victory in her grasp Japan not only secured lordship over Korea but also obtained other territorial concessions. However, these territorial gains were contested by Russia, Germany and France who demanded that Japan cede Port Arthur to Russia.

After entering into an alliance with Britain in 1902, Japan felt emboldened to challenge Russia and in 1904 Japan and Russia were at war, once again, over the control of Korea. With the outcome in Japan's favour, Korea was subsequently annexed in 1910.

Japan's extraordinary military adventures stunned the world. From the West's point of view Japan had become a force to be reckoned with; while throughout much of Asia she became an object of admiration.

In the 1920s Manchuria, in China, became the focus of considerable Japanese military activity. The area aroused Japanese interest on account of its mineral resources and in 1931, after a series of incidents, the whole of Manchuria was occupied by Japan. War followed between China and Japan. In 1932 Japan proclaimed the independence of Manchuria under the leadership of Pu Yi, the last Chinese emperor. In May of that same year, the Japanese Prime Minister Inukai was assassinated by military extremists, effectively terminating civilian rule.

Increasingly, the US opposed Japan's confrontation with China. US feelings were hardened when, after France was defeated in 1940, Japan concluded a Tripartite Pact with Germany and Italy. Soon thereafter, the US imposed a series of economic sanctions on Japan and in October 1941, Japan launched a surprise attack on Pearl Harbor provoking a war with America which ended in Japan's defeat in August 1945.

## ECONOMIC EVENTS

### The Edo Period (1603–1867)

From an economic perspective, these years had both positive and negative aspects and there is some debate over the degree to which the period contributed to Japan's economic take-off in the second half of the nineteenth century. A negative position has been upheld by Maddison who has argued that the Tokugawa regime stunted growth by imposing restrictions on internal trade, by regulating workshop production through the medium of guilds, by prescribing crop mixes to farmers and by generally hindering social mobility [Maddison 1969:6–7]. On the other hand, Nakamura believes that 'the origins of Japan's spectacular growth are to be found in this period' [Nakamura 1985:1].

What were the more positive economic aspects of this period? Nakamura suggests that national markets in some products (such as salt, cotton and cloth) had already been well established in the Edo era. Commercial activity was extensive, urban centres developed and trade between the regions became increasingly important. Class mobility was not as rigid as is sometimes thought: Many farmers also carried out work as artisans, the richer merchants being able to buy, or marry, their way into the samurai class. The infrastructure (transport, coastal shipping) was well advanced for the period. Education had attained levels which were superior to those of Britain. (In 1875 some 54 per cent of males had completed elementary school – a much higher percentage than in Britain.) A skilled and adaptable bureaucracy had come into existence and in the last ten years of the Edo period (1858–68) after the opening up to and confrontation with the West, there was a burst of economic activity. Furthermore, on the agricultural front, some technological improvements were beginning to be applied and food output yields had begun to expand.

Despite this positive legacy, Japan in the Edo period 'was a feudalistic agricultural-based country with most of her population at a little

above the subsistence level'. By contrast, at the start of their industrialization processes, per capita incomes in some western nations were
on average five times greater than that of Japan in 1868 [Nakamura
1985:4].

## Economic Transformation in the Meiji and Post-Meiji Era (1869–1938)

### Meiji Reforms

The first 15–20 years saw Japan embark on what can only be described
as a stunning transformation of its socio-economic structure. Here we
single out the following:

### The Abolition of the Class System
As part of the Meiji regime's modernization drive, traditional social
rankings and feudal proprietary rights were abolished, leaving society
with only two social groupings: a small aristocracy and an undifferentiated
mass of commoners. Freedom of movement both for individuals and
general merchandise was guaranteed. Farmers were given full crop
growing discretion and had access to land property rights, whereas
entry into new occupations became universally accessible, subject to
non-discriminatory conditions. These changes, combined with reforms
in the education system, paved the way for a remarkable degree of
social mobility and the establishment of a largely merit based hierarchy.

### The Overhaul of the Education System
A Ministry of Education was created in 1871 and education was standardized throughout the country. In 1886, four years of schooling were
required and by 1907, this was increased to six years.

### Monetary Reforms
Critical innovations were introduced in the financial and fiscal arena.
A key event on the monetary front was the establishment in 1882 of a
central bank (The Bank of Japan) with sole powers to issue banknotes,
and in general, the growth of banking was given top priority. To enable capital to be raised on a scale larger than was possible by one
family, the joint stock company was created. As early as 1873 joint
stock companies were represented in transportation, finance, land rec-
lamation and the silk industry.

*Government Sponsored Industrialization*

The government assumed a leading role in the industrialization process by establishing an extensive industrial infrastructure, including a national post and telegraph network, a railway system and a steam vessel shipping service. Furthermore, given an initial dearth of private entrepreneurial resources, the government itself set up new industries in a sequence which complied with national priorities. As Allen noted, 'there was scarcely any important Japanese industry of the Western type during the latter decades of the nineteenth century which did not owe its establishment to state initiative' [G.C. Allen as quoted by Lockwood 1954:14]. Under state patronage, the first modern silk filature was opened in 1870. Other industries founded included cotton spinning, iron and steel, cement, sugar, beer, glass and a variety of chemicals. Mining was also energetically pursued, particularly in coal and copper. Many enterprises were both state financed and operated, but, from around 1880, as private individuals increasingly became willing and able to perform entrepreneurial functions and as many of the state run industries were beginning to record low profit margins, the bulk of state owned enterprises were privatized. Most of such corporations were taken over by former daimyō and samurai who had acquired capital funds in return for renouncing annual stipends which the new regime was initially prepared to provide. Funds received (given in the form of bonds) were equivalent to four to six years of traditional annual payments. The ex-samurai among the new rich 'possessed a strong national consciousness', which motivated them when investing to do so on the basis of social and not necessarily personal interests [Morishima 1982:92].

The divestment of public companies did not imply that henceforth unbridled market forces were to be given full sway. In fact, strategic industries remained under close government supervision and were assisted by a combination of tariffs and subsidies.

Most of the privatized enterprises became economically sound institutions and formed the embryos for the birth of giant industrial conglomerates, known as zaibatsu. From the outset, these firms continued to retain close links to the government and generally heeded official advice. Their transformation into industrial colossuses was facilitated by the complete absence of any anti-trust legislation or other impediments against monopolization. Perhaps this was just as well, for the zaibatsu, which enjoyed large scale production economies, contributed greatly to Japan's capital formation.

## The Contribution of Agriculture

Between 1880 and 1920, agricultural output rose at a faster pace than the population, with the respective annual growth rates being 1.8 and 1.2 per cent [Hayami 1988:29]. This enabled industrial workers to be recruited from the countryside without imposing unduly large food import bills on the state. Of no less importance, the agricultural sector had also provided both material inputs and markets for Japan's budding industrial complex and contributed to the country's export effort, especially in the output of raw silk.

In the initial strides towards industrialization, the agricultural sector made an invaluable contribution to tax revenues. Thanks to the 1873 land tax reform which determined rural tax rates in accordance with newly assessed land values, the land tax 'furnished over 90% of State tax revenues in the early seventies. Twenty years later it still accounted for as much as 60%' [Lockwood 1954:17]. With the advent of the twentieth century, the average farmer paid taxes amounting to 28 per cent of his income compared to a 14 per cent share for the average merchant and industrialist [26].

## Opening Up to World Trade

Throughout the entire Meiji era silk was Japan's dominant export commodity. Output of raw silk rose from 7.5 million pounds in 1883–93 to 27.9 million pounds in 1909–13. In the latter period three quarters of the quantity produced was exported, enabling Japan to surpass China and her European competitors and to become America's major supplier [Lockwood 1954:27]. Other early export goods included tea, rice, copper, coal and miscellaneous handicrafts such as pottery, paper and lacquer. Eventually, the cotton textile industry rose to prominence, taking second place to silk. The industrial revolutions in Europe and North America were largely based on textile manufacturing and in this respect, Japan was no exception. In the immediate pre-World War I years, the textile industry employed around 40 per cent of the manufacturing work force.[1] (Most of the remaining workers were situated in traditional occupations, with the newer large scale enterprises in fields such as metal products, machinery and chemicals employing only a small fraction of industrial labour.) By 1913, Japan had captured a quarter of the world trade in yarn and was already making strong inroads into the exportation of cotton cloth. In 1913, combining silk and cotton, Japan's textile industry accounted for approximately 60 per cent of total exports.

*1912–1938*

The First World War provided a welcome boost to the Japanese economy. The Allies began to place large orders in Japan for munitions and other products, whereas many Asian countries who met with difficulties in obtaining manufactures from Europe, turned to Japan to fill part of the ever widening gap. Having lost access to German drugs, fertilizers and dyestuffs, Japan's chemical industry greatly expanded. Of no less significance, its iron and steel making capacity was rapidly enhanced, with the number of the country's steel mills rising from 21 in 1913 to 208 by 1918 [Sheridan 1993:98].

After the war, Japan was able to build on its enriched industrial experience and growing technical capabilities. In the early 1920s, in the field of engineering it had acquired the 'ability to manufacture electrical apparatus, railway equipment, bicycles, and industrial machinery of relatively simple and standard designs' [Lockwood 1954:48].

At the beginning of the 1930s, while the Western industrial world languished in the midst of one its worst and most crippling depressions, the Japanese, under the leadership of its astute finance minister, Mr Takahashi, pre-empted the universal adoption of Keynesian policies by resorting to widescale deficit financing, largely in pursuit of an armaments' policy. The armament process yielded significant economic results, chief among which was the mushrooming of the metallurgical, machinery and chemical industries. Between 1930 and 1936, the output of producer goods increased by 83 per cent, enabling Japan to be almost self-reliant in capital good manufacturing [71].

During the 1930s, the economy was geared for the waging of war. To this end a number of legislative and administrative innovations were introduced. These included the Vital Industries Control Law (1931), The Oil Industry Law (1934), the Munitions Industry Mobilization Law, Emergency Provisions Relating to Imports and Exports and the Law for the Emergency Procurement of Capital (all three in 1937). In 1938 the National General Mobilization Law and the Electrical Power Administration Law were enacted to be followed in 1939 by the issuing of price control ordinances. 'By 1940 the government and the army had taken a complete hold over the Japanese economy' [Morishima 1982:130]. Their power was used to effect a huge reordering of resources, elevating the metal, engineering and chemical industries to the pinnacles of economic activity. 'From this great experiment the Japanese government, industrialists and workers all learnt how to achieve industrial change' [131], a factor which stood them in good stead in meeting postwar economic challenges.

Finally, one needs to stress that one of the ultimate sources of Japan's economic transformation was a persistent investment effort which was upheld from the outset of the twentieth century. For instance, from 1900 to 1937, the proportion of national income directed towards net capital formation averaged 18–19 per cent annually [Sheridan 1993:61]. It is largely thanks to such an investment record that the Japanese economy progressed from a state of sheer backwardness at the start of the Meiji Restoration to one with the makings of an industrial force by the end of the 1930s.

## The Early Postwar Period and Occupation Reforms

When the Second World War ended, Japan was in dire straits. Close to two million souls including both military and civilian personnel had perished, while materially speaking, about 40 per cent of Japan's total urban structures had been devastated.

> For all practical purposes, the Japanese economy was at a standstill. Such factories as remained more or less intact stood idle for want of raw materials. Fuel of any kind was so scarce that the few taxis still running operated on the gases generated by unwieldy charcoal burners mounted on their tails. Public buildings went unheated, and as the first bitter postwar winter set in, a Japanese family counted itself fortunate if its members were able to huddle around a small, barely glowing charcoal brazier. Most terrible of all was the hunger. [Christopher 1983:18]

In the autumn of 1945, the rice crop failed and practically everywhere people desperately scavenged for food. In the process, many scurried to the countryside in search of relief. Throughout the nation at large, people were scantily clad, disease was rife and many suffered from malnutrition.

To make matters worse, with the demobilization of seven million soldiers plus the repatriation of large numbers of Japanese who had previously been resident in Korea, Taiwan and China, the ranks of the country's unemployed swelled to around 13 million. The outlook for Japan certainly seemed gloomy and many an observer forecast that at best, Japan might secure a slightly above average Asian standard of living.

Yet from its ashes, Japan rose like a phoenix to become the world's second largest industrial power. Its citizens currently enjoy one of the world's highest per capita incomes and it has attained competitive supremacy in fields such as steel, shipbuilding, automobiles, computers, other electrical goods and optical devices. How this 'miracle' was achieved is a central theme of this book but at this stage we note that much of the groundwork was certainly prepared by the occupying allied powers headed by General MacArthur.[2]

## The Reparations Issue

The occupation, which lasted some seven years, ended in April 1952. Although it had been an essentially benevolent occupation, it first seemed that severe retributive measures were to be exacted. In October 1945 a US mission headed by Edwin Pauley arrived in Japan to recommend a reparations programme. Pauley proposed that about a thousand of the factories that were more or less still intact, including electricity-generating plants, shipyards and steelworks, be dismantled and sent to the Asian countries that suffered at the hands of the Japanese. The Pauley plan would have limited Japan's industrial capacity to its 1928 level. Luckily for Japan, Pauley's suggestions were never seriously implemented. Instead, in April 1948, the Johnstone Committee argued that a more lenient recovery programme be installed and that any emphasis on punishment be markedly toned down.

Several factors were operative in causing the Americans to have a change of heart. First, by 1947–8, economic conditions had become almost intolerable. The 1947 GDP was just over half the level attained in 1937. Supplies of coal and electricity were below critical levels and raw materials were in very short supply. Inflation was rampant, unemployment widespread and the labour movement was, to say the least, restless. Second, with the emergence of the Cold War and the ascendancy of the Chinese communists, Japan began to be regarded as potentially a valuable member of the Western alliance. Although its newly founded constitution denied it the use of arms, a Japan restored to relative prosperity could nonetheless play a stabilizing role in Asia. Third, the futility and inconsistency of pursuing a policy of both reparations and aid (which was needed to avert a complete economic breakdown) became increasingly evident. As the Johnstone Committee realized, the US was effectively paying the reparations bill to the extent of some $400 million per year.

## The Occupation Reforms

It is convenient to group the occupation reforms into those that were essentially socio-political and those that were essentially economic, although the distinction, as we will see, is not always clear cut.

## Socio-Political Reforms

Of the socio-political reforms, the enactment of the 1947 constitution made a lasting impact on Japanese society. The constitution allowed for the election of both houses of the Diet (Japanese parliament) by an electorate consisting of all men and women aged 20 and over. The peerage system was abolished and standard democratic rights such as the right of free assembly and of a free press were guaranteed. Where the constitution departed from other democracies was in its renunciation of the right to resort to war and the curtailment of defence expenditures to 1 per cent of GNP. Furthermore, as part of the general democratization process, shintoism lost its claim to be the state religion and the emperor, who essentially became a mere figurehead, renounced his divine status.

Yet another important aspect of social reform was instigated in the sphere of education. Obligatory schooling was extended to nine years. Chauvinistic and bellicose teachings were expunged from the curriculum. Options available to students and methods of teaching were made more flexible and the university system was reformed somewhat more along American lines (the education system is discussed in Chapter 13).

Among the economic reforms were those relating to land, labour and monopoly powers, as well as the Dodge stabilization measures and the Sharp tax reforms. Let us consider each one separately.

*Land Reform.* Land reform is discussed in considerably more detail in Chapter 12. Here we will simply provide a few salient points.

Soon after the occupation commenced, the Japanese government itself proposed a measure of land reform but General Macarthur, the Supreme Commander for the Allied Powers (SCAP), felt that the proposals were not far reaching enough. In his Memorandum Concerning Rural Land Reform, MacArthur directed the Japanese government 'to take measures to insure that those who till the soil of Japan shall have more equal opportunity to enjoy the fruits of their labor' [as quoted by Kosai 1986:19]. Agreement was reached in July 1946 and subsequently all land owned by absentee landlords was bought and transferred to tenant farmers at less than the purchase price, which in any case had been below market values. In addition, the landholdings of resident landlords not engaged in cultivation and of landed tenants were strictly limited. As Kosai noted, due to these changes the 'farmers' will to work rose and the basis for a conspicuous rise in agricultural productivity was created. The land reform reduced the income share of the parasitic landlords to zero and by distributing the land virtually gratis, it forced the farmers engaged in cultivation to take up the entrepreneurial role in their former landlords' place.' [22]

*Labour Reforms.*   The labour reforms focused primarily on the promotion of trade unionism. Trade unions had been relatively insignificant in the prewar years and in 1940 were in fact banned. The Trade Union Law of 1945 guaranteed the rights to organize, to bargain as a collective and to strike. In 1946, legislation was extended to provide for the resolution of labour disputes and in 1947, basic labour standards were enshrined in law. These measures greatly encouraged the growth of trade unionism and indeed by 1948 over 50 per cent of the work force was unionized.

The unions, which came under the sway of both communists and socialists, began to be stridently militant and as a consequence, the country was plagued by a rash of strikes. The US authorities viewed these developments with grave misgiving. When a general strike was planned for 1 February 1947, SCAP agonized over the prospective turn of events and on the strike's eve, an order was issued banning it. Later in that year, national civil service employees were deprived of the right to strike and in 1949 legislation was amended disqualifying union officials from receiving salaries from their companies. In short, by 1948, the attitude of the US authorities had changed from a rather radical to a much more conservative position and this re-evaluation probably contributed to the subsequent non-confrontational approach of large sections of Japanese labour (see Chapter 7).

*Anti-Monopoly Measures.*   From the start the US attached much importance to the objective of destroying the power of the zaibatsu. They believed that: 'unless the zaibatsu are broken up, the Japanese have little prospect of ever being able to govern themselves as free men. As long as Zaibatsu survive, Japan will be their Japan' [Kosai 1986:24].

Accordingly, the zaibatsu families were forced to surrender their holdings in exchange for minimal compensation. In turn, these holdings were sold and dispersed to a large number of individuals and associations. Former executives of the zaibatsus were also barred from holding any official position in their companies and were severely constrained in their general industrial endeavours.

Cartels and other control associations were also dissolved. Business leaders who had maintained a close association with the military were purged. Legislation was also passed to dissolve companies which exercised excessive economic power.

While the US authorities first undertook the task of tackling monopolistic forces with gusto, by 1948 they had begun to waiver and the deconcentration campaign was subsequently waged with less vigour. This was partly in response to constant Japanese opposition and lack of cooperation. In late 1947, a leading Social Democrat argued that with the passing of the anti-monopoly legislation 'Japan will not be able to compete against foreign competition' [Yamamura 1990:22] and that the country's recovery would be aborted.

The ultimate impact of the anti-monopoly legislation is difficult to assess. It probably served to reduce the degree of economic concentration and to increase industry competitiveness. It almost certainly reduced the degree of income inequality, as did the land reforms. Nevertheless, after Japan regained full independence a series of reversals occurred.

*The Dodge Plan.*    Early in 1949, a Detroit banker, Joseph Dodge came to Japan as a financial adviser to the SCAP. He made a number of recommendations which were readily adopted. The proposals, known as the 'Dodge Plan', aimed to curb inflation and to stimulate export growth. The plan's principal elements entailed: a balanced budget to be realized mainly through an increase in tax receipts, wage stabilization, price controls, sharp credit limitations, and the replacement of a multiple exchange rate system by a single rate one set at 360 yen to the dollar.[3] The Dodge Plan is widely credited for helping place Japan on a solid postwar recovery path. It reined in inflation from 73 per cent in 1948 to 25 per cent in 1949 and then to 7 per cent in 1950. For around the next 15 years the country maintained a budget close on balance and the exchange rate remained constant until 1971.

*Tax Reforms.*    In May 1949 a team of tax specialists headed by Carl Sharp visited Japan to advise SCAP on tax policy. Its report, released in September that year, made a number of recommendations. Personal, broad-based income (including capital gains) taxes were to be the centrepiece of the tax system. To achieve equity, progressivity was to be retained but the wartime top rate was to be reduced from 85 per cent to 55 per cent. The repeal of numerous excise taxes as well as the excess profits tax was considered desirable. Taxes on corporations and on persons were slated for coordination (for example tax credits were recommended for persons on dividend income). Finally a net worth tax (properly indexed to inflation) as well as a value added tax were also proposed. Except for the value added tax, all of the Sharp proposals passed into legislation in 1950.

## The Early 1950s and the Postindependence Period

The years spanning 1950 to 1953, constituted a watershed for the postwar Japanese economy. In June 1950, the Korean War broke out evoking a huge demand for Japanese goods. At first, the chief items in need included trucks, vehicle components, cotton cloth and coal. 'Between July 1950 to February 1951 alone, orders worth nearly $13 million, placed for some 7079 trucks, stimulated the revival of the Japanese automobile industry' [Johnson 1982:200]. 'In 1952 the GHQ permitted the manufacture of armaments and these then became the largest item in demand' [Morishima 1982:163]. These 'special procurements' gave such a boost to the iron and steel industry, as well as to textiles, coalmining and machine tools, that by 1951 their production levels surpassed prewar ones. The 'special procurements' also included US payments for the stationing of troops in Japan. Between 1951 and 1955, income from these sources financed around 30 per cent of Japan's import requirements [Allen 1981:21].

In response to the onrush of demand for goods in the wake of the Korean War, a programme of massive accumulation of capital goods was embarked upon. In key industries such as steel, the formation of new plant and equipment ultimately gave Japan a competitive edge but even without the replacement of war damaged facilities, enough capacity had survived to enable supply to respond readily to the increased demand, provided energy and basic inputs were on hand. In the textile industry, for example, some 30–40 per cent of capital equipment escaped destruction. Not only did the country have idle capital to draw upon but because of the large unemployment situation, labour was available for the asking. The investment drive and the general influx of funds associated with the Korean War also gave rise to a welcome consumer boom which lasted throughout 1952 and into 1953.

## Rapid Economic Growth (1955–70)

Between 1955 and 1970, the Japanese economy sustained an average real growth rate of close on 10 per cent. This extraordinary spurt of economic activity was largely made possible by exceptionally high investment rates. Starting from a situation in 1955 whereby gross fixed capital formation amounted to 16.4 per cent of GDP, by 1970 a ratio of 39.4 per cent was recorded. The latter figure exceeded by far, the best investment performances of all other industrial countries.

The rapid accumulation of capital had a salutary effect on the Japanese economy by virtue of its enhancing the country's productive capacity, by its overcoming of a then growing labour shortage (because it increased the capital intensity of manufacturing production processes), by its facilitation of the adoption of more modern equipment leading to improved technological capabilities, and by its stimulation of consumer spending through standard multiplier effects [Kosai and Ogino 1984:7–11].

Investment was spurred on by a growing local market in which customers were eager to acquire basic consumer durables such as refrigerators, television sets and washing machines and by a very large personal propensity to save which released resources for capital formation. Between 1955 and 1970, personal savings as a proportion of GDP rose from 13.4 to 20.4 per cent. Public and corporation savings also rose but without the lead given by personal savings, higher profit rates (entailing lower wages) or higher taxes and less government spending would have been needed.

*1970–94*

From the early 1970s onwards, while Japan's growth rate generally exceeded those of other industrial countries, it remained at best at around half its previous hectic pace. A combination of circumstances contributed to this change, which included successive oil price shocks, a rise in the relative cost of labour, a lessening in the flow of Western technological transfers, successive yen appreciations and a slackening off of export prospects, due among other things to increased trade barriers. Events in this period are given special attention throughout this book.

SUMMARY

**Pre-postwar Socio-Political Landmarks**

- 1603 Inauguration of Tokugawa regime
- 1853 Commodore Perry enters Tokyo Bay
- 1868 Meiji Restoration
- 1894 War with China

- 1904 War with Russia
- 1931 Occupation of Manchuria
- 1941 War with America and Allies
- 1945 Defeat and surrender to the Allies.

**Economic History**

- **In the Edo Period** despite various restraints of trade, progress had been recorded in the establishment of a national market for certain goods, such as cotton and cloth. Improvements were evident in transport infrastructure and agriculture, while the bureaucracy and education system were relatively well developed.
- **In the Meiji era**, the State made strenuous efforts to industrialize and modernize Japan. The feudal system was abolished, education reformed and many economic institutions, such as the Bank of Japan, were introduced. After first establishing various projects and industries under state control, the government transferred most of them to private hands. During this period, the agricultural sector bore the brunt of the transformation process releasing resources for the rest of the economy. It was also a time of a massive trade expansion with the rest of the world.
- **Between 1912 and 1938**, the Meiji restoration gains were consolidated. Japan consistently upgraded its manufacturing potential and by the 1930s, the country's ability to produce a range of industrial products in areas such as shipping and aeroplanes, was on a par with the west.
- **In the early postwar years**, conditions in Japan were abysmal with most goods being in short supply. As a result, inflation was rampant. Thanks to a series of reforms, including the implementation of the Dodge Plan and others entailing radical changes in agriculture, trade union organization, the dismantling of the zaibatsu and the lessening of monopoly power, Japan was both equipped with institutions befitting a democratic industrial state and more capable of meeting ongoing economic challenges.
- **The Korean War** gave the Japanese economy a welcome boost in rapidly augmenting demand which in turn stimulated investment.
- **From 1955 to 1970** the economy experienced a period of high growth with GDP rising on average by 10 per cent per year. This prolonged boom was stimulated by an exceptional investment effort (made possible by an equally impressive personal saving rate) and by a great eagerness on the part of the Japanese people to acquire a range of consumer durables.

- **Since the mid-1970s,** although the Japanese economy generally continued to outpace other industrial countries, its growth rate very much slackened being beset by oil price shocks, increased labour costs, an appreciating yen and a less buoyant world market.

# 2 The Macro Institutional Framework

## INTRODUCTION

As a prelude to a review of macroeconomic trends and policy (see Chapter 3), here we provide a brief description of relevant facets of Japan's macroeconomic institutional environment.

Japan's financial sector has been subject to an extraordinary degree of regulation which has had a bearing both on policy formulation and resource allocation. With this in mind, we commence by summarizing some of the financial regulatory constraints and the process by which modifications were introduced. This is followed by a section describing most of Japan's key financial institutions, a major purpose of which is to emphasize the extent to which these institutions were compelled to cater for a well-defined market niche.

Next there is a discussion on relative capital costs, which arises from the fact that cost differences between Japan and say the US, illustrate one of the ways in which regulations and the specific characteristics of Japan's financial sector yielded outcomes which might not normally have been expected had complete free market forces held sway.

Finally, we briefly probe into the fiscal arena to highlight the small size of the public sector, sources of supplementary funds and the taxation system, all of which have been influential in the determination of fiscal strategy.

## THE FINANCIAL SECTOR

### The Evolution of the Financial System

Up to the early 1970s, that is until the era of high speed growth had ended, Japan's financial system was highly regulated and highly compartmentalized. The system then in place may be characterized by the following features:

(a) Foreign exchange control was maintained on both inward and outward capital flows.

20

(b) Financial institutions were rigidly segmented: 'on the liabilities side, the permitted methods of raising funds were defined and, on the assets side, the form of loans that could be extended and other assets acquired were both circumscribed' [Takeda and Turner 1992:11].

(c) There was barely any active secondary securities market. This reflected three institutional facts: Japan's financial isolation from the rest of the world, the predominance of indirect financing (that is corporate borrowing through the medium of financial institutions) and the small public sector deficit (which meant that the general flotation of public bonds was minimal). Furthermore, because of the lack of a securities market, open market operations were not an important policy instrument. Instead, the monetary authorities relied on the determination of bank credit to the corporate sector as their primary intermediate target.

(d) Banks were at the centre of the system, with the commercial banks accounting in 1970 for nearly 40 per cent of all financial institution lending. The household sector tended to have a substantial financial surplus (savings) which was mostly held with the banking system. By contrast, the corporate sector was in substantial deficit, financing the excess of its own investments over its savings by borrowing heavily from the banks.

(e) Commercial banks and bank credit were subject to rigid controls. Interest rates on their deposits and on their prime lending were regulated. They were also subject to varying reserve requirements and to quantitative control over (ceiling on) their lending to the private sector. Such lending was also indirectly controlled by the Bank of Japan (BOJ) in part by changes in reserve requirements but primarily through its own lending policies manifested in the discount rate at which it lent and the volume it was prepared to lend at that rate. The efficacy of such lending policies was, moreover, reinforced by the fact that the banks as a group, tended to be 'overloaned' in that their reserve positions (cash less borrowings from the BOJ or deposits less loans) were negative.

(f) The lack of an active capital market and of alternative sources of short-term credit outside the banks also meant that, at the given bank lending rate, there was an excess demand for credit. Credit rationing was thus an important feature of the financial system whereby banks mostly lent to the business sector and hardly at all to private households.

(g) In addition to the commercial banks, numerous public sector institutions played a key role in the financing of specific economic sectors, business categories and public projects.

## Financial Deregulation

By the mid 1970s, various developments, both internally and externally, brought about substantial modifications both in Japan's financial institutions and the way in which they were regulated.

Starting with internal factors, two in particular stand out. First, with the demise of the high growth period, investments undertaken by the corporate sector tapered off. At the same time, to counteract the deflationary pressures brought on by the investment slump, public expenditures rose sharply, causing the government deficit to exceed 5 per cent of GNP (in the 1960s it was less than 2 per cent of GNP). To finance its outlays, the government began to issue bonds in large quantities which promoted the development of open financial markets. The strengthening of open markets naturally enabled open market operations to become a practical technique of monetary control. Furthermore, with a decline in corporation borrowing, changes in bank credit became less effective as a means of regulating the general level of macroeconomic activity.

Second, not only did large firms tend to borrow less but they increasingly began to rely on the issuing of shares to meet their financial requirements. This tendency plus the growing bond market stimulated security transactions and a securities market which called for new financial instruments and a more liberal framework, that is the deregulation of various controls, including various interest rate payments.

With the city banks losing out on some of their traditional corporate business, they began to take an interest in servicing other groups which had hitherto been beyond their basic jurisdiction. In this regard they began to compete with institutions which had specialized in lending to small firms and they had also begun to lobby for permission to enter other fields which would normally have been reserved for institutions dealing in securities. Some of these pressures were reflected in legislative changes and the creation of devices for poaching on 'foreign' terrain. For example, in terms of legislation adopted in 1992, banks and securities houses are now allowed to enter each other's areas of business through the creation of appropriate subsidiaries.

Turning to external factors, from the mid 1960s, Japan began to record persistent current account surpluses which in turn brought about forces that made for a yen appreciation. To stave off these pressures, controls on outward capital flows had to be relaxed and by 1980 exchange control was formally abolished. With the liberalization of capital flows, many Japanese companies began to take advantage of greater opportunities to raise funds from abroad on more favourable terms than were available locally and at the same time, many institutions increasingly diversified their financial portfolios by acquiring overseas assets. For example, 'by the end of the 1980s, the foreign securities holdings of Japanese life insurance companies represented almost 34% of their total holdings' [Takeda and Turner 1992:19]. On this account alone, so as not to disadvantage local finance institutions, a fair amount of deregulation had to be effected.

Below we set out in point form a few (that is a sample) of the major financial reforms introduced since 1980:

1980    Foreign exchange controls abolished. Large security companies allowed to borrow in the call market.
1981    City banks allowed to buy in the gensaki market (market for repurchasing bonds.)
1983    Banks allowed to sell government bonds over the counter.
1984    Banks allowed to deal in the secondary market for government bonds.
1985    Interest rate ceilings on large term deposits lifted. Government bond futures market established.
1986    Ceilings on certificates of deposits removed.
1987    Market for certificates of deposits established.
1988    Financial Futures law enacted.
1989    Tokyo International Financial Futures Exchange established.
1990    Banks allowed to sell securitized corporate loans to institutional investors.
1991    Pensions funds and investment trusts allowed to buy securitized corporate loans.
1992    Securities and exchange surveillance commission inaugurated. Banks and securities houses allowed to establish subsidiaries to widen their field of activity.
1993    Interest rates on time deposits completely liberalized.
1994    Interest rates on non-time deposits (including postal savings) liberalized.

The important thing to notice is not simply that this or that change had been introduced but over the years there has been a near unbroken chain of reforms to the financial system making it more responsive to ongoing needs. The list almost exclusively contains measures relating to the internal financial market but a similar list could easily be drawn up indicating numerous changes which have integrated Japan more closely into the international financial system.

## Key Financial Institutions[1]

Japan's financial institutions may be classified into the following seven categories:

### Commercial Banks

There are two main types of commercial banks in Japan; city banks and regional banks.

**City banks,** which locate their head offices in a large metropolitan area, maintain a national branch network. Not counting the Bank of Tokyo (which performs distinct functions) 12 city banks are currently in existence. They are the Daiichi Kangyo Bank, the Fuji Bank, the Sumitomo Bank, the Mitsubishi Bank, the Sanwa Bank, the Tokai Bank, the Taiyo Kobe Bank, the Mitsui Bank, the Kyowa Bank, the Daiwa Bank, the Saitama Bank and the Hokkaido Takushoku Bank. These banks have in the past lent mainly to large corporations and in turn most of their deposits were drawn from big business. They 'have been at the centre of the private financial sector in Japan ever since the Meiji period', and 'have an extremely large influence on the national economy' [Suzuki 1987:171]. With the relative demise of large corporation bank borrowings, city banks are now avidly courting small businesses. They have also increased the scope of their international operations and a bank like Daiichi Kangyo, for example, has dozens of branches scattered throughout the world.

**Regional banks** are headquartered in large or medium-sized cities and function mostly within a given prefecture. By mid 1985, there were 64 such banks. Their main borrowers have been small and medium enterprises and most of their deposits originate from private individuals.

Japanese commercial banks differ from most Western ones in that they tend to depend on longer term deposits, and in turn, they are more predisposed to making medium and long-term loans. They therefore not only foster credit creation but they also perform the function of credit intermediation. Like their Western counterparts, they also facilitate payment transfers but instead of being primarily based on cheques, most transfers are executed by direct transfers from the sending bank into the bank account of the recipient.

### Long-Term Credit and Trust Banks

**Long-term credit banks** are private banking institutions organized under the Long-Term Credit Bank Law of 1952, with the objective of specializing in issuing long-term loans. They have concentrated on lending for plant and equipment as well as long-term working capital and in so doing, have played an important role during Japan's high growth period. These banks have been rather restricted in the source of their funding and were generally only permitted to accept deposits from government and public bodies, their own borrowers and other specified groups. After the first oil crisis (in 1973) they tended to canvass loans to the distributive sector and engaged in international financial operations.

**Trust banks** are entrusted with money or non-monetary assets (such as land for example) which they manage on behalf of the owner. The money trusts include pension trusts, securities investment trusts, and so on. Currently 16 trust banks are in operation and although they also engage in ordinary banking business, the two types of businesses have to be managed separately. Since the early 1960s, trust banks have expanded rapidly and like long-term credit banks, they provide long-term finance.

## Specialized Foreign Exchange Banks

As the designation suggests, specialized foreign exchange banks, established under the Foreign Exchange Bank Law of 1954, are concerned with foreign exchange transactions and foreign trade transactions. They do not make loans which are unrelated to trade and foreign exchange. The use of plural terms is perhaps unwarranted since currently there is only one such bank, the Bank of Tokyo.

## Financial Institutions that Cater to Small Business

Here we have a number of such bodies, namely sogo banks, shinkin banks, credit cooperatives and some others. We will briefly refer to the first two.

**Sogo banks,** based on the Sogo Bank Law of 1951, have serviced small and medium-sized firms. Unlike the regional banks which also pandered to small enterprise, sogo banks were originally exclusively confined (by legislation) to businesses below a certain size threshold, defined in terms of number of employees and fixed capital. In the course of time, they were permitted to relate to slightly larger establishments and by February 1989, all but one of the 69 sogo banks then in existence were reclassified as regional banks.

**Shinkin banks** emerged out of former urban based credit cooperatives by virtue of the Shinkin Bank Law 1951. They are organized on a membership basis with credit being available to members only. To become a member, one must be a small business owner and reside or function within the geographic area served by the bank. During the late 1980s, the value of loans which could be issued to each member had been capped at 20 per cent of the applicant's capital or 800 million yen, whichever was smaller.

### Financial Institutions Linked to Agriculture, Forestry and Fishing

The agricultural sector is organized on the basis of a federation of cooperative movements that are federated at the prefectural and national level (see Chapter 13).

**The Norinchukin Bank** is the central financial institution for the co-operative movement. It may receive deposits from organizations that may, according to the Norinchukin Bank Law of 1923, contribute capital and in principle its lending is confined to such organizations. Most deposits emanate from agricultural bodies.

### Securities Companies

Securities companies engage (*inter alia*) in the trading, intermediation and underwriting of financial securities such as stocks and bonds. They are in principle prohibited from engaging in non-securities operations. Of the 224 or so securities companies in Japan, there are four that command overriding dominance. They are Nomura, Nikko, Yamaichi and Daiwa. The securities market had not only been inhibited by structural factors, such as an early dependence on indirect financing and small quantities of floated government bonds, but had also been impeded by heavy taxes on equity transactions. From 1988 such taxes were greatly reduced.

### Government Financial Institutions

Leading bodies reviewed in this category include the post office, the Japan Development Bank, and the Export-Import Bank of Japan. Japan's central bank, the Bank of Japan and the Fiscal Investment Loan Program are dealt with in other sections that follow below.

**The Post Office** has been accepting savings deposits from as far back as 1875, making it one of Japan's first modern financial intermediaries. With some 24 000 branches scattered throughout the country, it is well placed to collect small scale deposits from private individuals, which is in fact its determined role. By law, individual deposits were limited to a set ceiling (three million yen in the mid 1980s). Until 1988 interest on post office deposits was tax exempt. Theoretically, savers could only open an account at a particular branch but 'checks to prevent people holding more than one tax-exempt account were not particularly rigorous and evasion was endemic' [Takeda and Turner 1992:42]. Post office fixed time deposits, which constitute around 90 per cent of all deposits, represent a particularly attractive asset. They are fully redeemable after six months yet they may be held for up to ten years at relatively attractive interest rates. In other words, they combine high yield with high liquidity. Not surprisingly, throughout the postwar period, postal deposits grew faster than total deposits and by March 1985 they stood at 'about the same level as the personal deposit balances of all banks in the country' [Suzuki 1987:290].

**The Japan Development Bank,** founded in 1951, supplies long-term loans (ranging in maturity from one to as many as ten years), for the promotion of industrial development and the country's general economic progress. Its function is to provide or augment funds to projects which might normally encounter difficulties in meeting all or most of their needs from private bodies. Since 1985, its charter was amended to allow it to support activities relating to the research and development of high technology.

**The Export Import Bank of Japan** was originally set up in 1950 for assisting export promotion but in 1952, it also began to concern itself with import finance and in that year the institution had a name change from 'The Export Bank of Japan' to its present name. Apart from trade support, it now provides loans for various foreign investment projects. Firms turn to it not only for loans but also for liability guarantees.

While the above list of Japan's financial institutions is not all inclusive, for example we could also have mentioned insurance companies, money market dealers and some others, it does at least highlight the segmentation of the financial sector, which has been very much more in evidence in Japan than elsewhere.

## THE BANK OF JAPAN

The Bank of Japan, which was founded in 1882, now essentially functions in terms of the Bank of Japan Law 1942. Like other central banks, the Bank of Japan has at least four clearly delineated roles. These are: the issuing of currency; the provision of banking services to financial institutions; serving as the government's banker and being responsible for the formulation and conduct of monetary policy. In terms of the latter objective, the bank has not only pursued price stability but has also been concerned with economic growth, full employment and the balance of payments.

The Bank's highest decision making authority, the Policy Board, consists of the Bank's Governor, two government representatives (from the Ministry of Finance and the Economic Planning Agency) without voting powers and four non-government members representing the city banks, the regional banks, commerce and industry and agriculture. Although the bank is theoretically beholden to the Minister of Finance and in fact regularly consults with the government, in practice, it tends to regulate monetary policy from a fairly independent stance. (Some of its major postwar decisions are documented in Chapter 3.)

**The Cost of Capital**

Many Americans, particularly from the business community, have asserted that throughout much of the postwar period, Japanese firms derived an 'unfair' competitive advantage in that they obtained capital at lower costs than their overseas rivals. This issue has been thoroughly investigated and in a recent review of the literature, Frankel concluded that in the 1970s and 1980s the cost of capital in Japan was indeed lower than in the United States but since 1990, relative costs have been more or less equal [Frankel 1993:60–1].

Essentially, the cost of capital to a firm is the weighted sum of borrowing and of equity costs. Therefore, if capital costs were lower in Japan, either the cost of borrowing (that is the interest rate) was lower, the cost of equity was lower or the debt financing (that is borrowing) weight was higher than in the US (on the grounds that debt financing is generally less burdensome than equity financing). Apparently, all three of these options applied. Let us examine each in turn.

*Interest Rates*

On paper, between 1967 and 1988 Japanese real interest rates fell short of US real rates but the extent of the gap is subject to dispute. This is so since during the 1960s and 1970s many bank borrowers were required to lodge 'compensating balances' for which no interest was forthcoming. Accordingly, most observers considered that the interest rate differential that then existed was of a small order of magnitude. By the early 1980s, when actual interest rates could be taken at face value, US interest rates exceeded those in Japan by a widening margin but towards the decade's end the gap narrowed and then closed. Low Japanese interest rates were made possible by capital loan rationing at preferential rates but above all by the voluminous savings of private individuals who willingly lodged their nest eggs in various banking and post office time deposits.

## The Cost of Equity

On the basis of a study undertaken by Ando and Auerbach, it would seem that between 1967 and 1983 the overall rate of return on capital (that is the sum of dividend payments and capital gains) was lower in Japan than in the US [Ando and Auerbach 1988]. But on the other hand, other studies such as by Baldwin (1986) and by Kester and Luehrman (1989) were rather inconclusive. Where there is no room for doubt is that the share price to dividend ratio has generally been much higher in Japan. In the late 1980s it became even more inflated (see Chapter 3) which meant that equity financing became increasingly cheap. (The floating of new shares yielded large quantities of cash inflows with relatively small dividend commitments.)

## The Debt to Equity Ratio

Throughout the postwar period, Japanese corporations have sustained a much higher ratio of debt to equity than have US firms. For example, during 1970–2, 'debt-equity ratios in Japan were four times as high as in the United States' [Frankel 1993:27]. Reasons for this are given in Chapter 6. In the meanwhile, what needs to be stressed is that under normal circumstances, equity-financing is more costly than debt-financing to compensate investors for a higher risk exposure. Of course, when as recently occurred in Japan, equity prices race far ahead of dividend payments, the opposite becomes the case. Therefore, consequent to the stock market boom in the tail end of the 1980s, Japanese debt to equity ratios plummeted.

Summing up, as the above paragraphs indicate the cost of capital in Japan had often fallen short of comparable costs in the US. This in part reflected controlled interest rates and an institutional bias in favour of indirect finance, both of which no longer apply.

## SOME ASPECTS OF THE FISCAL SYSTEM

### The Relative Size of the Budget

One of the many distinguishing features of Japan is that although the government has a high economic profile, public revenue and expenditure are relatively small. 'Even during the rapid growth period of 1955 to 1964, with considerable government investment in construction to support economic growth, the Japanese tax burden was only 18.5 per cent of the GNP, compared to 26.5 per cent in the United States.' [Vogel 1979:69] Between 1971 and 1990, Japanese government revenue as a percentage of GDP averaged 27.7 which was much less than the 39.8 average for all OECD countries (excluding the US). Similarly, the figures relating to government expenditure as a percentage of GDP amounted to 29.8 and 41.0 respectively.[2]

A closer look at comparative expenditure breakdowns indicates that Japanese public outlays have been held in check because of more limited government commitments to defence and welfare. For example, the aggregated ratio to GDP of 1985 military, educational, health, welfare and housing appropriations amounted to 6.03 per cent for Japan as opposed to 12.82 per cent for the United States and 15.95 per cent for the United Kingdom.[3] On the other hand, the Japanese ratio of public fixed capital formation to GDP was two to three times higher than the ratios obtained in the United States, United Kingdom, Germany and France [Sakakibara 1991:25]. Japanese government budgets are evidently much more heavily weighted towards directly productive economic activities.

### Budget Balances and the Fiscal Investment Loans Program

As shown in Figure 2.1, from 1988 to 1992, Japan's general government balance was in surplus but thereafter deficits appeared. For the entire period, Japan's budget situation seemed to be healthier than that of the average lot of the leading seven OECD countries and this is usually taken 'as giving Japan an exceptional degree of fiscal flexibility' [OECD 1993:81].

However, one of the quirks of the Japanese government financial arrangements is that along with the traditional budget, a 'secondary budget' in the form of the annual Fiscal Investment Loans Program (FILP) is also submitted to the Diet for ratification. This supplementary budget technically involves government borrowing, and therefore,

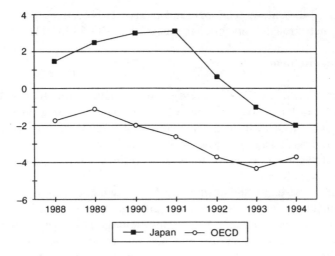

*Figure* 2.1    Central Government Budget Balances as Percentage of GDP

*Source*: OECD 1993, Table 23, p. 81.

the true measure of the overall government budget balance is not quite as rosy as would first appear.

**The Fiscal Investment Loans Program (FILP)** allocates funds to public corporations, government-affiliated financial institutions, special accounts and local governments. FILP funding, which generally accounts for a quarter of public investment, has been used for both industry related and social infrastructure projects, such as roads and urban renewal. Up to the mid 1970s emphasis was placed on furthering Japan's industrial growth but since then social investments have been given equal consideration.

The principal source of FILP funds are the postal savings as well as funds arising from various nationally administered insurance and pension schemes. These are supplemented by funds raised from government guaranteed bonds and other borrowings. Until 1972, Diet approval was not required for the administration of most of the FILP derived funds. However, since 1973, each FILP component is now officially listed and in need of Diet confirmation. Notwithstanding this, there is an elastic clause embodied in fiscal legislation which enables 'the government to react flexibly to changes in economic conditions that are difficult to foresee' [Suzuki 1987:274]. Over the period 1985–93, FILP expenditure grew from just over 6 to around 9 per cent of GDP and in the process 'has taken on many of the aspects of a second budget, being used to achieve economic and industrial objectives which could not be met through conventional means' [OECD 1993:91].

## Taxation Reform

Compared with the OECD average, the Japanese are lightly taxed. Currently, in Japan taxation from all sources amounts to approximately 19 per cent of GDP. By contrast, the overall OECD ratio is around 30 per cent. This is largely explained by Japan's relatively small government outlays but a tax collection system riddled with loopholes is also of some significance.

For the time being and abstracting from business cycle phases, total government revenues are normally sufficient to meet ongoing needs. However, in view of Japan's changing demographic age composition and the increasing recognition that the public infrastructure needs to be seriously upgraded, this is sure to change. For instance, while the ratio of the number of social security beneficiaries to contributors is now lower in Japan than in most other industrial countries, on account of a rapidly ageing population, by 2010 the ratio in question is expected to double. The implication of all this is that if the scale of social benefits is to be maintained at anything near their present levels, a general increase in tax receipts would have to be forthcoming. In 1988, partly to meet this challenge, the Japanese taxation system was fundamentally reformed.

The reform sought to extend the tax base by making personal and corporate earnings more taxable and by introducing a consumption tax. While wage earners have their taxes automatically deducted in each pay period, the self employed have long had a field day as far as both tax evasion and avoidance are concerned. Certain professional groups, such as doctors, had received highly favourable treatment while many small owner operators were able to dilute their tax burden by incorporating into their firms all household members. Up to 1988, capital gains arising from securities holdings were not taxed and earned interest payments were often exempt.

Tax payers were allowed four types of tax-free saving plans, which together meant that an individual could have held Y 14 million of his savings in non taxable forms. If the household had several members, the amount of non-taxable saving could be very much higher and over 70 per cent of all personal saving took advantage of tax-exempt vehicles of this type. [OECD 1993:100]

The 1988 Reform Act introduced a capital gains tax on individually held securities. Taxpayers may choose to pay a straight 20 per cent capital gains tax or be taxed at the rate of 5 per cent of the proceeds of security disposals. As for interest earnings, all tax exemptions were essentially abolished and interest income is now subject to a flat 20 per cent rate, regardless of other income. The corporation tax rate was reduced and the personal income tax schedule was simplified from 15 to 5 bands with tax rates ranging from 10 to 50 per cent.

In spite of many loopholes being closed these is one remaining problem and that is Japan has still not instituted a taxpayer identification system which would enable the administration to track and monitor all potential taxpayers. As a result, horizontal inequities persist. In an attempt to make the tax system somewhat fairer, a 3 per cent consumption tax was also introduced. The consumption tax was not well received by the public at large and in fact a series of demonstrations against it was organized. Nevertheless, taxes on goods and services in Japan are relatively very low. In 1990 they represented 19 per cent of all tax revenue as opposed to a 30 per cent share for all OECD countries [OECD 1993:99]. Recognizing the need to rectify this discrepancy, in September 1994, the government foreshadowed an increased consumption tax rate of 5 per cent which is to take effect in April 1997. If inequities and distortions in the payment of tax are to be further contained, an even higher consumption tax rate (with appropriate offsets in income tax) would seem to be justifiable. Yet other anomalies persist, such as those relating to excessively lenient inheritance taxes but unfortunately political considerations have limited the scope for general tax reform.

## SUMMARY

### The Financial Sector

- Up to the early 1970s, the financial sector was highly regulated and segmented.
- Activity was pivoted around the banks and corporations depended primarily on indirect financing.
- The market for secondary securities was very limited. Very few government bonds were floated.
- From the mid 1970s, as firms borrowed less, as government deficit financing was increasingly resorted to and as the country amassed

more foreign reserves, the regulatory system was subject to pressures for liberalization.

- In 1980 foreign exchange controls were abolished and thereafter the financial system was increasingly deregulated.
- Japan has a large number of specialized financial institutions that were originally established to serve specific market groupings.
- With the onset and continuation of deregulation, financial institutions became more able to compete across a broader spectrum of financial markets.
- One consequence of Japan's financial system was the prior existence of relatively cheaper capital costs.

## Fiscal Matters

- On the fiscal front, public expenditure and revenue has generally been far lower than in other industrial countries.
- To some extent, the activities of the Fiscal Investment Loans Program (FILP) mask the true extent of public outlays.
- The FILP has provided a greater degree of flexibility in central budgeting.
- In 1988 tax reforms somewhat streamlined the country's revenue raising system.
- The tax net was widened and made slightly more equitable. A consumption tax was introduced and certain privileges enjoyed by particular individuals, whether because of their occupation or mode of investment, were abolished.
- However, certain tax anomalies still persist.

# 3 The Macroeconomy

## INTRODUCTION

The evolution of the macroeconomy between 1960 and 1993 can be divided into three phases: the period 1960–70 during which the economy grew at a rate which far exceeded other OECD countries; the period 1970–2, characterized by the Nixon shocks; and the period from 1973 when Japan's growth rate settled at more modest levels, culminating in the 'bubble' and post 'bubble' recession. Finally, Japan's employment and price stability achievements are assessed.

## PHASE 1: 1960–70

### The Implementation of Monetary Policies

Until 1970, the prevalence of capital controls enabled Japan to pursue a relatively independent monetary policy paying scant regard to developments abroad. In other words, the conduct of monetary policy in the years to 1970 was not unduly frustrated by offsetting capital flows. That this was the case may be adduced from the following: (a) the interest rate effect on capital flows was 'weak'; (b) the offset coefficient (that is the degree to which monetary restrictions in the form of reductions in the domestic assets of the central bank were offset by an inflow of capital) was relatively low and (c) the covered short-term interest rate differential (that is the difference between Japanese and US short-term interest rates adjusted for the forward premium/discount) did not approach zero as would have been expected had international capital mobility been possible. In short, the system of capital controls allowed the Japanese authorities to control the growth of real bank credit. That being the case, the implementation of monetary policy was a relatively straightforward matter.

The ultimate objective of policy was to stabilize aggregate demand and in particular to reduce overheating in the economy, which tended to spill over into inflation and, at least until the second half of the 1960s, also into trade deficits. The economy was 'driven' by fluctuations in business investment, which was the most destabilizing component of demand. A boom (collapse) in investment activity would provoke restrictive (easier) bank credit policies and given in turn the importance of bank credit to the corporate sector, this would serve to restrain (encourage) investment and to stabilize the real economy.

Taking stock of the conduct of monetary policy, there were two key features of the way it operated until 1970. First, there was a tight control over bank credit. Second, there was a close and predictable relationship between bank credit on the one hand and prices, investment activity and the trade balance on the other.

**Fiscal Policy**

Until 1965 the prime fiscal objective was to ensure a balanced central budget. Public expenditure was to be contained within some 20 per cent of GNP. If taxes exceeded that level, tax schedules would be realigned to bring tax revenue in keeping with expenditure. The issuing of public bonds was accepted, within certain bounds, for expenditure on construction.

In 1965 in the wake of an ongoing recession, a special statute was enacted enabling the central government to issue bonds to finance current expenditures. However, this option was used sparingly. In fact, until 1973, the central government's financial balance was roughly zero over the business cycle.

PHASE 2: THE YEARS 1970–2 AND THE NIXON YEN SHOCK

By the second half of the 1960s Japan's current account had undergone a radical transformation, moving from a deficit into a persistent surplus. (Between 1966 and 1970 Japan's current account had moved to a surplus equivalent to 1 per cent of GDP.) With Japan's economy growing rapidly and the yen increasingly assuming an international role, the yen's value attracted much interest. In fact, by the end of the 1960s observers generally wondered whether the yen was not in fundamental disequilibrium, that is whether the yen was not undervalued.

Basically, there are two ways by which one might determine whether or not the yen was undervalued. The first involves an examination to ascertain whether at full employment in Japan and abroad, there was a persistent current account (or basic balance)[1] surplus (that is whether the surplus persisted over a whole cycle). The second relies on a relative purchasing power parity (PPP) test, to judge whether Japan's competitive position had been improving over a number of years. That is, had Japan's prices, after correcting for currency realignments, been falling relative to the country's major competitors?

On the basis of the first criterion, the evidence suggests that there had been a radical transformation in the current account position. By 1971–2 the surplus as a percentage of GDP had in fact more than doubled. A similar transformation was evident for the basic balance (see Table 3.1).

Evidence relying on the second test was less clear cut (see Table 3.2). Compared with other countries, Japan's consumer price inflation was substantially higher but her wholesale price inflation had (by the 1960s) began to fall behind the other major countries and her export price inflation had been less than her major competitors in both the 1950s and 1960s.

Generally speaking, it is fair to say that by the end of the 1960s, the yen was certainly undervalued and, therefore, under the IMF rules, it ought to have been a strong candidate for a formal appreciation. As long as the yen rate was expected to be maintained, small differences in interest rates brought about by differences in monetary policy did not induce large capital movements, protected as the economy was by exchange controls. However, the situation changed during 1971–2 when the Bretton Woods system was under attack. Fuelled both by the persistent surpluses on the current account and by foreign currency crises, there was considerable speculation in favour of the yen. Suddenly, in the face of potentially very large rewards from the purchase of yen denominated assets, Japanese exchange controls failed to insulate the economy, resulting in huge amounts of capital inflows being recorded in the course of 1971. These inflows added to the monetary base and to foreign exchange reserves.

Most of the above mentioned capital flows were stimulated by Japanese companies operating abroad. The subsidiaries of Japanese firms borrowed large amounts in dollars and then used them to remit prepayments for exports to parent companies or to purchase yen-denominated securities. Although there were controls on the receipt of advances for contracted exports, 'when huge profits over a very short period could be foreseen, the effectiveness of such controls was limited' [Fukao 1990].

To cap it all, on 15 August 1971, confronted with renewed attacks on the US dollar, President Nixon heralded a number of emergency measures which were to be taken to buttress the collapsing currency.

*Table* 3.1   Evolution of the Balance of Payments, 1946–72

|  | *1946–50* | *1951–55* | *1956–60* | *1961–65* | *1966–70* | *1971–72* |
|---|---|---|---|---|---|---|
| 1. Trade balance | −188 | −395 | 93 | 494 | 2862 | 8377 |
| 2. Current balance | 145 | 104 | 23 | −205 | 1310 | 6241 |
| 3. Long-term capital | −15 | −35 | −22 | 36 | −729 | −3803 |
| 4. Basic balance 2 + 3 | 130 | 69 | 1 | −169 | 581 | 2438 |

*Source*: IMF Financial Statistics

*Table* 3.2   International Divergence of Inflation Rates (Annual Average Percentage Changes)

| CPI | *1950–60* | *1960–70* |
|---|---|---|
| United States | 2.09 | 2.75 |
| Japan | 4.01 | 5.74 |
| Germany | 1.88 | 2.59 |
| France | 5.58 | 4.04 |
| Britain | 3.33 | 4.05 |
| Italy | 3.15 | 3.64 |
| Canada | 2.20 | 2.72 |

| *Wholesale prices* | *1950–60* | *1960–70* |
|---|---|---|
| United States | 1.50 | 1.52 |
| Japan | 2.21 | 1.28 |
| Germany | 2.03 | 1.32 |
| France | 5.00 | 2.86 |
| Britain | 2.87 | 3.08 |
| Italy | 0.54 | 2.49 |
| Canada | – | 1.77 |

| *Export prices* | *1950–60* | *1960–70* |
|---|---|---|
| United States | 1.26 | 1.52 |
| Japan | 0.29 | 0.28 |
| Germany | 3.89 | 0.76 |
| France | 4.80 | 2.49 |
| Britain | 2.60 | 3.11 |
| Italy | −0.55 | 0.55 |
| Canada | 1.28 | 2.16 |

*Source*: IMF International Financial Statistics, Supplement 1987

From Japan's perspective two decisions were particularly worrying, namely the imposition of a 10 per cent surcharge on imports into the US and the exclusion from a proposed investment tax credit of imported capital equipment.

It seems that the Nixon measures were essentially a bargaining ploy intended to force Europe and Japan to lower trade barriers and to revalue their currencies. The Nixon strategy had the desired effect and in December 1971 there was a general currency realignment. The yen officially appreciated by nearly 17 per cent *vis-à-vis* the dollar (although on an effective basis the appreciation was nearer the 11 per cent level).

Unfortunately, speculation in favour of the yen continued into 1972, making it necessary for the authorities to take additional measures to encourage capital outflows and to discourage capital inflows as a means of stabilizing the yen. (For details see Komiya and Suda 1991.)

Because of fears that the yen appreciation might induce a recession, fiscal policy was eased, while at the same time the money supply rose sharply. With regard to the latter, it is possible either that the spurt in monetary growth (from a yearly average increase of 17 per cent in 1968–70 to 23 per cent in 1971–3) was the result of a deliberate decision, or alternatively, given the expansion of the monetary base which the speculative inflows induced, the authorities may simply have lost complete control over the money supply and bank credit.

If the acceleration in the money supply had been intended then in retrospect it was clearly a major policy error. When the lagged effects of the easier monetary policy on inflation began to surface, the ensuing inflation rate was subsequently compounded by the commodity price boom, the oil price shock and the associated devaluation. To further complicate matters, large capital inflows enabled 'the city banks to repay their massive borrowings to the bank of Japan, thereby wiping out one of the major structural characteristics of the 1960s', that is overborrowing by the commercial banks [OECD 1972:69].

PHASE 3: 1970–95

**Adjustment to the First Oil Price Shock and its Aftermath**

In the wake of the first oil price shock, Japan suffered its worst recession since the early 1950s, with the 1974 GDP growth rate being –0.8 per cent. Fortunately, by 1975 the economy began to recover and by

1976 a 4.2 per cent growth rate was recorded. Although unemployment rose, the situation in Japan was appreciably better than in the OECD as a whole. In 1975 for instance, the respective unemployment rates were 1.9 and 5.1 per cent. The oil price shock also caused a substantial deficit in the 1974 current account (equal to 1 per cent of GNP). However, by 1975 the current account was virtually in balance.

In 1974 many adverse factors came to a head. Among them were the lagged effects of a previous acceleration in money growth, the worldwide commodity price inflation of 1972–3, the oil price shock itself which took its full toll in 1974, and the 1974 wage agreement whereby wages rose faster than productivity. As a result, consumer prices rose by 24.5 per cent in 1974 compared with a rate of 11.7 per cent a year earlier.

By 1975, with more favourable wage adjustments, a more restrictive monetary policy and the unwinding of the one-off direct effect of the oil price shock, the inflation rate halved. This then permitted a relaxation of monetary policy in 1975–6. As for fiscal policy, between 1974 and 1978, it was very expansionary, a situation justified in terms of the 1974 recession and then in terms of growing current account surpluses.

**Foreign Exchange Management**

With the institution of a flexible rate regime in February 1973, the Bank of Japan sought to reduce yen rate movements. Two principal methods were used. One was to vary the capital controls in place [Argy 1987]. When the yen was strong (weak) net capital outflows (inflows) were encouraged. The second method entailed sterilization procedures [Argy 1982]. When the yen was strong (weak) the Bank of Japan tended to buy (sell) US dollars in the open market (thus leaning against the wind) at the same time sterilizing the effects of the purchases (sales) on the money base.

How effective were these strategies? In seeking the answer, one might investigate the extent to which capital control changes achieved the objective of reversing capital movements. Assuming appropriate timing, if in fact the regulation of controls did alter the course of capital movements, the yen would implicitly have been stabilized. On the whole, the evidence does suggest that these objectives were realized (Argy 1987).

Did sterilized intervention succeed in stabilizing the exchange rate? There are two parts to this question. First, does sterilized intervention make a significant impact on the exchange rate? Second, if it did, did intervention act to stabilize the currency? These issues are very complicated. On the first question, there is now general agreement that sterilized intervention is likely to have a significant impact on the currency only if it impacts on expectations, that is acts to influence expectations about the course of the currency. On the second, there is evidence that intervention was on balance stabilizing (Argy 1994).

We conclude, therefore, that Japan's foreign exchange management policy was broadly successful in meeting its primary objectives.

**GDP Growth Performance**

We have already noted that there was a sharp drop in Japan's GDP real growth rate from the mid 1970s. The slow-down in real growth was not unique to Japan but was in fact common to almost all industrial countries. Table 3.3 shows the growth rates of output, total factor productivity (a weighted average of the growth in labour and capital productivity) and labour productivity for select groups of countries and periods. There was a significant slow-down in all regions but because Japan's real growth was so exceptional in the earlier period, it would seem that it receded much more dramatically. In Japan total factor productivity fell from 5.9 per cent in 1960–73 to 1.4 per cent in 1973–9; while labour productivity growth dropped from 8.6 per cent to 2.9 per cent.

In seeking explanations for these occurrences we should be looking not only for common elements but also for some elements perhaps unique to Japan.

Consider first the broad potential common elements. Shigehara (1990) has recently summarized the (older) conventional wisdom on the causes of the slowdown. He notes that the slowdown coincided with and is widely thought to have been caused by some combination of:

(a) the first oil price hike;
(b) some decline in research and development (R&D);
(c) rising female participation combined with a baby boom which left in their wake a less productive and efficient work force; and
(d) the collapse of the Bretton Woods System, associated with increased financial instability.

Careful studies, however, of the impact of the first three factors suggest that at most they could account for only a small portion of the slowdown. To quote Shigehara:

Table 3.3  Business-Sector Output and Productivity Data

| | Output 1960–73 | 1973–79 | 1979–90 | Total Factor Productivity[1] 1960–73 | 1973–79 | 1979–90 | Labour Productivity 1960–73 | 1973–79 | 1979–90 |
|---|---|---|---|---|---|---|---|---|---|
| US | 4.0 | 2.5 | 2.5 | 1.6 | −.4 | 0.2 | 2.2 | 0.0 | 0.6 |
| Japan | 10.0 | 3.5 | 4.3 | 5.9 | 1.4 | 2.0 | 8.6 | 2.9 | 3.0 |
| Europe | 4.9 | 2.4 | 2.3 | 3.2 | 1.4 | 1.3 | 5.0 | 2.7 | 2.1 |
| OECD | 5.3 | 2.7 | 2.7 | 2.8 | 0.5 | 0.8 | 4.1 | 1.4 | 1.5 |

[1] weighted average of the growth in labour and capital productivity

Source: OECD Surveys

For either energy prices or R&D to account for the bulk of the slowdown would require an impact that is greatly disproportionate to their weight in economic activity ... Similarly most calculations of the impact of demographic changes yield small effects ... Furthermore history has provided us with some further testing of these possibilities. In the 1980s all of these factors have been reversed without there being much effect on measured productivity. Oil prices have come down, spending on R&D as a per cent of GDP increased in many countries ... the work force is more experienced in most countries. [Shigehara 1992:21]

Shigehara proceeded to review more recent theories which try to account for the slowdown. These tend to assign a particularly important role to the decline in private and public capital formation but their estimated contribution to the decline is still not of much consequence. Shigehara himself contends that part at least of the slowdown 'may reflect such factors as high and variable inflation and increased structural rigidities' [1992:16].

Turning to Japan's own growth experience. A paper by Kasman (1987) examines the sources of Japanese growth and their change over time. Here Japan's full capacity growth is decomposed into various elements Typically we have:

output growth = $a_1$ capital stock growth + $a_2$ labour input growth + rate of technological progress.

($a_1$ and $a_2$ are the elasticity of output with respect to capital and labour respectively, that is the percentage change in output that results from a percentage change in one of those variables.) The rate of technological progress is the residual, that is the contribution to output growth not accounted for by the growth in the two factor inputs.

It is possible to calculate statistically the contributions of each of

*Table* 3.4  Composition of Japanese Potential Growth (Annual Rates of Change, 1980 Prices)

| | Potential Growth Rate | Labour Input | Capital Input | Technological Progress |
|---|---|---|---|---|
| 1967–73 | 9.0 | 0.1 | 6.5 | 2.4 |
| 1976–80 | 4.9 | 0.5 | 3.7 | 0.7 |

*Source*: Kasman (1987)

these three components to capacity growth. Calculations by Kasman are shown in Table 3.4.

As seen in Table 3.4, in the later period (1976–80) the potential growth rate almost halved. The growth of the labour input makes only a marginal contribution to the potential growth rate. The rate of investment fell in the second period and this contributed to a decline of nearly 3 percentage points in the growth rate, while the contribution of technological progress lessened by some 1.5 percentage points. Kasman attributes the slowdown in technical progress and in capital formation to 'maturation' of the Japanese economy. 'The gains from labor reallocation and from the closing of the technological gap between Japan and other industrial nations have largely been exhausted. An end to this "catching up" process appears behind the decline in rates of technological advance.' [1987:49]

**The Second Oil Price Shock – Adjustment and Aftermath**

The second oil price shock (in 1979) was about as large as the first but by then Japan's direct macroeconomic exposure had declined somewhat [Hutchinson 1991].

The economy was less heated than at the time of the first shock. There was no lagged accelerated money growth or a commodity price inflation with which to contend. Consumer prices had also been rising modestly in 1978–9. Monetary restraint was again applied but it was far less abrupt, falling now by some 3 percentage points on average. Moreover, in terms of real money balances, there was a fall of some 6–7 percentage points but this was nowhere near the 20 percentage point turnaround after the first shock. The most dramatic development occurred on the wages front. Wages rose very modestly at 6.7 per cent in 1979–81 and largely as a result, there was virtually no movement in the unemployment rate. Finally real growth in 1980 fell by only some 2 percentage points (see Table 3.5 and Figure 3.1).

*The Japanese Economy*

*Table* 3.5   Key Economic Indicators

| Year | Unemployment Rate | | Real GDP Growth Rate | | Consumer Price Inflation | |
|---|---|---|---|---|---|---|
| | Japan | OECD | Japan | OECD | Japan | OECD |
| 1960 | 1.6 | 3.2 | 13.1 | 7.1 | 3.6 | 1.9 |
| 1961 | 1.3 | 2.9 | 14.6 | 4.1 | 5.3 | 1.8 |
| 1962 | 1.3 | 2.7 | 7.1 | 5.3 | 6.8 | 2.4 |
| 1963 | 1.2 | 2.7 | 10.5 | 4.7 | 8.5 | 2.6 |
| 1964 | 1.2 | 2.4 | 13.2 | 6.0 | 3.9 | 2.4 |
| 1965 | 1.2 | 2.2 | 5.1 | 5.3 | 6.6 | 3.0 |
| 1966 | 1.3 | 2.3 | 9.8 | 5.5 | 5.1 | 3.5 |
| 1967 | 1.3 | 2.8 | 12.9 | 3.8 | 4.0 | 3.1 |
| 1968 | 1.2 | 3.0 | 13.5 | 5.5 | 5.3 | 4.0 |
| 1969 | 1.1 | 2.9 | 10.7 | 4.7 | 5.2 | 4.8 |
| 1970 | 1.2 | 3.3 | 10.9 | 3.1 | 7.7 | 5.6 |
| 1971 | 1.2 | 3.5 | 4.3 | 3.5 | 6.8 | 5.3 |
| 1972 | 1.4 | 3.5 | 8.4 | 5.4 | 4.5 | 4.7 |
| 1973 | 1.3 | 3.2 | 7.6 | 6.0 | 11.7 | 7.8 |
| 1974 | 1.4 | 3.5 | −0.8 | 0.7 | 24.5 | 13.4 |
| 1975 | 1.9 | 5.1 | 2.9 | −0.1 | 11.8 | 11.3 |
| 1976 | 2.0 | 5.2 | 4.2 | 4.6 | 9.3 | 8.6 |
| 1977 | 2.0 | 5.2 | 4.8 | 3.8 | 8.1 | 8.9 |
| 1978 | 2.2 | 5.1 | 5.0 | 4.3 | 3.8 | 8.6 |
| 1979 | 2.1 | 5.2 | 5.6 | 3.6 | 3.6 | 10.1 |
| 1980 | 2.0 | 5.9 | 3.5 | 1.3 | 7.5 | 12.7 |
| 1981 | 2.2 | 6.7 | 3.4 | 1.7 | 4.5 | 10.6 |
| 1982 | 2.3 | 8.0 | 3.4 | −0.1 | 2.7 | 9.2 |
| 1983 | 2.7 | 8.6 | 2.8 | 2.6 | 2.0 | 8.6 |
| 1984 | 2.7 | 8.1 | 4.3 | 4.6 | 2.5 | 7.6 |
| 1985 | 2.6 | 8.0 | 5.2 | 3.4 | 2.2 | 6.8 |
| 1986 | 2.8 | 7.9 | 2.6 | 2.7 | 0.4 | 5.8 |
| 1987 | 2.9 | 7.4 | 4.3 | 3.3 | 0.2 | 7.8 |
| 1988 | 2.5 | 6.9 | 6.2 | 4.5 | −0.1 | 7.4 |
| 1989 | 2.3 | 6.4 | 4.7 | 3.3 | 1.8 | 6.3 |
| 1990 | 2.1 | 6.2 | 4.8 | 2.6 | 2.6 | 6.2 |
| 1991 | 2.1 | 6.9 | 4.3 | 1.0 | 2.5 | 5.9 |
| 1992 | 2.2 | 7.6 | 1.1 | 1.6 | 2.1 | 4.8 |
| 1993 | 2.5 | 8.0 | −0.2 | 1.2 | 1.3 | 4.1 |
| 1994 | 2.9 | 8.1 | 0.6 | 2.9 | 0.3 | 4.1 |

*Sources*: OECD Economic Outlook

To sum up, Japan's recovery from the second oil price shock was particularly commendable. Of course general circumstances were much less unfavourable but monetary policy was applied more judiciously (less brutally) and wage outcomes were much more modest. Both of these factors contributed to a smooth transition and the avoidance of a recession.

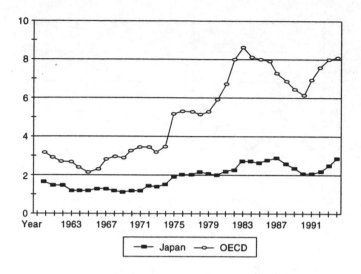

*Figure* 3.1   Unemployment Rate

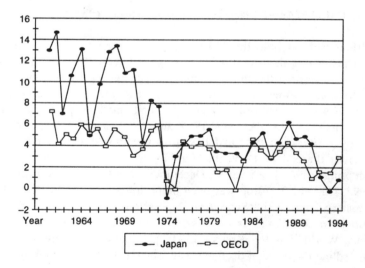

*Figure* 3.2   Real GDP Growth Rate

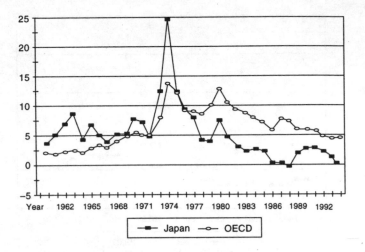

*Figure* 3.3　Consumer Price Inflation

## The Bubble (Asset Price Inflation-Deflation) 1986–95

Although throughout the 1980s the Japanese economy virtually grew at a faster rate than the OECD average between 1987 and 1990 when growth in Japan gathered momentum, the gap between its and the OECD's performance widened (see Table 3.5). Concomitant with this spurt in growth was an extraordinary rise in stock and land prices. As can be seen in Table 3.6, between 1985 and 1989, asset values more than doubled. (Between 1981 and 1989 they in fact rose by around fivefold.) Then at the end of 1989, the 'bubble' burst with the Nikkei average tumbling from 38 915 yen in December 1989 to 14 309 yen in August 1992. 'This 62.3% drop was even more dramatic than the drop of 44% registered during the Securities Depression of 1972, which had hitherto been considered as the most serious fall of Japan's stock prices since World War II' [Kon-ya 1994:1]. Land values were also greatly eroded but their rate of decline was to some extent moderated by government intervention.

There is little doubt that in the late 1980s, Japan was beset by a speculative mania which grossly inflated its asset values. However, even in the absence of such a phenomenon, some asset appreciation would have manifested itself in response to underlying fundamentals, of which low interest rates and high GDP growth rates were pertinent.

*Table* 3.6   Asset Values

| Financial Year | Stock | Land |
|---|---|---|
| 1981 | 81 | 128 |
| 1982 | 91 | 135 |
| 1983 | 107 | 139 |
| 1984 | 138 | 149 |
| 1985 | 169 | 176 |
| 1986 | 230 | 280 |
| 1987 | 301 | 449 |
| 1988 | 394 | 529 |
| 1989 | 527 | 521 |
| 1990 | 478 | 517 |
| 1991 | 373 | 504 |
| 1992 | 297 | 428 |

*Source*: Noguchi 1994: Table 1, p. 292

*Note*: Stock value is the total market value of stocks listed in the Tokyo Stock Exchange. Land value is the total residential land value in Tokyo

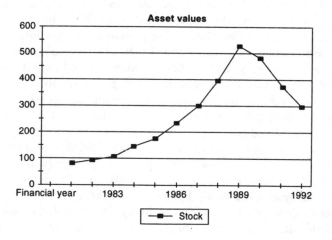

*Figure* 3.4:   Index of Asset Values

*Source*: As in Table 3.6

Also of relevance, the internationalization of the Japanese economy created an acute shortage of office space which was aggravated by a migratory flow from rural to urban areas.

Beginning in January 1986 the Bank of Japan initiated a succession of discount rate cuts. From January 1986 to February 1987 when the last cut occurred, the discount rate was halved from 5 to 2.5 per cent. Money growth accelerated substantially between 1986 and 1989. Whereas the growth of money had been of the order of 7.9 per cent in the three years 1983–5, in the four years 1986–9 it was some 10.6 per cent.

Various factors induced these changes. First, the US looked to Japan to maintain low interest rates to maintain needed capital outflows and when the yen rose even further, from 140 to the dollar in October 1987 to 120 in early 1988, a rise of Japanese interest rates seemed inappropriate. Second, by 1986 the economy was beginning to falter, in that the real growth rate was falling while unemployment was on the rise. Third, in 1986–7 the consumer price index barely rose. Thus, the combination of a stalling economy, negligible inflation and a strong yen constituted an attractive recipe for an easier monetary policy.

By 1988 real GNP growth accelerated and the unemployment rate fell significantly. Nevertheless, inflation continued to be very modest; averaging 0.3 per cent in 1986–8. The persistence of low inflation rates while asset values were racing ahead may seem paradoxical. The explanation lies in the yen appreciation which lowered import and input costs. A strong yen also forced Japanese producers to contain price rises by a combination of productivity enhancing measures and by impressing upon unions the need for wage restraint. Fortuitously, oil prices also declined.

The above mentioned set of circumstances yielded a 'normal' framework for asset value increases but other forces present fuelled a speculative bout. In the latter half of the 1980s, firms were increasingly capable of mobilizing funds by issuing stocks to a public, who on account of their generally improved living conditions and their accretion of wealth, were more willing to dabble in the share market than ever they were before. With a general rise in share values underway, between 1985 and 1990 companies amassed $638 billion by such issues 'in what seemed at the time like virtually free financing' [Wood 1992:6]. The companies in turn bought speculative shares as did practically all the financial institutions. In Kon-Ya's opinion, in response to more rigorous competition and performance disclosures facilitated by financial deregulation, mutual funds, insurance companies and other financial institutions sought profits from rising stock prices. This 'greatly increased the overall amount of money invested in stocks' [Kon-Ya 1992:5]. At the same time, the banks which were encountering smaller loan demands from large companies, turned their attention to the real estate sector and to smaller firms, both of which mainly borrowed on the basis of land as a collateral. By the time the 'bubble' burst, no less than 116 trillion yen had been lent to the real estate and construction sectors.

In 1989 the government realized that the economy began to be overheated. Inflation started to increase while asset price inflation began to be very worrying. Accordingly, by May of that year, it tightened monetary policy. Not only had interest rates been among the world's lowest but with rates consistently falling since 1980, there had been no other occasion in postwar Japanese history where rates had remained so low for such a time period. In retrospect, the Japanese authorities will now readily concede (at least in private) that monetary policy should have been tightened perhaps a year or so earlier and that the delay was a serious error of judgement.

What happened thereafter is well known. Asset values went into a tailspin and by 1991–4 there was a sharp decline in real income growth (see Table 3.5). The economy, which was in the doldrums, hardly spluttered above the 0.5 percentage GDP growth rate.

Opinions are divided as to the primary cause of the recession. One school of thought attributes most of the blame to the collapse of asset values, which through their negative wealth creating effects are thought to have dampened consumer spending and to have subdued investment prospects. At the same time, with the bottom dropping out of the land market, banks were left with a large volume of non-performing loans, making them think twice before entering into any new transactions and thus possibly giving rise to a credit crunch.

The other school of thought places more emphasis on the 1989 interest rate increase, a recession abroad and more importantly, on a needed adjustment to an over-expansion of productive capacity. 'Until 1983, the (real) ratio of private investment in plant and equipment to GDP was at a level of lower than 16 per cent. But from 1985 it surpassed 16 per cent. And during 1989 to 1990 when the boom in investment in land and equipment occurred, it reached an exceptionally high level: 21.7 per cent in 1990' [Noguchi 1994:318]. Similar trends were recorded for housing construction and for durable goods sales. That being the case, an economic breathing space was needed giving the recession the characteristic of a standard cyclical one. In fact, now that the asset speculative fervour has more or less been extinguished, the economy is poised to adopt generally more rational courses of action. Capital may be less frivolously wasted on showcase projects and lower land prices may serve in furthering urban social renewal projects.

Whatever the recession's cause, the government began to ease monetary policy in September 1991 and continued to do so on several subsequent occasions. By the second half of 1992 fiscal policy, which up to then had been fairly restrictive, was also eased. From August 1992 till September 1995 six separate fiscal expenditure packages have been introduced. The latest has been valued at 80 billion US dollars and has been coupled with the slashing of official interest rates to a record low of 0.5 per cent. Critics argue that the package fails to address Japan's banking crisis, the issue of general economic deregulation (a subject discussed in the concluding chapter) and tax reform and it remains to be seen whether it will help restore the economy to a reasonable growth path.

### The Kobe Earthquake

On 17 January 1995, a massive earthquake struck the Kobe area causing the loss of life of approximately 5000 people, destroying 150 000 homes and inflicting damage estimated to be around 2.0 per cent of GDP. Considering that Kobe Port, which was badly affected, normally handles 30 per cent of Japan's import and export containers and that the region itself represents 2.1 per cent of industrial output, initial expectations were that the earthquake would seriously compromise Japan's efforts to kickstart the post bubble economy.

However, the Kobe earthquake is now not regarded as constituting as serious a macroeconomic shock as first thought. The earthquake had in fact inflicted minimal damage on the region's industrial capacity, extra use of port facilities elsewhere averted any serious stifling of trade and in any event, Japan had been well cushioned given its huge trade surpluses and foreign reserve stocks. In the words of Saito, managing director of the Fuji Research Institute Corporation, 'the benefits to the national economy of demand for reconstruction should outweigh the negative factors of reduced industrial output and lower private consumption' [Saito 1995:15].

## A PARTIAL EVALUATION OF JAPAN'S MACROECONOMIC PERFORMANCE

As Table 3.5 shows, Japan's GDP growth has far outpaced that of the OECD as a whole. The manifold reasons for this are provided throughout the core of the book. Here we shall simply touch on Japan's record in unemployment and inflation.

### Unemployment

Judging from Table 3.5, since 1960 Japan has been blessed with what might be described as a situation of near full employment. Between 1960 and 1974, the unemployment rate never hit the 2.0 per cent level and from 1976 to 1994, it never touched 3.0 per cent. By contrast, the average OECD unemployment figure has typically been at least twice as high.

Before attempting to account for Japan's employment achievements, let us take heed of some issues relating to unemployment data. Unemployment data are drawn from national statistics which are not entirely comparable because countries define unemployment in different ways. The OECD has made an attempt to 'standardize' the unemployment data but this has applied only to some countries and for a limited time span. However, in practice the differences between national and standardized figures appear to be marginal.

Three difficulties which hinder inter-country comparisons are worth noting. First, in countries where a significant part of the work force is made up of temporary migrants, a fall (rise) in economic activity may manifest itself in the departure (arrival) of such workers. Where this occurs, less variation in the measured unemployment rate is recorded in comparison with countries undergoing similar economic changes but which depend less on migrant labour. As an illustration, let us take two hypothetical countries both with a work force numbering 100 and with an initial unemployment rate of 5 per cent. In the first country, five workers are foreigners, in the second all are local citizens. Assume that as a result of an identical economic downturn, five additional jobs are now lost in each country. In the second country (without foreigners) the unemployment rate rises to 10 per cent but in the first country, and assuming now that its five foreign workers are forced to leave, the unemployment rate rises marginally to 5/95 per cent. With the presence of migrant labour having been quite significant in several European countries such as Germany, Austria, Switzerland and Sweden but less so for Japan, Japan's relative employment record might be even better than what the figures suggest.

The second limitation in the statistics emanates from the fact that the unemployed may be absorbed into retraining schemes or put on the public payroll as disguised unemployed. This is relevant for Sweden, where it has been estimated that the true adjusted unemployment figure is much higher than the official one [see Calmfors and Forslund 1989].

Third, variations in the participation rate of the work force in response to cyclical fluctuations may differ substantially across countries and this could distort the true differences in unemployment performance. For example, suppose that when economic activity slumps, in country A the unemployed leave the work force (and thus are not counted among the unemployed) while in country B they remain in the work force and are thus counted as unemployed. B will show greater fluctuation in its official unemployed, but this will be deceptive. In terms of this illustration, Japan could be tagged an A type country for its labour participation rate is particularly sensitive to economic fluctuations.

Having noted some of the problems associated with making inter-country unemployment comparisons, we still think that it is perfectly reasonable to assert that Japan's rate of unemployment is both more stable and lower than that of most other industrial countries.

**Why is the Unemployment Rate Stable?**

We set out what appear to be the principal factors underlying this performance.

(1) Real wages in Japan generally appear to be more flexible in response to fluctuations in real demand than in most, if not all, other industrial countries [Taylor 1989].

Suzuki asserts that 'the Japanese economy behaves quite like the Classical model of a labour market. The critical point by which the Classical world and the Keynesian world differ is that in the Keynesian system nominal wages are sticky, while in the Classical world, real wages are flexible. The Keynesian assumption that nominal wages are sticky stresses such institutional factors as long-term wage contracts or a high cost of wage adjustments. We would argue that Japan is far from this assumption and is closer to the Classical world than the Keynesian world' [Suzuki 1985:3–4].

It is also believed that Japan can move to a lower rate of inflation with little impact on unemployment. In other words, the unemployment cost of a disinflationary policy is much lower in Japan than elsewhere, primarily because real wages are very flexible and adjust according to economic circumstances.

Why are real wages so flexible? According to conventional wisdom, the principal reasons are the following. First, unions (of which most in Japan are company ones) identify with their corporations and seek to maintain existing employment levels. Second, the bonus system (see Chapter 8) probably does inject an automatic degree of real wage flexibility. Third, although there is no formal incomes policy as such in Japan, the Japanese government does not detach itself entirely from the annual 'shunto' bargaining rounds. When deemed necessary it does participate directly, using a kind of 'informative incomes policy' (see Wagner 1989).

(2) Employment demand, given the real wage rate, is also very inflexible. Although the rate of change in production does fluctuate substantially in response to variations in demand this does not manifest itself in corresponding fluctuations in employment.

There are several reasons for this. First (as explained in Chapter 8), there is the institutional feature of life-time employment. Second, working hours are very flexible, providing an important element of adjustment. As Tachibanaki notes, 'Japan shows the highest standard deviation in working hours and the lowest in employment among the major industrial nations despite very high fluctuations in output' [Tachibanaki 1987:656]. Third, labour tends to be particularly mobile within the enterprise. Training tends to be more generalized, so that transfers within the organization also provide an element of adjustment.

(3) Labour supply is also highly flexible. There is a good deal of part-time work, primarily female, which is cyclically sensitive. Moreover, the participation rate is very cyclically sensitive, with many workers dropping out of the labour force during economic downturns to reappear when demand improves.

## Why is the Natural Unemployment Rate Relatively Low?

Apart from the high degree of wage flexibility in Japan, there are a number of social and cultural factors which contribute towards Japan having a low average unemployment rate. Some of these factors are listed below.

(1) Within agricultural and other sectors of the economy, such as in distribution, where a large proportion of the work force are self-employed, there may be a fair amount of disguised unemployment which eludes the statistician.

(2) In Japan, the teenage participation rate is relatively low.

(3) The education system in Japan may be more efficient in matching the supply and demand for different skills. Here we primarily refer to the high standard of education imparted in schools which makes for a more pliable work force.

(4) The relatively strict unemployment benefits system may have encouraged avid job hunting (see Hamada and Kurosaka 1987).

(5) Linked with the above mentioned point, the Japanese generally do not insist on working within their specific profession or calling to the extent that European or American employees do and on that account, they are more inclined to undertake retraining or to consider entering into alternative fields.

(6) Many public and private corporations may 'carry' a limited amount of elderly or low productivity workers manning reception desks, elevators and so on in fulfilment of some partial social responsibility towards such workers, rather than let them become completely redundant.

### Japan's Inflation Performance

As is clear from a perusal of the data contained in Figure 3.3, from 1977 onwards, inflation in Japan, as measured by changes in the consumer price index, was consistently less than in the OECD as a whole. Much of the credit must go to the Bank of Japan which has generally conducted its policies with an eye on price movements. Changes in the growth of the money supply have generally been associated with changes in inflation in Japan but at the same time, the rate of inflation has also been influenced by wage outcomes, fluctuations in the yen rate, commodity and energy price increases and taxes on commodities.

In 1987–8 monetary policy was too easy and this was in part responsible for the asset inflation of those years. However, in all fairness to the Japanese authorities, they were then subject to international pressure to ease policy and so perhaps this is more a commentary on politics and international coordination than on any misjudgement on the part of the Bank of Japan.

Generally speaking, monetary policy has been managed judiciously and competently. This much appears to be confirmed in a recent econometric study by Meredith (1992) who finds that, over the period 1980–91, had the Bank of Japan resorted to other monetary policy strategies (such as nominal income targeting, broad money targeting, a pure inflation targeting), the macro outcomes (as measured by fluctuations in output, inflation, short-term interest rates and exchange rates) would have been, on balance, inferior to those actually observed.

## SUMMARY

### 1960–70

- Because of capital controls, Japan's monetary policy was pursued with little regard for developments in the international economy.
- Changes in bank credit were used to stabilize economic activity.
- The major concern of fiscal policy was the attainment of a balanced budget.

### 1970–72

- As Japan recorded balance of payment surpluses, speculation against the yen emerged.
- In the wake of the Nixon shock, the yen appreciated by 17 per cent.
- Fears of a subsequent recession led to a relaxed fiscal policy and an expansionary monetary one unleashing inflationary forces.

### 1973–95

- First oil price shock in 1973.
- Economy recovered by 1975 when fiscal and monetary policies were eased.
- A flexible exchange rate introduced in 1973 and exchange stabilized by variations in capital flows and by trading in foreign reserves.
- The growth rate fell to more 'normal' levels on account of a changed world environment and because Japan had 'caught up' with the West.
- When the second oil shock appeared in 1979, recovery was much faster thanks in part to restrained wage rises and less inflationary pressures.
- In the late 1980s asset prices rose steeply both because of speculation and because of high GDP growth and low interest rates.
- The 'bubble' burst at the end of 1989 with the Nikkei Index falling by 62 per cent.
- Post 'bubble' recession most likely due to collapse of asset values, large non-performing bank loans, a previous rise in interest rates and the need to adjust to an over-expansion of productive capacity.

- To counter the recession the government has lowered interest rates and has introduced a series of large public expenditure programmes.
- The Kobe earthquake not likely to be as disruptive as first thought because most of Kobe's industrial capacity was left intact and because of the reconstruction activity.
- Unemployment in Japan is low and stable primarily because of wage flexibility and other characteristics peculiar to Japan such as a low teenage labour participation rate and more pliable workers.
- Inflation. From 1977 inflation in Japan has been less than the OECD average. To a large extent this is due to the Bank of Japan according price stability top priority.

# 4 Japan's High Savings Rate

## INTRODUCTION

Amongst industrial countries, Japan's saving rate is unusually high and this has facilitated exceptionally large investment rates during the period of rapid economic growth as well as large current account surpluses.

The phenomenon of Japan's high saving rate has attracted a good deal of interest and there is now a vast literature seeking to account for it. In particular, attention has focused on efforts to explain the wide gap in saving rates between the US and Japan. Although much light has been shed on these questions and we now have a better understanding of the principal forces underlying national saving behaviour, we are still far from fully comprehending either Japan's performance or her marked differences with the US. With these limitations in mind, this chapter seeks to provide some insight into Japan's saving behaviour.

The chapter commences by considering inter-country saving statistics and some of the difficulties associated with them. From there, it moves on to outline some general saving hypotheses and finally, savings within Japan itself are reviewed and some speculations regarding the future are offered.

## INTER-COUNTRY COMPARISONS

The national saving rate can be disaggregated into three components, namely public, household and corporate savings. Generally speaking, Japan's saving rate has been superior within all three categories, although its advantage is relatively smaller in the corporate sector (Table 4.1). Where Japan quite clearly excels is in household savings and this is borne out in Table 4.2.

### Measurement Problems

While the data in Tables 4.1 and 4.2 provide a reasonable approximation of Japan's relative saving performance, there are a few statistical problems.

*Table* 4.1　Saving (Gross Saving as a Ratio of GNP)

| | *1960s* | *1970s* | *1980s* |
|---|---|---|---|
| **United States** | | | |
| National | 19.7 | 19.4 | 16.3 |
| Public | 2.0 | 0.4 | −2.1 |
| Private | 17.7 | 19.1 | 18.5 |
| Household | 9.2 | 10.7 | 9.5 |
| Corporate | 8.5 | 8.4 | 9.0 |
| **Japan** | | | |
| National | 34.5 | 35.3 | 31.6 |
| Public | 6.2 | 4.8 | 4.6 |
| Private | 28.3 | 30.4 | 26.7 |
| Household | 13.3 | 17.9 | 15.6 |
| Corporate | 15.0 | 12.6 | 11.2 |
| **Germany** | | | |
| National | 27.3 | 24.3 | 22.5 |
| Public | 6.2 | 3.9 | 2.0 |
| Private | 21.1 | 20.4 | 20.5 |
| Household | 6.9 | 8.7 | 7.8 |
| Corporate | 14.2 | 11.8 | 12.7 |
| **France** | | | |
| National | 26.2 | 25.8 | 20.4 |
| Public | – | 3.6 | 1.3 |
| Private | – | 22.2 | 19.0 |
| Household | – | 13.6 | 10.3 |
| Corporate | – | 8.6 | 8.4 |
| **United Kingdom** | | | |
| National | 18.4 | 17.9 | 16.6 |
| Public | 3.6 | 2.6 | 0.1 |
| Private | 14.8 | 15.3 | 16.6 |
| Household | 5.4 | 6.1 | 6.0 |
| Corporate | 9.4 | 9.2 | 10.4 |
| **Italy** | | | |
| National | 28.1 | 25.9 | 21.9 |
| Public | 2.1 | −5.6 | −6.7 |
| Private | 26.0 | 31.2 | 28.3 |
| Household | – | 24.5 | 21.1 |
| Corporate | – | 6.6 | 7.5 |
| **Canada** | | | |
| National | 21.9 | 22.9 | 20.7 |
| Public | 3.6 | 2.7 | −1.6 |
| Private | 18.2 | 20.1 | 22.3 |
| Household | 7.8 | 10.4 | 12.3 |
| Corporate | 10.5 | 9.7 | 9.9 |

*Source*: Shafer *et al.* (1992), OECD National Accounts

*Table* 4.2    Net Household Saving as a Percentage of Disposable Household Income: National Definitions

|                 | *1975* | *1984* | *1991* |
|-----------------|--------|--------|--------|
| United States   | 8.9    | 8.3    | 4.9    |
| Japan           | 22.8   | 15.8   | 14.6   |
| Germany         | 15.1   | 11.4   | 12.6[a]|
| France          | 20.2   | 14.5   | 12.6   |
| Italy           | 26.9   | 20.5   | 15.6   |
| United Kingdom  | 11.4   | 11.0   | 9.8    |
| Canada          | 12.7   | 15.0   | 10.5   |
| Austria         | 9.9    | 8.2    | 12.8   |
| Belgium         | 16.5   | 13.7   | 17.0   |
| Denmark         | 7.1    | 16.7   | 14.7   |
| Finland         | 5.7    | 4.6    | 5.8    |
| Netherlands     | 3.9    | 2.0    | 0.6    |
| Norway          | 4.2    | 5.2    | 4.3    |
| Spain           | 11.8   | 6.5    | 8.7    |
| Sweden          | 4.7    | 1.3    | 1.9    |
| Switzerland     | 7.6    | 5.8    | 12.5   |
| Australia       | 14.9   | 9.8    | 8.4    |

*Source*: OECD Economic Outlooks. [a] Total Germany

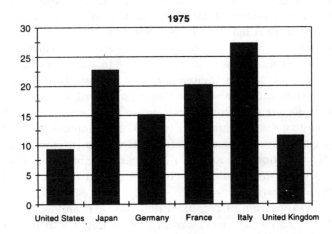

*Figure* 4.1    National Savings as a Percentage of Disposable Income

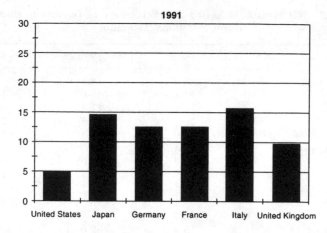

*Figure* 4.2   National Savings as a Percentage of Disposable Income

For a start, depreciation allowances are not all calculated in the same way. In the US depreciation allowances are (correctly) based on re-placement cost, whereas in Japan they are calculated on the basis of historical cost. Because Japan's depreciation allowances are understated (given the presence of some inflation), her net saving ratio (as shown in Table 4.2) is overstated relative to the US. When a correction is made for this, it turns out that the gap between the US and Japan net household saving ratio is reduced by 2 to 3 percentage points.

It can be argued that there is also a need to treat expenditure on consumer durables, such as automobiles, as saving. This is so since outlays on durables can be regarded as a process of setting aside in-come for future consumption, which amounts to saving. That being the case, only current consumption (that is, consumption minus dura-ble spending) ought to be deducted from disposable income. Since the US spends proportionately more on consumer durables than does Ja-pan, such a correction would likewise tend to narrow the gap in the household saving ratio.

Finally, as in the case of consumer durables, expenditure on educa-tion and on research and development (R&D) might also be consid-ered as a form of saving (investment).

Bearing all of the above mentioned points in mind, Shafer *et al.* (1990) standardized the national data for leading industrial countries. Their adjustments are shown in Table 4.3.

Table 4.3 starts with the gross national saving rates (as in Table 4.1) and then proceeds to make adjustments uniformly across coun-

*Table* 4.3   Gross National Saving Rates and Measurement Adjustments
(Percentage of GNP or Adjusted GNP)

|  | *1960s* | *1970s* | *1980s* |
|---|---|---|---|
| **United States** | | | |
| National saving rate | 19.7 | 19.4 | 16.3 |
| Adjustment for: | | | |
| Higher education expenditure(1) | – | 1.3 | 1.2 |
| Total education expenditure(2) | – | 5.1 | 4.6 |
| Durable consumer goods(3) | 5.2 | 5.3 | 5.5 |
| Business sector R&D | 1.6 | 1.3 | 1.6 |
| Total R&D(5) | 2.5 | 2.0 | 2.4 |
| Depreciation(6) | −8.9 | −10.3 | −12.6 |
| **Japan** | | | |
| National saving rate | 34.5 | 35.3 | 31.6 |
| Adjustment for: | | | |
| Higher education expenditure(1) | – | 0.5 | 0.6 |
| Total education expenditure(2) | – | 4.6 | 4.9 |
| Durable consumer goods(3) | – | 2.1 | 2.3 |
| Business sector R&D(4) | 0.6 | 0.7 | 1.2 |
| Total R&D(5) | 1.3 | 1.5 | 2.1 |
| Depreciation(6) | −9.4 | −8.7 | −10.8 |
| **Germany** | | | |
| National saving rate | 27.3 | 24.3 | 22.5 |
| Adjustment for: | | | |
| Higher education expenditure(1) | – | 0.7 | 0.7 |
| Total education expenditure(2) | – | 4.6 | 4.3 |
| Durable consumer goods(3) | – | – | – |
| Business sector R&D(4) | 0.7 | 1.0 | 1.5 |
| Total R&D(5) | 1.4 | 1.8 | 2.2 |
| Depreciation(6) | −7.4 | −9.4 | −10.9 |
| **France** | | | |
| National saving rate | 26.2 | 25.8 | 20.4 |
| Adjustment for: | | | |
| Higher education expenditure(1) | – | 0.7 | 0.6 |
| Total education expenditure(2) | – | 5.2 | 5.5 |
| Durable consumer goods(3) | – | 3.5 | 3.8 |
| Business sector R&D(4) | 0.7 | 0.8 | 1.0 |
| Total R&D(5) | 1.6 | 1.5 | 1.8 |
| Depreciation(6) | −7.0 | −8.8 | −11.9 |
| **United Kingdom** | | | |
| National saving rate | 18.4 | 17.9 | 16.6 |
| Adjustment for: | | | |
| Higher education expenditure(1) | – | 1.3 | 1.2 |
| Total education expenditure(2) | – | 5.8 | 5.2 |
| Durable consumer goods (3) | 4.2 | 4.5 | 4.7 |

*(continued on page 62)*

*Table* 4.3    *Continued*

|  | 1960s | 1970s | 1980s |
|---|---|---|---|
| Business sector R&D(4) | 1.1 | 1.0 | 1.2 |
| Total R&D(5) | 1.9 | 1.8 | 2.0 |
| Depreciation(6) | −7.5 | −9.6 | −11.2 |
| **Italy** | | | |
| National saving rate | 28.1 | 25.9 | 21.9 |
| Adjustment for: | | | |
| Higher education expenditure(1) | − | 0.5 | 0.6 |
| Total education expenditure(2) | − | 4.3 | 4.8 |
| Durable consumer goods(3) | − | − | − |
| Business sector R&D(4) | 0.3 | 0.4 | 0.8 |
| Total R&D(5) | 0.6 | 0.4 | 1.2 |
| Depreciation(6) | −8.3 | −9.7 | −11.3 |
| **Canada** | | | |
| National saving rate | 21.9 | 22.9 | 20.7 |
| Adjustment for: | | | |
| Higher education expenditure(1) | − | 2.2 | 1.1 |
| Total education expenditure(2) | − | 7.8 | 7.4 |
| Durable consumer goods(3) | 6.2 | 6.2 | 6.3 |
| Business sector R&D (4) | 0.3 | 0.3 | 0.6 |
| Total R&D(5) | 1.1 | 1.0 | 1.2 |
| Depreciation(6) | −10.6 | −9.8 | −11.2 |

(1) Public expenditure on higher education as a percentage of GDP.
(2) Total public expenditure on education as a percentage of GDP.
(3) Change in national saving rate as a result of adding consumer
    spending on durable goods to both the numerator and denominator.
(4) Change in national saving rate as a result of adding business-sector
    R&D to both the numerator and denominator.
(5) Change in national saving rate as a result of adding total R&D
    expenditure to the numerator and business R&D to the denominator.
(6) Change in national saving rate as a result of deducting depreciation in
    both the numerator and denominator.

*Source*: Shafer *et al.* (1990)

tries. Taking US and Japanese data for the 1980s as a basis for comparison, then after allowing for Shafer *et al.*'s adjustments, the national saving rate for the US becomes 19.0 instead of 16.3, while Japan's becomes 31.9 instead of 31.6. Although the saving gap between the two countries narrows a little, it is still unduly large. From this we conclude that we are dealing with a substantive difference in behaviour and not merely with a measurement problem (for a similar view, see Hayashi 1986).

## EXPLAINING HOUSEHOLD SAVINGS BEHAVIOUR

There are two leading theories of saving, both derived from neo-classical optimizing principles. The first is the so-called Life Cycle Hypothesis (LCH) associated with the work of Modigliani (1970). The second is the infinite-horizon model associated with the work of Barro (1974).

Savings can also be contemplated in terms of its dominant motives. Of these, three in particular are notable, namely saving for retirement, saving to meet uncertain contingencies (the precautionary motive) and saving to make bequests or intergenerational transfers [Sturm 1983].

The LCH model emphasizes the retirement motive, whereas the infinite-horizon model incorporates desires to make bequests and transfers. Finally, the precautionary motive is easily absorbed by either theory [Weil 1991].

Our own emphasis is placed on the three primary motives, but where possible, we explicitly integrate them with the two dominant theories.

### Saving for Retirement

According to the LCH in its purest form, households save exclusively for retirement. They accumulate assets (save) during their working years to run them down (dissave) in their post-working years. It is assumed that in general, no bequests are imparted. Thus, over an individual's expected lifetime, net savings are zero (which is another way of saying that lifetime consumption equals lifetime earnings).

In the long run, if there is no population or productivity growth (that is, if the economy is stationary) net savings will be zero. The working population will be saving but this will be exactly offset by the dissaving of the retired. On the other hand, let us suppose that real income per head rises. The working population will now be saving for their own retirement but since their real incomes are higher than the previous generation's, their saving, other things being equal, will be correspondingly higher. Saving by the working population will thus now exceed dissaving of the current retired, so net national saving will be positive. A similar conclusion could be reached assuming positive population growth.

In what follows we assume positive real growth. We also assume that there are no uncertainties about future income streams or about life's hazards in general (these assumptions are later relaxed).

Given the life-cycle framework and our base assumptions, variables that could be expected to influence household savings are listed below:

(i) *The retirement age*: The saving rate will tend to be lower (higher), the higher (lower) the retirement age.

(ii) *Life expectancy*: Given the retirement age, the longer the life expectancy the higher will tend to be the saving rate.

(iii) *The dependency rate*: The proportion of the dependent population (that is, both those who are retired and who are too young to be in the work force) is an important factor in determining aggregate savings. The higher (lower) the ratio of the dependent population, the lower (higher) will the saving rate tend to be. For example, other things being equal, an ageing population entails more dissaving and hence a lower national saving rate. Alternatively, a larger proportion of those below the work age gives rise to less relative saving by the active population.

(iv) *The rate of time preference*: Even if it holds that lifetime consumption equals lifetime earnings for the household, there is still scope for allocating lifetime consumption between working years and retirement. If, for example, people choose to spend more during their working years than during their retirement, less savings need to be set aside. Conversely, if they were to opt for better post-retirement consumption levels more savings would be required.

(v) *The growth rate of population and productivity*: Everything else being equal, the LCH also implies that the higher the real growth, the higher will be the household saving rate. This is so because the working population will now save at a faster rate relative to the retired dissavers.

(vi) *Social security and the tax system*: A link has been suggested between the availability and generosity of retirement benefits by the state and household savings. One would normally expect that the more generous the retirement benefit, the less the need to save and hence the lower the household saving rate.

(vii) *The availability of consumer credit*: It is conceivable that the availability of consumer credit will alter the time distribution of consumption between working life and retirement. The more that credit is easily on hand, the more the working population is likely to consume.

(viii) *Working hours*: If consumption and leisure are complements in the sense that longer working hours restrict the capacity to consume, then we might expect that economies with longer working hours would tend to save more.

(ix) *Inflation*: There are many subtle ways in which inflation could influence savings [Sturm 1983]. One possibility is that inflation can increase saving by reducing the real value of household wealth (which then has to be retrieved by setting aside more of one's income).

(x) *The participation rate of the aged*: The direction of the impact here is theoretically ambiguous. If more of the aged work savings might rise but since this effectively extends the retirement age, a lower saving rate is also possible.

(xi) *The real rate of return on savings*: Standard economic theory suggests that an increase in the real rate of return (governed by interest rates and inflation) will have an ambiguous effect on saving. On the one hand, a higher real return reduces the present cost of purchasing future consumption, which in turn ought to stimulate saving (the substitution effect). On the other hand, a higher real return reduces the need to save as much to achieve a given level of consumption in the future (income effect).

It is the substitution effect which is emphasized in life-cycle and infinite horizon models. Neo-classical theory, therefore, suggests that a higher return will tend to increase saving (more consumption in the future relative to consumption in the present). However, the empirical evidence is inconclusive [see Smith 1990].

(xii) *The distribution of income*: In all probability, a more egalitarian distribution of income results in a lower saving rate than would have been the case had incomes been more unequally dispersed.

## A Note on Precautionary Savings and Intergenerational Transfers

There are many uncertainties with which the average household has to contend. These may include uncertainties relating to future income streams, medical expenses and employment. Where individuals are risk averse, they are inclined to safeguard themselves by saving for possible future contingencies. In this context, the availability of private or government insurance is critical. For by mitigating uncertainty, the need to save is diminished.

Turning to intergenerational transfers, if a bequest motive is present, the saving rate would rise [Sturm 1983]. The relevance of the bequest motive, which is culturally determined, varies across countries.

JAPAN'S HOUSEHOLD SAVING RATIO

In considering Japan's distinctive household saving ratio, we first refer to aspects of the Japanese economy that have both a bearing on saving and which tend to be more marked in Japan than elsewhere. We recognize that this approach is subject to various difficulties. In the first instance, the theoretical underpinnings relating to each characteristic are subject to widespread ambiguities. Second, since there are so many individual variables, there is a likelihood that a multitude of explanations may be forthcoming and finally, given that some variable might exert a positive influence while others a negative. one, some means of assigning weights to them is imperative. Accordingly, we ultimately refer to various econometric studies for further evidence. Unfortunately, such studies are few in number, rather simplistic and do not accord with one another.

**A Survey of Explanations**

Japan's retirement age has tended to be somewhat lower than in other industrial countries, although differences are now diminishing. This would be expected to raise Japan's saving rate. Japanese life expectancy is the longest in the world and this again should make for a higher saving rate.

Table 4.4 shows the dependency ratios for the largest industrial countries. The ratio of the under 15 population to the working population (between 15 and 64) has not been exceptional in Japan. By the 1970s and 1980s there was considerable convergence in the rates. It is in respect of the aged population (the 65 and over as a ratio of the working population) that Japan's experience has been distinctive. (It is also distinctive when compared to a much larger group of OECD countries. See Hagemann and Nicoletti 1989.) This is strikingly so in the 1960s but less so in the 1980s. Japan's overall dependency ratio (the sum of the two dependency ratios) was particularly low in the 1960s and 1970s but substantially less so by the 1980s. No matter how Japan compares on average with other countries, its dependency ratio has been significantly below that of the US, although the gap has narrowed significantly between 1965 and 1985. We conclude then that dependency ratios have worked in the direction of lifting Japan's saving rate.

Very little of substance can be said about rates of time preference. It is conceivable that US households are more short-term oriented than Japanese households and this might just account for some small part of the gap in the savings ratios.

*Table* 4.4   Selected Demographic Variables, 1965–2025 (Percentages)

| Country | 1965 | 1975 | 1985 | Projections 1995 | 2005 | 2015 | 2025 |
|---|---|---|---|---|---|---|---|
| *Population under 15/population 15–64* | | | | | | | |
| United States | 51 | 39 | 33 | 34 | 29 | 29 | 30 |
| Japan | 38 | 36 | 32 | 25 | 28 | 28 | 27 |
| Germany, Fed Rep | 35 | 34 | 22 | 23 | 22 | 19 | 23 |
| France | 41 | 38 | 32 | 31 | 28 | 26 | 28 |
| Italy | – | – | – | 25 | 25 | 22 | 24 |
| United Kingdom | 36 | 37 | 29 | 31 | 31 | 31 | 31 |
| Canada | 57 | 41 | 32 | 30 | 27 | 25 | 28 |
| *Population 65 and over/population 15–64* | | | | | | | |
| United States | 16 | 16 | 18 | 19 | 18 | 21 | 29 |
| Japan | 9 | 12 | 15 | 19 | 26 | 33 | 32 |
| Germany, Fed Rep | 18 | 23 | 21 | 24 | 29 | 31 | 37 |
| France | 19 | 22 | 20 | 22 | 24 | 27 | 33 |
| Italy | – | – | – | 22 | 25 | 28 | 32 |
| United Kingdom | 19 | 22 | 23 | 23 | 22 | 24 | 28 |
| Canada | 13 | 13 | 15 | 18 | 19 | 25 | 34 |
| *Overall dependency ratio* | | | | | | | |
| United States | 67 | 55 | 51 | 52 | 47 | 50 | 59 |
| Japan | 48 | 48 | 47 | 44 | 54 | 61 | 59 |
| Germany, Fed Rep | 54 | 56 | 43 | 47 | 51 | 51 | 60 |
| France | 61 | 60 | 52 | 53 | 52 | 53 | 61 |
| Italy[a] | 52 | 54 | 45 | 47 | 50 | 50 | 55 |
| United Kingdom | 55 | 59 | 52 | 54 | 53 | 55 | 59 |
| Canada | 70 | 54 | 48 | 48 | 46 | 50 | 61 |

[a] Fund staff estimates for 1965–85

*Source*: Masson and Tryon (1990)

We have already noted that there are good theoretical grounds for believing that the higher the real growth rate, other things equal, the higher the savings rate tends to be. Japan has had a relatively high real growth rate, particularly in the 1960s and early 1970s. From the mid 1970s Japan's advantage on this score waned, so that a narrowing of the savings gap ought to have eventuated. As it happens, with so many other forces being at work, it is difficult to identify the changed growth rate's impact.

Japan's allegedly relatively underdeveloped social security system has frequently been cited as a partial explanation for Japan's high rate of savings. However, two points need to be made here. First, from about the mid 1970s Japan's social security system improved. Second, the precise role of social security in saving rates has not yet been clearly identified.

As to the impact of the tax system, with the matter being complex we shall simply focus on comparisons between the US and Japan under the following headings:

(1) tax breaks for saving;
(2) the overall tax burden; and
(3) the progressivity of the tax system.

Until April 1988, Japan offered special tax breaks for saving, up to certain amounts, in particular forms (bank deposits, bonds, debentures and certain types of investment trusts). This had the effect of sharply reducing the marginal tax rate on such income (down to something of the order of 10 per cent) and hence of increasing the return to saving. By how much, if at all, this increased household saving, remains unknown (see Horioka 1990, Balassa and Noland 1988). Since April 1988 these breaks have been limited to very special groups (such as the elderly, widowed and so on).[1]

Saito in comparing tax breaks in Japan (pre-April 1988) and the US, believes that 'any Japan-US comparison of saving-promotion policies must take into account the American treatment of private pensions and of mortgage interest payments' [Saito 1986:26]. This is ostensibly so because 'the deductibility of home mortgage interest and of contributions to private pensions, inasmuch as they make it easier for households to accumulate assets are similar in nature to Japan's tax free saving system' [23]. Saito concludes that, taking all tax breaks into account, 'the US favours saving under its tax system to a greater extent than does Japan' [25].

Some economists would argue (contentiously though) that the overall tax burden also has a bearing on household saving (the lighter tax burden being more favourable to saving). Until the mid 1980s, at any rate, Japan had a relatively lighter tax burden than the US (and substantially lower than Europe's). This might have acted to encourage more saving.

Finally, progressivity in the income tax system may reduce saving. For some time now, Japan's system has tended to be more progressive than in the US and this might have acted to discourage saving.

Consumer credit is said to be less freely available and conditions for borrowing are thought to be tighter in Japan than in most OECD member countries, so this could account for some small part of the relatively high savings rate. Table 4.5 provides evidence on this point. It shows that whilst consumer credit is not relatively restricted, housing mortgage loans are. Moreover, the downpayment for a housing mortgage loan is relatively high in Japan. Working hours are also longer in Japan and, as we noted, this could explain a relatively lower rate of consumption (and hence higher saving).

We have also argued that countries that are relatively risk averse tend to save more. Horioka notes that Japanese investors are very risk averse, having a strong cultural preference for safe assets such as bank deposits and postal savings accounts [see Horioka 1990]. The propensity to bequeath may also be higher in Japan than in most other countries. This is again a cultural phenomenon, reflecting the strong sense of community consciousness 'not only among members of the society but also among generations' [Horioka 1990:3].

Every variable thus far mentioned has tended to augment Japan's saving rate. We now cite variables which could have a negative effect on saving or which could go either way.

By reducing real wealth and by creating more uncertainty, inflation might well increase saving. But since in Japan's case, inflation since the mid 1970s has been relatively low, this ought to have acted to curb saving.

The participation rate of the aged is relatively high in Japan [Dean *et al.* 1989:43]. On balance this would be likely to lower the saving rate. Japan's income distribution is now one of the most egalitarian in the OECD [Horioka 1990]. Although this may be acting to reduce Japan's saving rate, its exact significance remains unclear.

Reviewing comparative Japanese and US interest rates, Frankel concluded that 'Japanese real interest rates were below US real rates virtually continuously from 1967 to 1989' [Frankel 1992:4]. Although from a theoretical point of view, this would have tended to depress relative saving in Japan, in practice its impact would most likely have been of little more than marginal significance.

Because of their importance in the Japanese context and because they have been widely commented on, we note two more potential influences on the saving rate: the bonus system and the high price of land.

It is frequently argued that a system of bonus payments would generate a bias in favour of savings, on the assumption that the propensity to consume out of bonuses is less than that arising out of the receipt of more regular income payments. While this notion has partly

Table 4.5   Indicators of Capital Market Development

|  | Consumer Credit Loans 1988 (1) | Housing Mortgage loans 1982 (2) | Downpayment for Housing Mortgage Loans (3) |
|---|---|---|---|
| Canada | 22 | 60 | 20 |
| France | 8 | 44 | – |
| Germany | 15 | 65 | 25 |
| Italy | 4 | 6 | 40–50 |
| Japan | 18 | 25 | 35–40 |
| United Kingdom | 10 | 45 | 15 |
| United States | 23 | 61 | 11–33 |
| Average | 14 | 44 | – |

Source: De Gregorio (1993)

Notes: (1) and (2) as a percentage of consumer expenditures

been supported by Ishikawa and Ueda's study [1984], Horioka asserts that 'bonuses have become institutionalized and are an integral and anticipated component of worker compensation' [Horioka 1990:66].

The price of land which is notoriously high in Japan rose very rapidly in the second half of the 1980s. Many believe that in order to secure a downpayment, the rise in land values have stimulated saving. The problem with this view is that if high and rising prices encourage more saving on the part of potential purchasers, an opposite effect might operate on existing property-owners. Because the latter enjoy wealth increases, this may act to reduce their saving rates.

**Econometric Studies**

Sturm (1983) undertook a comprehensive review of virtually all econometric studies (up to the early 1980s) which set out to explain cross-country differences in household or private saving rates. The range of variables used in those works included real income growth, dependency ratios, participation rates of the aged, length of retirement span, social security policies, income distribution and real (after tax) interest rates. What emerged was that all researchers confirmed the validity of the basic implication of the LCH, that more rapid growth entailed higher saving ratios. In addition, there was general agreement that high dependence ratios lower savings [Sturm 1983:178].

Later, Horioka (1986) made a further contribution in this area by

*Table* 4.6   Contribution of Each Factor to Japan's Higher Private Savings
Rate[1] (Percentages)

| Factor | Contribution |
|---|---|
| Higher growth rate of per capita income | +1.58 |
| Lower ratio of aged to working-age population | +11.47 |
| Lower ratio of young to working-age population | +3.15 |
| Higher labour force participation rate of the aged | −11.13 |
| Lower consumer price inflation | −1.65 |
| Proxy for land prices | +4.97 |
| Lower per capita income[1] | +3.88 |
| Residual | +0.06 |
| Total difference in private savings rate | +12.33 |

[1] Per capita income was found to have a negative impact on the private savings rate

*Source*: Horioka (1986)

seeking to explain cross-country private saving rates in terms of per capita income growth rates, dependency ratios, the participation rate of the aged, rates of inflation, a proxy for land prices per capita income, the retirement age and the public pension benefit rate. Concentrating on the US and Japanese private saving rates, where a 12.3 per cent gap emerged, Horioka was able to determine the relative contribution to this gap made by the variables under scrutiny. These are summarized in Table 4.6. Although most of his findings are in keeping with our earlier discussion, there are some surprises such as high land prices and lower per capita income adding to Japan's savings.

**Some Conclusions**

With Horioka and Hayashi both being the two greatest authorities on Japan's saving rate, we cite their judgements.

On the basis of his study, Horioka concluded that four factors appear to be especially significant and each seems to explain at least 2–3 percentage points of the gap between the saving rates of Japan and other countries. They are: conceptual differences and deficiencies (such as the calculation of depreciation and treatment of consumer durables), the age structure of the population, the bonus system and the rate of economic growth [Horioka 1990:84].

Hayashi, by contrast, rejects demographic, social security and real growth explanations. Instead, he places emphasis on the 'fact' that

'Japan's saving rate has been high because the Japanese desire to accumulate wealth in order for their children to live as well as Americans do' [Hayashi 1986:198–9].

Of the two explanations, we are inclined towards that of Horioka's.

## The Future Course of Savings in Japan

'A number of factors that may have contributed toward raising Japan's household saving rate in the past have become, or are becoming, less applicable, including: (1) tradition, (2) the low proportion of the aged, (3) the prevalence of the extended family, (4) the high share of the self-employed, (5) the unavailability of consumer credit, (6) the long working hours, (7) tax breaks for saving, (8) the underdeveloped social security system, and (9) the rapid rate of income growth.' [Horioka 1990:85] This means that Japan's household saving rate can be expected to decline even further. For one thing, the rapid ageing of the population alone will be enough to cause Japan's private saving rate to decline precipitously and to become negative by the year 2012. This will of course impact on Japan's balance of payments and investment potential.

SUMMARY

- Allowing for data deficiencies, Japan's saving rate generally exceeds those of other countries, especially in relation to household saving.
- Leading saving theories: Life Cycle Hypothesis and Infinite Horizon Model.
- Major saving motives: for retirement, to meet contingencies and to make bequests.
- Saving for retirement influenced by: retirement age, life expectancy, dependency rate (ratio of non-working to working population), rate of time preference, population and income growth rates, social security, working hours, inflation and interest rates.
- In Japan most of the above variables differ from those of other industrial countries and probably influence Japan's relative saving rate.
- Econometric studies indicate that data discrepancies, the age structure, the bonus system and economic growth have contributed to Japan's saving rate.
- Savings are likely to be negative by 2010 partly because of prospective changes in the dependency rate, lower growth rates, improved social security, less tax breaks and shorter working hours.

# Part II

# Industrial Policy and Entrepreneurship

# 5 Industrial Policy

## INTRODUCTION

The creation and execution of a comprehensive industrial strategy is one of the distinguishing trademarks of Japanese economic management. Many, including ourselves, believe that in Japan, public stewardship over industrial development was not only distinctive but also critically important in lifting the Japanese economy from its dismal postwar condition to its current industrial eminence.

It goes without saying that in the process of capitalist economic growth, entrepreneurial talents are indispensable. Also in the absence of sufficient incentives and of a mechanism for ensuring an appropriate allocation of resources, official plans or directives are more likely than not to be counterproductive. For this reason, economists are prone to concentrate on market conditions and on the nature of government activities which alter them, such as the imposition of tariffs, the provision of subsidies and so on. All these considerations are naturally important enough but in Japan so many subtle (and not so subtle) political and social factors also come into play, that without their inclusion, any analysis of Japan's industrial progress is bound to be deficient. That being so, while not neglecting basic economic factors we have also dwelt on so called 'non-economic' ones.

This chapter commences with a discussion of Japan's development state, the nature of industrial policy and the set of objectives that policy makers pursued. It incorporates a description of key bureaucratic organs, with a special focus on MITI (the Ministry for International Trade and Industry). The nature of Japan's industrial policy during the high growth period is explained and this is then contrasted with industrial policy as it is today. Finally, the contentious issue of the general effectiveness of Japan's industrial policy is reviewed.

## JAPAN'S DEVELOPMENTAL STATE

Unlike most other pre-industrial societies, Japan at the onset of its modernization drive was blessed with the evolution of what may be described as a capitalist developmental state [see Johnson 1982]. A precise definition of such a state is not readily come by, but essentially it is one which consciously fosters economic development. Overall economic leadership is assumed by the government but this does not necessarily imply large scale public ownership. The Japanese private sector has in fact been encouraged and treated deferentially, with the proviso that it moves in a direction judged to be socially desirable. Social objectives in turn have been determined in consultation with leading economic agents.

In Japan the most important postwar economic objective has been rapid industrial growth. An objective that has met with near universal public support, allowing politicians, government officials and industrialists to join forces in striving for its attainment.[1] Such a harmony of interests has bestowed an extra dimension of strength to the Japanese state, for without at least the backing of the country's industrialists, its power would probably have been attenuated.

To realize their aspirations, the Japanese devised and activated an intricate industrial policy. By the term 'industrial policy' we mean the adoption by the government of various means (such as legislative reforms or discretionary powers) to alter the general industrial structure and the relative acquisition of resources by specific sectors. In Japan this has usually been done in the interest of raising factor productivity and long-term growth but other, and at times conflicting, objectives have also been pursued. Policies within the latter category include those relating to employment maximization and the general minimization of the social costs resulting from structural economic changes.

The goal of industrial enhancement has generally had top priority even in circumstances where it might have negated the dictates of economic efficiency. In the early postwar years, instead of concentrating on labour intensive industries such as textiles, clothing, pottery and metal small wares and thus capitalizing on the country's relatively large and cheap work force, Japan's economic managers steered the economy on a totally different course [Allen 1981:85].

Dismissing the rational economic approach then favoured by the Governor of the Bank of Japan at the commencement of the 1950s and being convinced that the then market determined options would permanently consign Japan to a Third World status, the country's leading economic agents opted for an industrial complex based on capital intensive production techniques.

Two categories of industries (which were not necessarily mutually exclusive) were favoured. These were industries which had high world income-elasticities of demand and which were on the frontiers of technological progress. The first condition ensured that as world incomes grew, demand for the industries in question would expand at an even greater rate. The satisfaction of the second condition entailed a transfer and ultimately a self generation of technological know-how. If an industry also tended to seed the growth of satellite firms by virtue of it having widespread linkage effects, then so much the better. All told, the Japanese were judicious in the choice of their growth industries and were not enticed by white elephants that were technologically demanding but which were commercially dubious [Allen 1981:89].

Industries were nurtured by a combination of import restrictions and a package of fiscal and monetary incentives. The strategy provided for a limited gestation period (usually not beyond ten years) after which each industry was expected to be self reliant. Industries in temporary difficulties were assisted, but (with some exceptions) sunset ones and those not desired were encouraged to contract.

Over time the essence of industrial policy and the political framework in which it has been implemented have altered. In the first half of the postwar period, industrial policy was determined in the context of a three way partnership between the government bureaucracy, the ruling politicians and the leading industrialists.[2]

Each member of the above mentioned trio played an important role in its own right and constant two way communication occurred along each arm of this triangular relationship. However, at the apex and occupying a distinctly superior position sat the bureaucracy. It has wielded considerably more power and influence than have its counterparts in most Western countries, so much so that many non-Japanese observers have identified it as the ultimate seat of Japanese political and economic authority. In actual fact, such a perception is illusory, for instead of being vested in a single body, power in Japan has been diffused. Political and economic life has been enmeshed in an interlocking system whereby each of its components has been able to maintain a certain degree of autonomy. Nevertheless, the bureaucracy, somewhat like the British Prime Minister, can lay claim to being the first among equals.

## THE NATURE AND POWER OF THE BUREAUCRACY AND POLITICAL REALITIES

The executive bureaucrats and those eligible for elevation to executive positions, especially in economic ministries, constitute Japan's most prestigious and elitist body. Admission into this illustrious association is extremely restrictive. Only a tiny minority of the very best Japanese students are even likely to be considered. In 1977 for example, merely 1300 out of 53 000 candidates passed the higher civil service entrance examination [Johnson 1982:57]. Those that do, maintain a powerful *esprit de corps*. Aware of their special status, they imbibe a spirit of public service and devotion to their respective departments which is facilitated by constant interaction, frequent job rotations and a sense of solidarity with fellow entry cohorts. As promotion is based on age, each annual intake moves through the system in unison allowing for greater personal communication across each graded position.

The high ranking bureaucrats are a major source of policy innovation and seem to have had a fairly free hand in controlling and regulating the economy. Until fairly recently, they initiated and drafted virtually all industrial legislation which, unless it impinged on critical interest groups, was almost invariably rubber stamped by a compliant Diet. In the actual legislative process, parliamentary questions were often dealt with by ministry officials rather than by ministers. Similarly, instead of approaching Diet members, lobbyists were wont to petition the bureaucracy itself. All this was made possible by a supportive Liberal Democratic Party (LDP) which had held office from 1955 until 1993.

**The Liberal Democratic Party**

In no other democratic country has a single political party reigned for so long. Unlike most of the Japanese opposition parties who are beholden to single narrowly based interest groups, the LDP draws support from a wide cross-section of the population. Nonetheless, it is particularly responsive to entreaties from certain segments such as the farming community, ex-servicemen, construction firms, small and medium-sized manufacturers, small retailers and the medical fraternity. As for the LDP's relations to industry, it has consistently maintained a strong pro-industry position, standing ready to meet its requirements provided that the interests of its other protégés are not adversely affected.

Although the LDP is inherently conservative, it is remarkably undogmatic, preferring to base its decisions on pragmatic considerations that are in keeping with changing circumstances and public attitudes. Almost by default then, the bureaucracy had been granted considerable leeway to conceive and execute industrial strategy.

The LDP's rather loose organizational framework has also been to the bureaucrats' advantage. Within the Diet the party is fragmented into a number of clearly defined factions each headed by a senior politician. These divisions are primarily determined on the basis of personal allegiance to specific factional bosses, with ideological considerations having little, if any, significance. To attain the premiership, a candidate must not only be a faction head but must also secure the backing of at least one or two other party chieftains. This has resulted in a situation whereby many Prime Ministers have been incapable of manifesting strong and decisive leadership. Furthermore, cabinet posts have tended to be shuffled frequently. Under these circumstances, the civil service has been able to assert itself more vigorously than would otherwise have been possible.

**The Diet**

A primary function of the Diet, which is chosen on the basis of a universal franchise, has been to provide social ratification and thereby legitimization, to the bureaucracy's activities. In that regard, it has also provided a stable political environment which has fostered confidence in long-term planning and which has allowed entrepreneurs to expect a measure of economic policy consistency from one period to the next. The generally harmonious concord between the Diet and the civil service has been reinforced by the cooption into the legislative assembly of leading retired bureaucrats. There are more ex-government employees in the Diet than in any other legislative assembly. Their preferred party is the LDP where between 1955 and 1983, they occupied 21 per cent of its Lower House seats [Okimoto 1989:216]. More significantly, most of the postwar premiers have come from their ranks and between 1948 and 1977, they supplied 43 per cent of the cabinet ministers.

It would be an oversimplification to suggest that the Diet has always operated as if it were a paper tiger. On various occasions it has 'served as a mediator between the state and society, forcing the state to accommodate those interests that could not be ignored' [Johnson 1982:50]. In this light, it has assisted agriculture, rallied to the services of medium and small enterprises and has overcome the initial reluctance of the Ministry of International Trade and Industry (MITI) to combat pollution at the expense of some short-term economic growth. It has also deflected claims from a number of special interest groups which has enabled economic policy to be pursued with a minimum of interference from a multitude of conflicting lobbyists, an important condition for the smooth functioning of the developmental state.

## Government Ministers

In the day to day realm of running the country, cabinet ministers have tended to relate to the bureaucracy in a similar fashion to the way the Diet has, that is, the ministers have usually assumed only nominal supremacy. The standard practice has been for vice-ministers (the top ranking civil servants) to take full control over their departments' affairs. An indication of the power of the bureaucracy is provided by the fact that a conference of vice-ministers usually predetermines cabinet decisions. With respect to the annual budget, the convention is for finance ministry officials to concede politicians the right to determine marginal adjustments. If pressed to make more radical changes, they might typically proclaim that 'the budget is not a political matter' [Vogel 1979:67]. Their ability to withstand outside pressures partly explains why in Japan the tax system is reputed to be more coherent and less distortionary than in many other countries. For instance, 'declining, inefficient industries have failed to secure blatantly inequitable tax concessions' [Okimoto 1989:87].

Though they would normally have preferred their political masters to be as unobtrusive as possible, vice-ministers have also expected them to bear ministerial responsibility and to shield them from outsiders. As with the Diet, relations between the civil service and leading politicians have not always been cut and dry. Ministers with sufficient clout, especially those who were once themselves vice-ministers, have been known to assert themselves and to impose their will. Ikeda Hayato, for example, became famous for doing just that in both the Ministry of Finance and in MITI. Perhaps the incident that raised the largest public service outcry was the occasion in 1963 when the then MITI minister, Mr Fukuda, ignoring the outgoing vice-minister's advice, decided to replace him with a nominee of his own. Shocked officials who spontaneously went on strike demanded to know 'how is it that a party-politician minister, who knows nothing about the traditions of our glorious MITI, can pick a vice-minister we don't like?' [As quoted by Johnson 1982:262]

Nowadays, civil servants are more respectful towards their political masters. This change in attitude originated in the 1970s, when a subtle shift of policy influence occurred within the LDP, with the centre of gravity slowly moving from the factions to the zoku. (The zoku are senior politicians, not necessarily ex-bureaucrats, who have acquired intimate knowledge of certain ministries by virtue of their chairing of and involvement in specialist committees.) As a result, the LDP began to curtail the delegation of decision making to officials, and what currently seems to be emerging is an 'integrated party-bureaucratic structure' entailing intensive ministry consultations with the zoku.

## The Power of the Bureaucracy

Allowing for the odd occasion when the bureaucracy has had its feathers trimmed, either by the Diet or by the government, the fact remains that in its heyday it has had awesome powers. At its discretion it could award or withhold licences, subsidies, tax breaks or low interest loans. It had a large battery of devices which could be activated to direct economic life and to bring recalcitrant industries or firms into line and it did not hesitate to use them. Various public bodies have managed facets of Japan's industrial sector, but the one that has dwarfed them all, in terms of its scope and magnitude, is MITI, 'the pilot industrial agency'.

## MITI

In 1949 the Ministry of Commerce and the Board of Trade were abolished. Their functions and personnel were incorporated into a replacement ministry, the Ministry of International Trade and Industry (MITI). According to MITI's inaugural minister, Inagaki Heitaro, its chief objective was to transform Japan into a leading world exporter. To accomplish this, it was first necessary to attain a substantial increase in industrial output, the rationalization of enterprise and an upgrading of technical standards [Johnson 1982:193]. Hence MITI concerned itself with almost all aspects of Japan's industrial undertakings. (Some other ministries, such as those of Agriculture, Finance and Welfare, have been entrusted with responsibility for overseeing specific industries such as food-processing, alcoholic beverages and pharmaceuticals respectively but these 'non-MITI enterprises' represent a rather small proportion of Japan's total industrial output.)

MITI was well equipped to pursue its objectives for its progenitor, the Ministry of Commerce (known in the war years as the Munitions Ministry), had acquired a wealth of experience in economic planning. As the bulk of its leading administrators escaped the postwar purges, it maintained a continuity over time of senior functionaries. This enabled MITI to conserve the knowledge, experience and disciplinary tradition that its predecessors accumulated.

**MITI's Levers of Power**

The involvement of MITI in three areas in particular strengthened its domineering role. For one thing, it was entrusted with the task of scrutinizing and recommending all investment loan applications to the Japan Development Bank. Since access to Japan Development Bank finance prized open doors to the private banks, MITI's approval or lack of it sealed the fate of many an enterprise. Second, MITI had control of the resources of the Fiscal Investment and Loan Program, known as the 'second national budget'. As mentioned in Chapter 2, this account had been largely funded by the post office savings system and its annual receipts have often reached almost half the amount of those of the 'first budget'. Until 1973, its disbursements, which were channelled into projects that MITI deemed to be of national importance, were not subject even to token Diet consideration. To cap it all, under the terms of the Foreign Exchange and Foreign Trade Control Law, which was in force during Japan's rapid postwar economic growth period, MITI was the sole arbiter in determining the allocation of foreign exchange. Given that overseas capital equipment and inputs were urgently required, MITI's leverage over individual firms and industries was decisive.

**MITI's Structure**

By and large, MITI has been able to maintain a relatively high degree of autonomy. Unlike certain other ministries (such as those of Construction, Agriculture, Health and Transportation) MITI has remained moderately non-politicized. It has also been impervious to the influence and domination of any single industry or interest group. To some extent, this has been facilitated by an organizational structure divided into vertical and horizontal units. The vertical bureaux deal with specific industries while the horizontal bodies concern themselves with general matters. Within the overall framework, 'the tendency of vertical units to push for support for industries under their supervision is balanced by the broader vision of the functional horizontal ones' [Okimoto 1989:115]. If there is any outside body to which MITI must be especially heedful, it is the Ministry of Finance (MOF). MITI's expenditure is subject to strict MOF guidelines and without its cooperation, many of MITI's industrial policies would not have eventuated.

In general, MITI has applied its authority with considerable professionalism and care. It rarely utilizes the full battery of policy levers at its disposal and its various interventions seldom constitute a permanent increase in the application of state power [18 and 19]. Okimoto has described its degree of involvement with individual industries as following 'a curvilinear trajectory', being intensive during an industry's infancy, less so when the industry matures and more widespread as the industry declines [50].

To streamline its decision-making process, MITI regularly amasses an enormous volume of information through an extensive intelligence gathering network which now in fact spans the world. Work is delegated to specific divisions whose staff, across a wide spectrum of seniority levels, liaise both formally and informally with their counterparts in the private sector. On occasion, departmental officials take separate counsel from members of other sections or from outside specialists. Similarly, the business community may confer with its own experts so that MITI–industrial interchanges are commonly mutually informative and productive. In this regard, keidanren (the Japanese Federation of Economic Organizations) plays an important role. It mobilizes political donations and presents a united front to the government, imploring it to pursue measures which are supportive of industry in general. By acting as an umbrella organization, keidanren partially inhibits the formulation of policies that pander to narrow sectional interests. This does not prevent it from concerning itself with the particular needs of its constituents, for its one time Industrial Rationalization Council was composed of some 45 committees and 81 subcommittees spanning every industrial sector.

**MITI and the Industrialists**

In their routine and practical dealings with MITI, industrialists (as well as other members of the community such as academics and journalists) have been represented in the Industrial Structure Advisory Committee (from 1964 the Industrial Structural Council) whose subcommittees deliberate on matters relating to individual industries. By virtue of their inclusion, industrialists have been able to ensure that policy recommendations are usually not coercive and are in keeping with their needs.

This is not to say that relations between MITI and industry have always been smooth. Occasions have arisen when MITI has tried to impose its will upon reluctant participants. As it happens, when faced with concerted and united opposition, MITI, more often than not, has backed down. One such case relates to MITI's attempt in 1963 to pressurize the Diet to pass the Special Industries Law. This bill would have entailed the designation of industries in need of mergers. Since industrialists generally opposed it, the LDP did not endorse it. After two subsequent unsuccessful attempts, MITI conceded defeat.

## ADMINISTRATIVE GUIDANCE

Aside from deploying its armoury of discretionary powers and its ability to influence the pattern of industrial legislation, the bureaucracy, and MITI in particular, had frequently invoked administrative guidelines to elicit entrepreneurial cooperation. The form of the guidelines ranged from gentle hints to explicit requests, but in all instances they lacked the force of law. Even so, they were usually adhered to since few firms were prepared to risk the wrath of agencies on whose goodwill they were highly reliant.

Non-compliers had to contend with possible retributions by way of long delays in the processing of their licensing and other requests, with strong possibilities that in any case, their applications would ultimately be rejected. Furthermore, some corporations may have had reason to fear that unless they were forthcoming, MITI might well have delved into its vast storehouse of information to reveal publicly, hitherto undisclosed misdemeanours.

### Pros and Cons of Administrative Guidance

The practice of administrative guidance, which particularly came to the fore in the wake of the liberalization of foreign exchange, contained certain advantages. It forestalled the need for legislative changes or for budgetary adjustments, allowing for rapid responses to a constantly changing economic landscape. Since injunctions were also issued to specific firms, MITI was able to fine tune economic activities to a remarkable extent. On the downside, the process was an arbitrary one providing for little remedy in the event of bureaucratic abuse or blunder. In its defence, MITI might well have claimed, that since its general policy orientations were arrived at in consultation with key industrial players, only non-cooperative companies were likely to baulk at directives, which after all, were in the general interest.

Since 1984, MITI has used administrative guidance as a policy instrument less frequently. This resulted from a 1980 judgment of the Tokyo High Court (confirmed in 1984 by the Supreme Court) that compliance by firms with administrative guidance in violation of anti-monopoly legislation was not permissible. While MITI itself was not incriminated, it could no longer cajole industrialists into undertaking activities that were of dubious legality.

## Amakudari – The Cooption of Retired Civil Servants

Partly to provide themselves with a measure of self protection when the practice of administrative guidance was in full flurry, most large corporations began to recruit into their top ranks, retired senior civil servants. This process, known in Japanese as 'amakudari' (descent from heaven), affords a firm an effective channel of communication with respect to the ministries which are important to it. The recently acquired amakudari official maintains 'a personal acquaintance with government officials and a close familiarity with bureaucratic priorities' which 'are almost indispensable in reaching agreement to "adjust" policy' [Van Wolferen 1990:45].

The practice of amakudari has been criticized for 'promoting incestuous inbreeding and structural corruption' [Okimoto 1989:164]. To mitigate a possible tendency for government officials to favour companies to which they hope to 'retire', bureaucrats cannot transfer directly from the civil service to the firms in question. Instead, they have first to serve two years in unrelated corporations or in non-profit organizations.

An interesting case study of a firm which both tried to defy an administrative guidance directive and which initially refrained from employing amakudari bureaucrats has been documented by Johnson. The firm in question was Sumitomo Metals, which in 1965 refused to heed a MITI recommendation to prolong production cutbacks. (Sumitomo complained of foul play by rivals and of a positive MITI bias towards organizations that employed ex-MITI officials.) Sumitomo was given an ultimatum that unless it fell into line, MITI would restrict its imports of coking coal. Not only did the company yield, it subsequently invited a retiring MITI vice-minister to join its board of directors [Johnson 1982:59/60].

On the other hand, the absence of an amakudari bureaucrat can cut both ways. In the late 1960s, MITI attempted to extract promises from all automobile producers not to contemplate joint ventures with US companies without prior MITI consultation.[3] With Mitsubishi Motors, which desisted from employing former government workers, MITI lacked contacts at the personal level. It failed to win the company to its point of view and when Mitsubishi defied its wishes by announcing an agreement with the Chrysler Corporation, MITI's administrative guidance card momentarily proved to be of no avail.

## INSTRUMENTS OF INDUSTRIAL POLICY

Although individual enterprises eagerly responded to perceived investment opportunities and competed ruthlessly with rival corporations, it would be a gross distortion of reality to suggest that postwar industrial growth occurred within a free market environment. As the reader may infer from most of the above, economic events did not unfold in the absence of government involvement. In its quest for industrial advancement, the state consistently devised and activated a broad range of supportive measures. During the early occupation years, it even adopted an extremely interventionist stance.

### Early Postwar Steel and Coal Production Plans

In 1946 in response to a situation of critical coal and steel shortages, a priority production system was instituted entailing both material and credit rationing as well as explicit work force emplacements. Virtually all of the coal output was directed to the steel industry whose products in turn were restricted to coal. The underlying objective was a simultaneous expansion of both commodities so as to eliminate resource bottlenecks elsewhere.

### Import Restrictions

From the beginning, industrial development was highly dependent on import restrictions. Bearing in mind that in the 1940s and 1950s, Japanese expertise and productivity in the areas in which it later excelled were at such low and rudimentary levels, it should be obvious that there is no way in which many local industries would have survived had they not had protection. With regard to the automobile industry, for example, Cusumano has emphasized that it makes little sense to applaud Japanese management without taking into account the fact that it had virtually exclusive local market access. By permitting artificially high domestic car prices, protection helped to sustain profit margins and was an important factor in the industry's investment equation [Cusumano 1985:4 and 6]. The same could be said for steel, where throughout the 1950s, import flows were minimal even though local production costs exceeded those of the USA. As for the computer industry, various restrictions were imposed on IBM Japan to limit the scope of its operations to the advantage of local producers.

Import protection, which at one stage was among the world's highest, was maintained by steep tariffs and a comprehensive system of quantitative controls. The latter entailed a rigorous enforcement of foreign exchange rationing. In addition, the economy was made self reliant by a severe curtailment of foreign investment coupled with a close monitoring of imported technology.

## Other Forms of Industry Assistance

While import protection was the mainstay of industrial assistance, direct and indirect subsidies were lavishly bestowed. All industries benefited from an improved social economic superstructure containing new roads, ports, railways, power grids and telecommunication networks but certain companies received tailor made concessions. For example, in the government's bid to organize integrated factory and port systems, a factor which greatly reduced per unit costs, the Kawasaki Steel Company alone received some three million square metres of industrial land free [Johnson 1982:59]. Likewise, credit subsidies to shipbuilding played a significant role in enabling that industry to obtain international eminence.

Although generous industrial subsidies abounded, public largess was mostly directed elsewhere. Between 1955 and 1982, primary producers in agriculture, forestry and fisheries received over 80 per cent of national treasury handouts. Of the disbursements going to industry, a lion's share went to the small business sector rather than to high technology based corporations [Ogura and Yoshino 1988:122].

Within a fairly short time span, the state began to prefer issuing tax exemptions rather than awarding outright subventions, on the grounds that unlike direct subsidies, tax concessions need only apply once an enterprise does the government's bidding. Tax concessions were generous in the extreme. Investments that upgraded equipment were subject to very high depreciation rates as were export orientated activities. At one time, up to 80 per cent of export income was tax exempt. (In practice, as Itoh and Kiyono point out, the export taxation incentives actually realized appear to have amounted to a rather small fraction of the total value of Japan's exports.) [Itoh and Kiyono 1988:171]. As with subsidies, tax breaks were targeted not just in terms of specific activities (such as in research) but also in terms of specific industries. For this purpose, special laws were enacted, as was the case in 1956 for machine tools, in 1957 for electronics and in 1958 for the aircraft industry. Added to this, import duties on critical inputs were selectively waived, while excise taxes were occasionally lifted to meet individual industry needs.

An industry without the state's blessing would have been hard pressed to progress. It would have encountered difficulties in acquiring foreign exchange, investment funds and technology import licences. Unlike the nurtured ones, it would not be eligible for differential tax treatment nor would it receive development subsidies. By and large, the industries that became the country's dominant ones were those that received, in their infancy, MITI's endorsement.

## Public Control over Finance as an Instrument of Industrial Policy

Perhaps the greatest single ingredient in Japan's industrial success story was the government's command over the country's banking and financial institutions. In the early postwar years the state was the main source of industrial finance dispensed through various public bodies, such as the Japan Development Bank, and through the commercial city banks. As mentioned in Chapter 2, the private banks were highly regulated and had little autonomy in relation to the setting of interest rates and so on. They were expected to attend to the borrowing needs of industry. (Consumer loans were discouraged by tax levies on interest payments.) Japanese corporations, which had very low ratios of owned to total capital and which borrowed two to three times more than they raised through equity flotations, had an insatiable demand for bank loans. For major companies the risks associated with large scale borrowing were considerably lessened by the fact that the Bank of Japan had implicitly presented itself as their guarantor. That being the case, large commercial city banks were eager to finance companies operating within officially designated growth sectors. This factor stimulated new industrial entrants and thereby strengthened the competitive behaviour of existing firms.

## STATE ENTERPRISES

The government's limited direct hands-on approach to economic matters is reflected in there being a near complete absence of public enterprise in manufacturing. Public corporations do, of course, exist. By 1977 they numbered 113. In the forefront have stood Japan National Railways, the Nippon Telephone and Telegraph Corporation (now both 'privatized') and the Atomic Energy Corporation. Such bodies (termed kosha) tend to provide ongoing economic services. Others (classified as kodan) promote various construction projects while yet another group assist in financing regional development and small business ventures. As it happens, not all Japanese public corporations have been efficiently managed. Before it was reorganized and divided into six separate divisions, Japan National Railways which was grossly overstaffed, had an accumulated debt that exceeded the national debts of Brazil and Mexico [Horsley and Buckley 1990:197].

## GOVERNMENT PLANNING

Global economic objectives are disclosed in five or six year period indicative plans, released by the Economic Planning Agency (EPA), which was established in 1955. Formally, the EPA has no operational functions and no direct leverage over other economic agents. Considering that the EPA largely drafts voluminous reports, earning it the sobriquet 'the composition agency', it is not entirely devoid of influence. Its plans have provided a measure of flexible guidelines in determining allocations in finance, foreign exchange and imported technology and equally importantly, it has highlighted the industries which the state has sought to promote. For the industries in question, guaranteed government support made it almost inevitable that predetermined production targets would be exceeded. This partly explains why between 1956 and 1971, the growth rates that the economy actually attained were invariably higher than those projected. The industries that were at first singled out were electric power, ships, coal, steel and chemical fertilizers. Thereafter, synthetic textiles, plastics, petrochemicals, automobiles and electronics received the green light in that order.

Although at first neglected, a measure of regional economic balance has since been sought. By virtue of being the local authorities' major source of funding, the central government is able to ensure a reasonable degree of standardized public services (particularly in education) and a modicum of inter-regional equality. At the same time, local councils do have some scope for individual autonomous initiatives.

## MERGERS AND CARTELS

In 1947, in response to pressures by the occupying powers to eliminate restrictive practices and to foster more open and competitive market structures, the Diet passed the Anti-Monopoly Law. Modelled on US legislation yet being more comprehensive, the Anti-Monopoly Law 'prohibited holding companies, company ownership of stocks and bonds, directors of one company holding office in another concurrently, cartelization, and so on' [Minami 1986:151]. Legislation also provided for the establishment of a Fair Trade Commission to act as the law's enforcement agency.

Neither the Japanese bureaucrats nor the government were committed to the spirit of the law (a law described by former Prime Minister Yoshida as a shackle impeding economic recovery) [Trezise and Suzuki 1976:766], and in next to no time it was honoured mainly in the breach. In addition, legal loopholes were soon devised. These included the Exporters Association Law (applicable to medium and small producers) and the Major Export Industries Association Law, both permitting the formation of export cartels. More to the point, a 1953 amendment to the Anti-Monopoly Law allowed for cartels within depressed industries or within those undergoing structural transformations.

**Depression Cartels**

The 'depression cartels' were meant to provide a temporary mechanism for the alleviation and general sharing of losses. This entailed a coordinated supply reduction to moderate price decreases. Even before the Anti-Monopoly Law amendment, MITI orchestrated production cutbacks. These first occurred in February 1952, when ten cotton spinners were asked to curtail output. Shortly thereafter, output constraints were imposed on the rubber and steel industries. (Perfunctory complaints by the Fair Trade Commission were cursorily dismissed on the grounds that the law did not apply to informal advice.) With the eventual backing of legal authority, MITI's involvement gathered momentum. By the 1980s, some 2000 cartels (with varying lifespans) had come into existence [Horsley and Buckley 1990:53].

In their defence, it could be claimed that in most cases, depression cartels cushioned declining industries against harsh changes in market conditions and allowed for a more gradual and less painful contraction of their work forces. The cartels were normally expected to last for short periods only and where extended terms were sought, an industry was expected to demonstrate that a process of restructuring was clearly under way. Taking into account the fact that production quotas were usually allocated on the basis of prevailing market shares, the interests of leading corporations were well served. This does not imply that smaller firms were not also beneficiaries, for in many cases they were saved from extinction. In so doing, the cartels may be credited with forestalling, within specific industries, long run tendencies towards monopolization. On the other hand, while production quotas were being enforced, additional import curbs were imposed to prevent an influx of foreign products undermining targeted floor prices. (Additional aspects of depression cartels are covered in Chapter 8.)

**Excessive Competition**

Cartelization was also favoured in response to misgivings relating to 'excessive competition'. Unlike most other industrial countries, where observers have complained that there is an insufficiency of inter-firm rivalry, Japanese authorities have fretted with what was perceived as an unwarranted degree of market power contestation. They feared that excessive competition would be associated with excess plant capacity, predatory pricing policies and low profit margins. Faced with such a dilemma, the government believed that it had a duty to shape the country's industrial structure along lines similar to those of its leading competitors. More specifically, it wished to ensure that within critical industries, one or two leading firms would enjoy a large enough market to realize maximum scale economies.

The phenomenon of excessive competition mainly had its origins in Japanese industrial policy. Whenever the government designated certain industries as preferred ones and bestowed producers with attractive enticements (which of course included the government's commitment to the industry in the first place) corporate groupings as well as certain firms acting on their own, were persuaded that representation in such industries was imperative. Furthermore, the establishment of recession cartels, ostensibly to protect all industry participants, added fuel to the competitive flames. This was primarily due to the fact that recession cartels not only guaranteed an orderly response to difficult market situations but as each firm's production quota depended on its recent market share, each firm had yet another incentive to boost output. Occasionally this resulted in an industry's total supply capacity outstripping local consumer needs and thus generating a bout of cutthroat competition which, in the government's view, was to the producers' collective disadvantage.

## Encouragement of Mergers

By the early 1960s, the merging of firms that culminated in the dominance of a few giant complexes, was officially sponsored. To encourage such a process, the Japanese Development Bank indicated a willingness to assist financially. One beneficiary was Nissan Motors which secured an $11.1 million loan to arrange a tie-in with the Prince Automobile Company [Johnson 1982:268]. The government's resolve in this area was reinforced, when in 1964, Japan joined the OECD and committed itself to a more open and liberalized economy. At that time the country was beset by fears that once markets and institutions were deregulated, foreign enterprises would enter the country and would take over local enterprises. Hence the so called need for fewer, yet fiscally stronger, companies.

This policy was supported by a significant proportion of the private sector. More specifically, in March 1966 leading industrialists formed an Industrial Problems Research Association (SANKEN) which advocated mergers in areas such as steel, automobiles, machine tools, computers, petroleum refining, petrochemicals and synthetic leather. As a result, the 1970 Yawata-Fuzi merger materialized, leading to the creation of the New Japan Steel Company (then the world's largest). Interestingly, in the process, the Fair Trade Commission flexed its seldom used muscles. It insisted upon the two firms trimming back their strength and in a high court challenge, it succeeded in forcing each to divest itself of a plant as a merger precondition.

## Backtracking on Mergers

By 1974, for the first time in Japanese history, companies were prosecuted for violating anti-trust legislation.[4] This was followed by a 1977 revision of the Anti-Monopoly Law which further empowered the Fair Trade Commission to counter monopolistic tendencies. Among the changes, provision was made for the surcharging of unfair profits and for the enabling of the Fair Trade Commission to restore competition (by splitting or divesting companies of their assets) in oligopolistic industries where domestic sales exceeded 50 billion yen or where the market share of the largest or two largest companies exceeded 50 or 75 per cent respectively. These measures heralded a strengthening of the market mechanism which was manifested by a significant fall in the annual number of mergers, particularly horizontal ones, which as a percentage of the total, declined from 28.5 per cent in 1971 to 16.7 per cent in 1980 [Uekusa 1987:482]. As it happens, the enthusiasm for mergers had never been universal. Many a firm had successfully rebuffed MITI's entreaties in this regard, and to its chagrin, the number of independent industrial corporations has not significantly been altered.

## ECONOMIC LIBERALIZATION

Upon embarking on their postwar industrialization drive, the Japanese commandeered labour and resources with the same zest and sense of urgency as they had done earlier in their pursuit of military objectives. For all intents and purposes, the economy was marshalled in the interests of industrial progress, and to this end, it was fortified with a wide range of regulatory devices. Not until the late 1950s, by which time Japan had sought affiliation with various international economic bodies, did the government contemplate the introduction of liberalization measures. In 1960, in accordance with membership requirements of both the IMF and the GATT, Japan committed itself to the adoption of free trade policies. At first, it proposed an 80 per cent reduction in import barriers over a three year period but in response to IMF objections, it modified its offering to a 90 per cent target. Later it undertook neither to subsidize exports nor to resurrect (even on a temporary basis) trade controls under the pretext of balance of payment problems. To the dismay of MITI officials, foreign exchange rationing was terminated as were controls in international capital transactions but 'not until 1980, when the Foreign Capital Law of 1959 was finally abolished, could it be said that Japanese economic demobilization was more or less complete' [Johnson 1982:272]. The process was a lengthy one, on account of internal resistance, especially by government officials fearing a loss of economic control and possible departmental redundancies. Efforts were made to offset the liberalization measures by the introduction of complex exclusions but a critical and vigilant international community ultimately made it clear that prevarications would not be countenanced.

Once all the dust had finally settled, formal import barriers were reduced profoundly. Compared with the situation in 1962 when 466 product categories were subject to import quota restrictions, by 1975 only 27 items were listed. Of these just five applied to manufactured goods [Tsuruta 1988:55]. As for import tariff rates, by 1981 these amounted to an average of 2.5 per cent for all imports or 4.3 per cent for dutiable goods [Eads and Yamamura 1987:454].

## CONTEMPORARY INDUSTRIAL POLICY

### Outdated Policy Instruments

With the dismantling of trade and financial controls, the authorities sacrificed a package of policy instruments by which they coordinated industrial affairs. Gone is the government's ability to manipulate resource flows through the allocation of foreign exchange and import permits. Similarly (as already explained), MITI can no longer effectively orchestrate economic ventures, either broadly or in firm specific terms, by resorting to administrative guidance. Nor can it readily lend a hand in setting up cartels. GATT rules preclude the subsidization of exports, whether by direct monetary payments or indirectly by means of taxation rebates. While in the realm of finance, firms (other than small ones) which can now largely meet their fiscal requirements from retained earnings, the commercial banks or the stock market, are considerably more independent of the state. No longer is the government freely able to ensure the channelling of funds to targeted industries by counting on disbursements from the Fiscal Investment and Loan Program to seed an avalanche of commercial bank support.

### New Objectives

As it happened, the feathers of MITI and the other economic agencies were trimmed just when Japanese industry fully came of age. From then on, the need for an activist industrial policy was more frequently questioned and the overseeing of industry became just one aspect of general economic policy [Komiya 1990:306]. With the advent of economic maturity, the weight of objectives tilted from rapid growth towards the enhancement of the quality of life, with issues such as working conditions, leisure and welfare increasingly coming to the fore. Industrial policy currently focuses on redressing obvious market failures.

Matters which are now within its purview include problems associated with declining sectors, the reduction of capital risks in fostering advancements in research and development, the inadequacy of social overheads, the improvement of public services and of course, the promotion, wherever feasible, of high technology industries.

## Official 'Visions'

On its part, the industrial sector's expectations of public support have become more subdued. Instead of counting on concrete measures entailing favourable incentives, manufacturers look to government sources for detailed information regarding anticipated changes in industrial structures and predicted developments in high level technology. Such information is fed into their decision-making procedures and in fact now constitutes the core of contemporary industrial policy [Uekusa 1988:96]. The documents by which official views are imparted are referred to as 'visions'. The visions serve not only as vehicles for the disclosure of government assessments and aspirations but they also assist in forging a general consensus of expectations to facilitate government inspired inter-firm cooperation.

Although the scope for bureaucratic intervention is much reduced, this does not imply that the government is entirely incapable of influencing the course of industrial events. Being true to form, the state still musters whatever forms of economic control are still at its disposal. Within its reduced tool kit, it can still find the means to enhance the country's technological know-how and to afford a measure of hidden protection to favoured industries.

## Research and Development

Recently, MITI has given priority to the encouragement of research and development (R&D) in the private sector which shoulders most of the country's efforts in this regard. Government funds as a percentage of total R&D are relatively low, while the proportion of government funds accounting for the private sector's R&D budget is lower still. In 1987, for example, the respective figures were 19.9 and 1.7 per cent [Okuno-Fujiwara 1991:292]. Where MITI does make an imprint is through its involvement in the establishment of Technology Research Associations (TRAs). These are groupings of private firms (with government financial backing) organized on an *ad hoc* and temporary basis to conduct research in areas of interest to the companies in question.

TRAs are primarily constituted to enable firms to share both the capital costs and risks associated with major research projects and to benefit from a pooling of scientific personnel. The assumption is that in the short run, the advantages of any ensuing technological breakthroughs would be exclusively, or certainly mainly, appropriated by participant corporations.

A very high profile TRA was one centred on Very Large Scale Integrated Circuits (VLSI) which was active between 1976 and 1979 and involved five leading companies, namely Fujitsu, Hitachi, Mitsubishi Electric, NEC and Toshiba. Operating on a 70 billion yen budget (of which MITI contributed 29 billion yen), its major objective was the development of high-density high-speed semiconductors. The project yielded more than 1000 patent applications, some of which were considered to be in the forefront of world technology [Okuno-Fujiwara: 1991:284] and it has been credited with playing a key role in furthering the rapid increase in exports to the USA of 64K RAM chips [Eads and Yamamura 1987:457]. Equally impressive was the optoelectronics project, in force from 1979 until 1987, which incorporated 14 companies with cooperative access to a MITI provided laboratory. The ability of the Japanese to move within a six year period from a position of inferiority to virtual domination in the optoelectronic field is largely attributed to this project. Among its major beneficiaries were producers of video discs, optical fibres, laser beam printers, medical lasers and fax machines.[5]

Very much vexed by the success of Japan's TRAs, a success considered to be based on unfair competitive practices (taking into account their consortium nature and reliance on public support), the USA and other industrial countries demanded access to TRA generated patents and the inclusion in subsequent associations, of foreign firms incorporated in Japan. Meeting this criticism, projects are presently more oriented towards basic research, are less extensively subsidized and have far greater cross industry representation.

**Government Procurements**

An area whereby certain industries do indeed enjoy a measure of official protection and which is likely to endure, lies in the field of government procurements. This practice, which to some extent is more or less universal, has proven to be a godsend to certain Japanese industries. Computer producers in particular have reaped tangible benefits in that in 1982, for example, the four largest domestic manufacturers depended on government purchases for around 30 per cent of their sales [Shinjo 1988:337]. Even in this sphere, Japan has been subject to external pressures and has now committed itself to providing foreign manufacturers with a share of its procurement outlays.

## AN ASSESSMENT OF INDUSTRIAL POLICY

### Economic Theory and Industrial Policy

Standard economic theory provides little support for the application of an ongoing interventionist industrial policy. It does of course endorse the need for government actions to offset the perverse effects of price distortions and to rectify any inefficient resource allocations emanating from externalities. However, while economic theory emphasizes the necessity for the rectification of such market failures, it certainly does not justify the continued direct official involvement in industrial matters that have characterized the Japanese experience. That is not to say that Japanese policy makers have been misguided, for economic 'science' is by no means foolproof. Japanese officials, with some credibility, could well argue that economics is found wanting when advice relating to long-run growth patterns is sought. This is particularly so when conflicts between static and dynamic comparative advantages exist.

To illustrate the point, imagine some Third World country that has strong comparative advantages in primary products such as coffee and sugar. Assume further that it has virtually no manufacturing enterprises and that the market functions efficiently in that resources are deployed so that current incomes are maximized. A certain amount of savings may be generated annually but they are likely to be invested in existing activities, for by definition, alternative options are economically unattractive. Unless the manufactured sector is protected, entry into it would be unprofitable. Not only is capital likely to be confined to the primary sector but so is labour whose skills and training would have been geared to its needs. The economy may then be locked into a low income equilibrium level. It is possible that over many decades certain changes might be discerned. Aspects of industry might flourish based on natural protection and eventually various general manufacturing capabilities may be acquired but the time taken may exceed individual lifespans. Even the growth and changes attained may not be of the kind that maximize technological and labour productivity improvements. In short, it is possible for a competitive market economy to exist in a state free of price distortions and externalities and yet be in need of government guidance to direct it onto a more progressive course.

Although MITI did not begin seriously to theorize about the role of industrial policy until the 1960s, there was never any question of its commitment to one. Throughout the organization, officials were united in their view that the free market could not be relied upon to induce desirable economic changes without at least some form of government involvement. Many functionaries were convinced that existing corporations tended to perpetuate the status quo, for when faced with unfavourable market conditions, firms were believed to be more inclined to seek enhanced protection than to venture into new and uncharted fields [Johnson 1982:28]. Accordingly, the government had to assume responsibility for acting as a catalyst for galvanizing the forces and energy needed for economic restructuring and progress.

Furthermore, the Japanese practice of protecting and promoting industries on the frontiers of technology has recently met with the approval of some American economists. It seems that official assistance in enhancing world market shares in pioneer industries, where both producers and labour reap high returns, is regarded as an effective means of improving national welfare at the expense of foreign competitors [Dosi, Tyson and Zysman 1989:7].

## The Evaluation of Industrial Policy

Turning to the question of evaluating the effectiveness of Japanese industrial policy, it readily becomes apparent that the issue cannot decisively be determined. We know for certain how Japan fared when its actual policies were applied but we can never be sure how events would have unfolded had another course of action been pursued. No matter how sophisticated the theoretical and econometric analysis utilized, all estimated counterfactuals constitute nothing more than best guesses. With that in mind, the issue might partially be resolved by surveying the major arguments advanced by both some of the leading opponents and adherents of Japan's postwar industrial strategy.

### Critics of Industrial Policy

Ironically, many Japanese economists have taken a lead in challenging the widely held view that their country's economic success is in no small measure due to official industrial guidance. Instead, they would

like the Japanese economy to be perceived as a competitive market-
oriented one, dominated neither by big business nor bureaucrats and
in which growth 'was achieved *only* as a result of the high rate of
savings by the people, by their will to work, and by the vigorous efforts of Japan's entrepreneurs'.[6] It is quite possible that such a stance
reflects a desire among certain Japanese academics to downplay the
role of their country's industrial policy lest Japan be accused of resorting to 'unfair' practices. Alternatively, given that they are so extremely dismissive of industrial policy, the scholars in question may
simply be imbued with anti-interventionist economic philosophies.

Not only is Japan's industrial policy's contribution to growth accorded faint, if any, recognition but its detractors doubt whether there
ever were sufficient grounds to warrant it in the first place. According
to Komiya, official Japanese economic decision-makers believed that
an activist industrial policy was required to enable Japan, which in the
late 1940s was a very poor country (with little land, few natural resources and a large population), to 'catch up' with the advanced economies. However, Komiya asserts that 'from the perspective of economic
theory, differing resource endowments, being a latecomer, or undergoing reconstruction from war does not in itself constitute market failure' [Komiya 1990:291]. That being so, the case for state intervention
supposedly rested on a false premise, especially in light of Singapore's
experience. An experience which Komiya believes indicates that had
Japan relied exclusively on the market mechanism, it may well have
realized an ever higher rate of growth of industrialization [291].

A common tack taken by industrial policy opponents is the citing of
industries which seemingly did not enjoy any special government patronage and yet nonetheless thrived. Trezise and Suzuki list cement, paper, glass and bicycles as being among those sectors which received
scant public assistance but between 1955 and 1970 grew more than
threefold [Trezise and Suzuki 1976:794]. Other fields generally mentioned include radios, television sets, optical goods, motorcycles, pianos,
tape recorders, audio equipment, fishing gear, watches and clocks, cal-
culators, machine tools, communication equipment, cameras and robots
(in the case of robots, it took a decade and the participation of more
than 100 different firms until the government's blessing was obtained).
The success of the above mentioned industries is taken to indicate that
official support is unnecessary. In Komiya's opinion, for industries that
enjoy rapid productivity gains and for which the income of elasticity
of demand is high, growth would, in any event, occur spontaneously
[Komiya 1990:293].

Considering that Japanese industries are seemingly nourished by the free play of market forces, official attempts to moderate excessive competition are regarded by industrial policy opponents with disdain. For one thing, they identify competitive forces as a major factor in Japan's procurement of new technology and for another, they argue that from a general understanding 'of welfare economics and industrial organization, excessive competition seems a questionable and self-contradictory term' [Suzumura and Okuno-Fujiwara 1987:27].

Even if a hypothetical case for industrial policy were to be conceded, critics maintain that in practice it has been discredited. Because social and political imperatives compelled the authorities to serve the needs of certain economically inefficient interest groups, such as farmers and small shopkeepers, there was inevitably an element of inconsistency in Japanese economic management. Furthermore, some of the earlier policies had harmful environmental effects as well as adverse regional implications. (Note that the industrial zone between Tokyo and Kobe became increasingly congested at the time when other areas were being depopulated.) These factors, coupled with gross mismanagement of certain government corporations, the National Railways being a prime example, reflect some of the negative aspects associated with the overseeing of economic activity. In this respect, the Japanese record has been similar to those of other industrial nations.

In relation to specific features inherent in Japan's industrial policy, complaints have been levelled against the manner in which industrial resources have been channelled. During the 1960s, some favoured or strategic industries, such as steel, petroleum refining and petrochemicals, were reported to have yielded profit rates substantially below the industrial average. On this basis, Trezise and Suzuki maintain that 'it could easily be argued that the national income objective would have been better served by a different allocation of investment' [Trezise and Suzuki 1976:810]. Even more damning is Komiya's allegation that industries were singled out for special attention on account of their national prestige value. 'First, they had to be industries, symbolic of industrial might, that had already been developed by countries more advanced than Japan.' Second, these industries had to have a certain size, 'so as to be newsworthy' [Komiya 1990:295]. Finally, in association with the critics' dissatisfaction with the way in which the government determined resource use, a measure of strong scepticism has been voiced regarding the economic effectiveness of the granting of licences for the importation of technology. Considering that between 1949 and 1968, some 5000 applications were processed, it is not unreasonable to assume that bad as well as good decisions were made. The most frequently cited *faux pax* was the two year delay in the authorization of the importation of transistor technology, on the grounds that Sony (the applicant), was deemed to be incapable of putting it to good use.

## In Defence of Industrial Policy

A closer look at the above arguments indicates that many of them are found wanting or are defective in certain respects. Whilst it may be true that being in a situation of relative economic backwardness could be consistent with the satisfying of Pareto optimal efficiency criteria, it does not follow that there are not alternative global equilibria which may be attainable through the medium of state intervention. In any event, Komiya's reference to Singapore as a glaring example of *laissez-faire* capitalism is misplaced. Its government is well renowned for steering economic activity in predetermined directions.

The existence of successful industries which were not specifically targeted has virtually no negative bearing on Japan's industrial policy. By contrast, the opposite is more likely to apply. It is worth emphasizing that although the government wished to ensure that its designated strategic sectors would develop, there was never any official expectation that other sectors would also not do so. In that light, that both government nominated and non-nominated industries grew, is a tribute to the non-exclusionary nature of MITI's approach.

In reality, the non-targeted sectors were both direct and indirect beneficiaries of government policy. Throughout their formative years they were protected against foreign competitors. Some of them secured foreign technology with MITI's assistance and all enjoyed the benefits of a rapidly growing local market [Boltho 1985:196]. Internal economic growth was partly facilitated by exceptionally high rates of investment, for which the official underwriting of industrial progress in key areas had been an important determinant.

Taking up the issue of the prior neglect of the robot industry, ultimately the government rallied to its cause. It did so by the setting up of a support system which included accelerated depreciation allowances, the formation of a finance company to assist small enterprises and the endowment of research and development funds. The point being that even though the government does not usher in every promising industry, it does eventually promote those that are manifestly important.

As to Komiya's assertion that Japan's high growth industries would in any case have grown on their own accord, it would be foolhardy to deny that possibility. After all, the country was endowed with a well educated labour force and enterprising entrepreneurial talents. However, given the economic circumstances of the early postwar era, it is highly doubtful that their rate of progress would have been anywhere near the rates actually recorded. Capital equipment in the heavy and chemical industries was sparse and antiquated. High production costs ate into profits making it difficult, if not impossible, to mobilize sufficient funds internally to meet investment requirements. Externally (to the firms), capital markets were anything but perfect [Kosai 1988:38]. With this in mind, one may well question Trezise and Suzuki's view that because the steel industry made low profits, the public support it received was unwarranted. Apart from the fact (as is discussed in the next chapter) that in Japan, short-term profit rates were generally not regarded as critical investment indicators, progress in the steel industry had widespread ramifications. With government backing, it eventually outranked foreign rivals in terms of quality and productivity and thus supplied crucial inputs to the rest of industry at affordable prices. The automobile industry for one, owes a large measure of its success to Japanese steel.

Komiya's statement that the authorities were well disposed towards certain industries because of considerations of national status represents a distortion of MITI's selection criteria. That almost all of the targeted industries were both large and already in operation elsewhere is neither surprising nor condemnatory. Not uncommonly, when capital markets are imperfect, investment projects involving vast capital outlays and fairly lengthy gestation periods, depend more on public support than do smaller ones. Granted that a favourable product image would be regarded as an additional bonus, we are inclined to the view that Japanese officials were generally guided by considerations of economic efficiency and that MITI's industrial policy was essentially market conforming, a view strongly advanced by Eads and Yamamura as well as by Okimoto, among others.[7] Even critics of Japanese industrial policy have conceded that the 'civil service gave the country honest and competent administration', and that 'no amount of argument can show that the bureaucratic controls that it exercised so extensively could have been a net disservice to economic growth' [Trezise and Suzuki 1976:809].

Lastly, turning to alleged defects in the allocation of technology import approvals, one cannot deny, especially in view of the large volume of applications submitted, that certain errors occurred. Even so, the authorities were generally meticulously careful and with a few exceptions, they could normally be relied upon to distinguish between critically important and marginally useful technologies. Where MITI did seem to excel was in its ability (through its suppression of competitive inter-firm bidding) to extract favourable royalty terms on behalf of Japanese industry. A celebrated instance relates to the royalty for the oxygen-furnace process for steel (purchased from Austria) being set at 1 cent per ton of steel whereas US producers competing amongst themselves, secured the same technology at 35 cents per ton [Tyson and Zysman 1989:68].

It would be difficult to sustain the argument that Japanese industrial policies were either irrelevant or in fact largely harmful. Immediate postwar market signals would undoubtedly have placed the economy on a path which, at best, would have promised mediocre improvements and a minimal degree of advancement into the high technology sectors in which the country now leads. Instead, the era of an intensive application of industrial policies was in fact associated with world record breaking growth rates. Some observers suggest that postwar trends were simply a continuation of prewar ones. Whether this is true nor not, it is worth bearing in mind that even in the earlier years, the government had a hands on approach to industry. Policy errors undoubtedly occurred and some costs associated with the general implementation of industrial policy were borne. However, while other industrial countries have met with similar setbacks, they have not enjoyed anything like the scale of accomplishments that Japan has.

## The Applicability of Japan's Industrial Policy to Other Countries

Can the Japanese experience be applied elsewhere? This is a frequently posed question. In our opinion, the lessons to be learnt from Japanese industrial policy are rather limited because of the unusual co-existence of factors that made its success possible. Some of these factors relate to the special quality of Japanese human and other resources and the unique way in which they are organized. (These will be fully illustrated in the chapters that follow.) More importantly, one cannot realistically expect to replicate the complex socio-political factors which allowed Japanese officials to operate so efficiently and with such economic effectiveness. During the 1950s and 1960s, the country's underlying macroeconomic conditions were very favourable and since Japan lagged behind its rivals, appropriate target industries were relatively easy to identify. Also, in that period there was more leeway to utilize policy instruments which were able to deploy resources with pinpoint accuracy. Today, even Japan itself is hard pressed in maintaining an activist policy position which even faintly resembles previous ones, either in terms of procedures or capabilities. That does not mean to say that nothing the Japanese have done can be emulated. After all, the newly industrialized Asian nations have incorporated many elements of industrial policy which are very much like those of Japan.

## SUMMARY

* Within the Japanese developmental state the private sector was encouraged. Industrial policy was jointly determined by the government, bureaucracy and industrialists.
* The major postwar economic objective was to transform Japan into a leading industrial power.
* Industrial sectors singled out for special consideration were those whose products had a high income elasticity of demand and/or which embodied advanced technology.
* The bureaucracy was the leading force in the industrialization drive. It was given a measure of free rein by the government which was almost always headed by the LDP.
* MITI was largely entrusted with general industrial management. Given its capacity to recommend loans from the Japan Development Bank, to control the Fiscal Investment Loan Program and to allocate foreign exchange, MITI's powers were extensive.
* In addition, MITI also resorted to administrative guidance which foreclosed the need for constant legislation and which allowed for rapid policy adjustments. However, since the practice had an arbitrary aspect to it which was beyond appeal, it was eventually largely relinquished.
* Industrial incentives took the form of tariff protection and import quotas, taxation breaks, subsidies, preferential finance and the provision of industrial infrastructure, such as ports and communication systems.
* Anti-monopoly laws were not at first seriously enforced. In fact, depression cartels were authorized and with the government being concerned about the phenomenon of excessive competition, mergers were encouraged. However, by and large, corporations resisted pres-

sures to merge and from 1974 anti-monopoly legislation was taken more seriously.

- In the 1960s trade barriers were substantially reduced and by 1980 exchange control was abolished.
- Contemporary industrial policy has limited, if any, recourse to earlier policy instruments. Instead the government primarily relies on the issuing of 'visions' and financial subsidies. As for objectives, emphasis tends to be placed on research and development within high technology fields (partly through the sponsoring of technology research associations). Non-growth objectives such as quality of life, are now also taken into account.
- In the assessment of industrial policy we considered issues of market failure, problems relating to determining counterfactuals, incidences of inappropriate decision making and resource waste and finally factors redeeming Japan's industrial strategy.
- Assuming that Japan's industrial policy served the nation well, given the combination of special circumstances in postwar Japan, it would be foolhardy for other countries to attempt to replicate it lock stock and barrel.

# 6 Business Enterprise

## INTRODUCTION

In this chapter, we locate the Japanese corporation within its institutional setting and attempt to reveal the extent to which Japanese firms differ from Western ones both in terms of their objectives and the mode in which they are managed. Elsewhere, we shall deal specifically with personnel management, the development of technology and the capacity of Japanese firms to adapt to structural economic changes.

Firms in Japan are essentially categorized into large and small companies depending on the size of their work force, with those employing over a thousand workers being designated as large ones.

In general, there is quite a cleavage between the two groups. Large firms tend to be capital intensive and pay higher wages, whereas small firms are mainly labour intensive and are more reliant on less costly unskilled workers. Such differences have prompted observers to refer to Japan's economy as being dualistic. That is, it is split into modern dynamic and archaic static components. There is a fair element of truth in this depiction but like all generalizations, it is not quite that simple. Some small firms are fairly innovative, employ highly trained professionals and are scientifically based. Nonetheless, differences between the two polar extremes are immense and, therefore, we shall in this chapter deal with each group separately.

Starting with the large corporation, we shall cover topics such as inter-firm affiliations, relations with what are termed 'main banks', the status of shareholders and decision-making procedures, the competitive behaviour of firms and finally the proliferation and merging of corporations.

When dealing with small firms, we shall emphasize their distinctive characteristics and then we shall concentrate on subcontracting, an activity in which most small firms are engaged.

106

## THE LARGE CORPORATION

### Keiretsu Groupings

*Their Nature and Types*

By contrast with Western corporations, a very large proportion of Japanese firms maintain a degree of affiliation with others. Alliances tend to be formed among independent entities across different industries (horizontal alliances) and or with input suppliers as well as distributors (vertical alliances). Such groupings have had various designations, with terms like 'gurupu' or 'kigyo shudan' (firm group) often being used for the first type and keiretsu for the second. In keeping with what is becoming standard practice among Western writers, we shall label them all as keiretsu.

*Horizontal Keiretsu*

Horizontal keiretsu are effectively associations of large corporations which are clustered around a group city bank, a trust bank, a real estate agency, a life and a casualty insurance firm and one or more trading companies. Six groupings in particular dwarf all others, namely Mitsui, Mitsubishi, Sumitomo, Daiichi Kangyo, Sanwa and Fuyo.

Each keiretsu usually contains only a single firm from each industry, in order to promote, by mutual assistance and preferential transactions, the business interests of its members. Some exceptions to this rule occur among Daiichi Kangyo, Sanwa and Fuyo but in all instances, efforts are expended to incorporate representatives from every *major* manufacturing and service sector. The willingness of firms to sponsor products of fellow keiretsu members is largely conditional on being charged a price no higher than that of outsiders.

The horizontal keiretsu are loosely structured. Being voluntary associations of legally and financially separate firms, they are not controlled by any central authority. That is not to say that there is a complete absence of organizational coherence. The presidents of all the *major* firms (of each keiretsu) assemble monthly within a forum known as the presidents' council. There they deliberate on matters of common interest, such as the initiation of joint investments, the establishment of the group's presence in new industries or even on more mundane matters such as donations to charities and the general nature of the prevailing economic climate. These gatherings count less for the concrete decisions actually taken than for the social interchanges that occur.

Participation in the presidents' council tends to enhance each company's sense of group attachment but because it is limited to 'core' companies, inclusion in a presidents' council constitutes a sufficient but not a necessary condition for keiretsu membership [see Hoshi 1994:288].

*Interlocking Share Holdings*

Keiretsu group coherence is fostered by a system of interlocking directorates based on interlocking share holdings. Companies (particularly financial and insurance ones) hold 'friendly' shares of member firms. These are acquired less for ordinary commercial motives than for considerations of mutual solidarity. Such investments (which are rarely sold) serve to ward off non-group predators. In so doing, they afford companies a measure of long-term security and freedom from outside control, which enables them to indulge in long-term planning and to honour implicit lifetime employment contracts.

Mutually held shares are exchanged in small allotments throughout an entire grouping. However, financial interpenetration is more pronounced among the 'old guard' keiretsu, namely Mitsui, Mitsubishi and Sumitomo (see Table 6.1), which has induced some writers to argue that only those three constitute genuine keiretsu. The inclusion of the last three groupings in Table 6.1 is supposedly questionable because each member firm is only largely centred around a main bank and interaction among non-financial members is less extensive [see Odagiri 1992:174].

*Vertical Keiretsu*

As already indicated, vertical keiretsu consist of a collection of input manufacturers and or distributors (mainly small firms) attached to a large corporation. Their association is usually a long-term contractual one, with the satellite firms being indirectly linked to the corporation's horizontal sister companies. Relations between firms are highly stratified. At the apex rests a major corporation beneath which are its primary subcontractors. These in turn preside over a series of secondary and subsequent suppliers.

Vertical keiretsu came into being either by the inclusion of independent firms or by the hiving off from large corporations of new specialized sections. However, one of the prime forces underlying these formations is that in contrast to most Western firms, leading Japanese corporations tend to undertake less in-house activity, preferring instead to have a relatively larger bulk of their components tailor made by

Business Enterprise 109

Table 6.1  Financial Interpenetration within the Leading Keiretsu
(1987 Financial Year)

| | Average Interlocking Shares as % of Total | Average Intra-group Loans as % of Total |
|---|---|---|
| Mitsui | 17.10 | 21.94 |
| Mitsubishi | 27.80 | 20.17 |
| Sumitomo | 24.22 | 24.53 |
| Fuyo | 15.61 | 18.20 |
| Sanwa | 16.47 | 18.51 |
| Daiichi | 12.49 | 11.18 |

Source: Derived from Ito 1992, Table 7.1, p. 181

others. For example, in the period between 1979 and 1983, the proportionate value of total automobile manufacturing costs derived from a firm's own activities was 26 per cent for Nissan and 28 per cent for Toyota. Corresponding ratios for US firms were 43 per cent for General Motors, 36 per cent for Ford and 32 per cent for Chrysler [Cusumano 1985:38/9].[1] The flip side of this is that large Japanese firms usually employ less people per volume of sales. Comparing Toyota (in Japan) and General Motors, in 1986, the ratio of workers per final sales (expressed in trillion yen) was 10.8 thousand for Toyota and 50.9 thousand for General Motors. [Calculated from Komiya 1990:Table 2, p. 174.]

*Zaibatsu and Keiretsu*

The present day keiretsu are in fact descendants of prewar associations known as zaibatsu, some of which could trace their origins as far back as a century and more. They were controlled by holding companies belonging to rich and powerful families.

The holding companies held commanding shares of core companies which would include a bank, a trading, a trust and an insurance company. These in turn would have majority interests in yet other businesses. Members of the holding company assumed presidencies and directorships in the core companies. In many ways, in fact, a zaibatsu was akin to a giant conglomerate with a multitude of divisions. Each division had some limited autonomous decision-making capabilities but in the final analysis, the family holding company was the ultimate source of authority.

The zaibatsu were prominent in finance, industry and trade. By virtue of a previous near complete absence of capital markets, many independent companies in financial difficulties were ultimately drawn into their orbit [Allen 1981:125]. At one stage, its four domineering groups Mitsui, Mitsubishi, Sumitomo and Yasuda accounted for a quarter of all Japanese economic output.

Determined to dismantle what was seen as an excessively dangerous concentration of monopoly power, the Occupation Authorities dismembered the zaibatsu. Their holding companies were liquidated and other companies not dissolved were reconstituted into independent entities. The shares held by holding companies were all confiscated and sold to the general public, with the proviso that no individual was permitted to own more than 1 per cent of any company's shares. Only a nominal amount of compensation was paid to the zaibatsu families, who were effectively stripped of their wealth. At the same time, about over 3000 former senior zaibatsu executives were removed from office.

As it happened, within a short time span the remnants of the zaibatsu reassembled into horizontal keiretsu, some of which even retained their previous zaibatsu names. The renewed associations, plus a few that lacked direct antecedents, differ from the zaibatsu in several important respects: Resulting from the complete disappearance of the old family holding companies, keiretsu firms are very loosely interconnected, with each having complete autonomy and independence. That is, there is no central decision-making authority to which all keiretsu firms are answerable. Their boards of directors usually only contain a president or two of related companies who would merely be accorded junior status and who would primarily serve as a conduit for inter-company communications. Similarly, a given company would not own more than a few per cent of the total assets of any other individual keiretsu firm. To some extent, a certain amount of coherence is preserved by the group's bank, with which all associated companies deal. But even the strength of this tie is weakening, as member firms are increasingly resorting to supplementary assistance from 'outsiders'.

*Possible Keiretsu Advantages*

In this section we refer to horizontal keiretsu, the pros and cons of vertical ones are taken up below within the context of our discussion on the small firm.

Companies belonging to a keiretsu have benefited from the occasional pooling of capital, technological knowledge, personnel, office space and recreational facilities. This has proved to be particularly useful when member firms have entered into joint ventures with each other, for by dealing with fellow keiretsu firms, one starts off on the basis of long held associations which facilitate negotiations and cooperation. Information can freely be exchanged with full confidence in its confidentiality. Loans can readily be arranged through the group's main bank and other financial institutions, and the keiretsu's major trading company can be called upon for assistance in distribution and the acquisition of imported inputs.

However, on noting that on average, horizontal keiretsu firms appear to be no more profitable than non-keiretsu ones and with some actually being less profitable, Odagiri suggests that 'hardly any benefit seems to accrue from grouping' [Odagiri 1992:194]. By benefit, Odagiri must surely be referring to profit making ones only, for elsewhere [p. 196] he enumerates information pooling and in-group shareholding (which wards off take-over threats) as constituting at least two obvious keiretsu advantages. Moreover, in Japan, profit measurements have not always provided an adequate indication of firm performance. It is quite conceivable for profits to be restrained in order to provide greater employee benefits and/or to further high firm growth strategies. Nakatani, for one, believes that firms adhere to keiretsu groupings to augment monopolistic powers which are 'not necessarily used for the raising of profits', but rather for the maximization of 'the joint utility of its corporate constituents-employees, financial institutions, stockholders and management' [Nakatani 1984:228]. Not only are group profit rates lower than those of independent firms but in keeping with Nakatani's hypothesis, 'the average income received by the *employee* of the group firm is significantly higher than that of the independent firm' [229]. In this regard, reciprocal shareholdings, by weakening the influence of non-group shareholders, enable directors to pursue an independent agenda. Furthermore, Nakatani maintains that 'the variability of the performance of the group-affiliated firms is smaller than that of the independent firms' [228]. If this is indeed so, then one advantage of keiretsu membership lies in a greater degree of security afforded by the provision of mutual support under the watchful and protective eye of the keiretsu's main bank. This advantage extends to the economy at large, in that it enables Japan to adjust better to variable market conditions than most other industrial countries seem to be capable of doing. For instance, in previous economic crises, many workers in particularly depressed industries were successfully relocated within fellow keiretsu firms (see Chapter 8).

*The Relative Strength and Status of the Keiretsu*

The above stated arguments notwithstanding, reservations concerning the relative significance of the keiretsu (mainly the horizontal ones) have increasingly been expressed. Commentators have either questioned whether the keiretsu are still a force to be reckoned with or alternatively, whether their economic influence has now waned.

Keiretsu firms have never confined all their dealings to sister companies (especially when blatantly more attractive options lie beyond their grouping) and some firms appear to be associated with more than one horizontal keiretsu. Since the beginning of the 1980s, intra-keiretsu transactions as a proportion of total keiretsu transactions, have declined. In 1981, the average intra-group trade ratio for the six largest keiretsu was 11.7 per cent for purchases and 10.8 per cent for sales. By 1989, the ratios fell respectively to 8.1 and 7.3 per cent [Hoshi 1994:289].

The relative decline in intra-keiretsu activity and solidarity could have arisen from the fact that trading companies are becoming less relied upon (as many firms now tend to market their own products directly), that a recent drive to diversification has placed many member firms on a collision course (as they strive to capture the same fields) and finally, from the fact that bank loans now constitute a proportionally smaller source of corporate finance.

The latter observation implies that less reliance on keiretsu banks leads to a general weakening of keiretsu links. However, this assumption has been challenged by Gerlach (1987) who claims that other organizations belonging to the same keiretsu, such as insurance companies, have been buying more fellow keiretsu company shares. Since, as Gerlach argues, inter-keiretsu equity connections continue to be structured in long-term relationships based on group strategic considerations, the shift towards equity capital as such, has apparently not dented keiretsu unity.

Some evidence suggesting a fall in reciprocal shareholdings seems to be at hand. 'In the Mitsubishi group, for example, the rate of ownership of companies by other firms' in the group declined from 36.94 per cent in 1985 to 35.45 per cent in 1989, and this tendency was seen in other groups as well.' [Okumura 1993:15] However, the reputed change is of a very small order of magnitude and in any case, as Gerlach points out, such figures are based on overall shareholdings. 'If, on the other hand, we consider only firms' *leading*[2] shareholders, the percentage of internalization of ownership more than doubles' [Gerlach 1987:132].

As for the overall role of the keiretsu, it appears that in all probability while they have held their own in absolute terms, their share of total economic activity has dwindled. The keiretsu have maintained a high profile in raw material processing and heavy industries where capital requirements have been considerable. Sectors in which the six leading keiretsu have collectively held more than 80 per cent of market shares include rubber, shipbuilding, electrical machinery, nonferrous metals, textiles, drugs, petroleum, construction and chemicals [Okimoto 1986:146]. Needless to say, the relative importance of many of these industries has declined and many highly successful corporations in the forefront of innovation and growth such as Toyota, Honda, Hitachi, Sharp, Sanyo, Matsushita, Sony, Fuji Film, Canon, Rico and Seiko have been independent of the 'big six' [Abegglen and Stalk 1985:189–90].

## Dependence on Banks and the Main Bank System

From the mid 1940s to the late 1970s, most Japanese firms had depended on bank finance for more than 80 per cent of their capital requirements. Alternative capital sources were few and far between and considering that as a deliberate act of government policy, interest rate charges to industrial borrowers were set at low levels, firms sought to establish especially close ties with at least one bank. Having established an intimate link with a bank, even at the cost of some freedom of action and by offering fixed assets (which were grossly undervalued) as collateral, manufacturers were able to secure large loans on terms which enabled them to pursue long-term growth objectives.

In Japan, banks are permitted to hold up to 5 per cent of non-financial companies' stocks and financial institutions as a whole have of late laid claim to about 40 per cent of listed companies' shares [Aoki 1990:14]. As it happens, non-financial companies also hold bank shares but each individual company is likely to have a relatively smaller stake in any particular bank than that bank would have with it.

The bank with which a company is most closely connected is deemed to be that company's 'main bank'. Not only does a main bank provide routine financial services but it also undertakes at least two other key functions. One of which may include the organization and management of a loan consortium. Where inordinately large amounts of capital need to be mobilized, individual Japanese financial institutions are reluctant to be the sole or overwhelmingly significant underwriter. With a main bank committing itself to the project in question, it is often able to persuade other lenders to join in. Their willingness to do so is influenced positively by the fact that the main bank can be relied upon to have an intimate knowledge of the firm's affairs and that it is itself a significant firm shareholder. (Sometimes, one or two of a company's board members are main bank delegates.) In other words, 'the main bank acts as a signal to other banks of the financial health of the company, ensuring that the company is able to gain loans from other banks as well – a process known as "pump priming," or yobi-miz (lit., "calling water")' [Gerlach 1987:128]. Finally, in the establishment of a loan syndicate under main bank guidance, monitoring and administrative economies are yielded which could in practice be enjoyed both by the participating banks and the borrowing firm.

The other function assumed by a main bank is one of taking an interest in the general well-being of its client and being prepared to rally to its assistance when in need. (Their willingness to do so stems both from the main banks being prime lenders and company shareholders.) Apart from anecdotal evidence, there is some empirical support based on econometric analysis, which indicates that firms with a main bank relation emerge more smoothly from an economic crisis than do others [see Hoshi 1994:298].

Corporations in distress would secure the refinancing of old loans or the provision of new ones, provided that for the duration of the crisis, the banks would be given free rein to manage their affairs. Very likely this might involve the dispatch of bank personnel to replace existing directors for an interim period. Aoki believes that the potential threat of a bank takeover provides an important monitoring function of firm performance [Aoki 1990:15]. Such arrangements worked more harmoniously when the parties concerned were closely allied. Hence, keiretsu firms looked to their own grouping for their lead bank.

From the mid to late 1970s, the relative reliance of large corporations on bank finance began to decline. By 1984, for example, a sample of 621 leading companies suggested that bank loans formed only 14 per cent of current external funding compared with an average of 80 per cent during the 1960s [see *Economist*, 8 Dec. 1984:21]. This dramatic turnaround reflected a burgeoning use of alternative financial instrumentalities made possible by deregulation, such as shares and bonds, plus an increasing ability to generate internal savings.

Not only did companies begin to take advantage of new opportunities for mobilizing capital but some of them also became relatively less attached to a specific bank. Such an outcome was largely the consequence of company growth. The more a firm grew, the less inclined was its main bank to meet most of its financial requirements, for the simple reason that it was imprudent to commit undue loans to a single borrower. In the meantime, other banks were willing to step in.

## The Situation of Shareholders

### Small Individual Propensity to Buy Stock

The average Japanese citizen has a low propensity to buy company stock. In the late 1980s, the proportion of personal financial assets held in shares was 9.9 per cent compared with 45.3 per cent held in saving deposits. Within America, the equivalent amounts were 14.9 and 18.5 [Sakakibara 1991:10]. From the perspective of a typical Japanese firm, corporations loom larger than private individuals as stockholders. In fact, financial and non-financial companies combined carry roughly 70 per cent of issued shares. This has not always been the case. In 1949, for example, individuals held 69.1 per cent of listed companies' shares. That the proportion of individual share holdings fell to 23.2 per cent by 1991 can, among other things, be attributed to a growing preference on the part of private citizens for more secure forms of savings, to heavy estate taxes and to an increased demand for equity capital that original shareholders could not satisfy [Komiya 1990:161].

### Insignificant Power of Individual Shareholders

While, historically, many of Japan's large corporations were established by individual entrepreneurs, for the most part, their descendants have all but sunk into oblivion, having little, if any, representation on managing boards and relatively small company shareholdings. In virtually all large corporations, of the ten largest single shareholders, none are individuals. This contrasts with the US where in large corporations such as Ford and DuPont, the Ford and DuPont families have for years been principal stockholders.

With the top single shareholder of a high ranking company typically possessing less than 5 per cent of its stock, and with that shareholder often being a friendly keiretsu associate, most Japanese giant corporations are certainly not beholden to powerful individual capitalists. This of course influences the *raison d'être* of many Japanese firms. In the opinion of various Japanese scholars, the large Japanese corporation may be seen as primarily furthering the interests of its permanent employees. With rather few exceptions, board members tend to be selected from within the higher echelons of a company's managerial executives. In fact, in Japan there are no corporations in which outside directors constitute a majority. By contrast, in the mid 1980s, some 83 per cent of US corporations were in that position [see Odagiri 1992:40].

## Institutional Investors and the Small Shareholder

In both the US and the UK institutional investors have also attained prominence. However, leading institutional investors there such as insurance companies, pension funds and investment trusts, have virtually the same motives and expectations as have small shareholders. They all seek profitable returns. Considering that most of the institutional investors are effectively entrusted with individuals' savings, such a coincidence of interests is hardly surprising. This unity of purpose is a boon to small stockholders, who can generally count on the institutional investors to deploy their expertise and influence to ensure that company policies and practices are attuned to their collective needs. In Japan, by contrast (where pension funds are usually incorporated within a specific company's financial structure) a divergence of shareholder objectives frequently occurs. Many large corporations acquire the shares of other firms less for their expected dividends and more for the extraction of possible favours as prospective borrowers, customers or suppliers, not to mention mutual protection against takeovers. In the process, small shareholders are left to their own devices and as a result, their interests are often poorly served.

## Shareholders' Rights and Returns

Theoretically, shareholders are provided with adequate legal protection to safeguard their rights. The board of directors is obliged to report to them at annual general meetings and those mustering at least 3 per cent of total equity have access to the courts to evict wayward directors. Furthermore, critical managerial decisions which significantly affect the affairs of the company, require the endorsement of two thirds of the shareholders, which implies that a small minority is vested with significant veto powers [Clark 1979:99].

In practice, small shareholders are treated with scant regard and they are incapable of influencing the course of company events. Their access to information is limited at best, both as a result of shoddy financial accounting and reporting standards and more importantly, because annual general meetings have frequently been a sham. Invariably, these gatherings have been nothing more than mere ceremonies orchestrated by the board of directors [Okabe 1992:8]. In the not too distant past, gangsters who specialized in browbeating dissident shareholders (sokaiya) would be hired to ensure that everything ran smoothly and in over 90 per cent of cases, the meetings would be concluded within half an hour [Clark 1979:102–3]. Some exceptions are of course on record. In 1984, angry Sanyo shareholders remonstrated with their firm's board of directors for over 13 hours over the misguided adoption of the Beta VTR system. But even then, the management won approval for all its proposals, 'as is customary at virtually all shareholders' meetings' [Odagiri 1992:39].

Despite their rather circumscribed sphere of influence, individual shareholders expect some small percentage of the par value of their shares to be paid annually as dividends, and no matter how companies are placed, they all endeavour to meet that expectation. In that sense, Japanese shareholders are likened to US preferred ones. However, the amounts yielded have generally been far lower than what foreign share-holders have obtained. During the 1970s, first section Tokyo Stock Exchange companies paid an average dividend rate of only 1.5 per cent [Van Wolferen 1989:296]. The Japanese investor accepts this discrepancy with equanimity because when capital gains are taken into account, they reap very attractive long run returns. This is partly made possible by debt to equity ratios which vastly exceed those of US firms.

Although, as we had observed in Chapter 2 (when discussing capital costs), there is some disagreement concerning the relative return to Japanese and US equity investors, many believe that the acquiescent Japanese shareholder had not really been that hard done by. For instance, Abegglen and Stalk estimate that a 1000 yen investment placed in 1973 in a leading Japanese company would have yielded a 1750 yen profit by 1983. If during the same period, 1000 dollars had been committed to a mainstream US firm, a profit of only 390 dollars would have been realized. The Japanese shareholder comes out way ahead even though dividends would have accounted for 11 per cent of the returns compared to a figure of 85 per cent for the US firm [Abegglen and Stalk 1985:170].

If indeed returns to the Japanese shareholder are no worse than in the US, how does one explain the fact that in Japan, individuals are much more inclined to invest in interest bearing deposits? Aoki suggests that the answer partly lies in higher risks and transaction costs associated with share acquisitions. The annual rate of growth of capital gains is fairly volatile and brokerage 'fees charged by securities companies for trading shares are regulated and highly regressive' [Aoki 1987:278].

**Decision Making Procedures**

*The Demise of the Old-style Entrepreneur*

Like other industrial states, Japan has been graced with a supply of ingenious and inventive entrepreneurs. Some of its most enterprising concerns have been established single handedly by pioneers with humble origins and with limited formal schooling. The Matsushita Company, for example, was founded by its namesake, Kinosuke Matsushita, of peasant stock, who left school at the age of ten. At the age of 19, after having briefly been employed in an electrical apparatus firm, he set up his own business which eventually developed into a leading television and household electrical appliance producer.

Similarly, Soichiro Honda, son of a village blacksmith, started out, at the age of 16, as an apprentice automobile mechanic. At the end of the Second World War, he launched his own motor cycle company which met with immense success. Not content with that, he then (against MITI's advice) commenced automobile manufacturing.

The two above cited personalities do not by any means exhaust the list of Japan's distinguished business visionaries. Many corporations attribute their origins to a single, or, as in the case of Sony, a couple of men of distinction. Nor has the influence of the offspring of a firm's founding father totally been eclipsed. Take the Toyota Motor Corporation as a case in point. In 1992, half a century after the firm was founded by Kiichiro Toyoda, the firm's presidency was held by Tatsuro Toyoda, the younger brother of the former president, Shoichiro Toyoda. Their uncle, Tatsuro Toyoda was president before Shoichiro. All three are related to the company's founder, yet none is on the list of the company's top ten shareholders. 'Such unchallenged domination of a company's management without equity control is, to say the least, an *unusual* feature of Japanese corporate structure.'[3] [*Tokyo Business Today* Nov. 1992] More typically, almost all large Japanese corporations are administered by complex bureaucratic structures whose heads are appointed on the basis of appropriate qualification and experience.

*The Corporate Chief and Chain of Command*

The administrative head of a corporation is the president who fulfils a role similar to that of a chief executive officer (CEO) of an American firm or that of the managing director of a British one. It is the president who nominates candidates for the board of directors, including his own successor. Most directors have production and technological backgrounds, followed by those with marketing and export expertise. Those with financial and accounting experience are less prominent. This contrasts with the situation in the US and UK where financial training is more helpful in securing board membership. The probable explanation for this difference is that in Japan where lifetime employment (for professional employees) has been institutionalized, the human capital relating to technical and general operational procedures is rather firm specific and of irreplaceable value, whereas financial knowledge which is more universally attainable, is easier to acquire and of less intrinsic importance [see Odagiri 1992:45].

Ardent Western admirers of the Japanese method of business organization generally extol what they believe to be the widespread practice of group decision making. In particular, they are very much taken by the 'ringi-sei' process, which seems to reflect corporate democracy in action. In its ideal state, the 'ringi-sei' system involves a suggestion that may originate from within the relatively lower ranks of the firm. After it is exhaustively discussed, it is passed upwards, with each subsequent contact's endorsement or analysis. Finally, on the basis of accumulated reports, the company president issues a determination.

Intermediate stages where responses are passed downwards may occur, giving rise to a two way flow of ideas and information. Although the time-consuming aspects of the process are readily acknowledged, the system is credited with extending the involvement and understanding of company employees in important issues, so that ostensibly, once decisions are taken, they are rapidly and efficiently executed.

What might confidently be said on behalf of Japanese firm decision making is that it relies on a widespread dissemination of knowledge, with operating divisions coordinating their activities with another on the basis of shared information [Aoki 1990:3]. Less enthusiastic observers note that 'ringi-sei' could allow for the avoidance of responsibility or alternatively, instead of facilitating decision making, it may simply provide a vehicle for the mobilization of support or the dissemination of rulings already made [Clark 1979:126]. As it is, the system is not universally adhered to and contrary to what is frequently stated, able and efficient juniors do not routinely venture to make suggestions on behalf of less competent superiors.

Far from there being a widespread indulgence in joint decision making, the direction of many Japanese corporations is 'under the control or at least the preponderant influence of one man' [131]. This is well exemplified in the Nissan Corporation, which had not always been administered on a consensual basis. When in 1952, its then president Asahara, wished to forge close ties with Austin Motors (UK), he simply proclaimed his intentions as a *fait accompli*. Even though other board members disagreed with him, 'there was no debate over the matter since it did not seem that anyone would be able to change Asahara's mind' [Cusumano 1985:89]. Critical discussions or exchanges at board meetings tend to be subdued since directors being rated in accordance with their managerial pecking order, are hesitant in challenging those that outrank them. Okada, who was president of Mitsukoshi from 1972 to 1982, eventually 'became dictatorial and made decisions that worried several of the directors. Nevertheless, he was able to maintain his power by demoting directors with opposing views' [Odagiri 1992:41].

As already mentioned, managers pay little heed to individual shareholders. That being so and with the corporate shareholders taking little interest in the day to day running of the firm, plus the fact that large companies are well protected from potential takeovers in the event of their performance flagging, the question arises as to what brings an inefficiently run corporation into line. The answer is found in the threat of bankruptcy, which may involve the displacement of the existing management, much to their shame and chagrin, by main bank nominees. Furthermore, considering that the fortunes of the main core of employees are inextricably linked to the success and continuity of their firm, management has both a vested interest and a responsibility to ensure that the company's affairs are appropriately conducted. In Japan, social commitments are taken seriously and most managers would be mortified to have been instrumental in causing irreparable employee misfortune.

**The Corporation Within a Competitive Environment**

A distinctive characteristic of Japanese corporations has been their single minded pursuit of the expansion of market shares, an objective which is generally assigned more importance than short-term profit maximization. To appreciate why this is so, it is necessary to consider the competitive framework in which many large Japanese corporations operate.

Although Japan's modern consumer durable goods sector sustains a limited number of separate enterprises within each industry, there are generally still more participants than is common elsewhere. Take the automobile industry as a case in point. Within the United States, before the entry of Japanese firms, only three corporations were to be reckoned with, whereas in Japan there were at least nine. Not only is there usually a larger number of firms in each Japanese industry but they compete much more aggressively. This is best exemplified in the motorcycle industry where significant and rapid market position changes frequently occurred.

In the early 1950s (when the Japanese motorcycle industry had over 50 participants) Tohatso had the largest single share (22 per cent) followed by Honda (20 per cent). Within five years, Tohatso's share plummeted to 4 per cent while Honda's soared to 44 per cent. Honda's share peaked in the late 1960s at 65 per cent and then settled at around 40 per cent in 1981. By then, Yamaha, whose market share had swiftly risen from 10 to 35 per cent, openly launched a campaign (involving a massive increase in plant capacity) to overtake Honda. In response, Honda rapidly released 81 new offerings, which far exceeded Yamaha's 34 model range. As a result, Honda's market share increased to 47 per cent while Yamaha's receded to 23 per cent. Fearing a further battering, Yamaha publicly relented [Abegglen and Stalk:1985:43–50].

*Causes of Excessive Competition: The Quest for Large Market Shares*

Many observers subscribe to the view that unbridled industrial competition in Japan is in effect directly attributable to its industrial policy. By committing itself to the progress and sustainability of designated industries, and by being prepared to organize depression cartels to assist corporations in distress, the government had in essence encouraged undue industry entrants and the generation of excess productive capacity. There is a large element of truth in all this but the fact that excessive competition is no less rampant in non targeted industries suggests that there are still other, and perhaps no less significant, determinants.

The extraordinary rapid rate of GDP increases that Japan sustained during its high growth period, which far exceeded both its pre-world war growth rates and those subsequently notched up by its rivals, played a pivotal role in inducing Japanese firms to adopt extreme competitive positions. Had a firm responded to heightening demand pressures by raising its prices and thereby augmenting short-term profits, it would have been devastated in the long run. Successful business strategies required that prices be set not at what the market would currently bear but at a level low enough to achieve substantial cost reductions through economies of scale. Firms that raced ahead in anticipation of these scale economies not only invested heavily but also frenetically exhausted all other feasible cost minimization measures. In the long run, therefore, those companies that seemed to have thrown caution to the wind, ended up reaping profits at prices, which by then, faint hearted rivals were incapable of matching. Once this lesson was fully and widely grasped, industry after industry became engulfed in a competitive free for all.

Other factors that were more or less unique to the political economy of Japan gave added weight to the above mentioned process. First, firms were very much concerned with their public standing and since this was largely determined by their market shares, they were naturally keen to increase them. Second, the keiretsu likewise had a vested interest in ensuring that member firms excelled and that they held leading positions in important industries. Third, the willingness of institutional shareholders to accept low dividends meant that firms could concentrate on longer term objectives. Fourth, the high debt to equity financing that was so characteristic of many corporations facilitated rapid output growth at the expense of short-term profits. (Firms had less drawers of dividends to contend with and could mollify existing shareholders with promises of future capital gains.) Fifth, the commitment to lifetime employment (which will be elaborated upon in the following chapter) plus a previous constant desire to recruit young job seekers (both because their wages were low and because of fears of an impending scarcity of labour) meant that firms had to expand to accommodate an increasing work force. Faster growth rates also reassured permanent employees that their promotional prospects were reasonable and that upon retirement and if they so desired, they would have good prospects of obtaining temporary work. Also of some importance, a yearly infusion of new entrants (made possible by a high growth strategy) strengthened a firm's pension fund.

**Diversification, Subsidiaries and Mergers**

*Diversification: Then and Now*

Japanese corporations have generally had a tendency only to produce one or two distinct commodity lines (as opposed to numerous models), within a particular industry. There have been glaring exceptions to this rule. Canon forsook complete dependence on cameras to branch out into printers, computers, word processors, copiers and facsimile machines. Sony has been involved in life insurance, while Nippon Steel had taken to catalogue selling [Porter 1990:710]. Nonetheless, most Japanese firms have based their reputations and social standings in terms of their performances within given industries and they have usually been reluctant to transcend industrial frontiers.

Two factors largely account for this phenomenon, both of which are grounded in the institutional framework in which Japanese corporations operate. One relates to the 'lifetime' employment convention which makes it rather difficult for a firm to recruit the *experienced* skilled labour that may be required for diversification. (The skill composition of a standard Japanese company is fairly homogeneous and is in keeping with its product speciality.) The other factor stems from a firm's association with a keiretsu, which is usually structured to incorporate only one company from each leading industry. In the interest of keiretsu solidarity, firms had been inhibited from encroaching upon a fellow member's turf.

Whenever in fact diversification had been pursued, it was usually done through the spawning of separate and more or less independent subsidiaries. Such subsidiaries could well belong to different industry associations, enter into alliances with other companies and devise their own personnel policies. However, as Honda's foray from motorcycles into cars attests, not all diversification has taken place this way.

The past tendency for Japanese firms to eschew diversification is much less noticeable today. In 1970, only 47 per cent of Japanese firms had a diversification strategy as opposed to 65 per cent of US firms and while exact figures for the present period are not at hand, a recent study indicates that 'the difference between the United States and Japan has been reduced' [Koshiro 1994:238]. Between 1979 and 1986, the proportion of sales emanating from a company's traditionally main field of business fell from 85.8 per cent to 78.6 per cent for steel, 89.1 per cent to 60.8 per cent for nonferrous metals, 93.3 per cent to 83.6 per cent for electrical machinery and 59.1 per cent to 37.6 per cent for precision instruments [Komine 1991:88]. To no small extent, the growing need to diversify from traditional lines results from the ever increasing value of the yen and the consequent rise of offshore manufacturing (see Chapter 11).

*Mergers*

Mergers are limited by institutional considerations. With 60–70 per cent of a large corporation's stock generally being held by allied companies, 'it is virtually impossible to conduct an unfriendly takeover in Japan' [Sakakibara 1991:8]. Mergers that do occur, mostly do so within the same keiretsu or between organizations which previously maintained a business relationship of some sort. One of the most serious problems to which Japanese mergers give rise, concerns the integration of the staff of a recently acquired firm. The assimilation of a new set of employees whose previous relative positions were jealously guarded and who identified themselves utterly with a now defunct company, is a very problematic issue in Japan. Divisions between the two groups of personnel sometimes endure for years or even decades [Vogel 1979:77]. The problem is not just one of reconciling former loyalties or positions but also one of having to cope with human capital skills specific to each former enterprise.

Even so, mergers have of late been increasing. From the mid 1980s, companies began to accumulate cash in excess of their ability to expand internally. As a result, the acquisition of other corporations has increasingly appeared to be an attractive proposition. Most mergers have taken place as a means of furthering product diversification and have occurred among firms engaged in similar industries. Some observers see a latent threat to the Japanese economy if it were to begin indulging in mergers and acquisitions to anything like the extent to which it has been done in the West. Porter for instance fears that should Japanese firms shift their emphasis towards the buying and selling of existing assets rather than creating new productive capacity, the vibrancy and creativity of Japanese enterprise may partially be threatened [Porter 1990:710].

*Subsidiaries*

Apart from mergers, many large Japanese corporations have a tendency to launch subsidiaries as they progress beyond a certain point. The new corporations usually start off by being 100 per cent owned subsidiaries of parent companies. However, in the course of time, they might well extend their financial basis by floating shares bought by outsiders, so that eventually, the parent's stake may become considerably diluted with the companies emerging as independent units in their own right.

Motives for forming new subsidiaries are varied. In most cases, they represent a firm's response to a growing bureaucracy associated with previous bouts of expansion. As a firm's size increases, it encounters coordination and information exchange difficulties. Since the typical Japanese firm needs to excel in these areas in order to thrive, the moment its enhanced sized becomes dysfunctional, it adapts to the adverse situation by hiving off some of its activities into a newly created subsidiary. This helps 'to keep employees as homogeneous as possible in terms of career prospects, labor conditions, and so forth, thereby making human resource management easier' [Aoki 1987:285].

In addition to resolving problems of scale, new subsidiary formations also arise from efforts to economize on labour payments. With wages in Japan being firm-specific and with large companies being more generous than smaller ones, it occasionally pays to concentrate labour intensive activities within a smaller subsidiary and to boot, one which is located in a low-wage labour surplus area. Taking things to its logical conclusion, large Japanese corporations have displayed a growing readiness even to bypass local labour abundant areas by moving offshore to Asian countries.

Employees of parent companies also benefit from a proliferation of subsidiaries, in that it provides a mechanism for increasing the number of potential managerial positions to which they may be posted. Where individuals are offered senior openings in subsidiary firms, the parent company guarantees that transfers would not jeopardize their salary progressions nor their original pension and retirement termination payments. The practice of shunting off personnel to a subsidiary (termed 'shukko') is certainly widespread in corporations with a payroll in excess of 5000. In 1989, for example, 91.6 per cent of firms in this category had one or more of their employees working in other companies [Odagiri 1992:149].

THE SMALL FIRM

From the perspective of most Westerners, the notion of Japanese enterprise brings to mind images of large efficient capital intensive complexes utilizing the latest in modern computer and robotic technology. Certainly such complexes exist but in reality, more than half of industrial output and by far the largest proportion of employment in manufacturing are derived from small companies with a total work force of less than 300.[4] (See Table 6.2 for data relating to employment and the relative number of small commercial establishments.)

Not only is the small firm more pervasive in Japan than in Western countries, it also contains a far larger component of single handed or family operated enterprises. In the early 1980s these micro units employed 29 per cent of all Japan's work force compared with 9 per cent for the USA, 14 per cent for West Germany and 8 per cent for the UK [Patrick and Rohlen 1987:335].

Close to a million Japanese small 'enterprises' consist of self-employed, mostly female 'homeworkers', defined as individuals entrusted with the supply of goods for further processing or other care such as cleaning,

*Table* 6.2   Proportion of Employees and Firms Held by Small Business
Within Various Economic Sectors (1986)

| Industry | Percentage of Employees | Percentage of Establishments |
|---|---|---|
| Mining | 76.0 | 99.6 |
| Construction | 96.0 | 99.9 |
| Manufacturing | 74.4 | 99.5 |
| Wholesale/retail | 87.0 | 99.5 |
| Finance | 86.5 | 99.6 |
| Real estate | 98.0 | 100.0 |
| Transport | 88.1 | 99.6 |
| Utilities | 68.6 | 97.3 |
| Services | 67.1 | 98.3 |

*Source*: White Paper on Small and Medium Enterprises in Japan, Ministry of
International Trade and Industry, Tokyo, 1988, Tables 1 and 2

*Note*: Small and medium enterprises are defined as those with less than 300
employees (less than 100 in wholesale and less than 50 in the retail and service sectors)

repairing, sorting, etc. Most of the 'homeworkers' service the garment
and textile industries and they are essentially 'blue-collar workers who
work at home instead of in the factory' [Chalmers 1989:90]. They are
now declining in significance in the face of a global expansion of
labour saving technology and of a tendency for more women to seek
part-time employment [94].

On the other hand, there is another side to the small business sector
which consists of a large number of dynamic owner-managers endowed
with engineering and commercial talents. Operating within an internal
environment free of bureaucratic restraints, the owner-manager, who
closely resembles the classical entrepreneur, can formulate and execute
decisions more decisively than can most large firm executives. Thanks
to them, the relative importance of small business has been increasing
and there has been a slight shift in emphasis from light to heavy industry.

## Wages and Labour in the Small Firm

Since wage rates in Japan generally vary directly with firm size, there
are significant salary differentials between small and large companies.
Considering the issue from the perspective of two extremes, it would
seem that in 1974, workers in firms hiring 10–49 people received wage
payments that were on average less than 60 per cent of those working

in corporations employing more than 1000 [Allen 1981:50]. The situation did not subsequently improve. In 1987, for example, employees in firms with staff sizes in the 5–29 range (the only comparable classification available to the authors) earned on average 59.6 per cent of the salaries of those in firms that hired an excess of 500 people [MITI 1988:185].

Various factors account for these differences. Large companies attract more able and better qualified personnel. Their capital equipment is more sophisticated and extensive and partly as a result, value added per worker in firms with more than 1000 employees is nearly three times greater than in firms with less than ten [124]. Also, in response to a movement towards increased automation, large firms have shed some of their 'production workers', giving rise to a relative decline in the employment of low wage labourers.

Small firms tend to take on relatively more women, temporary workers and elderly retirees, all of whom generally command lower wages. Because the average length of tenure in small firms is shorter (due to more frequent job resignations and a higher ratio of part-timers), proportionally less workers accrue seniority based wage increments. Finally, the small firm sector is essentially non-unionized, leaving workers without satisfactory institutional safeguards to protect their interests. Partly as a result, 'working conditions in small factories and other establishments are often among the worst in Japan. Long hours, cramped spaces, lack of safety equipment, poor lighting, noise and so forth are common' [Patrick and Rohlen 1987:377].

If we were able to abstract from the major differences that appear in large and small firms in order 'to institute a comparison of workers of the same age, length of service and quality, the wage differentials (between firms of different sizes) would certainly be narrower than they appear in the statistics' [Allen 1981:151]. Nevertheless, sizeable gaps in relation to other aspects of worker compensation would still be apparent. For instance, bonuses in small firms are seldom more than a third of the amounts that large firms bestow. As for other rewards, such as lifetime employment and fringe benefits, considering the relatively precarious financial situation of many small firms, few of them can match the offerings of large ones. This does not, however, mean that no small firm offers comparable remuneration. Those at the upper end of the sector that produce high quality products based on precision engineering must, in order to attract and retain skilled labour, meet most of what such workers earn elsewhere.

Although small firms typically offer less material incentives, they do yield some non-monetary benefits which workers may value. One sort of intangible advantage may be a greater sense of belonging which is likely to occur in a small company where the owner is personally acquainted with everyone and where gifts are mutually exchanged on special occasions like weddings and funerals [Hendry 1987:139]. In relation to family firms, which are apt to employ all members available, those with employment further afield are provided with an assured safety net should ever they be in want of a job.

## Subcontracting and Dependence on Large Firms

*Definition and Nature of Subcontractor*

A subcontractor may be defined as a firm that supplies products to another firm under certain circumstances, these being that supply is in direct response to the buyer's request and that products are specifically tailored to meet the buyer's needs. Usually the products in question are components in the buyer's production process but subcontracting could also involve the supply of services. Not every input producer is a subcontractor, for some may simply be independent manufacturers. The critical difference is that in the case of subcontractors, each of their products is normally saleable to an individual buyer only and their control over its design is strictly prescribed [Uekusa 1987:500].

Subcontractors can and do supply different products to different buyers but until recently, they tended to deal mainly with one principal outlet. Many subcontractors have been 'partially if not fully integrated into the production system of the parent firm', and in the process have assumed a branch type character, accepting 'strict conditions and controls over such things as price and quality of product, and delivery and transaction terms' [Sheard 1983:52]. In the late 1970s, 40 per cent of subcontractors obtained some inputs from their parent firms and in about 20 per cent of firms surveyed, parent firms had some shareholdings or had dispatched to them, some personnel [52].

Firm dependence on mainly one buyer, involving the structuring of activities (both in terms of manufacturing and management) to meet a client's specific needs tends to create an exit barrier for the subcontractor [Kagono and Kobayashi 1994:97]. Accordingly, there has been a growing inclination on the part of firms with excellent technical and production management skills to widen the number of their parent companies [MITI 1988:74]. In fact, the average number of parent firms per subcontractor rose from three in 1976 to four in 1981 and then to five by 1986 [Yaginuma 1993:10].

*Incidence of Subcontracting*

More than half of all small manufacturing businesses undertake sub-contracting. The proportion of firms that have been so involved rose from 58.7 per cent in 1971 to 65.5 per cent in 1981, receding to 55.9 per cent in 1987 [Ito 1994:Fig. II.2]. Alternatively, over 50 per cent of all small firms depend on subcontracting orders for over 80 per cent of their sales. Clearly, 'the subcontracting relationship can be considered the most important relationship for medium and small firms in manufacturing' [Miwa 1991–2:42]. Of all small firms, those that employ less than ten workers are not only more likely to be subcontractors but are probably also more inclined to engage exclusively in subcontracting [Yokokura 1988:524].

Smitka [1990:66] attributes the unusually high incidence of subcontracting in Japan (especially in relation to the automobile industry) to attempts by producers, in the late 1940s, 'to lessen the power of the militant Japanese labor movement'. However, the growth of subcontracting is more of a reflection of a general shortage of parts manufacturers during the late 1950s and 1960s. Large corporations responded to these shortages by encouraging suppliers to join their own keiretsu and/or to enter into long-term relationships with them. On average, large companies call upon 67 subcontractors but some use very much more. Firms in the precision machinery industry regularly employ 132 suppliers and the Toyota Motor Corporation has had at one time, direct and indirect recourse to as many as 36 400 [Chalmers 1989:113].

*Subservient Position of Subcontractors*

The small subcontracting firm is normally placed in a subservient position with regard to its customers. Although nominally autonomous, the pace and standard of its operations are set in accordance with the exigencies of its patrons. With the introduction of 'kanban' or 'just in time' production technologies (see Chapter 8), the subcontractor's activities need to be synchronized with those of its buyers. Alternatively, the subcontractor may have to carry a large and varied range of inventories. Even the prices that a subcontractor levies are subject to buyer assent. By convention, full-cost pricing is applied. That is, a given markup over costs is allowed. The markup varies depending on the specific product and is sometimes generally raised to reward suppliers for efficiency improving efforts. By the same token, car manufacturers for one, do not accept increased labour or energy costs as a justification for component price hikes [Uekusa 1987:502]. In bidding for contracts, car parts firms are required to break down their production system into a series of individual steps and to price each process separately. This procedure allows automobile makers to 'compare costs for a given manufacturing step across firms and across time' [Smitka 1990:67].

The ability of large companies to override subcontractor interests is limited by the existence of competitive pressures to secure and retain reliable suppliers. Firms that produce key inputs that are not readily available elsewhere and firms that cater to more than one buyer are well poised to fend for themselves. Weaker firms may rely on the Subcontractors Protection Law which prohibits delays of over 60 days in payment for work and the refusal to take delivery of goods ordered. In addition, the act contains a number of other clauses that shield a subcontractor from outright exploitation.

*Advantages to Large Firms*

The advantages to large firms in using small firm subcontractors are manifold. They are able to capture scale economies with a certain amount of flexibility, for rigidities built into the organizational framework of large Japanese corporations by heavy debt financing and lifetime employment are counterbalanced by some give in the support structure of small firms [Okimoto 1989:131]. The system affords large firms an opportunity not only to reduce labour costs but also to lessen general labour supervision. In essence, small company managers act as proxy foremen on behalf of clients. Savings in the use of capital equipment are also realized. With many small firms possessing both sophisticated machinery and skilled operatives, large firms can confidently turn to them for high quality products promptly dispatched at competitive prices. Small firm owner operators have a much greater incentive to seek cost reducing measures than say divisional managers of large corporations and steady improvements in small firm efficiencies have been a boon to Japanese manufacturers in general.

*Advantages and Disadvantages to Small Firms*

The subcontracting system has turned out to be mutually rewarding. Many suppliers have secured long-term purchasing commitments from their customers which relieves them of marketing and distribution headaches. According to Aoki 'larger prime manufacturers with diversified finished products and financial viability function as partial insurers of business opportunities, earnings and employment for smaller subcontractors in exchange for insurance premiums in the form of semi-monopolistic gains' [Aoki 1987:284]. Payment by reputable corporations is more or less assured and financial assistance has also been forthcoming.

From a global economic point of view, leading companies have assumed some responsibility for upgrading the technological capabilities of their subcontractors by 'offering technical guidance in design, accounting, cost control, production management, automation and quality control' [Cusumano 1985:377]. Consequently, Japan boasts a significant collection of innovative and progressive firms within its small business sector. Some of these firms, by undertaking joint technical developments with their patrons, provide them with added technological resources [MITI 1988:76].

On considering the disadvantages of the subcontracting system, it seems that they virtually all fall on the supplier. Major handicaps include greater vulnerability to economic recessions, dependence on a restricted number of buyers and a strict requirement to accommodate customer needs, which limits the scope for small business inventiveness. Even so, it is not entirely clear that all subcontractors feel threatened by forging too close a tie with a parent company. On the contrary, 38.9 per cent of subcontractors surveyed in 1983 by the Shyoko-Chukin (the government financial corporation for loans to small and medium-sized firms) expressed a desire to strengthen relationships with a single parent firm in the hope of securing stable contracts [see Aoki 1984:29].

**Government Assistance to Small Firms**

The government has been very supportive of small business and has assisted and protected it by legislative and administrative means. According to an OECD report, by the late 1970s, of all the industrialized countries, Japan had assembled the most extensive range of policy tools for assisting small companies [OECD 1978:17]. In 1974 there were 18 separate statutes that fostered the well-being of small firms. These statutes were all consolidated in the Fundamental Law for Small and Medium Enterprise with the objective of rationalizing and modernizing small business and of safeguarding it from unfair treatment by large enterprises. By the late 1960s, no less than seven public bodies served small firm interests. The organizations in question were: the People's Finance Corporation, the Small Business Finance Corporation, the Bank for Commerce and Industrial Cooperatives, the Small

Business Credit Insurance Corporation, the Small Business Investment Company, the Small Business Promotion Corporation and the Environmental Sanitation Business Finance Corporation. Between 1966 and 1973, the combined loans of the People's Finance Corporation and the Small Business Finance Corporation 'consistently exceeded by a wide margin the loans of the Japan Development Bank' [Trezise and Suzuki 1976:775]. Among its general activities, the People's Finance Corporation disbursed funds (in terms of the No-Collateral Loan Program) to factories employing fewer than 20 workers. The Small Business Finance Corporation provided small companies with assistance in plant modernization.

In the early postwar years, small firms were not well served by the country's commercial banking sector, which had a pro big-business bias. But with government prodding and through the state agencies listed above, the share of small business in the total loans of the financial sector rose from 43.0 per cent in 1963 to 58.9 per cent in 1983. With these changes in mind and adjusting for risk and transaction cost differentials between large and small firms, Patrick and Rohlen concluded that 'there is now no substantial discrimination in financial markets against small enterprises' [Patrick and Rohlen 1987:363].

Finally, taxation rates for small businesses are lower than those for large ones. And in any case, small firms are known to evade taxes more widely.

### External Challenges

In the last few years, largely on account of the strengthening of the yen, Japanese exporters have run into difficulties. Many small firms have faced a fall in revenue because of reversals in both direct and indirect exports. Further erosions are threatened by growing imports of labour intensive products and by large corporations increasingly establishing overseas subsidiaries. The corporations in question, partly by choice and partly in response to host country pressures, have been procuring more and more of their inputs abroad. To safeguard their interests, many small firms have also moved offshore. Some have done so in order to continue subcontracting to their now partly foreign sited patrons, while others have been lured by access to cheap Third World labour and/or to be within easy reach of growing Asian markets. The small business sector as a whole is not seriously threatened but a fair degree of restructuring is inevitable.

SUMMARY

**Large Firms**

- Many Japanese firms belong to alliances known as keiretsu, which are spread across large corporations in different industries (horizontal keiretsu) or between a large corporation and input suppliers (vertical keiretsu).
- Each horizontal keiretsu usually contains a leading bank and other key financial bodies and is coordinated through a presidents' council.
- By a system of interlocking shares, horizontal keiretsu ward off unfriendly takeovers.
- Vertical keiretsu reflect smaller in-house manufacturing on the part of large corporations which secure components from independent suppliers with whom long-term ties are forged.
- The keiretsu are descended from the zaibatsu but unlike the zaibatsu, which were effectively large conglomerates run by controlling companies owned by wealthy families, the keiretsu consist of independent firms joined together in voluntary associations.
- The keiretsu provide a system of mutual support and a framework in which firms can undertake long-term planning. As a result, the output of keiretsu firms is less volatile than non-keiretsu firms in the course of a business cycle.
- Intra-keiretsu activity seems to be declining, probably because keiretsu firms were concentrated in sectors such as steel and shipping which are now less prominent.
- Most large corporations have a 'main bank' which handles the bulk of their financial services. It also had organized loan consortiums for its clients and in times of stress, the 'main bank' would bail out large clients by a combination of extra finance and direct managerial supervision. However, since the mid 1970s, large firms have become less dependent on bank finance.
- Individual stockholding is less extensive in Japan. Most stocks are held by other large corporations who are less concerned with profit and more concerned with mutual protection and mutual trading. As a result, the firm pursues objectives which do not give top priority to private shareholder needs. Although dividend payments are low, shareholders have been obtaining more than adequate capital growth.
- The president of a Japanese corporation has extensive powers. A large measure of group decision making occurs but in the final analysis, the president has the last word. Japanese corporations are thought to

be run with the interests of permanent employees very much in mind but fear of bankruptcy or falling into the hands of the 'main bank' provides a source of discipline and restraint.

- Excess competition in Japan had been stimulated (among other things) by industrial policy, high GDP growth rates enabling the lowering of prices to capture scale economies, a general firm desire for large market shares, the ability of firms to sacrifice short-term profits for growth (because of high debt to equity ratios and sympathetic large shareholders) and a desire to increase the ratio of young to elderly employees (through market expansion) which lowers average labour costs.
- At first, firms seldom diversified across industrial lines because of work forces geared to specific product types and because of not wishing to poach on other keiretsu members' turf. Now because of the ever appreciating yen many feel that they have no option but to diversify into more promising fields.
- Mergers are seldom undertaken in Japan. They create personnel problems in unifying staff from previously separate companies.
- Subsidiary formations enable core companies to maintain compact, homogeneous work forces which are easier to administer.

## Small Firms

- Small firms consist of a variety of types ranging from single handed operators to modern establishments employing 2–300 people.
- Wages in small firms are generally lower on account of the greater labour intensity of their production processes, the employment of more women, temporary workers and the elderly and less, if any, unionization.
- More than half of small firms enter into subcontracting relations in which they have to pay heed to client product specifications and delivery schedules.
- The subcontracting system benefits large corporations in that they need employ less labour, they can rely on their suppliers for quality products and in times of economic setbacks, they can pass on some of the adjustment costs to others.
- Small firms gain from subcontracting by obtaining technological transfers and training from large corporations, by having moderately steady sales outlets, by generally being paid on time and by being encouraged to seek cost reduction procedures of which they can be partial beneficiaries.

- The government is rather supportive of small firms and has assisted them by means of both legislation and administrative practices.
- Small firms are currently facing challenges posed by the appreciating yen and by their client companies increasingly moving offshore. In their defence, many small firms are following in parent firms' wakes.

# 7 Labour Management and Industrial Relations

## INTRODUCTION

The quality of Japan's human capital and the distinctive manner in which it is organized both go a long way in accounting for the tremendous economic success that the country has enjoyed. In a later chapter dealing with education, we show how Japan's school and university systems mould its labour force. Here we concentrate on personnel management within the large corporation, working conditions and remuneration, trade unionism and other related issues such as the lot of temporary workers, female employees and the firm's approach to staff when facing trying circumstances.

Our discussion opens with recruitment and training procedures. We do so because Japanese firms have been able to command a measure of loyalty and an almost unbridled enthusiastic application of effort on the part of their employees, which by far exceeds levels which their Western counterparts either expect or obtain. To some extent, this arises from the nature of Japanese society in general. That is, from people's attitudes, upbringing, beliefs and customs. However, the large corporation's conscious and sustained efforts to inculcate its workers with a value system conducive to its requirements, overshadows all else. Little is left to chance and much of that which is ascribed to the social environment, turns out on closer examination to be the product of skilful human engineering.

## RECRUITMENT

In this, and the next few sections, our attention is focused on career appointments, which generally constitute no more than a third of the total working population and which, as will soon become apparent, do not invariably even make up an *overwhelming* majority of a large corporation's payroll.

When it comes to choosing its permanent appointees or 'salarymen', the Japanese company is extremely meticulous. It has to be so, for

136

since each such new entrant is offered 'lifetime' employment and is subsequently vested with years of in-house training, recruitment errors would not only be difficult to rectify but would also be very costly.

The upshot of it all is that a prospective recruit faces a daunting set of hurdles and a complex filtering process. To gain entry into a prestigious corporation, it is virtually mandatory to graduate from an elite university or college. This in turn presupposes an outstanding high school performance. However, for many firms, such accomplishments merely satisfy necessary but not sufficient conditions. To cull the number of its applicants, firms frequently arrange their own formal examinations. Then, after carefully scrutinizing written testimonials, a candidate's background is scrupulously checked. Former teachers as well as even neighbours are consulted to establish whether any character defects can be detected and more sinisterly, questions are posed as to whether the person concerned is one of the 'burakumin' (an inferior caste) or even an adherent of a certain new religious order.

For its 1990 graduate intake, Fuji sifted through 20 000 applications, interviewed 2000 hopefuls and eventually settled on 300 of them [Horsley and Buckley 1990: 220]. Even taking into account non-graduate recruits, Fuji, like all other large corporations, prefers to enlist its new entrants directly from educational institutions and not from those who have already gained some previous work experience.


INDUCTION AND TRAINING[1]

After having chosen its fresh staff with extreme circumspection, the Japanese corporation proceeds, with no less thoroughness, to ensure that they are well and truly integrated within the organization. An individual's entry into the firm is likened to his or her admission into a new family. The rites of passage begin with a formal ceremony, presided over by the firm's president or deputy. There the novices are invariably given a rendition of the company's philosophy and tradition. Their privileged access into its fold is firmly stressed and their expected reciprocal obligations are clearly enunciated. Typically, a large portrait of the corporation's founder, who is likened to a familial ancestor, is prominently displayed.

Thereafter, an intensive initiation programme varying from two months to a year follows. Training during this period is sometimes undertaken in a remote location, such as at a firm's rural holiday complex. Alternatively, trainees may be lodged within centrally placed company dormitories. Whatever the case, the beginner is faced with a fairly rigorous daily routine. In extreme cases, a form of army training is replicated, which may entail submersions in an icy river or a 24 hour march but more probably the worst a newcomer could anticipate are early morning risings, the performance of various communal tasks and adherence to an early evening curfew [Van Wolferen 1989:160].

An intended by-product of the training process is the forging of close friendship ties among entry cohorts. As they progress and attain a measure of standing within the departments where they are ultimately placed, they will be able to relate to their peers elsewhere in an amicable and forthright manner. Herein lies part of the reason why communication and the exchange of information in a Japanese corporation is so widespread.

An overriding objective of the orientation programme is to ensure that recruits are modelled into employees who fully identify with and adjust to their firm's needs. With this in mind, a fair amount of emphasis is placed on company etiquette. Instruction is given on bowing procedures. (The norm is a 15 degree angle for colleagues of equal rank, 30 degrees for superiors and 45 degrees when apologies or awkward situations arise.) [160] The manner and timing of the exchange of business cards is clarified, as is the required physical placing in the presence of superiors and visitors. While such considerations are likely to be of little concern to Western firms, in Japan where rank and status are of grave importance, a solid schooling in firm protocol is imperative.

Except in regard to those with high technical and scientific qualifications, Japanese corporations pay little heed to a graduate's prior education and prefer instead to provide their own instruction. The permanent employment convention enables them to invest in human capital with an expectation that future returns would be more or less assured.

Much attention is of course focused on the acquisition of work and general management skills. Trainees are exposed to a broad range of activities and job rotations before their long-term career paths are finally determined. (For the first 15 years or so, they are all likely to be similarly graded and paid.) By undertaking a number of different tasks within different departments or sections, employees are more amenable and adjust more easily to job transfers. This has the effect of providing the firm with more flexibility in responding to changing market conditions and/or to new technological developments. It also has at least two other salutary by-products. One of which is the fostering of intra-firm communication and a general sharing of information. The other is the provision of many candidates for promotion leading to more employee rivalry and, presumably, more worker efficiency.

## DEVOTION TO THE FIRM

The ideal situation from a Japanese corporation's point of view, is for its employees to identify themselves wholeheartedly with their firm. Much to their satisfaction, many companies have attained a close approximation of this ideal. So much so, that if workers were to be asked how they earn a living, most would proudly reply that they serve a certain corporation rather than define themselves in terms of a particular profession or trade.

Companies project themselves as having intrinsic values. Among these is the supposition that one of their major objectives is the furthering of employee well-being. Those in positions of seniority take it upon themselves to adopt a quasi parental stance in relation to their subordinates. Section heads, for instance, might concern themselves not only with the integration of the staff under their care but also with their personal life and problems. Grateful juniors in turns, would respond by inviting them to their weddings and to other milestone family gatherings.

To foster a sense of communal association, many departments are allocated a modest budget to finance after hour restaurant and pub gatherings. Within the workplace itself, there is a constant semblance of joint decision making. Emphasis is placed on the unity and cohesion of each sub-work group with the hope that in such a setting, employees would manifest group loyalty and possibly even strive for peer approval.

An employee's identification with his or her firm is buttressed by a host of symbols and rituals. Companies devise their own coat of arms, design their own uniforms and widely distribute labelled caps and lapel badges. They organize group callisthenics, after hours sport and recreational activities, local excursions and even overseas company trips. Whenever the opportunity presents itself, workers are called upon to provide a gusty rendition of the company song.

Finally, as it were, most companies spice their symbolism with a dash of religion. Shinto shrines may adorn their roofs and religious ceremonies may be organized to commemorate special events or company landmarks. The intention is to bestow an aura of spiritualism to the corporation at large.

## WORK HOURS AND HOLIDAYS

Having obtained worker loyalty and dedication, the Japanese firm extracts relatively large quantities of effort on the part of its employees. In 1990, the annual number of hours worked per person in Japan amounted to 2052. This was about 10 per cent higher than in the USA and Britain and about 25 per cent more than in Germany and France [Institute of International Economics 1992:14]. In 1987 the government reduced the number of hours that may legally be worked from 48 per week to 46 'but enforcement of the law is less than zealous' [*Economist* 1991:28]. For more than half of the labour force, the workweek extends into Saturdays (until noon) and a small minority of unfortunates are also occasionally called upon to do a Sunday morning stint.

### Working Overtime

Rather than hiring more workers to meet sudden or temporary demand boosts, firms tend to rely on existing staff working overtime. This is largely (but not exclusively) an outcome of the lifetime employment convention. Unless there is a fair degree of certainty that a firm's increased activity is likely to endure, it would be risky to take on more career orientated personnel. Recourse to overtime thus provides a firm with output flexibility at minimum costs, especially since the need for extra staff training is averted.

In normal times, overtime is regularly expected. At a factory studied by Clark, most people put in an extra seven or eight hours per week [Clark 1979:193]. It is very difficult to avoid doing overtime and as a result family life suffers. In 1967 Hitachi corporation dismissed an employee for refusing to do overtime. The employee in turn tried to sue for damages and the case ultimately reached the Supreme Court which ruled 'that employees are obliged to work overtime, even against their will, if the request is reasonable' [Clark 1979:28]. In addition, at the conclusion of formal work activities, individuals are frequently subjected to strong pressures to socialize with their colleagues (usually in bars).

### Holiday Periods

Holiday allowances, which depend on seniority and on firm size, generally range from two to three weeks. Few utilize their full entitlement. In 1989, the average Japanese worker took only eight days [*Economist* 1991:28]. It would seem that many are hesitant in being away from the workplace for an extended period of time lest their loyalty be questioned and their promotion prospects be threatened.[2] However, the overall situation is not quite so gloomy. There are four public holidays within a week around the end of April and the beginning of May and about 56 per cent of manufactured firms and 34 per cent of all industries take this 'golden week' off and close their plants [Ito 1992:231].


LIFETIME EMPLOYMENT


In return for their efforts, Japanese workers are rewarded in various ways, one of which is the provision of lifetime employment. However, this privilege is largely confined to tenured workers who constitute no more than a third of the work force. Such workers are mostly concentrated in large firms but average job tenure across the entire spectrum of Japanese companies is significantly longer than in the United States. Many blue-collar workers are also lifetime employment beneficiaries and to some extent, the 'white-collarization' of blue-collar workers is a distinguishing feature of Japanese corporate industrial relations.

Far from being an integral part of Japanese culture, lifetime employment only became widespread towards the mid-twentieth century. It took root in response to labour shortages and the need for labour training. Before that, and in the Meiji period in particular, 'there was little sense of a common purpose or of reciprocal obligation between management and the workers, and the labor turnover was high' [Allen 1981:145].

Corporations have not legally bound themselves to lifetime employment but they adhere to it as accepted traditional practice. Only a very small number of employees considered eligible for lifetime employment have ever been formally dismissed and of these, most have either been dishonest or flagrantly negligent. In some instances, rulings have been given by a regional labour relations committee or a court that certain 'regular' employees have been wrongfully dismissed obliging the firms in question to reinstate them [Imai and Komiya 1994:21].

The lifetime employment bargain cuts both ways. Firms have an expectation that their professional staff will maintain allegiance to them. This they largely do out of a sense of loyalty but as it happens, there are a number of other considerations that dissuade workers from resigning. Company benefits that they enjoy or entitlements that they may accrue are generally not transferable. Furthermore, an individual moving to another firm is very likely to encounter a setback in seniority and or a slower promotion progression. Apart from not having established long-term intimate collegial connections, the person in question would probably be regarded with suspicion as an intruder. Also of relevance is the fact that because of the general provision of all round in-firm training, entailing exposure to a multitude of activities and tasks, the overall skills that employees acquire are largely firm specific. This has the effect of making it more difficult for them to move elsewhere.

In reality, the term 'lifetime employment' is a misnomer. For most male workers reaching the 55–60 age range, retirement is compulsory. Directors and managing directors are able to remain till their sixties while chairmen of the board stay on till their seventies. Nearly every retiree (who has served 30 years) receives a severance payment equivalent to three to four years' salary. Even so, many workers require continued employment after their 'retirement'. They may be re-hired by their original firms as non-regular staff and at a lower wage, they may join smaller companies (sometimes with assistance from their former employers) or they may become self-employed. In fact, some 35 per cent of them will continue to work beyond the age of 65. State old age pensions are only payable from the age of 70. To alleviate the plight of older workers, a 1978 law mandates firms with a payroll in excess of 100 to ensure that at least 6 per cent are over 55 years old. Partly as a result, the participation rate of workers in that category far exceeds the OECD average.

Employees who would least expect to remain with one firm throughout the bulk of their working lives are youthful blue-collar workers with lesser education. So large a proportion of people in this category attempt to transfer from smaller to larger companies (where the pay is higher) that it could be considered unusual for any of them not to do so [Clark 1979:151].


## SALARIES, ADVANCEMENT AND SENIORITY

### Salaries

In Japan there is no common wage rate applicable to workers of a given craft, profession or grade across an industry. Instead, pay awards are separately determined within each company. As we have already noted (in the previous chapter) larger firms generally offer higher remunerations than smaller ones due to greater productivity and to more pronounced trade union involvement.

Since earnings are governed more by one's rank and less by the specific tasks that are undertaken, the internal redeployment of staff may have little bearing on wages. Accordingly, companies wishing to restructure their activities meet with little worker resistance.

Emoluments rise with seniority and with age. Relatively low wages are accepted by young entrants on permanent track appointments, as they can confidently anticipate larger incomes in the course of time. Firms that sustain rapid growth are able to maintain a high ratio of youthful to more elderly employees, a factor that keeps their average labour costs in check. By contrast, stagnant firms with higher proportions of mature aged personnel, encounter increasing average wage payments. Faced with this dilemma, some companies have attempted to limit salary increments at the top end of the scale.

Within large corporations, on the job learning is essentially a never ending process, so that human capital is enriched over time. That being the case, seniority based wage payments do not flout the principle of rewarding workers in terms of relative labour productivity.

A remarkable feature of Japanese salary profiles is the existence of a comparatively narrow differential between the earnings of senior executives and those of junior employees. Although there were considerable differences in the past (in the late 1920s returns to those at the top were one hundred fold greater than to those at the bottom) [Abegglen and Stalk 1985:191], in the postwar period the gap narrowed appreciably. By 1992, it would seem that 'in Japan, the CEO (ie the president) makes less than 32 times the pay of the average factory worker.' In the US, by contrast the 'gap between the executive suite and the shop has widened to the point where the average American CEO makes an incredible 157 times what a factory worker gets' [*Business Week*, 26 April 1993]. The more modest rewards meted out to Japanese executives serve their organizations well in that they promote a sense of staff cohesion and company loyalty.

Still on the subject of salary differentials, differences based on formal education and occupation are smaller in Japan than in most other industrialized countries. Sasaki maintains that 'the gaps in the lifetime income among primary and/or middle school graduates, high school graduates, and university graduates are getting smaller' [Sasaki 1990:8]. This may arise from the fact that 'blue-collar workers in large firms have some skills similar to those of white-collar workers' [Koiki 1987:329]. In other words, in Japan, a fair degree of white-collarization of the blue-collar worker has taken place. (For this, the education system can claim much credit.)

## Bonuses

On two occasions each year, around the New Year at the end of December and around the midsummer festival (O-Bon) in June–July, corporations provide their employees with large financial bonuses. With 97 per cent of firms employing 30 or more employees paying bonuses, the system is essentially all pervasive. Bonus payments which amount to three to five months of a recipient's salary are generally assumed to be a function of profits, base salaries and seniority (the bonus to monthly salary ratio is higher for older workers). Ohashi has advanced the hypothesis that bonus payments constitute a reward for intensity of work effort. 'More specifically, when determining the bonus size, the firm will consider the level of activity, that is, the labor intensity experienced since the last payment' [Ohashi 1994:279]. However, given that the intensive use of labour is virtually bound to be associated with increased profits, we remain unmoved by Ohashi's proposition.

As a result of the bonus system, annual incomes are effectively derived from two sources, base salaries which are more or less constant and the bonuses themselves which vary from year to year depending on a firm's circumstances. Reliance on this method of payment bestows a number of advantages both to the firm and to the economy at large. First, it affords a large measure of labour cost flexibility, enabling staff expenditures (though not necessarily staff numbers) to be adjusted downwards in an economic crisis. Second, because it entails a large element of deferred remuneration, the bonus system in effect yields a temporary cash loan to the firm. Third, it allows retirement benefits, which are linked to base salaries, to be kept low. Fourth, since bonuses depend on profits, it provides all employees with a performance improving incentive. Fifth (as suggested in Chapter 4), by virtue of their being regarded as windfalls, bonuses may well be an important factor contributing to Japan's exceptionally high national savings rate.

## Perks

Apart from their salaries and bonuses, workers in the large Japanese company receive a variety of additional perquisites. These are dispensed to employees at all levels of seniority and may have both monetary and non-monetary components. Benefits most commonly available include supplementary allowances for education, transport and housing (including subsidized mortgages), cheap access to company holiday resorts, residential accommodation, sporting facilities and reception halls (for family celebrations), as well as price discounts for company products. Firms may supply medical care and children's crèches and may even organize cultural and recreational activities.

Rewarding employees in this form serves to forge closer bonds between them and their firms. To a certain extent, it may also allow a company to contribute to the well-being of their staff in an economically satisfactory way. For example, its outlays on housing and other forms of real estate for personnel usage, are in fact, valuable property investments. Considering that in the face of labour shortages, firms were obliged to seek workers from outlying rural areas, they were, at the very least, compelled to entice them with offers of accommodation and other basic amenities.

An interesting aspect of the provision of perks is that some of them continue to be available to employees even after they retire. For instance, retirees (from large companies) are generally able to continue to make use of their firm's medical and holiday facilities. In that sense, company ties are never severed.

**Promotion and Seniority**

Provided they do not step out of line or perform unduly poorly, graduate appointees can confidently anticipate semi-automatic career progression up to some intermediate level. Promotions tend to be made in a spiral, rather than in a linear way [see Komiya 1990:163]. That is, instead of simply moving up through the rank hierarchy, each promotion usually entails a transfer from one department or branch to a more senior position elsewhere. The length of stay in any particular post is roughly three years.

By convention, age cohorts tend to be promoted in unison with each other and where possible, every effort is made to ensure that the most senior official in any section, department or division, is also the most senior by age. Eventually, when a new president is appointed, his former executive peers retire.

Since the majority of one's fellow entry colleagues simultaneously attain a parallel status in other parts of the firm, inter-departmental communication is enhanced. In like fashion, with former classmates reaching comparable posts in the civil service and in other organizations, relations with important institutions and businesses are maintained through long-term and intimate personal connections.

The principle of promotion by age is not adhered to rigidly. There are occasions when extraordinarily able employees rise above those older than themselves but as this rarely occurs, their meteoric progress is generally accepted as a fitting tribute to their exceptional talents.

## The Ranking System

Each corporation maintains a well defined hierarchy in which everyone is appropriately placed. As already mentioned, the Japanese are very status conscious and meticulously observe rank protocol. That is, their bearing is modified according to the relative pecking order of those with whom they come into contact. Even seating arrangements reflect an employee's comparative stature. Considering the kudos attached to rank, striving for promotion is motivated nearly as much by the desire for enhanced social standing as for increased earnings.

A clearly defined ranking system provides a common frame of reference for workers in various branches of a company undertaking different tasks. Given that similar gradings apply in all large organizations, the standard ranking system also comes into play in inter-firm relations. Where two organizations are of comparable size, officials of the two bodies would liaise only with each other's counterparts. Should the two entities not be on equal footing, a high ranking official in the lesser one may have to contend with a nominal junior from the other.

One of the most significant positive aspects of slotting everyone into a graded post is that all company members are likely to envisage themselves 'as being on the same ladder, rather than as being in separate categories or classes' [Clark 1979:108]. In many respects, similar ranking systems are in force in Western universities and in the British Civil Service, where likewise there is a strong sense of corporate unity and fellowship.

Concomitant to the functioning of the hierarchical system, a strong and fairly independent personnel department is normally in place with full control over recruitment procedures, job rotations, employee monitoring and the determination of promotion criteria. Worker performance is measured in terms of contributions to the firm's general well-being and not specifically in terms of the execution of specific skills. Because staff are frequently rotated from one department or task to another, feedback is derived from a number of supervisors and in that sense, the overall assessment of any one employee is moderately fair and objective.


## TRADE UNIONS

At the beginning of the twentieth century various attempts were made to introduce trade unions into Japan. For the most part, such efforts were vigorously countered. After the Second World War, the occupying authorities not only permitted trade unions, they actively encouraged them as important props to Japan's then fledgling democracy. Former union organizers were either released from imprisonment or allowed to return from exile. Within next to no time, union membership skyrocketed from zero in 1945, to nearly seven million by 1948.

The ratio of trade union members to the total work force (the unionization rate) peaked at around 40 per cent by the mid 1950s. Thereafter, it slowly receded, falling to 33 per cent in 1978, 31 per cent in 1981 and 28 per cent in 1986. 'Today, more than half of Japan's work force has never belonged to a union', [Horsley and Buckley 1990:57] and of all the OECD countries, only the US has a lower rate of unionization. A growing proportion of workers who derive their livelihood within sectors which are not amenable to union membership (particularly small firms) and an increase in casual staff, largely explain the present situation.

Until 1987, the union movement had been structured around four loose national federations in which each affiliate's autonomy was sacrosanct. In that year, three of the federations merged into an organization named Rengo, which was expanded in 1989 to incorporate public sector workers. Currently, two federations exist, Rengo with an estimated membership of eight million and a pro-communist grouping called Zenro-Ren which has a following of 1.5 million [Ito 1992:228].


### Industrial Strife

As far as industrial disputation is concerned, Japan has been enjoying a period of relative tranquillity. In 1988, it lost 163 000 days through industrial action, compared with the US and the UK where 4 364 000 and 3 702 000 days respectively were involved [Bank of Japan 1990]. The country has not always maintained such an idyllic state of affairs, for in the early to medium postwar period, Japan was troubled by a series of bitter and protracted labour–management confrontations.

Right up to the mid 1950s, there was a spate of strikes, especially in the coal, electrical power, steel and automobile industries. Plans were even afoot to call a general strike for 1 February 1947, but this scheme was foiled by the intercession of the Occupying Authorities. On many occasions, workers found themselves pitted in pitched battles not only against the police but also against hired thugs. Such was the case with regard to the Yomiuri newspaper in 1946, Nissan Motors in 1953 and a Mitsui coal mine in 1960.

Of all the industrial turmoil that raged in the 1940s and 1950s, the clash, in the early summer of 1953, between the then National Car Workers Union (Zenji-Roren) and three automobile firms (Nissan, Toyota and Isuzu) represented a watershed in Japan's trade union history. After an interval of haggling, a settlement was reached with Toyota and Isuzu but the conflict intensified at Nissan where the union called for an indefinite strike and where production ceased over a three-month period. With financial backing (arranged through the Federation of Industrial Employers [Nikkeiran]) and with commitments by Toyota and other rivals not to poach upon its market share, Nissan dug in its heels. Leading a two prong attack, it mobilized all the means it could muster to intimidate the strikers, and at the same time, it organized a company union which very shortly eroded the industrial union's rank and file. Cusumano believes that Nissan executives were largely instrumental in fomenting the strike with the express purpose of supplanting the Car Workers Union with a union of their own [Cusumano 1985:142]. Whether this is true or not, Nissan has not subsequently lost a single day's output on account of industrial action.

## Company Unions

With the exception of associations encompassing seamen, teachers and groups of public workers, over 90 per cent of Japan's unions are company ones. In other words, there is a separate union for each corporation which includes all regular employees save those in managerial positions. Where multiple plants exist, each has its own union which is a constituent member of an umbrella organization representing the entire company's work force.

Not surprisingly, there is a fair amount of harmony between a company and its enterprise union. The union is invariably provided with office space and furniture and the company in turn draws many of its personnel officers from among union organizers. That active union involvement provides no barrier to career advancement is clearly suggested by the results of a 1981 survey which indicated that 74 per cent of firms questioned, reported having at least one board member with a trade union leadership background [Chalmers 1989:101].

Companies benefit from the enterprise union system in that they need only bargain with a single negotiating partner which appreciates in turn the link between wages and productivity. Given the lifetime employment convention (without which company unions would probably not exist), regular workers identify with the firm and have a direct interest both in its general well-being and in particular in its continued viability. This does not mean that the unions are complete pushovers. On the contrary, they are fairly assertive and effective in furthering their members' interests.

From a general point of view, enterprise unions have manifested certain anti-social traits. They are opposed to opening up membership to temporary workers, they show a general lack of concern with national welfare issues and they are indifferent to the plight of Japan's unorganized workers [Chalmers 1989:192].

THE SPRING WAGE OFFENSIVE

Since the mid-1950s, it has been the standard practice of Japanese trade unions to submit wage demands on an annual basis. This occurs between March and May in the context of coordinated and simultaneous bargaining rounds known as the Spring Offensive (shunto). In many instances, a one or two day strike precedes the wage negotiations which focus on basic pay awards.

Essentially, discussions are independently conducted within each enterprise but union federations play a role in orchestrating the overall campaign by urging their more powerful members, within the steel, railway, engineering and chemical industries, to take the lead. The terms which these forerunners secure provide guidelines for those that follow.

Although there is a flurry of union activity every spring, in actual fact a fair amount of sparring takes place from November onwards when both employee and management bodies begin releasing press statements detailing their basic positions. In the course of time, during which the media reports and comments on the views of authoritative economic players, a consensus regarding the range in which the average pay increase is likely to fall will emerge. This consensus usually provides a two to three percentage point band in which the subsequent shunto norm settles [Dore 1986:24].

With the conclusion of the Spring Offensive, the unions continue to take up other issues. Paramount among these are matters of overtime allowances and bonuses.

## TEMPORARY WORKERS

Most Japanese firms take on non-regular labour who are non-unionized and who are not only paid lower wages but are also ineligible for normal fringe benefits. Laws which regulate labour standards provide little protection to temporary workers and they are readily dispensable. The workers in question consist of staff officially designated as 'temporary' but who in practice, turn out to be regularly employed. For example, there is a tendency among certain firms to replace young female workers with older 'part time' women who, according to a 1982 survey, work on average seven hours per day for wages and bonuses which amount to 82 and 28 per cent respectively of the payments made to full-timers [Dore 1986:96]. Other non-tenured staff include seasonal workers and retirees re-engaged at lower salaries.

The widespread tendency to rely on temporary workers is believed to emanate from an assumed practice on the part of large Japanese corporations to distribute 'a certain proportion of the profit to the shareholders and the rest to "company members"' [Komiya 1990:170]. In other words, the employment of temporary workers whose productivity in certain respects is no less than that of others but who are excluded from profit sharing (given in the form of bonuses, regular perks and pensions) enables member workers to 'exploit' non-member ones [173].

Not only are temporary workers generally disadvantaged but because they can be hired or fired at a moment's notice, they also provide an employment buffer for permanent staff. Evidently, the job security that the small core of lifetime employees enjoy is largely at their expense.

## THE POSITION OF WOMEN

Japanese women, who represent no less than 35 per cent of the labour market, are more hard done by than their sisters in other industrial countries. Trade unions rarely concern themselves with their plight, which is distinctly inferior to that of the men folk. Not only do women commence work earning at at least 10 per cent less than men with similar skills but as time goes by the differential widens to more than 30 per cent.

Young women are expected to work for only a few years, marry and then leave to start a family. With this in mind, many seek openings in large prestigious firms in the hope of encountering potential partners with good career prospects. To realize their ambitions, many pursue a two year study course at junior college. This level of education is normally more than sufficient to meet company entry requirements for clerical female workers and yet not quite high enough to threaten the vulnerable ego of a prospective salaryman.

With the exception of those that have entered banks, finance and insurance companies, government service, departmental stores or foreign firms, women approaching the end of their twenties who wish to remain at work encounter little scope for advancement. Very few rise to the level of general manager and a woman member of a company's board of directors is all but unheard of. Considering the discrimination that women face, it is not surprising that many choose not to invest too heavily in tertiary education.

Discrimination against women is, of course, not exclusively practised by the business sector. Elsewhere, 'there are no women judges in the nation's highest courts, no heads of government department, none of the 47 prefectural governors is a woman and only two of the 3,000 city and town mayors are' [*Sydney Morning Herald*: 24 Nov. 1993]. Female representation in law, scientific research and medicine (that is, doctors and dentists) has in the late 1980s been only of the order of 3, 6 and 11 per cent respectively [Powell and Anesaki 1990:203].

While a woman's time in employment is ideally of limited duration, more than 60 per cent of women workers are married. In 1990, the female labour participation rate was around 50 per cent. This was slightly lower than in the US and Canada but more or less on a par with Britain and Australia [Maki 1993:81]. Some women, especially those involved in farming and shopkeeping, may have worked more or less continuously but most would have returned to the work force after a period of child rearing. On doing so, they cannot claim any seniority and (as mentioned in the above section), they usually earn less than they did previously.

A large proportion of women workers are employed on a part-time basis. To some extent, this has resulted from the fiscal system which allows a woman to earn up to one million yen (in 1993) without being subject to income tax. Above that amount, not only is the female employee taxable but her husband stands to lose the tax deduction for his spouse and also the spouse allowance paid by his company. With this in mind, many women adjust their working hours so as not to approach the taxation threshold.

To redress the woman worker's plight, an Equal Employment Opportunity Law was enacted in 1985. The law enjoins firms to treat all employees on an equal basis regardless of sex and to ensure that there is an absence of discrimination in hiring, promotion and dismissal. Unfortunately, no penalties were prescribed for non-compliance and little has since changed. Of the 300 graduates that Fuji selected for its 1990 intake, only 16 were women [Horsley and Buckley 1990:220]. There is no reason to believe that the situation is any different elsewhere. In 1994, the *Nikkei Weekly* reported that 'less than 5% of women workers are on career tracks', and in 1993, only 7 per cent of women graduates received career track offers [*Nikkei Weekly*: 21 Feb. 1994].

## DISMISSALS AND ADJUSTMENTS TO HARD TIMES

When faced with general economic downturns or passing shortfalls in the demand for its products, the Japanese firm has wide scope for reducing its labour costs. It can lower average wage payments by minimizing its biannual bonuses, and more drastically, by holding out for a real wage cut in the shunto negotiations. However, to secure trade union cooperation, management is expected to, and certainly does, preempt the talks by heralding significant executive salary reductions. This contrasts starkly with Western industrial economies where executive burden sharing is a rarity. In fact, there are frequent occasions when Western executives award themselves salary hikes while demanding sacrifice and restraint from others.

Additional means of lowering average wage costs include the imposition on employees, of immediate vacations on less than full pay, the curtailment of overtime and a general shortening of the work day.

Apart from altering the time that an employee is actively at work, firms are wont to shed their temporary and part-time workers. If difficulties still persist, they would make further adjustments. One option would be to dispense with the services of various subcontractors by assuming the production of certain components themselves instead of acquiring them externally. This enables firms to maximize the use of their slack but permanent staff. Alternatively, a firm might either arrange to transfer some of its workers to an 'affiliated' company in a more dynamic sector or hire them out. For example, during the mid 1970s, 'Japan Steel lent some of its surplus workers on rotation to Isuzu Motors – several thousands for a year at a time. (They kept their

Japan Steel wage and status and Isuzu paid Japan Steel a lump sum for their services.)' [Dore 1986:97]

After all other avenues have been exhausted and a firm still finds itself in an untenable position, it may, with considerable reluctance, declare part of its permanent labour force redundant. Accompanying such a declaration would be an indication of the number of 'voluntary' resignations that were being sought. (Employees resigning under these circumstances would be compensated with separation allowances.) Should an insufficient number not be forthcoming, irresistible pressures would be brought to bear to ensure the exit of additional staff with poor work performance histories. If all else fails, outright sackings would take place. Such an option is usually not taken until the firm in question experiences losses over at least a two to three year period [Odagiri 1992:60]. Holding a senior position is no safeguard against dismissal, for 'in times of business hardship expensive senior employees are often the most vulnerable' [Aoki 1987:263].

Finally, it goes without saying that in depressed periods, the recruitment of young hopefuls is markedly reduced. *The Financial Times* reported that in 1994, Toyota Corporation reduced its annual graduate intake from nearly 900 to 200 and that NTT, 'Japan's and the world's largest company', froze recruitment completely. Not unexpectedly, women have shouldered the main brunt of the cutbacks. 'Since 1991, the average number of job offers per female graduate has fallen from 1.98 to 0.87', and in 1994, 51 per cent of graduate recruiting companies totally suspended offers to female applicants [*Financial Times* 11 Nov. 1994]. So much for the Equal Employment Opportunity Law.

SUMMARY

- New full-time personnel are usually recruited directly from school, college or university. They are inducted with intensive in-house training for emphasis is placed on firm-specific skills.
- Work hours are longer in Japan than in Western countries. Overtime is an integral part of working conditions and full holiday entitlements are often not taken.
- Lifetime employment (usually until around age 55) arose in response to labour shortages. Only a small minority of workers have permanency of tenure.
- Salaries which are based on age and seniority are not related to

specific work tasks. Wage differentials between junior and senior staff are narrower in Japan than in the West.

• Bonuses are paid twice yearly. They provide for wage flexibility and are sometimes regarded as a reward for general effort.

• Perquisites are fairly extensive and function to strengthen employee ties to the firm.

• Promotion by age is almost automatic up to a certain level. The all pervasive rank system functions as a work incentive device.

• Trade unions were legalized after the war. In the late 1940s and 1950s industrial strife was widespread. After the workers' defeat by Nissan in 1953, company unions began to flourish. Company unions are cognisant of their employers' circumstances but they show little regard for general social issues.

• Wage increases are negotiated annually in the context of the shunto spring offensive in which certain wage leader unions set the tone.

• Temporary workers are non-unionized, receive lower pay and have no job security. They serve as an employment buffer for permanent workers who also derive other benefits at their expense.

• Despite the Equal Employment Opportunity Law of 1985, women continue to be discriminated against. They obtain lower salaries and face awesome recruitment and promotion hurdles.

• In trying times, firms reduce bonuses, resist wage rises, impose on staff holidays at less than full pay, rid themselves of temporary workers and reduce subcontracting orders. When all else fails, a certain amount of 'voluntary' resignations are arranged.

# 8 Productivity, Technology and Structural Change

## INTRODUCTION

In order for a country to achieve sustained economic growth, factor productivity needs to be constantly upgraded. A country's full production potential is determined by its input capabilities (assuming optimal resource allocation) and the value of the products it is capable of producing. In other words, there are two aspects to factor productivity. First, an input-output relation governed by the state of technology and second, the value of the resulting output determined by final selling prices. Therefore, to attain constant growth, not only must there be a steady rise in input-output ratios but the economy must regularly rearrange its output mix to ensure that it is concentrating on products which yield the maximum return. The latter process involves structural adjustments to changing economic circumstances. These in turn may require the winding down of some industries and the promotion of others, or alternatively, a realignment within a specific sector concentrating on areas in which the country may still be internationally competitive.

Japan has been extraordinarily successful in improving its technological capabilities and in undertaking timely and effective structural adjustments. In this chapter both these phenomena are considered. We commence with a discussion relating to technology, paying heed to improvements in production organization technology in which the country excels. Then we examine Japan's responses to external shocks (the microeconomic counterpart to the analysis in Chapter 3) and the country's general restructuring policies, closing with a brief review of the structural adjustment experience of some major industries.

## PRODUCTIVITY AND TECHNOLOGY

### Productivity

Considering that Japan is now the world's second largest economic power, it is somewhat surprising to discover that its average labour

155

productivity falls short of standards realized in countries like the USA and West Germany. In no small part this is due to inefficiencies in the service sector, and in agriculture. However, even if attention is confined to manufacturing, a 1985 survey concluded that output per worker in Japan was 32 per cent less than in the United States [Porter 1990:708]. Process industries such as paper, chemicals and metal refining seem to be relatively poor performers. Furthermore, the overall labour productivity average has been lowered by the relatively poor performance of the country's white-collar workers who have been rated as being 'only two-thirds as efficient as America's' [*Economist* 9 July 1993].

To Japan's credit, the productivity gap is rapidly dwindling. In the decade from 1977 to 1987, output per worker in Japan increased by 35 per cent while in the USA it rose by only 7 per cent [Yamada *et al.* 1990:91].

Japan's strengths lie in industries with intricate and multi-staged production procedures where productivity has been improved both through the successful adoption of equipment embodying the latest technology and as a result of the devising of superior production systems. This is well exemplified in the automobile industry where the number of vehicles produced per employee per year rose from 1.2 in 1955 to 7.4 in 1965 and then to 12.2 in 1973 [Allen 1981:170].

**Technology**

Japan in the aftermath of the Second World War embarked on its road to economic recovery with large technological handicaps. Having been isolated from the West at the very time when giant strides were being taken in areas such as household electrical appliances, there was a gaping gap between Japan's and the West's ability to produce such goods. Items like refrigerators for instance, were to all intents and purposes virtually unheard of. Even with respect to traditional industries, such as iron and steel and textiles, Japan fell far behind [Goto and Wakasugi 1988:183].

**The Importation of Technology**

Instead of trying to re-invent the wheel, so to speak, Japan, through the auspices of MITI, scoured the world in pursuit of technological know-how. It succeeded in acquiring, at bargain prices, the technology that it needed to upgrade and diversify its industrial complex. At the time, Western companies were more than willing to undertake techno-logical transfers, for they considered Japan to be too remote and with too small an internal market to concern themselves with exporting to it.[1] Revenue derived from the sale of technology was regarded as a welcome windfall and the prospects of Japanese industrialists eventually competing with them seemed non-existent.

Many well known firms and organizations obliged. Dupont helped in relation to nylon, ICI and Dow Chemicals in relation to plastic, while Bell Laboratories supplied transistor technology. During the 1950s, in the automobile industry, technical agreements were concluded between Nissan and Austin, Isuzu and Rootes, Hino and Renault and between Shin-Mitsubishi Heavy Industries and Willys-Overland. Between 1951 and 1984, Japan entered into 41 972 separate contracts for the importation of foreign technology at a total payment of just over $17 billion [Abegglen and Stalk 1985:127].[2]

While Japan has consistently imported technology, it has also increasingly supplied it to others, with the ratio of its exported to imported technology rising from 0.13 in 1970 to 0.30 in 1985 [Harris 1990:279]. Unfortunately, the data on which these ratios are based are calculated from royalty and licence payments. This means that the 'trade' figures for a particular year include that year's transactions plus financial settlements based on obligations stemming from earlier periods. This would very likely disguise the true extent of Japan's yearly technology export growth. On the other hand, as, in contrast to the United States, most of Japan's technology exports are directed to developing countries, they probably are on average still less sophisticated than the country's technology imports [Okimoto and Saxonhouse 1987:393].

For relying on external sources and for adopting the fruits of other countries' research and development, Japan has met with a certain amount of derision. However, had the country not done so, it would have taken considerably longer to have attained its current living standards. The rapid absorption and adaptation of modern technology is in fact no mean feat. It is certainly not an option open to the majority of countries in Africa and other Third World areas. In Japan's case, a combination of extremely large investment rates, a highly skilled and educated labour force and work practices that were receptive to the introduction of new production techniques, all facilitated the technological transfers in question.

**Research and Development**

In keeping with its strategy of securing technological know-how from overseas sources, Japan's early postwar expenditures on research and development (R&D) were not only relatively smaller than in other industrial countries (in 1965 its ratio of R&D outlays to GNP was half the ratio in the USA), but were also sparsely used for basic research. Projects fostering improvements in the country's technological adaptive capabilities were usually more favourably considered.

There are at least three reasons why basic research in Japan was not previously given pride of place. First, as already implied, it made little economic sense to devise at great expense technology that already existed. Second, government investments in R&D have been proportionally lower than in other industrial countries. This has partially deprived Japan of august public research institutions and has limited the role that universities could have played. Third, although Japan's population is highly educated by world standards, its output of pure scientists and graduates with doctoral qualifications has been less than sufficient.

Over time, Japan's relative commitment to R&D has risen and it is now almost unrivalled. Whereas in 1978, R&D expenditure as a percentage of national income amounted to 2.15 for Japan compared with 2.46 for the USA and 2.64 for West Germany [Allen 1981:100], by 1987, the respective figures were 2.8, 2.81 and 2.74 [Watanabe and Honda 1992:49]. Even by 1978, Japan's dedication to *industrial* development was probably not outmatched by the USA, for while some 45 per cent of US national research outlays were earmarked for defence, in Japan less than 3 per cent were. Among the industries in which, during the 1980s, the R&D to sales ratio had been exceptionally high were pharmaceuticals, telecommunications, electronics, electrical machinery, precision instruments and chemicals [Imai 1988:228].

The growing predominance of Japanese R&D outlays was clearly manifested from 1986 when, for the first time, aggregate R&D manufacturing expenditures exceeded capital investments. By 1987, 27 of the country's top 50 R&D leaders were spending more on research than on physical capital. 'For example, in the top company, Toyota Motor Corporation, R&D expenditure was 275 billion yen while its capital investment was Y225 billion. The Matsushita Company spent Y271 billion on R&D, but invested only Y66 billion in capital equipment. Hitachi spent Y262 billion on R&D and Y103 on capital investment.' [Kodama 1991:5]

In tandem with the above mentioned trend, Japan has become more preoccupied with basic research. Having largely caught up with the West, the technology that it now needs is not so readily available in the world market place, nor at such previously affordable prices. Realizing this, MITI has sponsored various joint inter-firm collaborative efforts. It is also set on improving conditions in universities and other national institutes so as to create centres of excellence capable of attracting top world class scientists. MITI's efforts in terms of joint firm projects have (as mentioned in Chapter 5) met with some resounding success. Accordingly, many now look upon Japan's technological prowess with a mixture of awe and admiration. Some have even gone as far as to declare that Japan has emerged as a technological superpower [Uyehara 1990:290]. Even allowing for some hyperbole, Japan maintains a leading position in opto-electronics and by the turn of the century it is expected to be second only to the US in computer chips, life sciences and new materials [295].

However, the general worldwide respect that Japan now commands ought to be tempered in view of glaring shortcomings within certain critical fields.

One area in which Japan is yet to make its mark lies in the domain of computer software. To some extent, Japan's comparative weakness in this market stems from work practices which partially muffle individual creativity, which is a necessary component in software production. Another factor inhibiting progress has been the tendency of Japanese computer manufacturers to try to lock their customers into their own programs. According to *The Economist*, this has 'fragmented the software market, killing any chance of an independent software industry emerging in Japan to supply programs for a common operating system such as Microsoft's ubiquitous MS-DOS' [*Economist* Oct 1992:78]. Weaknesses in Japan's computer usage come to light in noting that only 8.6 per cent (as opposed to 52 per cent in the USA) of personal computers are linked to networks and that the database market in Japan is a fifth the size of that of the United States [*Nikkei Weekly* 16 May 1994:1].

Where Japan has clearly been a recent pace setter, is in relation to breakthroughs in production organization which is best exemplified by the 'just-in-time', or 'kanban' system.

**The Kanban System**

The system which revolutionized Japanese factory procedures and which boosted labour productivity was the brainchild of Ono Taiichi, of Toyota

Motors. Often referred to as the 'just-in-time' system, a term which many erroneously believe captures its essence, it is in fact rather multifaceted. Basically, it has three major aspects: near continuous product processing, rapid equipment changeover times and the operation, by individual workers, of whole batteries of machinery.

In its most idealized state, the just-in-time system is so well synchronized, that inputs are produced and delivered precisely when required. More specifically, each production station responds to supply requests from the station above it. That is, all activity ultimately emanates from the needs of the final assemblers, or to be more precise, from the customers.

As a work unit utilizes a product component or an item of some kind, it hands over a production order card, or kanban, to the source supplying that unit. This serves as a signal to replenish that item. To do so, the supplying unit in turn draws upon other inputs, while conveying appropriate kanbans to sources further down the work chain. Some of these sources of course would be external subcontractors. For obvious reasons, the Japanese term this process a 'pull system'. Once final assembly production schedules are arranged, the need to organize and coordinate all intermediate stages is largely obviated.

Since inputs are now effectively manufactured and dispatched only to meet present needs, this has led to a dramatic reduction in inventories. In the automobile industry, a 1982 study revealed that in contrast to American firms that were holding three to five days' supplies of items such as heaters, radiators and brake drums, most Japanese manufacturers managed with stocks lasting one or two hours [Cusumano 1985:300]. As a result, not only have the Japanese been able to make do with 20 to 40 per cent less factory space, they have also been able to reduce traffic between warehouse and shop floor (since external suppliers now largely deliver, in small lots, directly to work stations). In financial terms, total 1980 work-in-process inventories per completed vehicle, averaged $74 in Japan compared with $584 in the United States [300].

The ability to reduce inventories, and for that matter, the ability to sustain the entire just-in-time system, rests on quick machinery changeover rates. In industries which manufacture a wide variety of different models, as in automobiles, machine tools have to be readjusted or changed when diverting output from one model to another. During the changeover period, the production flow ceases and workers are made idle. The longer the time interval, the more costly the whole procedure. To minimize the number of such pauses, models were originally produced in large batches but this necessitated the holding of large stocks of other models and parts to satisfy ongoing demand. Clearly, as models grew in number, the stock of inventories had also to rise.

In the 1950s, the Japanese domestic automobile market was rather small, yet strong inter-firm rivalry induced competitors to broaden the range of their offerings. In response to this challenge, Japanese automobile engineers focused their minds on drastically reducing changeover times. Their efforts soon bore fruit. By 1977, it took Toyota an average of 12 minutes to change dies for stamping hoods and fenders, when plants in the United States, Sweden and West Germany were still averaging four to six hours. Consequently, Toyota switched dies three times per day to produce one day's supply for most components, whereas the 'foreign plants found it economical to manufacture in lots equivalent to ten or 30 days' supply, and to reset equipment only once a day or every other day' [Cusumano 1985:285].

The capacity of the Japanese to move rapidly from the production of one specific product to another, that is, to work within a framework of what is known as a 'flexible manufacturing system', partly explains why in many firms, R&D expenditures now exceed physical capital acquisition costs. Thanks to technological advances in robotics, micro processors, electronics and high precision mechanics, industry's need for capital has been partly reduced. Whereas in the past, alternative machinery was required for the production of alternative goods, within a modern day Japanese plant geared to multi-product output, many if not most of its implements would be reprogrammed or readjusted rather than changed [see Kodama 1991:5 and 24].

The third aspect of the productivity raising techniques associated with the just-in-time or kanban system relates to multi-machine handling. Instead of simply controlling just one machine, workers have been trained to take care of a small number of them. Operators traverse a circular path to carry out functions on each machine sequentially. The installation of automatic cut-off mechanisms, coupled with alert or warning devices, facilitates multiple machine monitoring [Chalmers 1989:124]. With this arrangement, instead of checking for quality defects at the end of a production run, the system provides for inspections at each assembly point. Faults are automatically detected or noted by visual scrutiny. These innovations are believed to have raised worker productivity by no less than 30 per cent [Abegglen and Stalk 1985:100].

Although the just-in-time or kanban system is rated as a great success, it is not without its difficulties. In order for the production stream to be a fairly continuous one, all progressions from one step to another must be in unison. Sub-assembly stations ought not to serve more than one other unit and all changeover times should be comparable. Achieving all this constitutes no mean feat.

Strict delivery schedules are imposed on subcontractors, who must be located within reasonable reach of their buyers. What is more, because suppliers are expected to undertake daily deliveries, they have, to some extent, become inventory holders on behalf of final product manufacturers.

Finally, work routines, even if now less monotonous, have become more arduous. The tasks at hand demand more precision and alertness. In addition to operating several machines at once, the same workers also attend to maintenance and repair problems and, as already mentioned, serve as proxy inspectors.

Despite all these complications, the just-in-time system is not only now fully entrenched within a wide band of Japanese industries but foreign industrialists are attempting to emulate it, or at least incorporate some of its key features. However, raising factor productivity is only one of a number of necessary steps that have to be taken for an economy to be able to sustain viable and significant growth rates. Economies must, amongst other things, also be capable of reacting and favourably adjusting to changing situations, whether they be externally or internally induced.

Before considering Japan's major adjustment measures and policies, an outline of the country's general reaction to some recent external crises is first presented.[3]

**Responses to External Shocks**

The 1973 oil price crisis severely jolted the Japanese economy. By 1974, industrial output receded by 9 per cent, company profits went into a tailspin and some 11 000 firms went to the wall. The oil shock dealt a direct and immediate blow by virtue of sudden and exorbitant increases in energy costs and indirectly on account of a decline in international trade. To meet this challenge, Japan had to cope with energy problems, shed non-viable industries and reinvigorate its corporate structure. It accomplished all three of these objectives.

MITI, which was vested with special powers to ration electricity and enforce consumption cutbacks, led an energy conserving campaign. Firms installed improved thermal insulators and limited, where possible, their energy use. Electrical power stations, which had previously relied on oil for 71 per cent of their output, switched to liquefied natural gas, so that by 1989, they were only 34 per cent oil dependent. Similarly, the steel industry which converted its blast furnaces for coke inputs only, was able, by 1980, to be totally oil free. Lastly, the aluminium industry, another voracious energy devourer, moved to limit the scale of its operations to that of a mere fraction of its pre-1973 levels.

Many producers facing difficult times because of radically altered economic conditions, divested themselves of large numbers of employees, through a combination of staff redeployments to subsidiaries or allied firms and by temporarily suspending or curtailing new recruitment intakes. To regain the upper hand, they reorientated their production strategy and concentrated in market segments where their comparative strengths were greatest. For instance, the shipbuilding industry, when faced with drastic falls in the demand for supertankers (which technologically speaking were relatively easy to construct), zeroed in on high grade vessels, leaving the tankers to countries like Korea.

Apart from shearing their labour forces and reviewing their product market strategies, Japanese firms rapidly set about putting the rest of their affairs in better order. General management practices were improved, especially in inventory control which was largely computerized. The kanban production system was increasingly adopted, along with more extensive factory automation. Firms' financial standings were strengthened by extended issues of shares and of convertible bonds, all of which weakened the hold that commercial banks previously had over them. With all these changes in place, Japanese industry emerged from the 1973 oil crisis storm relatively unscathed.

When in 1979 Japan was hit by the second oil crisis which led to a much sharper deterioration of its terms of trade than that experienced by its American and European rivals, the country pulled through even better than it had previously. On this occasion (when wages were restrained) worker layoffs barely materialized and because of productivity raising investments in Japan's processing-assembly industries, its relative international advantages were strengthened boosting its export performance [Bank of Japan 1983:7]. Between 1975 and 1981 the ratio of Japan's fixed investments to GDP exceeded that of its major competitors and while over the period 1979–81 labour productivity in Japan rose annually by 4.7 per cent, it fell or barely rose in the US, UK and Germany [13]. Thanks to general oil usage economies and to changes in the country's industrial structure, between 1974 and 1981, the ratio of oil consumption to real GNP fell annually by 6.1 per cent [4]. Between

1980 and 1988, when total output increased by 40 per cent, oil import volumes actually fell by 25 per cent [OECD Survey 1989:70].

By the mid 1980s, the country's resilience was once more put to the test. Between 1984 and the end of 1985, the Japanese currency appreciated in value from around 240 to 150 yen to the US dollar. This had a devastating effect on exports.

Firms responded by further streamlining their managerial practices. They 'rationalized personnel, plant, and inventory and reduced the burden of fixed expenses, enabling them to make a profit even at rather low production levels' [Komine 1991:81]. Turning the strengthened yen to their advantage, they expanded overseas production facilities and imported manufactured inputs from cheap labour sources. To a large extent, all these modifications helped to restore the country's international competitiveness.

Internally, the quest for local market shares intensified, partly as a way of seeking compensation for falling sales abroad and partly in order to hold the line against an influx of more affordable imports. In the course of events, corporations increasingly began to venture across traditional industrial boundaries and became more disposed towards product diversification. An intensified process of structural adjustment was in fact occurring.


## INDUSTRIAL TRANSFORMATION AND RESTRUCTURING

To become a fully fledged industrial power, the Japanese economy had to be thoroughly transformed. It had to wean itself from an overwhelming dependence on rural pursuits and to engage more in manufacturing. It began to do all this from the mid to late nineteenth century onwards, with the process continuing in the postwar period. As can be seen from Table 8.1, from 1956 to 1990 there have been fairly radical changes in the contributions to GNP by the major broad sectors of the economy. Agriculture's percentage share fell from 17.4 to 2.2, industry's rose to 37.6 (peaking at 41.7 in 1972) while an increase from 48.1 to 60.2 was recorded for the service sector.

Changes of course were not confined to the general representation of specific sectors, for within each broad grouping various activities waxed and waned. With manufacturing as an example, between 1954 and 1977 (which takes us from the beginning to just over the end of Japan's high growth period) textiles' contribution to total output fell from 13.1 to 4.8 per cent. By contrast, goods classified in the machin-

*Table* 8.1   The Percentage Contribution of Economic Sectors to GNP

| Year | Agriculture | Industry | Services |
|------|-------------|----------|----------|
| 1956 | 17.4 | 34.5 | 48.1 |
| 1972 | 5.1 | 41.7 | 53.2 |
| 1980 | 3.3 | 39.0 | 57.7 |
| 1990 | 2.2 | 37.6 | 60.2 |

*Sources*: OECD Surveys various editions plus Patrick and Rosovsky 1976:16.

*Note*: Agriculture includes forestry and fishing. Industry includes mining and construction

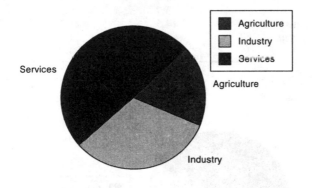

*Figure* 8.1   1956 Sector Shares of GDP

*Source*: Table 8.1

ery category increased their share of output from 14.5 to 23.2 per cent (see Table 8.2).

Generally, Japanese firms responded to basic changes in market conditions. Big corporations had an incentive to adjust and even to diversify into new product lines in order to honour the job commitments given to their permanent employees. Internal reorganizations were eased by staff willing to be both retrained and relocated. Small firms were not quite so flexible, and in point of fact, overall changes in the composition of their aggregate output has mainly been achieved by the exit of bankrupt ones and the inauguration of new ones.

*Table* 8.2   Percentage of Manufacturing Output Produced by Various Industries

| Industry | 1954 | 1977 |
|---|---|---|
| Food and drink | 11.4 | 10.3 |
| Textiles | 13.1 | 4.8 |
| Clothing | 1.2 | 2.1 |
| Wood products | 3.7 | 2.5 |
| Furniture | 1.0 | 1.8 |
| Paper products | 4.0 | 3.0 |
| Printing | 5.6 | 5.1 |
| Chemicals | 16.5 | 11.2 |
| Leather goods | 0.4 | 0.6 |
| Ceramics | 5.7 | 5.0 |
| Metals | 10.6 | 8.0 |
| Metal goods | 3.7 | 6.5 |
| Machinery and instruments | 14.5 | 23.2 |
| Transport equipment | 6.8 | 11.0 |
| Others | 1.7 | 4.7 |

*Source*: Allen 1981:104

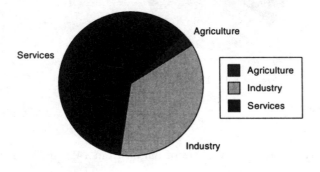

*Figure* 8.2   1990 Sector Shares of GDP

*Source*: Table 8.1

## Handling Industries in Distress

The government and MITI in particular, have constantly rallied around industries in distress. Their involvement in depression cartels has already been noted (Chapter 5). However, it was not until 1978 that major legislation specifically relating to such industries was enacted. The act in question was entitled 'The Law on Temporary Measures for Stabilizing Depressed Industries'. It listed seven 'structurally depressed industries', which were to come under its terms. Later, seven others were added. To help alleviate some of the travail confronting the designated industries, the law authorized the provision of low interest rate loans for investments opening up new fields of endeavour, concessional finance for redundancy retirement schemes and new loans to redeem those which were based on outdated plant and equipment used as collateral. Additional assistance was forthcoming by way of another 1978 law which sanctioned government subsidies to firms in designated industries which were striving to modify their work forces. Also of note, small firms within depressed industries were not overlooked, and those wishing to move on to fresher pastures were plied with low interest loans and tax credits.

The depressed industries were to be stabilized by significant reductions in output capacity. Supply was to be brought down to match the lower level of demand so that some form of equilibrium would prevail. In this regard, provision was made for industry-wide cooperation and action. More specifically, within each troubled industry, a Basic Stabilization Plan was formulated which determined capacity reduction objectives and the extent to which each firm would play its part. The government further lent its support by ensuring that the depression cartels would be exempt from prohibitions prescribed in the Anti-Monopoly Law. All in all, the aims of each industry Basic Stabilization Plan were to be realized within five years, by which time the Law on Temporary Measures for Stabilizing Specified Depressed Industries would have expired. Of the various dispensations that were made available, untied loans issued to replace those with a lien on plant and equipment were perhaps the most effective. Considering that a very high proportion of corporations' real estate and machinery was used as collateral for commercial bank loans, without government help, neither the debtor firms nor the creditor banks would have readily countenanced the scrapping of surplus plants [Saxonhouse 1979:307].

By 1983 when all industries covered by the 1978 legislation were due to have completed their restructuring, the Law on Temporary

Measures for the Structural Adjustment of Specified Industries was passed. Essentially, this was an updated version of the 1978 act. It arose in response to the 1979 oil price hike which ostensibly upset the timetable of previously designated depressed industries and which threw others into turmoil. Of the 22 industries specified, 11 had been listed earlier. Like its predecessor, the new law was to be valid for five years only and served to reduce output capacity. Some differences can be discerned in subtle shifts of emphasis which allowed for mergers, the encouragement of narrower product ranges and the promotion of new technology. Though MITI strove to eliminate each industry's dead wood, it hoped that all would re-emerge in a more modernized and efficient state.

The 1983 law also explicitly ruled out the use of import restrictive measures in coping with depressed industries. Japan had in fact claimed that even beforehand, it had abided by GATT and OECD guidelines in not introducing additional trade restraints in the guise of structural adjustment policies. This certainly seems to be borne out with regard to most of the 1978 designated industries. Examining ten of the 14 industries concerned, Peck and others noted that in four instances tariff rates were actually reduced, whereas no tariff rate increases were observed elsewhere [Peck 1987:111]. They delved closely into the matter since they were puzzled by a seeming inconsistency between the government's desire to shore up local prices and its commitment to free trade. For items like aluminium and ferrosilicon, imports had in fact risen markedly and in the case of synthetic fibres, exports remained competitive. However, in terms of chemical fertilizers, there are indications that some form of import protection had been at play. Suspicions arise from the fact that after quoting lower landed prices in Japan than the local producers, US urea exporters were yet unable to capture a significant share of the Japanese market [117].

**Factors in the Relative Success of Japan's Industrial Restructuring**

In assessing the relative success of Japan's approach in handling industries in distress, the following points should be borne in mind:

(i) Both key legislative acts stressed the temporary nature of the availability of public assistance and in both cases, a five year deadline had been set.

(ii) Within distressed areas, unemployment rates remained low by

Western standards. To some extent this was due to the fact that in industries such as wool and cotton spinning '71 per cent of the workers were women who often withdrew from the labor force when discharged' [Peck 1987:102]. But more importantly, a near universal full employment rate allowed the bulk of displaced workers to be rehired.

(iii) Direct government financial support was limited. In contrast to Europe, declining industries were not sustained by large public handouts. Instead, they had more or less to rely on their own devices and to form capacity reducing cartels. In this respect, some of the adjustment burdens were borne by consumers but to the extent that Japan did not increase trade barriers, price increases were moderated by international competition.

(iv) No industry was completely wound down but most became more narrowly market focused and efficient.

## EXAMPLES OF INDUSTRY ADAPTATIONS

Although Japan has had a better industrial restructuring record than have most other Western economies, this was not uniformly realized. In some industries the outcomes were quite satisfactory and in others rather less so. To help appreciate this, a few brief industry sketches are provided.

### Textiles and Clothing

The relative decline of the textile and clothing industries (shown in Table 8.2) has already been remarked upon. These industries had in fact been subject to two distinct adverse external developments. In the early 1950s, Japanese textiles began to penetrate the US market at an exceedingly rapid rate. For example, between 1953 and 1955, exports of cotton cloth increased more than four fold. As a result, fearful US manufacturers clamoured for and soon secured import protection. This initially took the form of voluntary Japanese export restraints, which were eventually institutionalized within the Multi-Fibre Agreement. Just over a decade later, the industries were dealt another blow by virtue of the increasing competitiveness of neighbouring Asian states which were able to capitalize on cheaper labour resources. The problems of the Japanese producers were also compounded by the yen appreciating in 1971, 1973 and 1978.

All of the above mentioned events brought about a reduction of Japanese textile exports and a considerable increase in imports. In 1960, textiles comprised 30 per cent of Japan's total exports. Twenty years later, their share had fallen to less than 5 per cent. An unprecedented acceleration in overseas sales of products generated by the country's more dynamic sectors was partly responsible for the relative demise of textiles but the influence of the other factors is evident in that the ratio of textile exports to output had itself declined. Similarly, imports as a percentage of output rose from .03 per cent in 1960 to 13.6 per cent in 1980 [Dore 1986:154].

The industries in question initially responded by reducing output capacity. This occurred as a result of a number of small firms falling away, a large drop in the textile work force (from 1 200 000 in the early 1960s to 655 000 by 1981 [Abegglen and Stalk 1985:21]) and the scrapping of excess plant and equipment. By investing in countries such as South Korea, Taiwan and Hong Kong, textile manufacturers shifted their less sophisticated activities offshore. Within Japan itself, they concentrated more on higher valued synthetic products. In the process, they modernized their factories with the introduction of faster and more efficient spindles and looms and they upgraded their work practices. To maintain adequate levels of profitability, textile companies diversified into other fields, mainly in the area of petro-chemicals. Here they moved swiftly, for in contrast to the situation in 1968 when only 11.8 per cent of the output of six leading synthetic-fibre corporations were non textiles, by 1978, 35.7 per cent were [Allen 1981:110].

Not did only firms undertake most of the changes under their own volition but the overall level of government involvement was fairly limited. Official intervention centred around the coordination of and partial provision of compensation for plant reductions as well as supplying limited grants for modernization. To its credit, Japan lowered tariffs to such an extent that by 1971, it was deemed to have had 'the lowest import duties on textile products in the world' [Yamazawa 1988:413].

Despite the severity of the aforementioned external shocks, the relatively limited amount of public assistance, as well as Japan's adherence to freer textile trade, the textile and clothing industry is currently in a reasonably healthy condition. Between 1960 and 1980, absolute output had in fact risen by 60 per cent. The industry's ability to emerge moderately unscathed is largely attributable to its timely undertaking of appropriate adjustments. Nevertheless, some other factors have also had a positive bearing. Unlike foreign suppliers, local producers readily replace defective merchandise. Furthermore, locally made cloth is officially graded at inspection stations run by the quasi government Cloth Inspection Association. Since importers are excluded from the inspection system, they cannot offer the same guarantees as domestic producers [Dore 1986:186]. This means that Japanese consumers tend to be wary of foreign goods and as a consequence, local producers are more advantageously placed. These advantages are coupled with 'a fastidious willingness' on the part of the Japanese consumer 'to discard clothes at an earlier age of wear' [193]. Japanese clothing and textile producers face a buoyant local market protected by certain non-tariff trade barriers.

**Steel**

The chronicle of events in Japan's postwar steel industry epitomizes the country's unrelenting effort to industrialize and to place itself on the frontier of technological progress. From a situation in 1950 of sustaining an output capacity of only five million tons, the industry acquired the status of a world colossus, capable by 1980 of yielding an annual yield of 150 million tons.

Behind an import protective wall and with ample access to finance, the industry set about constructing steelworks that were integrated from blast furnaces through to finishing mills (in 1971, Japan already had 12 such mills to two in the USA) [Abegglen and Stalk 1985:74]. Likewise, in the late 1970s, Japan had no less than 25 blast furnaces each with a two million ton capacity when there were only seven comparable ones in the EEC and none in the US.

By taking advantage of scale economies and of the latest technology, labour productivity soon surpassed US ratings. On top of all this, it became standard practice to locate steel plants at deep water sites so that with investments in overseas iron ore mining, the industry had ready access to the world's cheapest iron ore and coal, not to mention its ability readily to ship out final products. This alone placed the Japanese industry in a better position than its US rivals, which had invested in local high priced ores and which were located inland. Thanks to all these factors, other Japanese manufacturers could attain steel inputs at prices ranging from 15 to 20 per cent less than those confronting US producers [77].

The industry's achievements are a result not only of government support and of a large capitalization process but they also reflect a readiness to adjust to changing market realities. During the oil crisis, the shift to coal use was prompt and efficient, with the industry utilizing less coal per ton of produced steel than was the case in Western countries. In response to the 1985 yen appreciation, the five largest companies (Shin Nippon Steel, NKK, Kawasaki Steel, Sumitomo Metals and Kobe Steel) 'set goals to increase the sales of their non-steel divisions to as much as over half of all sales' [Komine 1991:85]. By 1986, almost half of its R&D expenditure was being directed to non-steel products [Kodama 1991:7]. While retaining its lead in high quality steel, the industry has been making its mark in ceramics and non-ferrous metals.

## Shipbuilding

With the onset of the 1973 oil crisis the shipbuilding industry was badly mauled. The magnitude of the disaster became evident when new orders for ships plunged to such low levels that towards the end of the 1970s, they were *less than one tenth* the 1973 amount.

In 1978, after a few desultory attempts in coordinating an industry-wide response, the Ministry of Transport declared the industry structurally depressed. A stabilization plan was then formulated which called for output capacity reductions, the discarding of workers, a credit fund and devices to stimulate demand.

The 61 leading companies capable of producing large ships were prevailed upon to lower their production capacity by 35 per cent. They acceded to this request (with the seven largest ones cutting back by 40 per cent and the others by lesser amounts depending on their original sizes). These commitments were honoured by February 1982. To no small extent, the establishment of an official body known as the Association for Special Stabilization Measures for the Shipbuilding Industry eased the contraction process. Funded by both the Japan Development Bank and private ones, many shipyards were bought out at market prices.

Along with the contraction in capacity, the labour force was reduced. Between 1973 and 1982, the total number of workers employed fell from 184 000 to 116 000. Most firms encouraged their staff to consider 'voluntary' retirement, by enticing them with a full year's salary in addition to their normal retirement benefits. Also, a number of employees of some of the large companies were transferred to sister keiretsu firms. For example, the Mitsubishi Heavy Industry Company secured openings for many of its workers in the Mitsubishi Automobile Company.

Even so, numerous labourers were dismissed outright leaving 25 000 shipbuilders on the 1978 unemployment roll. Putting this into perspective, in that year the total number of unemployed originating from all depressed industries was 47 000 which was less than 5 per cent of the million then unemployed in Japan as a whole. More notably, by 1979, only 19 000 workers of *all* designated depressed industries were still officially jobless [Peck 1987:101].

The shipbuilding industry entered the 1980s with renewed vigour and confidence. Most large companies were still intact and the berths that remained in their hands were the most modern and best equipped. By revamping their production procedures with the use of robots, numerically controlled cutting machines, computer-aided design systems and so on [Uekusa 1987:496], the industry clawed back most of its world market share. In 1975 it commanded just over half of all shipping tonnage. By 1979, it held only 36.6 per cent but by 1985, its stake rose to 45 per cent [Peck 1987:109]. Rather than being substantially financed by the public purse, the industry itself bore the brunt of the adjustment costs. Most official assistance took the form of loans which were in the main subsequently repaid.

Government support was certainly not inconsequential. Apart from generally rallying to the industry's defence and propping it up with legislative and administrative backing, the Ministry of Transport played a key role in engendering a revival of demand by arranging new orders and by persuading shipping companies to replace older vessels. In that sense, a measure of non-tariff protection had been provided.

**Automobiles**

Perhaps even more so than with steel, the assumption by the Japanese automobile industry of a leading role in world markets, symbolizes for the average Western citizen Japan's economic might. Here progress has certainly been no less remarkable, for from an output of 1594 cars in 1950, the industry turned out 7 151 888 by 1983. (In 1974, Japan overtook West Germany as the largest car exporter and six years later it became the largest producer.)

The early postwar years were not very auspicious ones. In companies such as Nissan, labour productivity was flagging. The corporation in 1947 was manufacturing fewer vehicles than it had been doing in 1941, yet its work force had risen from 7550 to 8500 [Cusumano 1985:73]. With the industry in general being beset by limited markets and high production costs (of which the then poor quality of Japanese steel was one ingredient) its future did not seem rosy. Somehow, through a combination of government financial support, the shedding of surplus labour and a timely boost in orders from the US armed forces at war in Korea, the industry began to see the light of day.

Various elements were responsible for the industry's long-term rise to prominence. Chief among these were high levels of import protection, a fast growing domestic market (once the era of rapid economic growth had been inaugurated), large scale investments and the industry's absorption of foreign technology.

Although the automobile industry is currently one of Japan's leading export earners, it initially catered almost exclusively for the home market. In the 1950s, it barely exported 4 per cent of its total output and even by 1970, 80 per cent of its sales were domestic ones. Without import protection, the industry would have been doomed, yet to its credit it blossomed into a fiercely international competitive force. By the 1980s, when more than 50 per cent of its output was sold abroad, US automobile manufacturers who had been thrown into a state of panic, successfully lobbied for Japanese 'voluntary export restraints'. In so doing, they essentially conceded that they had forfeited their ability to match their newfound Japanese challengers.

A major ingredient contributing to the success of the Japanese automobile industry lies in the internal maintenance of competition. In the 1960s, there were no less than 11 separate car companies, each jostling for a larger market share. Other factors include a smaller degree of plant integration which enabled leading companies to invest in costly labour saving equipment (such as robots) while acquiring inputs cheaply from labour intensive subcontractors, and of course, pioneering work in production processing (such as the kanban system).

Being such an efficient industry, it was not assailed by external shocks to the extent that others (like textiles or shipping) were. When confronted with disturbances, it was able to meet the challenges head on. In the wake of the oil crises, it upgraded its technical efficiency and vastly improved labour productivity. It was able to take advantage of comparative weaknesses in small car manufacturing in the US and with an adroit advertising campaign, it began to penetrate the US market. When 'voluntary export restraints' were imposed, it responded by selling more high priced prestige vehicles. Finally, in response to import restrictions and a post 1985 appreciating yen, it established plants offshore, producing directly in North America, Europe and Asia.

## Aluminium

The steep rise in oil costs in 1973 and a series of yen appreciations around the same period of time, both dealt the Japanese aluminium industry a crippling blow. Higher oil prices translated into higher electricity prices, while the strengthening of the yen meant that aluminium imports were becoming cheaper. Considering that the aluminium industry absorbed large quantities of electricity which was priced abroad at far lower rates, the Japanese industry ceased to be internationally competitive. This was clear even by the early 1970s, when imported ingots were landed at 129 000 yen per ton compared with local production costs of 170 000 to 190 000 yen per ton [Uekusa 1987:497].

Instead of moving towards a complete closure of the industry, it was decided to retain it, albeit in a reduced form. Government authorities argued that its retention was necessary for the following reasons: Its continuation provided some assured supply; some leeway in negotiating long-term contract prices; the availability of high quality specialized products and the potential to be a world player in the event of cost conditions taking a turn for the better [Dore 1986:143].

With this in mind, the 1978 industry stabilization plan hoped that of the 1 653 000 tons of capacity that the industry was estimated to have had, 1 100 000 tons would ultimately be salvaged. When in 1981, in the face of further falling import prices, this target proved to be unrealistic, it was downgraded to 700 000 tons. However, the situation continued to deteriorate, and by 1985 a new reconstruction plan called for cutbacks to 350 000 tons [144]. All the while, the industry received tariff protection. Producers were party to a tariff-quota system. That is, they were permitted to import certain amounts of aluminium at reduced tariffs. The savings on these tariffs were paid into the Association for the Promotion of the Structural Improvement of the Aluminium Industry. Later, producers were given tariff exemptions and were allowed to pocket the savings directly [Peck 1987:109].

The industry reacted to events by investing in overseas plants (by 1983, nine offshore projects were initiated), diversifying into other product areas such as fine ceramics and even by trying to develop a refining process which would generate electricity with the use of carbon monoxide produced as a by-product when melting bauxite ore and coke in blast furnaces.

As for the workers, their numbers fell from 15 000 in 1975 to 4000 in 1983. To their good fortune, at least half were re-employed within fellow keiretsu firms [Peck 1987:89].

The keiretsus not only rallied around their respective aluminium industries by mopping up many of the displaced workers but they also shouldered a large burden of the financial costs of the industry's general contraction. For instance, the losses associated with the dissolution of Sumikei Aluminium, amounting to 19 billion yen plus its outstanding bank borrowings which were in excess of 80 billion yen, were borne by a group of firms within the Sumitomo keiretsu, to which Sumikei belonged [Sheard 1992:132].

## Coal

Notwithstanding a 1968 decision to phase out the coal industry on the grounds that it was internationally inefficient, it has continued to be protected. This has involved the setting of consumer prices at levels in excess of foreign ones. In fact, the situation worsened in the 1980s as production costs rose as a result of increased wages (coal mining in Japan is relatively labour intensive) and the mining of deeper deposits. The industry is mainly in Hokkaido and Kyushu and 'the largest mines are located inland, huddled together in relatively isolated areas' [Lesbirel 1991:1084]. Workers, whose average age in the 1980s was 41.4 years, fear that if retrenched they would have to bear high costs resulting from temporary unemployment, retraining, job searches and the lower wages that they would ultimately obtain [1084]. Deferring to industry pressures, the state's eighth coal programme covering the period 1986–91, provided for slightly more stringent protective arrangements.

## A Verdict on Japan's Adjustment Experience

As can be seen from the above summaries, the Japanese present outstanding examples of industries that have coped with unfavourable external events by adjusting positively. The scope of adjustments has included a tendency to concentrate on higher value added activities (as shown in textiles, cars and shipping), a movement into new product lines (particularly as in steel) and a large reduction of output (as in aluminium).

For the most part, restructuring occurred without increases in import restrictions and with limited government outlays. Thanks to the keiretsu system, sister firms have stepped into the breach to provide assistance to troubled industries or firms. That this has not only been the case in the aluminium industry is indicated by the rescue operation of the Mazda Corporation whose keiretsu (again Sumitomo) in the wake of the 1973 oil crisis, provided it with a guaranteed customer base and a massive infusion of capital. 'The contrast with the (US) government-led rescue of Chrysler could not be more striking' [Bergsten and Noland 1993:111].

Unfortunately, as the coal industry indicates, the notion that the Japanese ruthlessly rid themselves of industries that were uncompetitive, is simply not universally valid.

## SUMMARY

- Even by the mid-1980s the average productivity per labourer in Japan was less than that of the US and Germany but the gap is rapidly closing.
- At first, in keeping with a policy of importing most needed technology, research and development expenditures were contained at relatively low levels. But having recently acquired most of what the West has to offer, basic research in Japan has been stepped up. Japan now claims the lead in certain fields, such as opto-electronics but lags behind in areas like computer software.
- Japan is very strong in industrial organization technology exemplified by the kanban system. The latter encompasses continuous production processing, rapid equipment changeover times and multi-machine handling.
- In response to external oil price and yen appreciation shocks, Japanese firms economized on energy, shed unprofitable plants, reorganized work practices, introduced new equipment, diversified output and increasingly moved offshore.
- Economic restructuring is a common feature of all growing economies. It is characterized by a relative decline in the agriculture sector and relative increases in manufacturing and services. Within Japan's postwar experience, manufacturing sectors like clothing and textiles subsided while others such as machinery and transport flourished.
- Japan's industrial restructuring strategy incorporated the identification of depressed industries, the formation of depression cartels and industry loans. Government assistance was meant to be of a temporary nature and import restricting measures were usually shunned.

### Some Industry Examples

- The textile industry was hit by a fall in exports and a rise in imports. In turn, it reduced its productive capacity, invested abroad, moved into higher value added products, installed new plants and upgraded its work practices.

- When confronted with oil price hikes, the steel industry substituted coal for oil and began producing non-steel products, such as ceramics and non-ferrous metals, in increasing quantities.
- Faced with a precipitous fall in their markets, Japanese shipbuilders shed their excess capacity and transferred redundant workers to fellow keiretsu enterprises. They modernized their remaining plants and conceded less sophisticated products, like tankers, to their Korean rivals.
- Japanese automobile companies defended their besieged foreign markets by directly producing standard models in the US and Europe and by producing high quality luxury cars at home.
- Within the aluminium industry output was severely curtailed. Much help was forthcoming from fellow keiretsu firms who absorbed surplus workers and who rallied round companies in serious financial stress.
- Coal represents one example of a lack of progress in restructuring. As in other industrial countries, it has been propped up in the interests of ageing workers who would find it difficult to relocate elsewhere.

# Part III

# International Economic Relations

# 9 Trade and the Balance of Payments

## INTRODUCTION

Within the global economy Japan is a leading player. In 1992 it was, after Germany and the USA, the third single largest exporter, dispatching 9.5 per cent of all internationally traded goods. As an importer, it ranked fourth, purchasing 6.1 per cent of world exports [World Bank Report 1994:187].

This chapter elaborates on the nature and characteristics of Japan's trade. After taking stock of the broad determinants of the country's exports and imports, it considers the overall current account and the extent to which currency movements and general macroeconomic variables bear upon it.

## THE COMMODITY COMPOSITION OF EXPORTS

A striking feature of Japan's export structure is that it is overwhelmingly dominated by manufactured items. Referring to Table 9.1 and abiding by the standard convention which regards the Standard International Classification System (SITC) categories five to eight as representing manufactured products, it is apparent that in 1992, they incorporated 97 per cent of Japan's exports. The exports of no other industrial country, not even the resource poor ones of Hong Kong and Singapore, were quite so reliant on manufactures.[1] Such has been the Japanese situation throughout the postwar period. Furthermore, a rather small cluster of industries (in terms of the three-digit level of the SITC) account for at least 50 per cent of Japan's total exports. In 1985, only six such industries fitted the bill, whereas it required nine in the USA, 18 in France and 13 in Germany [Lincoln 1990:32]. That exports are more highly concentrated in Japan is confirmed by UN computations of 1984 concentration indices. The figures in question were 0.209 for Japan, 0.110 for the USA, 0.085 for France and 0.136 for Germany [33].

*The Japanese Economy*

Table 9.1   Commodity Composition of Exports (Percentage Breakdown)

|  | 1972 | 1977 | 1982 | 1987 | 1992 |
|---|---|---|---|---|---|
| SITC Sections: | | | | | |
| 0. Food and Live animals | 2 | 1 | 1 | 1 | 0 |
| 1. Beverages and Tobacco | 0 | 0 | 0 | 0 | 0 |
| 2. Crude materials | 2 | 1 | 1 | 1 | 1 |
| 3. Mineral fuels | 0 | 0 | 0 | 0 | 0 |
| 4. Animal and Vegetable oils | 0 | 0 | 0 | 0 | 0 |
| 5. Chemical products | 6 | 5 | 5 | 5 | 6 |
| 6. Manufactured goods* | 29 | 26 | 23 | 13 | 11 |
| 7. Machinery and Transport goods | 48 | 56 | 56 | 65 | 72 |
| 8. Miscellaneous manufactures | 12 | 10 | 13 | 14 | 8 |
| 9. Other | 1 | 1 | 1 | 1 | 2 |

\* Classified chiefly by materials used

*Source*: OECD Economic Surveys of Japan, various issues

## Japan's Changing Comparative Advantages

In broad terms, significant changes in the composition of Japan's exports can be perceived. Judging from Table 9.1, exports have been increasingly concentrated in SITC category 7, machinery and transport goods, which embody more capital and technological know-how than the withering general manufacturing categories (SITC numbers 6 and 8).

The relative change of fortune of some specific industrial sectors is highlighted in Table 9.2. In the early postwar years textiles ruled the roost. By the mid 1970s textiles were eclipsed by iron and steel, electrical machinery, road vehicles and ships. Towards the late 1980s, the relative demise of textiles continued, accompanied by sharp reversals of fortune in steel and ships. A lead has been taken by road vehicles followed by electrical machinery, while steady progress has also been made in the precision instrument group.

Resorting to the use of an index measuring 'revealed' comparative advantage (the ratio of a country's world share in the exports of a particular commodity to its world share of total exports) Balassa and Noland noted certain broad changes for Japan between 1967 and 1983 [Balassa and Noland 1988:31]. Their observations, which are in line with what has already been mentioned, suggest that in that time span, very large reversals in comparative advantage occurred in textiles, clothes, leather and stone, clay and glass products. At the same time, gains had been

*Table* 9.2    Percentage Export Shares of Some More Specific Commodity
Groupings

|                      | 1955 | 1975 | 1987 |
|----------------------|------|------|------|
| Textiles             | 37   | 7    | 3    |
| Iron and steel       | 13   | 18   | 5    |
| Electrical machinery | –    | 11   | 18   |
| Transport equipment  | –    | 26   | 27   |
| Road vehicles        | –    | 15   | 25   |
| Ships                | –    | 11   | 2    |
| Precision instruments| –    | 5    | 9    |

*Source*: MITI, *Japan Statistical Yearbook 1990*, OECD 1989 Survey of Japan

*Note*: After 1987 the commodity classification was revised

made in machinery, transport equipment, instruments and related products.
This complements data presented by Petri, which indicate that in
1988, 53.3 per cent of Japan's exports were technology intensive
products, compared with 40.7 per cent in 1970. For labour intensive
goods, the ratio changed from 17.4 per cent in 1970 to 6.4 per cent in
1988 [Petri 1991:64].

## THE COMMODITY COMPOSITION OF IMPORTS

Just as Japan is an outlier in the composition of its exports, so is it
with respect to its imports. In 1992, manufactured products constituted
only 48 per cent of all its incoming goods. At that time, the weighted
average ratio of manufactures to total imports for all 23 World Bank
defined high income countries was 76 per cent. Most countries reported ratios exceeding 80 per cent and the country with the closest
reading to Japan's was Italy at 69 per cent [World Bank, *World Development Report 1994*:189]. In earlier years, Japan imported even relatively less manufactures. The 1970 ratio was a mere 0.25 against the
then high income countries' average of 0.58.

As Table 9.3 indicates, mineral fuels and raw industrial materials
had previously predominated, but more recently, their relative importance has waned. Falling crude oil prices, the introduction of energy
saving measures and the contraction of large primary product input
users, such as the textile, steel and aluminium industries, are all factors in the equation. In addition, the growing representation of SITC

*Table* 9.3   Commodity Composition of Imports (Percentage Breakdown)

|  | 1972 | 1977 | 1982 | 1987 | 1992 |
|---|---|---|---|---|---|
| SITC sections: |  |  |  |  |  |
| 0. Food and live animals | 15 | 13 | 11 | 13 | 14 |
| 1. Beverages and tobacco | 1 | 1 | 1 | 1 | 2 |
| 2. Crude materials | 30 | 20 | 14 | 15 | 12 |
| 3. Mineral fuels | 24 | 44 | 50 | 26 | 23 |
| 4. Animal and vegetable oils | 0 | 0 | 0 | 0 | 0 |
| 5. Chemical products | 5 | 4 | 5 | 8 | 8 |
| 6. Manufactured goods* | 9 | 7 | 7 | 12 | 11 |
| 7. Machinery and transport goods | 10 | 6 | 6 | 12 | 16 |
| 8. Miscellaneous manufactures | 5 | 4 | 4 | 9 | 13 |
| 9. Other | 1 | 1 | 2 | 4 | 1 |

* Classified chiefly by materials used

*Source*: OECD Economic Surveys of Japan, various issues

sections 5–8 is partly a reflection of Japan's changing comparative advantages, whereby industrial activities are increasingly centred in spheres which are more technology and capital intensive, yielding scope for the further importation of more labour intensive goods. Finally, the large yen appreciation in the latter half of the 1980s, not only led to a reduced oil import bill (in local currency) but it also provided a boon to foreign consumer good manufacturers.

## THE GEOGRAPHIC COMPOSITION OF TRADE

A quick glance at Tables 9.4 and 9.5 readily indicates that the United States is Japan's most important trading partner. Over the period covered (1960–89), the USA usually purchased no less than a quarter of Japan's exports and generally supplied it with a comparable proportion of its imports. Japan trades with no other single country with anything like the same degree of intensity. For example, in 1989, its second, third and fourth largest single country markets were South Korea, Germany and Taiwan which respectively bought 6, 5.8 and 5.6 per cent of its exports.

In general terms, the tables also reveal the growth of Europe as a market for Japan's exports, the relative diminishing importance of both Latin America and Africa and a moderate degree of constancy for South and non-Communist East Asia. Trade relations with Europe strength-

Table 9.4   Geographic Composition of Exports (Percentage Breakdown)

|      | USA | Europe | Latin America | Asia | Mid. East | Africa | China |
|------|-----|--------|---------------|------|-----------|--------|-------|
| 1960 | 27  | 12     | 8             | 32   | 4         | 6      | –     |
| 1970 | 31  | 15     | 6             | 25   | 3         | 5      | 3     |
| 1980 | 24  | 17     | 7             | 24   | 11        | 4      | 4     |
| 1989 | 34  | 21     | 3             | 27   | 3         | 1      | 3     |

*Source*: Japan Statistical Yearbook 1990. Statistics Bureau, Tokyo

Table 9.5   Geographic Composition of Imports (Percentage Breakdown)

|      | USA | Europe | Latin America | Asia | Mid. East | Africa | China |
|------|-----|--------|---------------|------|-----------|--------|-------|
| 1960 | 35  | 8      | 7             | 20   | 10        | 2      | –     |
| 1970 | 29  | 5      | 7             | 16   | 12        | 4      | 1     |
| 1980 | 17  | 7      | 4             | 23   | 32        | 2      | 1     |
| 1989 | 23  | 17     | 4             | 25   | 10        | 1      | 5     |

*Source*: As in Table 9.4

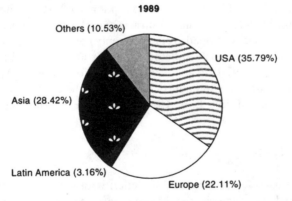

**1989**

Others (10.53%)

USA (35.79%)

Asia (28.42%)

Latin America (3.16%)

Europe (22.11%)

*Figure* 9.1   Geographic Composition of Exports
Shares refer to those in Table 9.4

ened in the 1980s as Japan plied it with its leading technological based products while buying ever increasing amounts of chemicals and transport vehicles. Closer ties were knit with the Middle East in response to oil price rises, but as they receded, so did Japan's trade with that region, not only in relative but also in absolute value terms. The Asian region forfeited its dominance as Japan's largest export outlet, as Japan's export

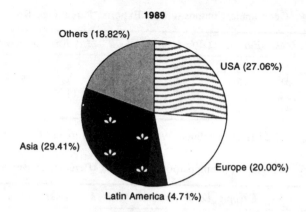

*Figure* 9.2    Geographic Composition of Imports
Shares refer to those in Table 9.5

products became more sophisticated and capable of carving further niches within North America and Europe.

The temporary relative decline in exports to the USA in 1980 did not reflect absolute setbacks but an exceptional effort on the part of Japan to boost Middle East sales contracts. Similarly, in the same year, imports from the USA slipped (relatively only) as the value of Japan's oil import costs was grossly inflated. Looking at imports (Table 9.5), the relative fall in 1970 of goods originating from the USA, Europe and South and East non-Communist Asia seem to be explained by larger sourcing from the Middle East, China and Australia (not represented in the table).

## Triangular Trade

For the most part, Japan runs a trade deficit with some of its main raw material suppliers, such as the Middle East, Australia, Canada, the Philippines, Brunei, Indonesia, Malaysia and Brazil while running sizeable surpluses with the USA and Europe. Many observers term the Japanese practice of largely sourcing its primary products from one group of countries while turning more emphatically towards the USA and Europe to vent its manufactured exports, as 'triangular trade'.[2]

## SOME DETERMINANTS OF JAPAN'S TRADE

To put the matter rather simply, a country's export performance is a function of the rate of growth of the foreign demand for the basket of goods that it offers, their prices *vis-à-vis* those of overseas competitors and certain more nebulous concepts, such as quality and product or firm reputation. In the case of imports, values depend on local demand and on foreigners' prices as well as their general competitiveness. Trade flows are of course also influenced by the extent of the import protective measures that trading partners maintain.

Changes in the prices of traded goods are, among other things, governed by changes in relative factor productivity (particularly labour) and by real exchange rate movements. At this stage, we will consider productivity growth. Exchange rate realignments will be taken up later.

### Productivity Growth and Improved Competitiveness

Turner observed that during the period 1975 to 1989, Japanese labour productivity, in manufacturing as a whole, grew by 5 per cent per annum compared with a yearly average of 3.5 per cent for Europe [Turner 1991:19]. In some industries, such as electrical machinery and general machinery, Japan's labour productivity grew at more than twice the pace of practically all other European rivals [see 20].

Similarly, comparisons with the USA point to impressive Japanese gains. Although 'all Japanese industries had lower levels of productivity than their US counterparts in 1960', by 1985, Japan had closed the productivity gap in at least 12 major manufacturing sectors [Jorgenson and Kuroda 1992:216]. Furthermore, for most of the 1960–85 period, 'the Japanese economy has been more competitive than the US economy' [212]. Both relatively lower wages and lower real costs of capital, played significant roles.[3]

In the words of Michael Porter, Japan 'contains some of the most competitive firms and industries in the world' [Porter 1990:394]. This is borne out by the fact that in 1985, 50 separate manufactured products, which collectively represented 48.5 per cent of Japan's exports, all commanded at least 30 per cent of the world market. Some, like motorcycles, TV recorders, cameras and gramophones had respective shares amounting to 59 per cent and more [385]. The extent to which Japanese producers surpassed US ones for certain OECD export shares is shown in Table 9.6. Naturally, there is also a group of industries in which the US is dominant. This too is listed. What Table 9.6 also

Table 9.6   OECD Export Shares (by Percentage)

|  | Japan 1975 | Japan 1988 | USA 1975 | USA 1988 |
|---|---|---|---|---|
| Group A |  |  |  |  |
| Computers | 3.2 | 26.3 | 26.7 | 24.6 |
| Telecommunications | 16.8 | 41.5 | 18.6 | 15.3 |
| TVs and recorders | 47.3 | 59.8 | 5.6 | 4.3 |
| Cars | 14.8 | 25.4 | 18.3 | 10.6 |
| Machinery | 8.1 | 18.8 | 21.9 | 16.1 |
| Iron and Steel | 26.0 | 20.7 | 6.3 | 2.9 |
| Group B |  |  |  |  |
| Aircraft | 0.3 | 0.8 | 68.9 | 50.8 |
| Medical products | 2.1 | 2.7 | 14.5 | 15.7 |
| Chemicals | 9.9 | 7.4 | 20.5 | 17.6 |

Source: Turner 1991, Table 7, p. 23

demonstrates is the rapidity of progress made by certain Japanese sectors such as those in computing, machinery and cars. Taking cars as a case in point, exports rose from under 400 000 units in 1967 to 1 000 000 in 1970 and to around 6 000 000 in the early 1980s. 'The shift in American preferences from large to smaller vehicles helped but the export performance of the Japanese automobile industry would not have been possible without better designs and cost reductions' [Cusumano 1985:132].

With regard to imports, Japan has a reputation for being impervious to foreign manufactured products. In 1990 the import share of domestic consumption of manufactures (in percentages) was 5.9 for Japan, 15.3 for the USA, 15.4 for Germany and 17.7 for the UK [Bergsten and Noland 1993:66]. Except for a handful of products (which include chemicals) import penetration rates for most industries are considerably lower than in the USA and Europe (see Table 9.7).

**Import Barriers and Import Liberalization**

Early in its postwar development drive, Japan resorted to widespread import limitations to protect local producers. Specific measures adopted included a system of tariffs, quotas, exchange controls and outright import bans. By the end of the 1950s, 'only about 20 per cent of Japan's imports were free of bans or quotas' [Horsley and Buckley 1990:63]. The general effectiveness of such restrictions may partially be appreci-

*Table* 9.7   1988 Import Penetration Rates (Value of Imports Divided by GNP)

|  | Japan | USA | Europe |
|---|---|---|---|
| Total manufacturing | 2.96 | 7.24 | 17.11 |
| Computers | 0.07 | 0.17 | 0.59 |
| Telecommunications equipment | 0.05 | 0.22 | 0.33 |
| Medical and Pharmaceutical goods | 0.09 | 0.07 | 0.26 |
| Aircraft | 0.07 | 0.11 | 0.30 |
| Electrical machinery | 0.18 | 0.65 | 1.17 |
| Cars | 0.13 | 1.52 | 2.02 |
| Chemicals | 0.26 | 0.20 | 0.92 |
| Iron and Steel | 0.16 | 0.24 | 0.78 |
| Clothes | 0.24 | 0.45 | 0.82 |
| Paper | 0.04 | 0.17 | 0.56 |

*Source*: Turner 1991:Table A-1, p. 49

ated by noting that between 1951 and 1961, the ratio of imported cars to domestic sales fell from 44.6 to 0.7 per cent [Cusumano 1985:387].

From the beginning of the 1960s, Japan began to liberalize its trade regime. The process was a gradual one but at least it consistently moved in the appropriate direction. By the end of the 1980s, the weighted average tariff rate for industrial products (excluding petroleum) was 1.9 per cent [Bergsten and Noland 1993:72]. By 1991 quotas on beef and citrus fruits were converted into tariff equivalents and in general terms, the country is now *formally* no less open to imports than any of its major trading partners. In fact, even by 1986, a smaller proportion of Japan's imports were subject to non-tariff barriers than was the case in the USA [see OECD Survey 1988:88]. As if to guarantee trade openness, the government has officially been encouraging its citizens to buy more imports. Judging from recent trends, this has not been necessary. Between 1985 and 1990, partly thanks to the yen appreciation and to heightened economic activity, import growth rates exceeded export ones (the respective percentage increases were 81 and 63). That part of the import increases reflected a real reduction in trade barriers is suggested by the fact that the surge in consumer goods imports 'was well in excess of what might have been expected on the basis of developments in overall consumer demand and relative import prices' [Crocker 1991:9]. The reader should bear this in mind in considering US charges that Japan's markets are still largely impenetrable. These accusations are discussed in the following chapter.

## JAPAN'S TRADE DEPENDENCE

In this section, we partly deviate from our underlying theme (factors influencing Japan's trade and current account) to consider the extent to which the Japanese economy relies on international trade. As it happens, such a diversion is not entirely unrelated to our main area of concern.

Because Japan is a titan among the world's leading exporters and because its internal raw material resource base is so limited, it is widely assumed that Japan is inordinately dependent on foreign trade. In truth, it is and it isn't.

There is no question that Japan counts on obtaining almost all of its vital basic inputs which include oil, natural gas, iron ore, coal, copper, lead, bauxite and nickel from abroad. Even in terms of foodstuffs, it imports large quantities of animal feed, fish and wheat. In that sense, Japan is certainly more dependent on external suppliers than say the USA, France or the UK.

However, if Japan's relative trade involvement is measured as a ratio of either imports, exports or both to GDP, it turns out that no matter which ratio one selects, Japan would seem to be considerably less trade dependent than virtually all other industrial countries (see Table 9.8).

### Trade as an Engine of Growth?

Given Japan's low ratio of either exports or imports to GDP, one might well wonder whether and to what extent, trade functioned as an engine of the country's postwar growth. According to Kosai and Ogino, after the war, trade and industrial progress developed at the same pace. What is more, they claim 'that one might go as far as to say that Japan's industry has been actually led by the development of foreign trade' [Kosai and Ogino 1984:64]. Here Kosai and Ogino seem to be treading on very thin ice. A more common view is that in most industries, 'exports increased substantially *only* when the domestic market became mature' [Porter 1990:405]. That is, domestic demand saturation was a major impetus for many industries' export drives (for corroborating evidence see Johnson 1982:230 and Abegglen and Stalk 1985:60). One need only turn to automobiles to see how small a role foreign trade played in stimulating manufacturing in the early postwar period. Between 1946 and 1957, Nissan and Toyota, the country's two leading automobile companies, exported only about 2 per cent of their annual output [Cusumano 1985:131]. In fact, as Allen explains, it took

*Table* 9.8   Measures of Trade Dependency (1992)

|  | Exports/GDP | Imports/GDP | Exports and Imports/GDP |
|---|---|---|---|
| Ireland | 65 | 52 | 117 |
| New Zealand | 23 | 22 | 45 |
| Israel | 19 | 27 | 46 |
| Spain | 11 | 17 | 28 |
| Australia | 13 | 14 | 27 |
| UK | 21 | 24 | 45 |
| Netherlands | 43 | 42 | 85 |
| Canada | 26 | 25 | 51 |
| France | 18 | 18 | 36 |
| Germany | 24 | 23 | 47 |
| USA | 7 | 9 | 16 |
| Sweden | 25 | 23 | 48 |
| Japan | 9 | 6 | 15 |

*Source*: Calculated from data in Tables 3 and 13, World Bank, *World Development Report 1994*

until 1959, when general industrial output had already exceeded prewar volumes by a factor of two, for export flows merely to equal previous levels [Allen 1981:160]. Without question, 'during the post-war period, the main stimulus to growth was provided by industrial investment and . . . exports played a secondary role' [158].

However, it seems that at the tail end of the 1958, 1962, 1965 and 1971 recessions, export increases partially offset internal demand shortcomings. Because of their positive impact on the balance of payments, surges in exports also 'enabled authorities to embark on a reflationary policy earlier than would otherwise have been prudent' [158]. After 1975, net exports certainly contributed significantly to economic growth, at least until 1985. During 1980–85, net export increases were responsible for 42 per cent of the annual GDP increment [Balassa and Noland 1988:6]. In the same time frame, exports became crucially important in sustaining output for a number of key industries. For example, by 1985, 'exports provided markets for 30 per cent of the domestic production of iron and steel, for 42 per cent of electronic communications equipment and electrical machinery production, 48 per cent of automobile production, and 54 per cent of precision machinery production' [13]. In that sense, export progress had become imperative for the profitable viability of many leading Japanese corporations.

Between 1986 and 1990, when economic activity continued to expand, the contribution of net exports to the growth rate was consistently negative. Large yen appreciations worked to discourage exports and to stimulate imports.

## THE CURRENT ACCOUNT

The last occasion that Japan experienced a current account deficit was in 1980, when it was still reeling under the impact of the 1979 oil price hikes. Since then, overall balances have always been positive. They rapidly advanced to a level of $87 billion in 1987, dropping off to $35.8 billion in 1990 and then rebounding to a record $117.5 in 1992 (3.2 per cent of GDP. See Table 9.9). In very broad terms, the setbacks in the latter half of the 1980s can largely be attributed to sizeable appreciations of the yen, and in the case of the post 1990 recovery, to an economic recession which led to an absolute fall in imports.

Within the net services and transfers category, transport and travel deficits rose from $6.2 billion in 1985 to $32.5 by 1992. The Japanese increasingly took advantage of the strong yen to travel abroad while at the same time, foreign tourists were deterred from visiting Japan. In the past few years, Japan has become a rather generous foreign assistance donor and had its foreign investment income not risen so swiftly, its net services and transfers account would have been even more in the red.

### The Current Account as the Excess of National Saving over Investment

In macroeconomic terms, the size and sign (positive or negative) of a country's current account is theoretically equivalent to the difference between its total savings and total investments. To appreciate this we take a very simple case where the current account involves only traded goods and services and not financial transfers such as returns to foreign investment. (In the appendix to this chapter we show how the inclusion of financial transfers may be accommodated.)

Consider a country's gross domestic product (Y) which is defined as being equal to the sum of its consumption (C), investment (I) and exports (E) minus its imports (M). (Exports and imports include services such as foreign travel.)

$$\text{Symbolically presented: } Y = C + I + E - M \tag{1}$$

*Table* 9.9   Japan's Current Account (Billions of US Dollars)

|       | Trade Balance | Net Services and Transfers | Current Balance |
|-------|---------------|----------------------------|-----------------|
| 1980  | 2.1           | −12.9                      | −10.8           |
| 1981  | 19.9          | −15.2                      | 4.7             |
| 1982  | 18.1          | −11.2                      | 6.9             |
| 1983  | 31.5          | −10.7                      | 20.8            |
| 1984  | 44.3          | −9.3                       | 35.0            |
| 1985  | 56.0          | −6.8                       | 49.2            |
| 1986  | 92.8          | −7.0                       | 85.8            |
| 1987  | 96.4          | −9.4                       | 87.0            |
| 1988  | 95.0          | −15.4                      | 79.6            |
| 1989  | 76.9          | −19.8                      | 57.1            |
| 1990  | 63.9          | −28.1                      | 35.8            |
| 1991  | 103.0         | −30.1                      | 72.9            |
| 1992  | 132.3         | −14.8                      | 117.5           |

*Source*: OECD Economic Surveys of Japan, Various issues

Rearranging equation (1) (by bringing C to the left hand side) we get:

$$Y - C = I + E - M \qquad (2)$$

Since income minus consumption is equivalent to savings (which is symbolized by S) the left hand side of equation (2) is relabelled:

$$S = I + E - M$$

Now transferring I to the left hand side we arrive at:

$$S - I = E - M \qquad (3)$$

Equation (3) informs us that saving minus investment is equal to the exports minus imports, that is the current account balance.

We can now move a step further and disaggregate saving and investment into three components, that is the savings and investments undertaken by private corporations (c), by private households (h), and by the government (g) and present equation (3) as:

$$(Sc - Ic) + (Sh - Ih) + (Sg - Ig) = E - M \qquad (4)$$

Finally, if equation (4) is divided by Y (to make every component a ratio of national income) we land up with:

$$\frac{(Sc - Ic)}{Y} + \frac{(Sh - Ih)}{Y} + \frac{(Sg - Ig)}{Y} = \frac{E - M}{Y} \qquad (5)$$

Table 9.10    Sectoral Savings–Investment Balances
(as a Percentage of GDP)

| | 1960–64 | 1965–68 | 1969–73 | 1974–79 | 1980–85 | 1986–91 |
|---|---|---|---|---|---|---|
| **Corporations** | | | | | | |
| Saving | 16.1 | 17.9 | 17.4 | 10.1 | 11.2 | 12.2 |
| Investment | 24.4 | 21.9 | 25.5 | 17.1 | 16.4 | 20.0 |
| Saving-investment | −8.3 | −4.0 | −8.1 | −7.0 | −5.2 | −7.8 |
| **Households** | | | | | | |
| Saving | 11.8 | 12.4 | 14.8 | 19.7 | 16.1 | 13.8 |
| Investment | 6.8 | 8.6 | 6.3 | 9.3 | 6.9 | 4.6 |
| Saving-investment | 5.0 | 3.8 | 8.5 | 10.4 | 9.2 | 9.2 |
| **Net private** | | | | | | |
| **Sector balance** | −3.3 | −0.2 | 0.4 | 3.4 | 4.0 | 1.4 |
| **Government** | | | | | | |
| Saving | 7.7 | 6.2 | 6.9 | 3.0 | 3.5 | 7.6 |
| Investment | 5.2 | 5.3 | 5.7 | 6.4 | 6.5 | 6.0 |
| Saving-investment | 2.5 | 0.9 | 1.2 | −3.4 | −3.0 | 1.6 |
| **Current account** | −0.8 | 0.7 | 1.6 | 0.0 | 1.0 | 3.0 |

*Sources*: Lincoln 1988:72, Economic Planning Agency and Bank of Japan

In Table 9.10 we present Japan's average saving and investment to GDP ratios for various periods between 1960 and 1991. What emerges is that although the corporate sector has generally maintained a rather high savings rate, its investment ratio has invariably been larger, so that it has consistently been a net borrower. By contrast, private householders have regularly generated net savings which, after 1968, were able to offset corporate deficits. As for the government sector, net average savings have only been negative between 1974 and 1985.

In the early 1960s, the current account was in deficit because of a shortfall in net private savings. When exceptionally large public sector deficits appeared in the periods 1974–9 and 1980–5, a large rise in household savings and sharp falls in corporate investments held the day, averting current account deficits. In the ultimate period (1986–91) a very sharp turnabout in the government deficit seems to have been largely responsible for Japan's exceptionally high current account surplus.

## Comparisons with the United States

Japan's large current account surplus and the trade balance component in particular, has for some time been a bone of contention between it and the USA. In the past few years, by contrast with Japan, the United States has been running large global trade deficits, an appreciable proportion of which stems from unbalanced US–Japanese bilateral trade. Although (as we shall show in the next chapter), US officials charge that this stems from sharp and unfair Japanese practices, in actual fact, divergent macroeconomic conditions are the primary cause.

Just looking at say the comparative situation in 1992, Japan's national savings as a ratio of GDP was 34.0 per cent while in the USA it was 15.0 per cent. Japan also maintained a very high investment ratio of 31.0 per cent but net savings were still positive. In the USA, the investment ratio at 16.0 per cent was almost a half of Japan's, but nonetheless it still exceeded the savings one, creating a shortfall equal to 1.0 per cent of GDP. In the United States, not only are household savings meagre but for year after year, government sector finances have been deficient. In 1992 the deficit equalled 4.9 per cent of GDP [see World Bank, *World Development Report 1994*:179 and 181].

## Is Japan's Persistent Current Account Surplus a Matter of Concern?

A not inconsequential number of American commentators, including some academics, describe Japan's global surplus as 'a major problem'. For instance, Bergsten and Noland would have us believe that because 'Japan is now the only surplus country in the G-7 and is running the only large surplus in the world', it 'is maintaining domestic output and employment at the expense of other countries, whose external deficits have risen as a counterpart to the increase in the Japanese surplus' [Bergsten and Noland 1993:5]. Such an assertion seems to lie at odds with another statement by Bergsten and Noland (within their very same book) that over the past decade, wide swings in US–Japan bilateral trade imbalances are correctly attributed by most observers 'to fluctuating macroeconomic conditions in the two economies' [23].

We have already noted that disparities in savings–investment ratios between countries are associated with differing current account outcomes. On that basis, it is not clear why, if Japan chooses to have a high rate of savings relative to the US, the current account reflecting that choice, should be contentious. A neutral stance would of course require the assumption that there be no distortions affecting private saving and investment decisions, no externalities and that saving–investment decisions are made rationally. In other words, the market mechanism is assumed to function efficiently. Moreover, since public sector saving is a very important component of national saving, the problematic issue of determining what constitutes an appropriate public sector balance, would also have to be addressed [see Argy 1994:Ch. 34].

In light of Japan's proclivity to wish to save more than it proposes to invest, many eminent economists, both native and foreign, argue that 'it may remain appropriate for Japan to run a modest current account surplus, of the order of 1.0 to 1.5 of GNP' [Balassa and Noland 1988:149].

## Some Policy Implications

If either the US or Japanese governments or both wish to reduce their bilateral trade imbalances, it would be appropriate for them to pursue policies that would ensure at least one of the following outcomes:

(1) A reduction in private savings in Japan and/or an increase in private savings in the US.
(2) An increase in private investment in Japan and/or a reduction in private investment in the US.
(3) A reduction of public sector savings in Japan and/or an increase in public sector savings in the US.
(4) An increase in public investment in Japan and/or a reduction in public investment in the US.

American economists generally advocate the curtailing of their country's budget deficit and the boosting of local private savings. Their governments, by contrast, emphasize the desirability of the Japanese reducing both their public and private sector savings. In so doing, US officials point to Japanese public sector deficiencies (such as an inadequacy of roads and other forms of public infrastructure) or to the 'need' for Japan to become more consumer-oriented.

Apart from the impropriety of meddling in other countries' affairs, there is no scientific way of determining optimal saving or investment levels. Even if there were, changes in saving rates may simply alter investment outcomes in such a way that no new net change is effected.

## Some Shortcomings of the Savings–Investment Approach

Essentially, the savings–investment approach to the current account draws on an identity that does not in itself reveal anything about the direction of causation. For instance, a larger current account deficit might result from an expansion of imports induced by a larger public sector deficit. Alternatively, a fall in exports (which increases the deficit) may lead to a fall in national income and hence taxation, which in turn worsens the budget deficit. As Tyson and Zysman put it, 'both saving and investment depend upon current levels of economic activity and these in turn are affected by trade' [Tyson and Zysman 1989:107].

## MORE ON GENERAL TRADE DETERMINANTS

Earlier on, we had given some thought to relative productivity in relation to changing trade competitiveness. Now, after briefly considering income changes, we shall turn our attention to some of the ways in which Japan's trade balance has been altered by exchange rate movements.

### Income Changes and the Trade Balance

The impact that income changes exert on Japan's trade balance is a function of relative GDP growth rates and export and import income elasticities. Export (import) income elasticities are defined as the percentage change of exports (imports) divided by the percentage change of income. (For exports, the income changes are those of Japan's overseas markets; for imports, Japan's own growth rate is taken.)

Assuming all else to be constant (that is, exchange rates, relative wages, productivity growth, tastes etc) then starting from a position of a zero trade balance (exports equal imports), if income elasticities are the same at home and abroad, then when growth in real demand is also the same, the trade balance will remain constant.

If foreign income growth exceeds local growth, the trade balance will improve and conversely, if foreign income growth falls short of home growth, the trade balance will worsen.

A study published by the Bank of Japan [1991] indicates that in the second half of the 1980s, the country's income elasticity of demand for exports fell from around 1.5 to 1.0, while the income elasticity of demand for imports rose from around 0.9 to 2.5. This means that *ceteris paribus*, unless Japan grows slower than her trading partners, her trade balance is likely to deteriorate.

The decline of Japan's income elasticity of demand for exports is in no small part due to a rapid expansion of overseas manufacturing subsidiaries which have significantly displaced direct sales from home based parent plants. This has certainly been the case in the automobile industry, where firms such as Toyota now maintain production networks operating in and supplying the North American and European markets. To this, one should add the moderating effects of various restrictions that have been imposed on Japanese exporters, foremost of which are the so called 'voluntary export restraints', which are discussed in the following chapter.

Increases in Japan's income elasticity of demand for imports also reflect the impact of direct overseas investment, which by capitalizing on cheaper foreign labour sources, particularly in Asia, provides the homeland with both lower priced manufactured inputs and finished products. However, in overall terms, the changing composition of Japan's imports, characterized by a marked shift from raw materials to manufactured goods, probably accounts for most of the recent rise of the income elasticity of import demand.

A knowledge of relative export and import income elasticity dimensions, enables us to forecast trade balance changes on the basis of prospective GDP growth rates, provided of course the *ceteris paribus* assumption holds. Needless to say, this does not apply. One of the variables that are frequently subject to change, is the exchange rate. Precisely how this affects the Japanese trade balance is, to some extent, still an open question.

## Exchange Rate Changes and the Trade Balance

Indices of the real exchange value of the yen (that is Japan's trade weighted exchange rates adjusted for relative national price level changes) are shown in Figure 9.3.

From Figure 9.3 it would seem that in the early 1980s, the real value of the yen was more or less stable. After 1985 it appreciated markedly, reaching a high point in 1988. It then receded over the following two years, only to bounce back with renewed vigour from 1991 onwards. The 1985–8 appreciation was larger than the one experienced in 1975–8 when the yen recovered from the first oil crisis [Petri 1991:51].

Leaving aside the familiar J-curve effect which accounts for a short-term trade balance deterioration (improvement) in the face of an exchange rate depreciation (appreciation),[4] the normal expectation is for a medium to long-term improvement in response to a depreciation and of course a worsening in response to an appreciation. Projected changes would be based on known or estimated export and import elasticities of demand, which in Japan's case are considered to be of magnitudes capable of ensuring appropriate outcomes.

## Pass-Through Magnitudes and Effects

In the past, especially when confronted with yen appreciations, the trade balances that were registered, even when allowing for lagged time effects, differed from the balances that were forecast. It soon became apparent that either export or import price changes did not fully reflect exchange rate variations. Technically, this phenomenon became known as an 'incomplete pass-through'. That is, the price effects of exchange rate variations were only partially transferred to consumers.

Very basically, the concept of the 'pass-through' may be grasped by considering how an appreciation of say the yen dollar exchange rate translates into a new set of dollar prices for Japanese exports. It may well be that the Japanese exporters simply maintain the original dollar prices. To do so, they would have to reduce their *yen* export prices by amounts that are proportional to the appreciation. This usually results in a situation in which the yen export price drops below the yen price for the same goods sold internally. Alternatively, they may not yield on *yen* export prices, in which case, dollar prices would rise by the extent of the appreciation. An intermediate case would be represented by some increase in the dollar price and some fall in the yen one. The extent of the pass-through may be measured by the percentage change in the foreign currency price divided by the percentage change in the exchange rate. A zero pass-through would imply that the foreign quoted price is completely insensitive to exchange rate changes while a complete pass-through would indicate that a yen appreciation raises dollar denominated Japanese export prices by the same proportion.

Major factors determining the pass-through include: the financial strength of the enterprise (the stronger, the lower the pass-through), the degree of competition in export markets (the less the competition the larger the pass-through), the export to domestic sales ratio (the higher the ratio the larger the pass-through), the degree to which emphasis is placed on maintaining market shares (the greater, the lower the pass-through), the extent to which export contracts are written in US dollars (the more so, the less the pass-through) and the extent to which foreign producers raise their prices (this facilitates pass-through).

Estimates of the aggregate pass-through in Japan vary but a 50 per cent figure is generally accepted as being reasonable, at least as far the 1985–8 period is concerned. (At an earlier stage, such as during the yen appreciation from November 1976 to November 1978, the pass-through was thought to be much higher [Balassa and Noland 1988:144].) The ability of Japanese exporters to absorb roughly half of the impact

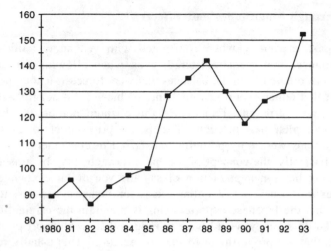

*Figure* 9.3   Index Values of Japan's Real Exchange Rate 1985 = 100

*Source*: IMF International Financial Statistics, various issues

of the 1985–8 appreciation was partly due to the cost reducing effects of rapidly falling oil prices. Unfortunately, after 1990, when the yen once more gathered strength, Japanese producers were less able to curtail pass-throughs. A JETRO survey established that this resulted from a number of reasons, of which the major ones were: The fact that company streamlining and cost-cutting measures had reached their limits, that the local recession limited the scope for internal markets to subsidize external ones, the export ratio is now higher than before and that there has been a fallback in competitiveness so that 'higher quality is no longer enough to justify higher prices' [JETRO 1993:33].

With Japan's trade prices now much more responsive to currency movements, the post 1985 appreciations have been biting into its trade balance. Imports have been rising at all time records and 'during 1985–89, Japanese real export growth was the slowest for any five year period of the past three decades' [Crocker 1991:6].


SUMMARY

• Much more so than in other countries, Japan's exports are overwhelmingly manufactured goods. On the import side, Japan tends to have an unusually high concentration of primary commodities.

- The United States is Japan's biggest trading partner, buying around 25 per cent of Japan's exports and supplying a similar proportion of imports.
- Japan maintains a triangular trade relation in which it runs trade deficits with its major primary product suppliers and surpluses with most industrial countries.
- The ratio of imports to final demand in Japan is exceedingly low. Probably because of high trade barriers; but since the 1960s these have *formally* been reduced to levels comparable to or even lower than those in the West.
- Contrary to general belief, trade as a ratio to GDP in Japan is rather low and in the high growth period it was mainly to the internal market that producers turned for sales outlets. Subsequently, exports became very significant for certain individual sectors and between 1980 and 1985 net export growth was responsible for 45 per cent of the growth of GDP.
- A current account balance of payments surplus has been recorded for every year since 1981. This can be explained in terms of savings in Japan exceeding investment. Likewise, deficits in the US can be considered to be the outcome of investment exceeding saving.
- A fall in Japan's export income elasticity of demand and a rise in income elasticity of demand for imports is likely to contribute to a deterioration in the current account balance.
- In the past, an appreciation of the yen did not give rise to expected price movements reflecting incomplete pass-throughs. This is now expected to change considering that the internal Japanese market is depressed and that production cost saving measures have just about been exhausted.

## APPENDIX

Here we present the derivation of a variant of equation (5) in the chapter's text, this time allowing for the inclusion of a flow of funds in the current account resulting from foreign held assets.

As before, we commence with:

$$Y = C + I + E - M \qquad (1)$$

Disaggregating consumption and investment expenditures into private (p) and government (g) ones, equation (1) is rewritten as:

$$Y = Cp + Ip + Cg + Ig + X - M \qquad (2)$$

Before we proceed further, let us assume that in the hypothetical economy that we are investigating, there are no external transfers in the form of aid or remittances by migrants, etc, no profit or interest payments made to foreigners and that earnings from abroad accrue only to the private sector in the form of interest payments on overseas held assets. In other words, the current account consists of the sum of the trade balance $(X - M)$ plus interest on overseas assets.[5]

Now, in what may seem to be a digression, let us define private disposable income (YD) as:

$$YD = Y + r*EFA + rdB - T \qquad (3)$$

where r* is the foreign interest rate, FA stands for foreign assets denominated in foreign currency, E is the exchange rate (defined as units of domestic currency per unit of the foreign currency) rd is the domestic interest rate, B represents holdings of government bonds and T is taxation.

Equation three indicates that disposable private income is equal to the gross domestic product plus interest payments on foreign assets and government bonds less taxes.

Private disposable income is absorbed by either private consumption (Cp) or private savings (Sp). That is:

$$Sp + Cp = Y + r*EFA + rdB - T \qquad (4)$$

If we now insert the value of Y (as given in equation two) into equation four and rearrange the terms somewhat, we may land up with:

$$Sp + (T - Cg - rdB) = Ip + Ig + (X - M + r*EFA) \qquad (5)$$

Equation five indicates that *national* savings which are made up of private savings plus government savings (taxes minus government outlays) is equivalent to national investment plus the current account surplus (or deficit).

Alternatively, the current account is equal to the difference between national savings and investment:

$$Sp + (T - Cg - rdB) - Ip - Ig = X - M + r*EFA \qquad (6)$$

Finally, let us divide private sector savings and investment into household (h) and business (or corporate) components (c). If we then take each component part in (6) and divide by GDP (Y) we end up with:

$$\frac{X - M + r*EFA}{Y} = \frac{Sc - Ic}{Y} + \frac{Sh - SI}{Y} + \frac{Sg - Ig}{Y} \tag{7}$$

$$(Sg = T - Cg - rdB = \text{government savings})$$

# 10 Trade Conflict

## INTRODUCTION

This chapter approaches the question of Japan's persistent current account surplus from yet another perspective. It focuses on institutional, cultural and historical factors believed to be instrumental in enabling Japan to sustain such a surplus. With regard to imports, Japan is alleged to have perpetuated informal and invisible barriers, while on the export front, aggressive and predatory tactics have seemingly been deployed. In other words, Japan's trade surplus is 'explained' by her 'under importing' and 'over exporting'.

A rift between Japan and the US has persisted for over a quarter of a century, tending to become more acute as bilateral imbalances widen, as happened in 1969–72, 1976–8 and from 1981 onwards. These three periods correspond to the three big 'waves' of US–Japan trade disputes, which by threatening to undermine relations between the world's two largest economic powers and by strengthening protectionist forces within the US, have cast a shadow over the entire international economy.

As noted in the previous chapter, Japan now has very few formal barriers to manufactured imports. That is beyond dispute. What in fact is in dispute, is whether in other respects Japan's trading system generates outcomes which would not normally be expected to result from impersonal market forces. In the discussion that follows, we shall mainly confine ourselves to manufactured goods. (Agricultural products are dealt with in Chapter 12.)

Essentially, we consider charges that Japan unofficially impedes import flows and the methods adopted to remedy the situation. Then we survey the controversy relating to Japan's rapid export penetration into the US market with special reference to American reactions and to cap it all, we question whether in the ongoing dispute with Japan, the US also is not beyond reproach.

## DOES JAPAN MAINTAIN INVISIBLE IMPORT BARRIERS?

The charge that Japan has in place a series of invisible import barriers may be evaluated in various ways. One could review anecdotal evidence or undertake a more disaggregated case-by-case study of particular restrictive practices in relation to specific commodity groups. Alternatively, one might point to or identify Japanese cultural, historical or structural characteristics which might impede imports. Finally, at the aggregate level and employing standard statistical procedures, one might try to gauge whether, allowing for Japan's unique structural-economic characteristics, the country's import to GDP ratios differ appreciably from those of other industrial countries.

In trying to disentangle Japan's web of import barriers we commence by considering some of the restrictive devices employed by official-dom, often in collaboration with local entrepreneurs.

### Product Standards, Testing and Certification Procedures

Until the early to mid 1980s, the Japanese system of setting standards for the importation of certain products was quite blatantly trade restrictive. Standards, determined by committees in which local but not overseas suppliers were represented, were frequently and of course deliberately drafted so as to curb imports. They were often not only arcanely worded but also frequently inaccessible [Christelow 1985/86]. Rulings relating to import licence applications were arbitrarily determined and long delays in certification were the order of the day. Below are some examples which illustrate the sort of obstacles with which foreign suppliers had to contend.

Instead of merely testing a sample of incoming products, an inspection of each individual unit was often insisted upon. In the case of cars, each vehicle had to be examined upon arrival in Japan. Fastidious officials were quick to find fault with even the smallest of items, such as the location of mirrors or door handles [Vogel 1979:241]. Considering that by the time the cars in question would have arrived in Japan, production would have already been standardized, this made it more costly for the foreign car manufacturer to incorporate any adjustments required by the Japanese.

Previous testings of imported pleasure boats afford a good instance of discrimination against outsiders. Foreign vessels were occasionally dropped from a given height to observe how they would fare under such conditions. Needless to say, this procedure, the cost of which had to be borne by the supplier, did not apply to local manufacturers.

A number of interesting cases appeared in the health industry. As soon as foreign kidney dialysis machines made inroads into the Japanese market, partly because of their ability to complete the procedure in a fraction of the time taken by local equipment, the Ministry of Health authorized payments for dialysis to be made on the basis of time actually expended [Vogel 1979:24]. The importation of pharmaceuticals had for many years been very problematic. At one stage, no drug could be imported until it had been tested within Japan itself, irrespective of how many responsible overseas authorities had vetted it.[1] Eventually, in 1982, the authorities relented and 'agreed to accept foreign drug-testing data so long as the tests were run on Japanese living abroad' [Vogel 1992:143]. Likewise, entry was denied to a widely acclaimed hepatitis blood test kit. When faced with a barrage of protests, officials later agreed to license it but only after intensive clinical trials were run on Japanese in Japan [144].

In a similar vein to the supposed need to make allowances for unique Japanese characteristics, it was seriously suggested that because snow in Japan was supposedly different to snow in Europe and North America, American and European ski equipment standards were inappropriate. Even more ludicrous was the claim by a former Japanese agriculture minister that Japanese beef consumption was naturally limited by the 'fact' that the Japanese had longer intestines than foreigners [145].

The arbitrariness of decision-making is highlighted by the experience of a US manufacturer of soft drink dispensers who had plied his wares in Japan over a ten year period. Suddenly, and for no given reason, product standards were changed in such a way that only one local producer was able to meet the new requirements [Cohen 1991:199].

The dispute over the importation of metal baseball bats from the US in the early 1980s has now become something of a classic. After some considerable delay, a US firm was finally given approval to sell aluminium bats in Japan. Shortly thereafter, safety standards were altered to preclude US goods. The matter was then referred to GATT and as a result, standards were again changed, allowing US firms access to the Japanese market. Then the rules were modified once again causing a rise in import costs. Ultimately, the conflict was resolved [Butler 1991:25].

Some barriers have been exceedingly petty. According to Woronoff, 'it was necessary to specify the number of fruit in canned fruit. Mineral water had to be heat pasteurized. To collect imported drugs, pharmaceutical companies had to present the personal health certificates of all their executives. When labels indicated both centimetres and inches or kilos and pounds, the latter had to be erased' [Woronoff 1983:66].

By the mid 1980s, Japan had liberalized her practices and accepted foreign tests and certification by importers. Accordingly, the country now more or less conforms to general international standards. However, although complaints have subsided, they have not altogether disappeared.

**Customs Practices**

Customs procedures were often cumbersome, irritating and on many an occasion, unashamedly manipulated to restrict imports. Classifications were frequently ambiguous and to the chagrin of suppliers, a product might arbitrarily be regraded in order to command a higher level of tariff duty or to be subject to more stringent entry requirements. For example, American apple butter was first classified as a jam but then later to protect local manufacturers, it was reclassified as a fruit paste puree, the imports of which were subject to quotas. Similarly, a type of potato chip which initially was designated as a processed good, was later declared to be a confectionery and liable to much higher tariffs. In this instance, despite the absence of proper and clearly defined appeal procedures, the American exporter in question challenged the reclassification. The appeal was eventually successful but as typically has been the case, the disputation was drawn out over such a lengthy period, that in the interim, a local manufacturer was able to enter the market and establish a strong foothold [Woronoff 1983:64].

Even when a product's classification and status had duly been approved, customs officials were ever on the lookout for the flimsiest of pretexts to bar it. On one occasion, a container of Philippine pineapples was rejected because in the documentation, a hyphen appeared between pine and apple [Cohen 1991:198]. Fortunately, significant abuses now rarely occur.

**Inadequate Protection of Intellectual Property Rights**

Conflicts over intellectual property rights involve disputes over alleged violations of patents, trade marks and copyrights. It has been contended that Japan's copyright laws have been inadequately enforced and that tardy registration procedures deprive would-be claimants of reasonable periods of exclusiveness. At stake have been billions of dollars of lost revenue on the part of US and other foreign companies.

The lack of protection of US intellectual property rights became a *cause célèbre* in the mid 1980s when IBM charged Fujitsu of illegally copying its software. Deferring to the American Arbitration Association, Fujitsu subsequently paid IBM $400 million in compensation. Not every US company received its just due. A large part of the problem lies in patent application procedures. Eighteen months after applications are filed, they are automatically made public, irrespective of whether they are approved or not. 'This means that an inventor cannot even exploit his invention as a trade secret in Japan if he or she fails to receive a patent' [Johnson 1990:111].

The glacial speed with which applications are processed constitutes a boon to local entrepreneurs, just as they are a major source of annoyance and inconvenience to foreign claimants. Take Texas Instruments as a case in point. In 1960 it filed an application for patent protection of the integrated circuit invented by Kilby and Royce. Twenty nine years later (in 1989), the patent was finally granted [Johnson 1990:111]. Similarly, Corning Glass had to wait ten years (from 1971) for the patent protection of its optical fibre technology. In the interim, local industrialists, with government backing and support, were able to develop their own know-how [Mastanduno 1992:734].

**Government Procurement Practices**

Government procurement practices, which have long vexed US manufacturers, have continued to constitute formidable import barriers. A tendency for government bodies to rely on single tenders or short bidding time frames, plus the imposition of complex qualification procedures and a general lack of transparency, has placed outsiders at a distinct disadvantage. To make matters worse, a 'catch 22' eligibility condition, which requires suppliers to have domestic market experience, has often been imposed [OECD 1989:90].

The Nippon Telephone and Telegraph Corporation (NTT), which for the most part has been a public enterprise,[2] and which has earned a reputation for excluding foreign bids, has been at the centre of controversy with the United States. Despite officially bowing to US pressure in 1981 to accept overseas tenders, contracts continued to be awarded to Japanese firms only. Further US protestations (lodged with GATT) did not bear fruit, for NTT stipulated that optical fibre supplies had to conform to a Japanese design. Not until 1989 was this exclusory provision withdrawn.

By resorting to various devices, the government tried to exclude US participation in the $8 billion Kansai International Airport Project in the late 1980s. This became the subject of a protracted and acrimonious exchange between the US and Japan. Similar exclusions occurred for work on the Osaka Airport and on the Tokyo bridge. Eventually in 1992 an agreement was reached that would presumably increase foreign firms' access to Japan's construction market.

Finally, when it came to Japan's computer industry, government procurement has been very protective. For example, when in 1988 the Japanese Ministry of Education announced its intention to purchase large amounts of personal computers for Japanese schools, by insisting that only Japanese type designs would be considered, foreign competitors were effectively precluded.

## Official Administrative Guidance

A good illustration of the use of administrative guidance to limit imports is provided by the Lions company. Towards the late 1980s, the company's president, Taiji Sato, sought to import a small quantity of gasoline from Singapore with the intention of letting it be sold at a limited number of gasoline stations at prices below those normally imposed by Japan's major petroleum refiners. Although MITI could not explicitly prohibit the firm's imports, it is believed to have applied tremendous behind the scene pressures. As a result, the bank financing the project withdrew its support 'and the discount gasoline proposal folded' [Cohen 1991:191].

## Collusive Practices

For a good case study highlighting attempts to crowd out foreign goods from the Japanese market, one need look no further than the soda ash industry. Soda ash represents a product in which the US has a clear and natural comparative advantage, for in the US where deposits are seemingly endless, extraction costs are a fraction of those in Japan. In the early 1980s, after being frustrated with the fact that their share of the Japanese market kept hovering around 2 per cent, the US industry complained that it was subject to restrictive practices, a charge hotly denied by the Japanese government. After strong prodding on the part of the US administration, the matter was formally investigated by the Japanese Fair Trade Commission (JFTC). In 1983 the JFTC did indeed officially substantiate US complaints but significantly, no fines or penalties were imposed on local producers for what amounted to a breach of Japanese law. Consequently, American exports did in fact rise (to around 17 per cent of the market) but collusive practices were suspected to have lingered. US suspicions were vindicated by a second JFTC investigation which in 1987 reported a continuation of 'problematic' practices. This enabled US exporters to increase their market shares to 22 per cent of the total.

Few believe that the activities of the soda ash cartel were unique. Similar incidents 'have been reported in many other sectors and undoubtedly play a major role in restricting imports from the United States and other foreign countries' [Wolff 1990:154].

## Cultural and Structural Barriers to Imports

It is widely thought that keiretsu associations and the structure of Japan's distribution system discriminate against imports. On the face of it, vertical keiretsu, in which large manufacturing plants source inputs from allied subcontractors, would seem to deprive foreign part producers of potential market outlets. There may be a grain of truth in this but when comparisons are made with US firms in which production is more integrated, that is, where more inputs are in-house supplied, it would seem that the 'problem' is two sided. In other words, many Japanese subcontractors would have limited prospects of exporting to the US, simply because there are fewer inter-firm transactions there for the type of items that they produce.

Turning to horizontal keiretsu, it is argued that a tendency to place orders with sister firms, constitutes a restrictive practice. Again, there is some substance here and this has partly been corroborated by Lawrence [1991], who reported that there has been a significant difference in import behaviour between enterprises that belonged to a keiretsu and those that did not. Lawrence's findings have been challenged by Saxonhouse [1991] (on both conceptual and methodological grounds). However, leaving aside the academic arguments, it ought to be stressed that intra-keiretsu fraternity tends to wear very thin when outside firms are significantly more price competitive. In addition, even among Japanese firms themselves, a large number have no keiretsu affiliation, while certain foreign corporations have actually been coopted. On balance, we would contend that while keiretsu groupings probably do contribute to a lessening of imports, the chances are that their influence is somewhat less than what foreign critics purport.

On turning to Japan's distribution system, it is easier to identify features which are likely to hinder import flows. For one thing, imported goods are overwhelmingly marketed by local distributors who take title to them abroad and who subject them to much higher markups than they do to locally made products. Referring to a 1985 Japanese government survey, Lawrence notes that for some products in particular, such as whisky and men's clothing, markups were double those on domestic goods and that 'the Japanese distribution system operates like a privately administered set of tariffs' [Lawrence 1991 a:30]. An abundance of small stores not willing to cross swords with their local mainstream sources and the willingness of many Japanese producers to take back unsold stock, pose additional problems to would-be foreign exporters. As if to compound matters, extremely high land acquisition costs present outside corporations with even more burdens in doing business in Japan.

Purely cultural import constraints are difficult to identify but few would doubt that they are operative and effective. The Japanese demonstrate that they are quite willing to buy foreign products that are either exotic, fashion or trend related (as in clothes and music) or clearly prestigious (like luxury cars or costly beverages). But when it comes to run of the mill consumer durables or capital goods, there seems to be a universal consensus, shared by private citizens and public officials alike, that it is beholden upon each and everyone to make every effort to buy locally made goods. Where no close substitutes are available, the bureaucracy often prevails upon buyers to defer, where possible, making their purchases until the local deficiency is made good. Such a situation is consistent with the occasional public relations campaign undertaken by leading politicians to mollify foreign anxieties. From time to time, a prime minister or someone with comparable standing, would make a flourish of wearing a French tie and or eating Belgian chocolates but we are yet to see them driving a small American sedan or opting for a US personal computer.

## Statistical Studies of Japan's Import Behaviour

As in many areas of economic inquiry, investigators have not reached unanimity as to whether statistically it is possible to demonstrate that Japan's actual import effort is consistent with an effective activation of invisible trade barriers.

There is full consensus that Japan's total and/or manufactured imports as a ratio to GDP is far lower than that of most other industrial countries. However, when allowance is made for specific country characteristics, like distance from major suppliers, dependence on foreign primary products, local demand, etc, Bergsten and Cline are quite emphatic 'that Japan's ratio of imports to GNP is almost precisely what would be expected for a country of its economic size'. Furthermore, they maintain that 'statistical tests incorporating transport costs and natural resource endowments confirm that Japan's import–GNP ratio is normal by international standards' [Bergsten and Cline 1987:124]. Similarly, Saxonhouse and Stern, on reviewing a number of different studies, concluded that although Japan's imports appear to be relatively low, 'there is no convincing case' that non-tariff barriers were responsible [Saxonhouse and Stern 1989:333].

Scanning much the same literature, Lincoln, by contrast, tends to be more agnostic. While accepting that some of Japan's relatively low import propensity 'can be passed off as the product of ordinary economic variables', he goes on to state that 'these variables fail to explain all the peculiarities' [Lincoln 1990:37]. In other words, something other than Japan's unusual structural characteristics seems to be at play, particularly when Japan's intra-industry trade record is considered.

**Intra-industry Trade**

Intra-industry trade occurs when a country simultaneously exports and imports products pertaining to the same industry. A country might, for example, be both an importer and exporter of say automobiles. With such a diversity of car products, there is scope for a country like France to sell Peugeots to say Germany, while at the same time buying Volkswagens from it. As trade barriers came tumbling down in Europe, as well as throughout the entire industrial world, the incidence of intra-industry trade has increased, so much so that today, most of advanced countries' manufactured trade is in the intra-industry category. For Western European and North American countries, intra-industry transactions constitute over 60 per cent of their trade flows. For Japan, it is less than 30 per cent. To the dismay of Europeans, Japan has been able to make inroads into their markets without them being able to reciprocate. 'In one year, 1976, Japan exported 400 000 cars to the EC while Europeans sent only 25 000 to Japan.' [Horsley and Buckley 1990:163]. On the other side of the Atlantic, economists bemoaned the fact that 'despite the reduction of formal barriers to entry to the Japanese market over the last decade, the basic patterns of Japanese trade have not altered' [Tyson and Zysman 1989:100].

Accepting that Japan's intra-industry trade is lower than that of other countries, Komiya and Irie proclaimed that 'low ratios do not constitute scientific evidence for the closeness of a country's domestic market' [Komiya and Irie 1990:88]. In their view, Japan's limited intra-industry trade can be explained by Japan's 'strong comparative advantage in manufactured industries', the absence of other industrialized countries with comparable income levels within geographic proximity to Japan, the fact that Japan's export products are highly differentiated and finally, the fact that European and US entrepreneurs are oblivious 'to the kinds of products and services wanted by Japanese consumers' [88]. Needless to say, all of these arguments are completely spurious. Japan is not the only country with a strong comparative advantage in manufactured goods. If distance from markets limits Japan's imports, why does this not apply to its exports? The existence of differentiated products is actually a major determinant of intra-industry trade and lastly, the notion that the composition of local demand is beyond the ken of foreigners would only be plausible if the Japanese consumption of goods and services was significantly at variance with that of other advanced countries.

Japan's low intra-industry trade involvement is of concern not only because it is so small but also because in contrast to its trading partners, it has actually shown signs of becoming still smaller [Lincoln 1990:48].

To conclude our discussion relating to general observations about Japan's low level of imports, we would like to draw to the reader's attention the well known and undisputed fact, that many of Japan's own export items are cheaper abroad than in Japan itself [Johnson 1990:110]. For this to endure, some mechanism must exist which prevents arbitrage. That is, the re-entry of exported goods by dealers wishing to take advantage of price differentials, is somehow stifled. That alone suggests that existence of some invisible import barrier.

## EFFORTS TO OPEN THE JAPANESE MARKET

Perceiving itself as the victim of Japan's seemingly closed door policies, the US has conducted a number of campaigns to obtain greater access to the Japanese market. Belief in the need to do so was reinforced by observations that the *formal* dismantling of Japanese import restrictions was largely due to foreign pressures. Internally, there had been virtually no lobbying by consumer interests, the bureaucracy was not committed to a free trade regime and in any event, in practically all instances, the easing of entry restrictions in relation to specific goods, was granted only after Japanese producers had become internationally competitive [Cohen 1991:196].

## The Super 301

An important component of the US's armoury in its trade war with Japan, has been legislation, which has authorized the administration to initiate retaliatory measures in response to unreasonable foreign trade behaviour. At first, the US Trade Act of 1974, or more specifically, section 301 of that act, constituted the primary legal basis for intervention. In 1988, the Omnibus Trade and Competitiveness Act was adopted, which contained the Super 301 clause. Super 301, which added more meat to the 301 clause of the 1974 law, empowered the US Trade Representative to name countries engaging in unfair trading practices (previously only issues relating to individual products could be cited). If, after 18 months of negotiations, a satisfactory resolution of US grievances is not obtained, the US government is authorized to impose import sanctions against products of the country or countries in question. In May 1989 the US designated Japan (as well as India and Brazil) as countries exercising unfair trade practices. Discussions with Japan, which centred on super computers, satellites and forest products, registered enough progress so as to obviate the need for further action. However, lest the reader concludes that US trade laws have been effective free trade weapons, Bayard and Elliott's 1992 paper should be borne in mind. There they reported that between 1975 and 1992, in only slightly over half of the 82 instances of the activation of clause 301 (of which 13 involved Japan) was there subsequently even a partial improvement in market access. Critics of the 301 procedures regard them as a violation of the spirit of GATT which called for multilateral consultations in the event of trade disputes. Instead, the US is seen as taking upon itself the role of sole prosecutor and judge [Ito 1992:376].

## Market-Oriented Sector Specific Talks

As a result of US frustration at the seeming inability of a number of its internationally-competitive industries to make any significant headway in the Japanese market, a series of US–Japan bilateral discussions was inaugurated. The deliberations, which commenced in 1985, were known as 'Market-Oriented Sector Specific Talks' (MOSS). They aimed at identifying invisible trade barriers covering four broad sectors and at procedures which the Japanese could adopt to eliminate or reduce them. The categories in question were: electronics, telecommunications, medical and forest products.

By and large, the talks led to some alterations of the ground rules for trading in Japan and to a semblance of acceptable monitoring arrangements to ensure Japanese compliance with agreements reached.

Within electronics, the Japanese, who were prevailed upon to provide more support for intellectual property rights, responded by affording a 50 year copyright protection period for computer software and a ten year safeguard for the original (US) chip design. In the medical field, Japan agreed to accept foreign clinical test data in considering pharmaceutical approvals. Some significant concessions were extracted in relation to telecommunications in the form of a reduction of technical standards for terminal equipment, a partial deregulation of cellular telephone services, an easing of rules defining how computers must interconnect within networks and an allowance was made for partial US entry into the satellite communication market. As for forest products, a modest quantity of tariff reductions was obtained.

Given some reluctance on the part of the Japanese to concede that significant invisible barriers actually do exist, the MOSS talks seem to have been quite successful. 'From 1985 to 1987, US exports to Japan in the four product categories combined, increased by 46.5 per cent, well above the 24.8 per cent in total US exports to Japan over the same period' [Lawrence 1991a:35].

## Structural Impediments Initiatives

In 1989, the US embarked on special bilateral negotiations with Japan under the broad rubric of the 'Structural Impediments Initiative'. These deliberations aimed to bring about changes in the structure of the Japanese economy which would result in a significant reduction of informal import barriers, and in a sense, they were a global extension of the MOSS talks. Essentially, the US prevailed upon Japan to rationalize her retail networks, to reduce the anti-competitive features of the keiretsu system by tightening the country's anti-trust laws, to increase public works expenditures (as a way of reducing savings and thus lowering Japan's trade balance) and to take measures to reduce land costs. A formal agreement was soon reached in which Japan undertook to meet the gist of the above mentioned demands. In return, and as if to emphasize that there was a two way give and take, the US promised to reduce its budget deficit, encourage more private savings and to allocate more resources to education and research. These US obligations were less binding than the Japanese ones.

Aside from the proceedings yielding little by way of tangible results, the whole process has been criticized as an unwarranted attempt on the part of the US to intrude upon Japanese internal affairs and as 'a grandiose public relations scheme to allow American politicians to blame the US trade deficit on the structure of Japanese society' [Bovard 1991:252].

## Demands for Quantitative Import Changes

After having made numerous and varied forays (including those mentioned above) in attempting to eliminate all Japanese trade obstacles, the US is still not in reach of what it would regard as a completely satisfactory outcome. Typically, the Americans complain of exhausting negotiations, which at the eleventh hour culminate in a handful of concessions yielded with seeming reluctance. To make matters worse, new and more ingenious import barriers seem to replace restrictions that were previously identified and ostensibly removed.

For the US administration, one of the last straws came in the guise of Motorola's attempts to gain freer access to Japan's prime market locations. Despite its complaints having officially been tabled on three separate occasions, Motorola, which normally commands at least 50 per cent of the world market for cellular telephones, has not been able to obtain more than a 1 percentage share of sales in the Tokyo-Nagoya region [*Nikkei Weekly* 28 Feb. 1994]. With this instance very much in mind, the US began to press Japan to accept specific import targets for certain products, rather than simply agreeing to further implementations of trade liberalization reforms.

Appropriately, Japan has rejected what has become known as the 'results-oriented approach', on the grounds that it would inflict damage both on Japan and on other trading partners. Had Japan acquiesced, it would have become necessary for its economy to have been subject to a greater degree of government control. MITI would have had to encourage the formation of buying cartels and in general, the sum of policies needed to guarantee the results in question, would have edged the economy back to a system which the Americans themselves regard as unacceptable [Lawrence 1991a:11]. From a third party's point of view, a commitment by Japan to ensure that imports from the US would rise at certain rates or would command a certain share of the Japanese market, would almost certainly be at the expense of US rivals.

In other words, there would very likely be some trade diversion from other sources to US suppliers. Hopefully, the 'results-oriented approach' will remain a non-starter.

## REACTIONS TO JAPAN'S EXPORT DRIVE

Within official US circles, a feeling has long since persisted that Japanese products have entered their country 'on the backs of a closed market and an unfair business system' [former US Secretary of Commerce P. Peterson, as quoted by Holbrooke 1991/2:45]. That such beliefs are based on distorted perceptions is unfortunately beside the point. In practice, what matters is that the widespread adherence to them encourages US administrators to be unduly obdurate in their dealings with Japanese counterparts.

### 'Voluntary' Textile Export Restraints

Ever since the Japanese economy began its postwar recovery and its exports began flowing in significant amounts, Japan encountered pressures, mainly but not exclusively from the US, to limit its overseas shipments. There is a touch of irony in all this, in that while Western countries have constantly pressurized Japan to minimize government intervention and to give market forces complete free rein, they never hesitate in insisting that the Japanese government ought to use every means at its disposal to curtail export volumes.

At first, textile exports constituted the main area of contention. Having been a significant textile exporter in the prewar years and taking advantage of its then abundant and cheap labour supplies, Japan in the 1950s, was swiftly able to regain ground in the US market. From a low level of two million square yards of cotton material shipped to the US in 1951, export volumes soared to 140 million square yards by 1955. Awed by the extraordinarily rapid rate at which Japanese exports rose, and noting that the prewar peak had already been exceeded in 1955 (when unemployment in the US was then widespread), American textile workers and management joined forces in pressing for import restrictions [Goto 1990:15]. The US government response was immediate and forceful, and on the heels of intensive negotiations, the Japanese agreed to impose 'voluntary' export restraints (VERs). The agreement which was first reached in December 1955, turned out to be insufficiently restrictive. This induced further discussions and by January

1957, the Japanese acceded to much more stringent controls. As a result of both this accord and a subsequent multilateral agreement, known as the Long-Term Arrangement Regarding International Trade in Cotton Textiles (LTA), 'Japanese cotton shipments to the United States were contained and the Japanese share of US imports of cotton products continued to decline' [18]. Next, Japan's synthetic textile exports became subject to Japan–US wrangles following a considerable increase of imported synthetics into the US. Fulfilling an election campaign promise, President Nixon, in October 1971, secured Japanese acquiescence to limit exports involving 18 different fabrics and clothing categories. The American Textile Manufacturers Institute claimed that imports 'were putting many of the blacks among their employees out of work' [Johnson 1982:285]. However, Cohen points out that imports averaged only 5.1 per cent of all the US consumption of synthetic textiles products in 1969–70 and that Japan accounted for less than one-third of the import bill, or 'less than 2 per cent of the total value of the US market for man made textiles!' [Cohen 1991:21]

**Restrictions in Steel Exports**

A dispute over steel exports erupted in the latter half of the 1960s, when cheaper Japanese products posed a threat to US producers. After some initial pressure, Japan in 1966, began to lessen steel export sales. Even though in 1969 Japan tightened its voluntary steel export restraint (VER), the US was not placated. In the acrimonious exchanges that followed, Japan attempted to parry American demands for even more limitations. Faced with prospects of the US actually imposing harsh steel import quotas, Japan ultimately capitulated and a third VER came into force between 1972 and 1974. The matter did not rest there, for in January 1976 the US Trade Commission determined that imports of speciality steel posed a serious injury to the domestic industry and called for the installation of a five year import quota. Japan's reluctant willingness to retard exports over a three year period, forestalled the adoption of the Trade Commission's recommendations.

**Television VERs**

No sooner had the textile dispute run its course than the next major controversy, centring around television sets, emerged. (Although the steel issue was a highly contested one, compared with television, it was less dramatic.) From a base of 2000 Japanese television sets delivered to the US in 1962, export numbers raced to 700 000 in 1964 and then to 4 million by 1971 [Goto 1990:27]. Five years down the track (in 1976), Japanese colour TV sets commanded 40 per cent of the US market. In the intervening period, 'more than 60 000 jobs were lost in the US colour TV industry, and the number of manufacturers dwindled from twenty to five' [Cohen 1991:29]. Cohen believes that the Japanese TV export onslaught was deliberately engineered and that it involved large-scale dumping and price collusion [30].[3] Not surprisingly, US protectionist forces were activated and in July 1977, an understanding was reached in the framework of the Orderly Market Agreement (OMA), whereby Japan undertook to limit colour television set exports to less than 1.75 million units for the next three years. Abandoning the interests of TV workers, the US producers canvassed to clamp down only on Japanese goods and not on TV imports in general. The reason being that they themselves were moving offshore to countries like Korea and Taiwan. Ultimately, Japanese firms were partially able to defend their market positions by establishing production facilities in the US itself.

**Automobile Export Limitations**

Following television sets, Japanese automobiles were placed high on the US administration's negotiating agenda. The issue reached boiling point in 1980 when output in the US automobile industry plunged to its lowest level since 1962, the work force contracted by 25 per cent and one of the 'Big Three', namely Chrysler, was on the verge of bankruptcy. As the share of Japanese cars in the US market grew from 8.5 per cent in 1974 to 22.3 per cent in 1980 [Cohen 1991:35], Japan's successful performance was readily identified by the US automobile makers, and by protectionist forces at large, as the prime cause of the American industry's distress. Deferring to such views and unprecedentedly not paying heed to the International Trade Commission's ruling that industrial mismanagement and not imports were at the source of the problem, President Reagan sought to curb the inflow of Japanese cars. Realizing that by fair means or foul, the US would implement import restrictions, the Japanese saved Reagan the ideological embarrassment of explicitly intervening against market forces, by offering, in May 1981, to 'voluntarily' restrain its car exports. A ceiling of 1.68 million vehicles was set for 1981. Over the next two years, the ceiling was to rise by 16.5 per cent of the growth of the US car market. In time, the VER (at 2.3 million cars) was extended to March 1985 and although the US then let it be known that it was not interested in subsequent restrictions, the Japanese took it upon themselves to keep the VER in force, then making it truly voluntary. In 1992 MITI reduced the VER quota from 2.3 to 1.65 automobiles, enforcing the same limit again in 1993.

Although the VER on cars did indeed stem Japanese exports to the US, it had a number of unintended and unforseen consequences which in the long run did not bode well for US automobile producers and consumers alike. To some extent, the partial Japanese withdrawal from the US market paved the way for a smoother entry by Korean manufacturers who produced cars which were compact and fuel efficient, and which were thus comparable to Japanese models. Of greater moment, by reducing supply, the VER enabled Japanese (and US) producers to command higher prices than would otherwise have been the case had normal market forces held sway. To maximize revenue per exported vehicle, the Japanese brought about improvements in quality and tilted sales towards the prestigious luxury end of the market. In both cases, a higher premium was forthcoming. Excess profits were amassed and these were 'ploughed back into investment in new plants, equipment, and research and development, making the Japanese firms even more formidable' [Bergsten and Noland 1933:106]. Finally, Japanese car producers engaged their US competitors in a flanked assault by establishing production facilities within the US.

## Semiconductors

The most recent of the *major* export conflicts has related to semiconductors. Despite the fact that the US was a pioneer in the semiconductor industry and that in the early 1960s, it was the first to invent and distribute integrated circuits, by the late 1970s, it was subject to devastating Japanese competition. Thanks in part to government research sponsorship, the availability of cheap loan finance and to import protection, the Japanese semiconductor industry (explicitly targeted by MITI) made significant inroads into the US market. In the field of memory chips, imported Japanese products constituted close to 90 per cent of total 1986 US sales. Unable to match Japanese price discounts, six of the nine US companies that produced memory chips forsook the product.

Not unexpectedly, in June 1985, the US Semiconductor Industry Association filed a petition with the US government complaining of restricted access to the Japanese market and of widespread dumping on the part of Japanese firms within the US, a practice at variance with clause 301 of the 1974 Trade Act [Okuno-Fujiwara 1991:287]. It was pointed out that while US firms were able to achieve more than 60 per cent of third country purchases, they were rarely able to attain more than a 10 per cent share in Japan. That such an anomaly persisted was taken as proof that, despite undertakings to the contrary, foreign entry into the Japanese market was still heavily proscribed. In what amounted to an unusual step, in December 1985, the US government itself filed a dumping suit against Japanese producers. Then in May 1986, the International Trade Commission ruled that dumping had indeed occurred and that anti-dumping duties could legitimately be imposed. Within another two months, Japan reached an understanding with the US.

In essence, Japan agreed to a procedure which would maintain explicit semiconductor floor prices in the US as well as third party countries (to avoid indirect dumping). It also undertook to increase imports from the US to enable US market shares to reach a 20 per cent level. The first commitment turned out to be a two-edged sword, for by guaranteeing high prices to all producers, profits of the efficient Japanese firms were augmented. Furthermore, since the Japanese were free to charge lower prices in their home market, 'the agreement helped Japanese manufacturers that use memory chips by reducing the competitiveness of US, European, and other memory chip users' [Baldwin 1994:131]. Not surprisingly, when the agreement was renewed in 1991, 'the floor prices were abandoned due mostly to strong opposition by US users of memory chips' [131]. As for the entry of US products into Japan, a 20 per cent market share was eventually accomplished by the end of 1992.

At this point, we have covered almost all of the major US–Japan trade disputes. Among others that could have been dealt with are those relating to bicycles, nuts and bolts, flatware, baseball gloves, ceramics and machine tools. Also in 1995 the Americans, by threatening to impose prohibitive tariffs on Japanese luxury cars, managed to persuade the Japanese to commit themselves to increase their purchases of imported spare car parts. However, the reader has been presented with sufficient examples to appreciate the underlying concerns that have propelled the US into seeking redress from its Japanese trading partner. What remains to be done is for us to stress that the US has not acted alone in trying to dam the flood of Japanese exports. The European Community has imposed 27 different voluntary export restraints against Japanese products such as passenger cars, trucks, steel, machine tools, video tape recorders, ball bearings, cotton fabrics and pottery [Turner 1991:22].

## HAS THE US BEEN CULPABLE?

In its ongoing trade conflict with Japan, the US has tended to project itself as an innocent victim seeking redress from a belligerent trading partner which refuses to comply with internationally accepted trade norms and with impersonal market forces. The question that we now pose is: to what extent has the US been above board? A full and precise answer is not provided but what is abundantly clear is that the Japanese could readily and justifiably compile a list of charges against the US which would not easily be rebuffed. As is well known, 'the United States maintains formal quotas in a number of agricultural products including dairy products, sugar, peanuts and cotton' [Bergsten and Noland 1993:70]. Apart from specific restraints directed against Japan, 'the United States also maintains a variety of sanitary regulations, standards, testing and certification requirements, and other practices that could be classified as non-tariff barriers' [70]. As Cohen reminds us, 'liberal import policies seldom are practiced beyond the point where foreign competition causes disruption', and that 'the uncertainties and imprecision of US trade and regulatory law are viewed in Japan as de facto trade barriers' [Cohen 1991:176–7].

The US does not hesitate to activate legislation against countries accused of dumping or resorting to other unfair trade practices. In determining whether in fact the practice of dumping can be established, the US occasionally resorts to procedures which blatantly favour its position. For example, in considering export and home prices, comparisons are sometimes made between goods which are not strictly identical in quality or in other attributes [Bovard 1991:119]. Alternatively, problems may arise in concluding whether or not a certain foreign enterprise is the beneficiary of government assistance. The US criteria for imposing countervailing duties on foreign products thought to be receiving foreign subsidies are both broad and vague. In short, the US is not an innocent bystander.

## SUMMARY

### Japan's Restriction of Imports

• In the past a variety of practices was devised to restrict imports, some of which have more or less been abandoned while others still persist. These include: the setting of unreasonable product standards and certification procedures, obstructionist customs inspections, inadequate protection of intellectual property rights (which deprived Western producers of potentially large sales within the Japanese market), the favouring of local suppliers in government procurements, the use of administrative guidance, collusion among Japanese firms against outsiders and the manipulation of cultural traits to ward off imports.

- Statistical studies which attempt to throw light on Japan's import behaviour are couched in controversy. Some point to objective factors (like Japan's dependence on primary product imports) as explaining Japan's low manufactured import bill. Others are more agnostic, citing Japan's small and decreasing involvement in intra-industry trade as grounds for suspicion.

## Efforts to Open the Japanese Market

- Super 301 (1988) which enables the US to name a country employing 'unfair' trading practices and to authorize sanctions against its products.
- Market Oriented Sector Specific talks (MOSS) (1985) aimed to identify invisible Japanese trade barriers in electronics, telecommunication, medical and forest products and to persuade Japan to eliminate them.
- Structural Impediments Initiatives (SII) (1989) aimed to induce structural changes in the Japanese economy (a sort of global MOSS) in the interests of reducing informal import barriers.
- Demands for quantitative import changes. A results oriented approach which is currently being applied (for example 1995 US car part exports to Japan) and which concerns third party countries concerned that Japan might respond at their expense.

## US Reaction to Japan's Export Drive

- Voluntary export restraints imposed on textiles (1955), steel (1972), television sets (1977), automobiles (1981) and semiconductors (1986).

## US Culpability

- The US is also at fault in that it maintains formal quotas on agricultural imports, defines dumping in terms that favour its case and it indulges in exporting subsidized wheat at the expense of traditional wheat exporters.

# 11 Japan's Foreign Direct Investment

## INTRODUCTION

As a foreign investor, Japan's performance has been extraordinary. From a situation of near total insignificance in the late 1940s, it laid claim in the late 1980s to around 17 per cent of the world's stock of foreign direct investment (FDI). By 1989 it was the single largest current FDI source, with outflows amounting to $67 billion compared with $40 billion from the US and $35 billion from the UK [Balasubramanyam and Greenaway 1992:180].

The involvement of Japanese firms in the world economy has had important consequences for both Japan and host countries alike. Within Japan it certainly is a subject of immense interest, where it is seen as either a threat to or saviour of the country's industrial competitiveness.

To provide the reader with the necessary background and understanding of such a key aspect of Japanese economic activity, this chapter is divided into three sections. In the first section we survey the postwar growth of Japan's foreign direct investment (FDI) in Asia, the US and Europe (where 78 per cent of the total is placed); section two assesses the general impacts of Japan's FDI and in section three we briefly take up the issue of FDI inflows into Japan itself.

## 1 JAPAN'S FDI AND ITS CAUSES

### Global Investment Trends: An Overview

At the conclusion of World War II, Japan forfeited all her overseas held assets so that on re-entering the foreign investment arena it had to start from scratch. This largely explains why even nowadays, Japan relies relatively less on foreign investment than on direct exports to maintain overseas sales. (Its ratio of export to overseas subsidiary sales, though declining from 4.3 in 1977 to 1.64 in 1988, is still higher than that of the US or UK (0.15 and 0.20 in 1988.) [Tejima 1993:45]

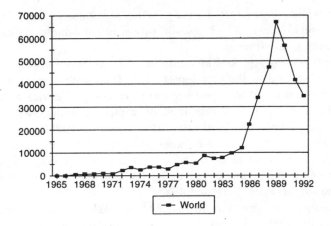

*Figure* 11.1    Japanese Direct Investment (in Million US Dollars)

The flow of postwar Japanese foreign direct investments recommenced in 1951 but little headway was made until the end of the 1960s. Foreign exchange controls which were tightly enforced throughout the 1950s and most of the 1960s, an internal investment boom and a 'lack of experience in undertaking FDI as well as a lack of firm-specific assets such as technology and management know-how', all combined in limiting Japanese FDI involvement [Urata (b) 1993:274].

After 1965, total investment flows began to gather momentum, rising from $227 million in 1966 to a peak of $3494 million by 1973 (see Table 11.1). This resulted from Japan's balance of payments moving into surplus in 1965, a total lifting of foreign investment restrictions in 1971, a 14 per cent yen appreciation in 1973, newly introduced pollution controls (which encouraged offshore production), an increased availability of funds at lower interest rates, as well as a bout of investment promoting legislation in Asia.[1] At the same time, in response to increasing wage costs and a lessening of Japan's ability to compete in certain labour intensive industries, such as textiles, interest increasingly began to be shown in establishing plants for export purposes in Asian newly industrializing countries (NICs).

With the advent of the 1973 oil crisis, the investment boom ended. Internally, the oil shock, which curbed business activity, resulted in large liquidity shortfalls and current account deficits. While externally, the world economy was in a state of recession. In Asia in particular, conditions favouring Japanese FDI worsened. Some countries, such as Indonesia and Thailand, became more overtly hostile towards Japanese capital, while others adopted more exacting regulations concerning local equity, employment and production ratios, all of which tended to inhibit foreign investments.

Capital outflows picked up again in 1978 as Japan coped with the energy crisis and as the yen appreciated. Then with a reversal of the value of the yen and with problems in developing countries associated with the debt crisis, FDI remained on a plateau until 1981, when it was nearly double the 1980 rate. After receding slightly in 1982, it rose steadily until 1985 and between 1986 and 1989, it surged ahead, rising by a factor of close to three. In the latter interval, cumulative investments totalled more than twice the nominal sum of all investments made between 1951 and 1985.

A number of elements contributed to the high investment rates recorded in the 1980s. Starting from a fairly modest surplus of $4.3 billion in 1981 (compared with a deficit of $8.2 billion the year before) the current account rose constantly until 1987 to reach $87 billion. Such a trend reflected a high degree of saving relative to internal investment which partly resulted from a decline in the country's GDP growth rate and the consequent fall in local investment opportunities. At the same time, the 1980 deregulation of exchange controls paved the way for banks, financial security companies and institutional investors such as life insurance firms to invest abroad. In the latter half of the 1980s, their ability to do so was greatly augmented by the yen appreciating (*vis-à-vis* the dollar) from 238 in 1985 to 168 in 1986, 144 in 1987 and 128 in 1988. That is, between 1985 and 1987, the yen appreciated by 46 per cent. The yen appreciation not only extended the means to invest but considering that it adversely affected exports, it also provided an FDI incentive.[2]

After having increased consistently since 1983, Japan's foreign investment growth was negative in 1990, 1991 and 1992. The fallback can be attributed to the bursting of the 'bubble' at the end of 1989, the prior implementation of major production projects in the US relating to steel and automobiles and to a more pessimistic prognosis regarding ongoing economic prospects throughout the developed world. Within both the US and Europe there was a slump in real estate markets and in general, affiliates in America were yielding poor returns.

When in the postwar period Japan first engaged in FDIs, most were related to the manufacturing sector (to overcome Asian trade barriers) and to primary products (to obtain a secure source of raw material inputs). Accordingly, between 1951 and 1960, the Third World absorbed 68 per cent of total investments. By 1986–90, the combined share of manufactured and primary resource investments fell to 27 per cent (from 78 per cent in 1951–60) and North America and Europe attracted the same proportion as the Third World once had, that is 68 per cent.[3]

## Investment in Asia

For all intents and purposes, the term 'Asia' within the framework of this chapter refers to the countries of Taiwan, South Korea (henceforth Korea), Hong Kong, Singapore, Malaysia, Indonesia, Thailand, the Philippines and China.

### Investment Trends and Country and Sectoral Breakdowns

Until the mid 1980s, the general pattern of Japan's FDI in Asia more or less conformed to overall trends, for in the main, the factors that influenced total FDIs were also instrumental in influencing those in Asia. Until then, Asia's share of Japan's FDI stood at around the 25 per cent mark but from the mid 1980s with advanced countries attracting most of the FDI increases, its share fell to 12 per cent.

The relative importance of individual countries as destinations of Japanese FDI is shown in Table 11.1, where it can be noted that Indonesia (except for the period 1986–90) has been the most significant destination. Lately, Malaysia, Singapore, Thailand, China and Hong Kong have all be vying for second place.

Turning our attention to the sectoral composition of Japan's Asian investments (indicated in Table 11.2), the manufacturing sector has consistently been the largest. In earlier years, mining also carried much weight but from the late 1970s onwards, the service sector (including real estate, commerce and finance) has attracted increasing interest and currently it accounts for around half of all FDIs.

In earlier years, textiles constituted the single largest group of Japanese Asian manufacturing investments. Even by 1973, 39 per cent of all Japanese direct investment in Asia went into textiles. In the late 1970s, the emphasis changed towards steel, non-ferrous metals and chemicals, reflecting increasing costs of anti-pollution measures which made it less economical to import raw materials for processing locally. After 1980, chemicals continued to be in the limelight but attention shifted to transport and electrical machinery, with electronics now in the foreground. See Table 11.3.

228                    *The Japanese Economy*

*Table* 11.1   Japanese FDI Destinations (Percentage Breakdown)

| Period | Ind | Mal | Phil | Sing | Thai | Chin | H.K. | Kor | Tai |
|--------|-----|-----|------|------|------|------|------|-----|-----|
| 51–73 | 36 | 9 | 6 | 8 | 7 | 0 | 10 | 18 | 6 |
| 82–85 | 26 | 7 | 3 | 18 | 5 | 4 | 25 | 7 | 5 |
| 86–90 | 11 | 8 | 2 | 16 | 12 | 9 | 25 | 9 | 8 |
| 91–92 | 23 | 13 | 3 | 11 | 12 | 14 | 14 | 4 | 6 |

*Source*: Ministry of Finance. Ind = Indonesia, Mal = Malaysia, Phil = Philippines, Sing = Singapore, Thai = Thailand, Chin = China, H.K. = Hong Kong, Kor = Korea, Tai = Taiwan

*Table* 11.2   Japanese Sectoral Investment in Asia (Percentage Composition)

| Industry | 1951–76 | 1977–86 | 1987–92 |
|----------|---------|---------|---------|
| Manufacturing | 43.4 | 36.7 | 44 |
| Agriculture | 3.0 | 1.1 | 0 |
| Mining | 36.6 | 27.5 | 4 |
| Construction | 0.5 | 1.4 | 2 |
| Commerce | 3.1 | 6.7 | 11 |
| Finance | 3.2 | 5.3 | 13 |
| Branch offices | 0.9 | 1.6 | 2 |
| Other | 9.5 | 19.5 | 24 |

*Sources*: Morris-Suzuki 1991, Table 7.2 and Ministry of Finance sources. Other includes services, real estate and transport. Agriculture includes fisheries and forestry.

*Table* 11.3   Japanese Manufacturing FDI to Asia. Industry Composition (Percentages)

| Industry | 1951–70 | 1976–80 | 1986–92 |
|----------|---------|---------|---------|
| Foodstuffs | 07 | 02 | 07 |
| Textiles | 33 | 10 | 07 |
| Wood and Pulp | 05 | 02 | 03 |
| Chemicals | 06 | 16 | 18 |
| Metals | 11 | 39 | 09 |
| Machinery | 05 | 06 | 09 |
| Electrical goods | 14 | 08 | 27 |
| Transport | 04 | 06 | 08 |
| Other | 15 | 11 | 12 |

*Source*: Ministry of Finance–Monthly Financial Reports

*Some Characteristics of Japanese Manufacturing Enterprise in Asia*

A large proportion (probably in the 40–50 per cent range) of Japanese production plants in Asia are fairly small scale. This is partially explained in terms of small input suppliers moving abroad in unison with or shortly after their parent firms did so, as well those moving independently and on their own initiative.

By virtue of the expansion during the 1980s of assembly plants in electrical, general machinery and transport industries, the demand for local parts increased. As indigenous suppliers were generally incapable of meeting all of the extra demand, small and medium sized Japanese companies filled the gap. They were driven to establish an Asian presence rather than engage in directly exporting from Japan because of host country local content policies and because of the high value of the yen.

The other distinguishing attribute of Japanese firms in Asia is that joint ventures between indigenous and Japanese partners (which have been encouraged by host country regimes) are more common in Asia than in North America and Europe. In 1993 for example, an Export-Import Bank Survey disclosed that 58.8 per cent of Japanese concerns in ASEAN countries were joint ventures, which compares with figures of 26.3 per cent for North America and 31.5 for Europe [Tejima 1994:24].

*Possible Causes of Japanese Direct Manufacturing Investments in Asia*

Historically, the Asian region has constituted a large market for Japan's exports and in the prewar years, most of its foreign investments were sited there. Comparing American and Japanese early investment experiences, it seems that both countries directed their funds 'disproportionably to geographically nearby areas' [Mira Wilkins as quoted by Encarnation 1992:166]. After the war, Japan's exports (such as textiles) were predominantly labour intensive and the Asian market was of importance to them. As one Asian country after another moved to impose import restrictions, Japanese producers were compelled to enter the region as producers of products they had previously been exporting. Thus, at first the circumvention of trade barriers was the major motive for Asian FDIs in manufacturing. (It is of course axiomatic that Japanese firms were confident that they possessed sufficient firm-specific assets to override the disadvantages associated with the establishment of foreign based factories.)

Later, relative changes in production costs encouraged Japanese firms to shift to Asia. For example, on the basis of a 1989 survey of small and medium Japanese firms, low ASEAN wage costs were cited by 61 per cent of respondents as a factor of importance to them in having committed themselves to the region. Access to the ASEAN market was mentioned by 40 per cent. Of those *contemplating* investing, 58 per cent were struck by the region's minimal wage rates but the second most important consideration was the intention of shipping foreign made products to Japan [Tokunaga (a) 1992:17]. The latter factor reflects structural changes that were underway in the Japanese economy in which some labour intensive industries were being shed to make way for knowledge intensive ones. In any event, it is still consistent with cheap Asian labour being an important consideration. Setting Japanese 1986 average real wage as being equal to 100, the Bank of Japan (1994) reports comparable measures for Asian countries. They were: Korea 21.3; Taiwan 23.5; Hong Kong 21.8; Singapore 21.7; Philippines 5.4; Indonesia 4.5; Malaysia 8.6 and Thailand 7.0 [45]. The rates given for most ASEAN countries seem extremely low but even if they were in fact three to four times greater, they would still be far lower than the Japanese average.

The entry of Japanese manufacturers to Asia was also prompted by Japan–US trade conflicts. As Japanese textiles and other products such as electronic goods became subject to import quotas, shifting to Asia presented one way of sidestepping such barriers. In 1974 for instance, Japanese textile and electronic subsidiaries operating in Asia exported over half of their output (in roughly equal measures) to Japan and to other countries, of which the US was the main one [Encarnation 1992:170].

Finally, Asian countries themselves have encouraged foreign investment by offering a range of inducements. These have included the establishment of export processing zones which provide foreign firms with facilities, such as good air and sea ports, power, roads, telecommunications, factory and warehouse space and so on and often at subsidized rates. In addition, the investors are offered certain tax concessions, exemptions from many labour regulations and a minimum of bureaucratic interference. Such enticements have undoubtedly played an important role in the selection by Japanese investors of specific destination countries and regions.

**FDI in the United States**

Prior to 1978, FDI in the US tended to fluctuate quite sharply, with the share of Japanese FDI going to the US moving from say 31.3 per cent in 1966 to 10.4 per cent in 1970 and then to 25.2 per cent a year later and so on. After rising to an average share of 31.5 per cent in the early 1980s, investments took off in the second half of the decade from $5.4 billion in 1985 to $10.2 billion in 1986 and then to $32.5 billion in 1989 when the US commanded 48.2 per cent of Japan's overall FDI. In 1990 and thereafter, mainly as a result of the fall in Japan's stock and land prices, FDIs were drastically curtailed.

*The Sectoral Composition of Japanese FDIs in the US*

Before the Second World War, virtually all of Japan's FDI to the US was undertaken by general trading companies in the interests of promoting US–Japan trade. After the war, general trading companies and financial institutions were the first to restore their investment links and by the mid 1970s, foreign investment trade activities were still predominant. The sectoral composition of Japan's FDIs in the US (indicated in Table 11.4) is characterized by a very high concentration in commerce, banking, finance and real estate, which places the Japanese at odds with European and Canadian investors, who had been more inclined to favour manufacturing.

The emphasis on commerce reflects an earlier preference to export from Japan rather than to cater for the American market by supplying locally produced goods. In that light, a strong interest was developed in the service sector and in real estate to help foster trade but in any case, an appreciation of the enhanced role of services in industrial society also came into play. Since many services cannot be traded internationally, Japan extended its FDIs in this field to obtain an increasing stake in so buoyant an area [see Emmott 1992:39].

With regard to manufacturing, 93 per cent of investments accumulated up to 1989 were undertaken in the years 1981–9. That is, Japan only recently seriously began manufacturing within the US. Of the industries in question, electrical machinery has been the leading one followed by transport equipment, with the two sectors combined receiving 41 per cent of the total (see Table 11.5). As would be expected, interest in the labour intensive industries, such as textiles, has been minimal. The food investments that were undertaken were in part stimulated by the US in the early 1970s extending its fishing rights to 200

Table 11.4 Sectoral Composition of FDIs into the US (1951–89)

| Sector | Sector Share (in Percentages) |
|---|---|
| Manufacturing | 30.0 |
| Construction | 1.0 |
| Commerce | 13.1 |
| Finance and Insurance | 15.9 |
| Services | 11.2 |
| Transportation | 0.4 |
| Real estate | 23.1 |
| Resources | 1.8 |
| Others | 3.5 |

Source: Ministry of Finance

Table 11.5 The Commodity Composition of FDIs in Manufacturing (1951–89)

| Industry | Share of Total (in Percentages) |
|---|---|
| Foods | 5.0 |
| Textiles | 2.0 |
| Wood | 2.0 |
| Chemicals | 11.0 |
| Iron and Metals | 11.0 |
| Machinery | 10.0 |
| Electrical machinery | 27.0 |
| Transportation equipment | 14.0 |
| Others | 18.0 |

Source: Ministry of Finance

miles off its coastline. To maintain direct access to US fish, the Japanese acquired a number of American processors. Later some forays were also made into grains, beef, fruit and wine [Emmott 1992:25].

## Automobile Investments

The Japanese automobile industry has invested in the US on a grand scale. Currently, there are eight major Japanese transplant assembly facilities in the US (three in Canada) as well as some 270 transplant automotive parts suppliers [Florida and Kenney 1991:91]. Honda was the first to produce in the US, commencing in 1982, with Nissan and NUMMI starting in 1983 and 1984 respectively. By 1989, all other incumbents were in place. The projected production capacity of all US based plants is 2.2 million vehicles employing 30 000 workers. Most firms deliberately selected rural sites free of automobile workers, 'in a well-defined "transplant corridor" which drifts slightly south of the more traditional North American auto belt' [93]. Of the eight assemblers, four are non-unionized. One unionized firm, NUMMI (a joint Toyota-GM venture), which occupies an old GM plant, had granted hiring preference to ex-GM workers. In all plants, workers are remunerated at rates comparable to those offered by the 'Big Three' American corporations. Staff have generally been amenable to flexible labour deployments, even the unionized ones, and absenteeism has been much lower than in the purely American owned corporations. For example, in Freemont, California, when working solely for GM, the staff had an absenteeism ratio of 20 per cent. Later, when much the same body of workers began serving in the NUMMI plant, the absenteeism ratio declined to 2 per cent [Goto 1990:177].

Apart from possessing various ownership-specific advantages, such as a reputation for quality, ingenious production process technology and so on, the competitiveness of Japanese firms is also derived from specific features embedded within the Japanese economy. One of these is the ready availability of skilful and flexible small subcontractors capable of supplying the input needs of large corporations both speedily and comparatively cheaply. Many an observer had concluded that in the absence of these facilities, Japanese automobile producers would, when operating in the US and Europe, be hard pressed to maintain an edge over native firms.

On finding that in the main, indigenous part suppliers could not be counted on to comply with 'just-in-time' delivery schedules or to meet Japanese quality requirements, traditional suppliers were induced to migrate to the US. Three categories of Japanese suppliers are now in place. Those that provide original inputs, those that manufacture replacement parts for vehicles imported from Japan and those that make capital goods demanded by assemblers [Goto 1990:96].

Once reliable component manufacturers were at hand, Japanese automobile firms were able to tackle the problem of persuading American workers to comply with the best of Japanese work practices. Job classifications have been kept to a minimum, ranging from just two at Mazda to four at Nissan and NUMMI compared with over 90 at the Big Three. Work teams are now the norm, as are worker rotations, decentralized decision making and worker quality control circles [Goto 1990:98]. Partly as a result, by the late 1980s, the productivity levels of transplants compared favourably with those of Japanese based plants

and of course, significantly better than the Big Three [Goto 1990:101].
The Japanese plants are now in the process of becoming ever more
autonomous by setting up their own American based R&D facilities
and subsidiary managers are independently responding to and planning for the dictates of the local market.

*Some General Observations Regarding Japanese Subsidiaries Within
the US*

In the mid 1980s, 76.5 per cent of Japanese investment projects in the
US incurred costs of less than $10 million and 81.9 per cent employed
less than 300 hundred people, which means that most Japanese affiliates have been moderately small in scale. Profit rates obtained by Japanese
manufacturing subsidiaries in North America have generally been less
than those enjoyed by Japanese firms in Asia. In 1981 for example,
only 63.2 per cent of the Japanese companies situated in North America
attained a positive current surplus compared with 72.2 per cent in Asia.
Such a difference is probable due to a larger proportion of new operations in North America, the existence of less government preferential
measures and higher production costs. All such factors notwithstanding, Japanese firms have not performed as well as other foreign rivals
in the US. In 1988 while the average rate of return of Japanese subsidiaries in the US manufacturing sector was −0.5 per cent, the overall foreign company average rate of return was 6.6 per cent [Takaoka
1991:74].

At first, most Japanese subsidiaries in the US preferred to establish
greenfield plants or to enlarge their own pre-existing ones. However,
in the latter half of the 1980s, when Japanese liquidity was extremely
high and the yen very strong, acquisitions became quite common. Many
of which, like Sony's adventure into Hollywood, turned out to be of
dubious economic worth.

*Factors Affecting Japanese Manufacturing FDI in the US*

Very often, firms first establish themselves as exporters to specific
regions before undertaking foreign investment to support and expand
their market positions there. This has seemingly been the case for Japanese
firms entering the US [see Caves 1993:284].

However, increased US import barriers unquestionably precipitated
a massive onrush of Japanese manufacturing FDI in the period 1978–
84, during which time the ratio of manufacturing FDI to Japan's total
US investments rose from 16.1 per cent to 49.6 per cent. After 1978,

in response to trade restricting threats, Japanese semiconductor producers set up a succession of manufacturing bases in the US. Likewise, five producers of colour TVs began US operations within two years of the commencement of the 1977 colour TV voluntary export restraint (VER) agreement. With regard to automobiles, in 1981, in response to strong US pressure Japan agreed to a VER in automobiles, limiting exports to 1 680 000 vehicles per annum for the next three years.[4] Up to then, almost all Japanese automobile manufacturers preferred to produce vehicles destined for the US in Japan. Such a preference reflected an absence of cost advantages from siting production in the US. In fact, in talks with MITI in April 1980, Toyota and Nissan spokesmen rejected suggestions that their firms produce in the US on the grounds that such investments were unwarranted 'in a market characterized by high relative wages and poor labor-management relations, and where prevailing forecasts predicted that US automakers would themselves begin compact-car production' [Encarnation 1992:130]. Despite their reservations, with trade restrictions soon in force, automobile companies realized that future access to the US market could only be assured through the establishment of local production plants. Their decisions to do so were heartily endorsed by the US automobile industry which assumed 'that the strong Japanese competitiveness would be weakened when they had to produce their cars with union labour and with various inefficiencies, such as the high absenteeism of American workers' [Goto 1992:173]. With the Japanese automobile plants transferring to America and confronted with import barriers specifically directed to them, Japanese steel producers began moving into the US from 1984 onwards.

Besides wishing to have a production presence in the US to ensure market access, a number of Japanese firms, particularly in areas such as chemicals, optical goods and electronics, seem to have acquired US corporations in order to obtain a direct channel to sought after technology. This is partly corroborated by Kogat and Chang (1991) who claim to have detected a positive relation between the level of a Japanese industry's involvement in the US and the extent of R&D associated with that industry, both in Japan and the US. Endeavours to keep abreast of the latest technological developments, do not necessarily entail direct acquisitions or joint venture agreements. The mere presence within the US of a fully owned Japanese subsidiary confers upon the firm in question the ability to employ world top flight engineers and scientists and the facility to be tuned into trends associated with affluent and sophisticated consumer trends. 'Even some Japanese textile firms (have been) building their own textile mills in the United States for the purpose of quickly monitoring the rapidly changing fashion market for high-value fashions-oriented lines of products' [Ozawa 1979:53].

Finally, it should be borne in mind that the US offers many attractions to potential foreign investors. These include: a large: and growing market, few bureaucratic restrictions and regulations that impede corporate activity, an excellent social infrastructure, low energy costs and an educated labour force. Most state governments and municipalities have welcomed foreign investment, particularly from Japan. In furthering Japanese investment, numerous states and cities have solicited prospective firms by lobbying within Japan itself, indicating public benefits available and highlighting their areas' relatively favourable aspects. The State of Ohio induced Honda to establish a production plant there by offering a site development grant (of $2.5 million), reductions in property taxes, guaranteed railroad improvements and even free English tuition for Japanese staff and their families [Encarnation 1992:133].

## Europe

Not until the early 1980s, did Europe attract a particularly large proportion of Japanese FDI. In 1981 only close on 9 per cent of total direct investments were placed there, yet by the decade's end, Europe's share had risen to 21 per cent.

In relation to specific countries, the UK has been the single most favoured FDI destination followed by Holland, Luxembourg, Germany and France, in that order. Switzerland and Spain were also moderately successful (see Table 11.6). Table 11.6 refers to total FDIs. In order to consider the country distribution of FDIs in manufacturing, the reader is referred to Table 11.7. While confirming the UK's leading status, it suggests that with it, France, Germany and Spain have also been in the forefront. The UK's leading position can be explained in terms of a preference to locate in a country where English is spoken,[5] relatively low wages, favourable public investment incentives and an absence of strong local rivals in automobiles and electronics. France offered a central location and a large internal market, Germany a good industrial relations record, high labour skills and centrality, and finally, Spain, which is endowed with cheap labour, initially commanded a relatively large Japanese production presence because of its high import barriers. At the sub-national level, there have been clear locational patterns. 'In

Table 11.6   Country Composition of Japan's FDIs in Europe (1951–89)

| Country | Percentage Share of FDI in Europe |
|---|---|
| UK | 35 |
| Holland | 22 |
| Luxembourg | 12 |
| Germany | 08 |
| France | 06 |
| Switzerland | 04 |
| Spain | 03 |
| Others | 10 |

*Source*: Ministry of Finance

*Table* 11.7   Country Distribution of Japanese Manufacturing Plants in the EC, 1989

| Country | Number of Plants |
|---|---|
| UK | 92 |
| France | 85 |
| Germany | 67 |
| Spain | 41 |
| Holland | 27 |
| Belgium | 23 |
| Ireland | 19 |

*Source*: JETRO data as reported by Morris 1991:198

the UK, for example, the peripheral regions dominate – in particular Wales, Scotland and the North-east of England' [Morris 1991:200].

Turning to the sectoral composition of Japanese FDI in Europe, the role of the manufacturing sector has been even smaller than has been the case in the US. In 1989, for instance, manufacturing represented only 22 per cent of FDI, with the lead taken by finance at 44 per cent.

Within the manufacturing sector, nearly two thirds of the total have generally been accounted for by machinery, electronics and transport equipment (see Table 11.8). Of these, electronics has been the sector of most importance.

The electronics industry tends to maintain large scale plants and is a relatively large labour employer. Most investments have been of the greenfield variety, with the exception of those directed to Spain, where joint ventures have been far more prevalent.

*Table* 11.8   Percentage Composition of Japan's Manufacturing FDIs in Europe

| Sector | 1982 | 1989 |
|---|---|---|
| Foods | 01 | 05 |
| Textiles | 04 | 06 |
| Chemicals | 28 | 17 |
| Iron and Non-ferrous metals | 05 | 02 |
| Machinery | 09 | 23 |
| Electronics | 38 | 24 |
| Transport equipment | 13 | 15 |
| Other | 02 | 08 |

*Source*: Ministry of Finance

*Motives for Manufacturing Investments in Europe*

As in the US, Japanese industrialists have mainly invested in Europe because of trade restrictive measures. The issue is simply not trade restrictions in general but growing trade obstacles to goods in which Japan has had distinct comparative advantages. This point seems to have been missed by Nicolaides and Thomsen who had claimed that despite the US being less protectionist than Europe, it received disproportionally more of Japanese manufactured investments and therefore by implication, trade barriers have not been significant FDI determinants [Nicolaides and Thomsen 1991:636]. By contrast, a study by Heitger and Stehn showed that Japanese FDI in European manufacturing was positively linked to effective protection (which is high in areas of interest to the Japanese) and to favourable Japanese firm-specific non-tangible assets (equated with revealed comparative advantages) [Heitger and Stehn 1990:11]. A few years later, still questioning the relevance of protection, Thomsen conceded that in cases where exports had reached a certain level, newly imposed trade barriers might 'accelerate the transfer of production to the host country' [Thomsen 1993:309]. However, in Thomsen's opinion, over the long term, had there been a continuation of free trade, the same investment process would in all probability have eventuated. Such a view is based on the notion that an 'acute sensitivity to consumer tastes' induces Japanese manufacturers to produce in markets where their goods are sold in appreciable quantities, since this enables them to shorten production lead times and to respond more appropriately to consumer needs and whims [308]. To support his contentions, Thomsen argues that within

Europe, 'firms will establish plants in or near the largest markets' [311]. Acknowledging that there is a poor correlation between Japanese FDI in Germany and market size, Thomsen concedes that other factors 'also affect the equation', such as a country's locality in relation to neighbouring markets. Sadly for Thomsen's analysis, for the UK where Japanese FDI is larger than in any other European country, both the locality factor and market size were given low to medium ratings by Japanese investors [313].

That many Japanese producers would probably have preferred to have continued exporting to Europe rather than to have invested in it, is inferred by estimates over the late 1970s and early 1980s, that Japanese automobile producers had a landed cost advantage over European firms of between 20 and 30 per cent. In addition, colour TV and VCR production costs were far cheaper in Japan [Dicken 1991:36]. With regard to colour TVs, the UK imposed a VER in 1973 and by 1981 a European community-wide VER came into effect. Given that the Japanese had already installed a wide network of distribution facilities (which enhanced their knowledge of local conditions), once these VERs were enforced production plants in Europe were set up in next to no time.

Again, like in the US, some manufacturing investments have also occurred in response to a need to acquire foreign technology. Investments based on such motivations have been concentrated in the chemical and pharmaceutical areas where they have also taken the form of acquisitions rather than *de novo* establishments.

With cumulative 1951–90 FDIs in European manufacturing amounting to $12.5 billion in Europe as opposed to $40.3 billion in North America, it is obvious that Europe very much played second fiddle to the US. This may have resulted from the lesser importance of Europe as a market for Japanese exports[6] and from an unfriendly European investment climate that ensured that some funds which 'ordinarily would have gone to the EEC had ended up in America to finance American exports to Europe' [Sullivan 1992:27].

## 2   THE EFFECTS OF JAPAN'S FDI

**Some General Observations**

The extent to which Japanese investments influence a host country's general economic well-being depends on a number of circumstances. Among important determinants are the nature of the investments themselves, whether or not they reflect takeovers, whether the incoming corporations possess certain firm-specific skills, the factor intensity of the investor's operations, the internal linkage effects generated and the framework in which the investments are made. The latter incorporates the extent to which investors are socially subsidized, the economic incentives that motivate them, the firms' long-term commitment to the host country and their willingness to share in rents associated with patents, goodwill, monopoly power and so on. There is no prior assurance that foreign investment *per se* will turn out to be socially rewarding.

Normally, the range of benefits that host countries anticipate includes technological and capital transfers, a wider access to foreign markets and an expansion of employment in manufacturing. When it comes to making an assessment as to whether and to what degree such hopes are realized, one is immediately beset by a host of intractable data problems, interpretation disagreements, an inability to determine long-term effects and so on. Were economists frank and honest, they would readily admit that estimating FDI effects 'is impossible rather than extremely difficult' [Yamamura 1989:21]. In the final analysis, one can do no more than offer assessments based on informed judgements.

## The Impact of Japan's FDI on Asian Countries

### Employment and Capital Formation

Estimates of the number of people employed in Japanese subsidiaries and the ratio of Japan's FDI to domestic capital formation for the year 1988 are provided in Table 11.9.

Before proceeding any further, the reader is cautioned that one cannot confidently assume that the data in question are even remotely accurate. Take investment ratios as a case in point. The Japanese statistics are derived from reported FDIs, which do not necessarily translate into actual ones. Even when a corporation lays claim to a specific outlay, it is not patently clear whether the transaction represents a transnational capital flow, for there is now a fair amount of evidence that a very large proportion of foreign investment outlays are locally financed. What can safely be assumed is that invest ratios shown in Table 11.10, almost certainly err on the high side. The most we can deduce is that Japanese FDIs in Singapore, Malaysia and Thailand have had some significant influence on capital formation and at any rate, more so than in Korea and Indonesia.

Table 11.9   The Influence of Japanese FDI on Asian Countries.
(Data for the Year 1988)

| Country | Invest Ratio | Total Employ | Manuf. Employ |
|---------|-------------|--------------|---------------|
| Hong Kong | na | 38,494 (1.4) | 18,306 (2.2) |
| Taiwan | na | 171,851 (na) | 166,424 (na) |
| Korea | 1.0 | 179,269 (1.0) | 162,386 (3.5) |
| Singapore | 10.0 | 67,441 (5.5) | 54,087 (15.3) |
| Malaysia | 6.0 | 70,324 (1.1) | 57,456 (6.1) |
| Philippines | 2.0 | 36,181 (0.2) | 24,414 (1.0) |
| Thailand | 7.0 | 109,831 (0.3) | 96,115 (4.0) |
| Indonesia | 3.0 | 61,611 (0.0) | 52,257 (0.9) |
| China | na | 28,775 (0.0) | 21,283 (0.0) |

*Sources*: Urata (a) 1993:285, ILO *Statistical Handbook* 1992, Ministry of Finance, IMF *International Statistics Yearbook* 1994.

Invest ratio is the percentage of Japanese FDI to domestic gross fixed capital formation
Total employ is the number employed in all Japanese subsidiaries in 1988.
Manuf. employ is the number employed in Japanese manufacturing enterprises in 1988. Figures in brackets are the percentage of the country's total workforce.

As for their impact on employment, it seems that in 1988, in the manufacturing sector, Japanese FDIs have been quite a sizeable factor in Singapore, of some importance in Malaysia and have made a small dent in Thailand and Korea. It has been argued that since Japanese subsidiaries generally pay higher wages than do local firms, their contribution to employment income is naturally greater than the proportion of workers that they employ [Sekiguchi 1983:14].

*Procurement Practices of Japanese Firms in Asia*

During the 1980s, Japanese manufacturing establishments tended, on average, to procure an increasing proportion of their input components from within their host countries. This is in line with host country aspirations and encouragement. But since many Asian countries have expanded their industrial capabilities on the basis of relatively cheap labour, it is also in keeping with good commercial practice. Where local inputs had not been purchased, Japan had been, by far, the largest foreign source. As Table 11.10 demonstrates, between 1980 and 1989, local procurement increased in all the listed industry groupings except for electronics and the miscellaneous 'others' category. In the

*Table* 11.10   Procurement Sources of Japanese Firms in Asia
(Percentages)

| Industry | 1980 Host Country | Japan | 1989 Host Country | Japan |
|---|---|---|---|---|
| Manufacturing | 42.2 | 41.5 | 49.8 | 38.9 |
| Food | 75.4 | 1.6 | 87.7 | 3.3 |
| Textiles | 38.9 | 29.3 | 43.1 | 22.4 |
| Wood | 65.2 | 1.8 | 92.5 | 2.3 |
| Chemicals | 53.3 | 30.8 | 56.3 | 34.7 |
| Iron and Steel | 26.6 | 53.5 | 36.0 | 56.1 |
| Non-ferrous | 20.6 | 42.1 | 59.3 | 18.1 |
| Machinery | 44.5 | 54.8 | 53.6 | 42.5 |
| Electronics | 49.6 | 46.0 | 42.4 | 44.6 |
| Transport | 38.2 | 61.1 | 57.7 | 41.8 |
| Precision mac. | 12.1 | 74.8 | 42.1 | 45.2 |
| Petro-chemical | n.a. | n.a. | 89.5 | 10.5 |
| Others | 40.5 | 27.8 | 36.0 | 48.4 |

*Source*: Statistics on Foreign Investment, MITI, Japan no. 1. 1981 and no. 4 1991

Non-ferrous = non-ferrous metals. Precision mac. = precision machinery

case of electronics, even though the proportion was down, considering that the scale of activity had risen so much, on an absolute basis, local purchases are almost certain to have been increased.

Compared with the situation in the US and the EC, Japanese Asian subsidiaries secure more of their inputs locally. Urata advances two reasons for this difference. In the first instance, 'Japanese FDI has a relatively long history, compared to that in the United States or the EC', and secondly, there has been a greater application of local content requirements on FDI in Asia than elsewhere [Urata (b) 1993:287]. Also, in advanced countries the desire to gain access to local markets is by far the major consideration. In that light, limited local sourcing may reflect attempts primarily to import production kits for assembling at local points of sales.

*Technology Transfers*

One potential advantage of direct foreign investment to a host country lies in possible technological transfers. Since a comprehensive definition of technology is elusive and a clearcut identification of technological flows is not feasible, we assume that technology is transferred by a variety of means. One might be through the introduction of advanced capital goods requiring skill enhancement for operation and maintenance purposes. Another might be through a transfer of expertise across a whole spectrum of activities such as design, production control, marketing, finance and so on. Or yet another might be through a transfer of patent rights. Still other channels exist but we will not attempt to spell them out.

In forming a judgement of the role of Japanese FDI in technological transfers to Asia, it is worth bearing in mind that irrespective of the willingness of Japanese corporations to promote such transfers, transfers actually effected are also influenced by local conditions. Of these, the quality of supporting institutions, general cultural attitudes, the pool of entrepreneurial talent and the level and diffusion of technical education are very important [Chew *et al.* 1992:113]. Having said that, it has been alleged that Japanese firms are fairly restrictive in providing native staff with access to advanced technology. It has been alleged that 'the whole structure of Japan's overseas investment strategy relies upon the export of "second hand", less mature technologies', with the latest know-how retained for application within Japan itself [Morris-Suzuki 1991:147]. Considering the ASEAN region, and partly relying upon Yamashita's paper, Ishigami concluded that Japanese firms 'have transferred only small parts of technology at a non-advanced stage, such as operational techniques, maintenance and quality control. They are reluctant to transfer the advanced stages of technology, such as dies, design, new products and developments of manufacturing equipment' [Ishigami 1991:27]. There may of course be legitimate reasons for such behaviour, for the most up to date machinery may be too sophisticated and too capital intensive to suit the volume of local Asian operations [see Lim and Ping 1983:80].

There is a perception of Japanese firms in Asia as being more inclined 'to employ a large number of Japanese as compared to, for example, US or European subsidiaries' [Chew *et al.* 1992:119]. Adding strength to this perception is the belief 'that Japanese subsidiaries are reluctant to train local managerial and higher-level technical personnel' [119]. However, a number of Japanese firms do provide on-the-job training and even dispatch some of their technical staff to Japan to undertake short-term courses. The courses are usually of only three to six months duration. A good deal of the time is 'lost' by virtue of the fact that the trainees also receive some rudimentary basic Japanese linguistic tuition. In most instances, the trainees are not bound to their firms for any definite period and as many do seek alternative employment on attaining enhanced skills, the firms are understandably reluctant to treat them on the same basis as their lifetime Japanese employees. Nevertheless, training has continued and one electronic firm (in Malaysia) has even sent as many as 160 trainees to Japan [Lim and Ping 1982:76]. Companies such as Matsushita and Sony have established training centres in Singapore to which employees attached to ASEAN branches are sent. On completing their studies, certain technicians are then posted to Japan for further instruction [Tachiki and Aoki 1992:37]. In Thailand, Canon is planning to recruit local engineering graduates to be given supplementary training in Japan, to enhance their design, production and sales capabilities [*Tokyo Business* 1992:25].

Although the Japanese in Asia are accused of monopolizing executive posts, Japanese staff have a lower profile there than in the US. In 1989, Japanese nationals constituted only 1.2 per cent of the total work force of Japanese companies in Asia, compared with a 3.7 percentage figure for the US.[7] In all probability, this is partly explicable in terms of the greater prevalence in Asia of joint ventures with local entrepreneurs.

*Japanese Manufactured Firms as Exporters and their Effect on Asian Trade*

In the late 1980s roughly 64 per cent of the output of Japanese Asian subsidiaries producing manufactured goods was sold within host countries. Another way of putting it, is that 36 per cent of total sales constituted exports, which compares very favourably with Japanese firms in the US and EC where, in 1988, only 5 per cent of output was exported [Urata (b) 1993:284]. Between 1977 and 1986, the exports of Japanese affiliates as a proportion of all Asian exports, rose from 7.6 to 13.5 per cent [Plummer and Ramstetter 1991:244], which suggests that Japanese FDI does stimulate Asian trade. Certainly, there has been an impressive showing in the machines and electronic sectors where by the end of the 1980s, the proportion of output exported reached 43.1 and 62.6 per cent respectively.

**The Impact of Japan's FDI on the United States**

In considering the effects both good and bad that Japanese FDIs may have on the US economy, cognisance should be taken of the relatively small scale of Japanese investments. In overall terms, 'FDI still represents a small fraction of the US economy. In 1990, it represented less than two per cent of the total output. In 1990, FDI stock as a percentage of the total net worth of non-financial corporations amounted to 10.5 per cent, while US affiliates of Japanese firms amounted to 2.17 per cent of the total. The total stock of FDI in the US in 1990 stood at $403.7 billion of which $108 billion was UK FDI and $83.5 billion Japanese FDI' [Georgiou and Weinhold 1992:764].

Starting with employment, in 1987, one estimate put the number of American workers hired by Japanese firms at 285 000, of which 82 000 were in manufacturing [Takaoka 1991:68]. Alternatively, Reid, citing figures from Knight, reports a manufacturing employment figure of 182 447 [Reid 1991:68], which is still but a minuscule fraction of the total US work force. Even though Japanese firms may enhance employment opportunities in the towns and regions to which they have become attached, their net contribution to overall employment is difficult to gauge. In the first instance, they may displace workers from previously existing firms. Secondly, they may be more efficient users of labour and thirdly, they may have a propensity to import more inputs. A lack of precision in determining employment impacts is illustrated by two studies concerning the automobile industry. In one, commissioned in 1986 by the United Auto Workers Union, a net loss of 200 000 workers (more incidentally than it seems Japanese companies employ) was forecast for the year 1990. Alternatively, a 1988 study of the United States General Accounting Office 'calculated that the impact of Japanese auto-related investment on jobs could range from a net job loss of 45 000 to a net job gain of 112 000' [Reid 1991:86].

Turning to the sourcing of inputs, in 1989, Japanese corporations in the US purchased 62 per cent of their requirements from Japan and 36 per cent locally. Within the electronics industry, imports from Japan amounted to as much as 79 per cent of input purchases. The situation has been appreciably better in the automobile industry where local content ratios reached a level of 60 per cent or more for companies such as Honda, Nissan and NUMMI but even so, Japanese firms still continued to source more inputs from abroad than did native ones. Over time, overseas Japanese sourcing can be expected to decline. Operative variables include the stringent enforcement of local content rules in compliance with NAFTA requirements,[8] the high value of the yen which discourages imports from Japan and the institution of 'just-in-time' production procedures which necessitates local supply sources.

As for exports, Japanese firms supply more than six times the value of other foreign firms per worker [Georgiou and Weinhold 1992:769]. However, in 1988, for instance, although Japanese affiliates exported goods worth $24.5 billion compared with $23.6 billion for all European

Table 11.11   Some Relative Characteristics of Japanese and US Owned
              Automobile Plants in North America, 1989

| Characteristics | Japanese Owned Plants | US Owned Plants |
| --- | --- | --- |
| Hours per vehicle | 21.2 | 25.1 |
| Defects per 100 vehicles | 65.0 | 82.3 |
| Days stock of sample parts | 1.2 | 2.9 |
| Rate of absenteeism | 4.8 | 11.7 |

Source: J. Womack, D. Jones and D. Roos. *The Machine That Changed the World.* Harper, New York, 1990 as reported by Bergsten and Noland 1993:109

affiliates, they simultaneously ran up an import bill totalling $75.9 billion, which vastly exceeded the $52.1 billion import costs incurred by European American based subsidiaries [JETRO 1991:17].

Where Japanese manufacturing subsidiaries have left their greatest mark is in encouraging local rivals to reappraise their production methods. This has certainly been the situation in the automobile industry where Japanese affiliates have shown 'that problems of low productivity in the US-owned plants are not due to poor US workmanship', for when operating in the US, Japanese plants outranked locally owned ones in terms of production efficiency [Bergsten and Noland 1993:112]. See Table 11.11. As a result, native firms began emulating Japanese manufacturing procedures and in the process, their competitiveness in design, performance, safety and price has much improved [118].

Apart from beneficial demonstration effects, there have been a number of occasions where through joint ventures with local companies, problem industries have been revived. A case in point has been in electrogalvanized steel sheets where technological cooperation in the area of continuous casting has assisted the US industry in recovering lost competitiveness [Watanabe 1987:67].

The discussion of the benefits of Japanese FDI to American industry would be incomplete without mentioning some of the hostility which it has encountered. For one thing, there is widespread resentment at the fact that virtually all top executive posts in Japanese controlled firms are held by Japanese. Even in posts usually offered to locals, such as sales and personnel managers, less than 50 per cent of the incumbents have been American. 'By comparison, US affiliates in Japan are almost entirely staffed by Japanese' [Prestowitz 1989:80]. To some extent the placing of Japanese personnel in key positions follows from the practice of rotating staff from Japan in order to maintain good communication channels between parent firms and subsidiaries. It also follows from the widespread use of the Japanese language within senior circles, as many Japanese posted abroad are not sufficiently conversant with host country languages. Friction and misunderstanding may also arise in relation to trade unions. Apart from Japanese corporations being accustomed to dealing with their own company unions, Japanese work practices may not readily be accepted by foreign workers without patient and tactful handling. Finally, most Japanese corporations subcontract work to small satellite input suppliers with whom long standing relations are sustained. This arrangement is difficult to replicate abroad. Where firms encourage the migration of their home country suppliers, they run the risk of antagonizing host country ones.

Japanese firms in the US are also assailed for systematically transferring US technology to Japan and for 'following a strategic plan whereby they scan US technology and purchase small firms not only to enhance their own position, but also to deny US competitors access to this technology' [Krause 1989:114]. The prevalence of such suspicions brought about a situation causing Fujitsu to withdraw a 1986 offer to purchase the Fairchild semiconductor company. 'That the objection was to Japanese, as opposed to foreign, ownership was underscored by the fact that Fairchild was owned by Schlumberger, a large conglomerate headquartered in France' [Makin 1989:42].

**The Impact of Japan's FDI on Europe**

Of the three regions under survey, cumulative Japanese investment in Europe has been the smallest both in absolute and relative magnitudes, with their impact on European economic affairs being negligible. In 1986, for example, only 11 200 British workers were employed in Japanese plants, an amount which fell short of Ford's work force at Dagenham and of the 450 000 employees of US owned plants [Dicken 1991:15]. 'By 1990 only four per cent of *total* direct investment in Britain was Japanese, and only seven per cent of the foreign investment in that year came from Japan' [Eltis and Fraser 1992:3]. For Europe as a whole, Japanese firms at the end of the 1980s, employed around 100 000 people.

Local content usage has been low with many plants importing the majority of their inputs. This has resulted from the relative newness of Japanese European plants, a shortage of satisfactory indigenous suppliers and a lag in small scale investments undertaken by the Japanese companies' traditional suppliers.

R&D activities have been kept to a minimum and for the most part, branches have been tightly regulated by their Japanese based head offices. However, some firms, such as Nissan and Sony, have been moving towards full-scale manufacture, local R&D and greater autonomy for European managers [Morris 1991:204]. Nissan is in fact now able to boast that barring the production of automatic transmissions, all of its main in-house activities are undertaken in Europe. 'Similarly, in the semiconductor industry, both NEC and Jujitsu have, or are going through the process of, transferring the very complex and capital intensive wafer fabrication process to their operations in the EC' [207].

Some of the beneficial effects of Japan's manufacturing presence in Europe are illustrated by Japanese electronic and automobile companies as they have functioned in the UK. Taking the colour television industry, in 1967, eight of the ten then existing TV corporations were locally owned. In 1973, when an industry VER was negotiated, the first Japanese firm, Sony, arrived to be followed by Matsushita (1976), Toshiba (1978), Mitsubishi and Hitachi (1979), Sanyo (1981), and NEC and JVC (1988). Over time, the locally owned firms proved to be incapable of withstanding competitive pressures and by 1988 all had folded. By 1990, eight of the then ten firms in Britain were Japanese, the remaining two being French and Taiwanese [Eltis and Fraser 1992:7]. Such a turnaround testifies to the strength of the Japanese firms' intangible assets. Although Britain lost its entire native TV industry, it gained by its 'consumers obtaining the highest quality television sets the world could supply', and by the country moving from a trade deficit in colour TVs to a surplus in 1991 of £446 million [8]. Similarly in automobiles, just when local suppliers were in the doldrums with production falling by 54 per cent between 1972 and 1982, the entry of Toyota, Nissan and Honda brought about an industry revitalization. Between 1984 and 1991, 400 000 more vehicles were produced in Britain at a time when the market was stagnant. A large part of the output has been exported helping to offset an industry trade deficit. Cars made in the UK are now more competitive in price and quality. In fact, labour productivity attained by the majority of European vehicle producers is perhaps 'half (of) that now being achieved by Japanese companies in the United Kingdom' [12].

## The Impact of Japan's FDI on Japan Itself

Concern has been expressed by some commentators, both Japanese and Western, that because FDIs promote the industrial potential of other countries, Japan would reap a number of undesirable consequences. What they primarily have had in mind is a 'hollowing out' of internal manufacturing activity and jobs, as well as some lessening of export competitiveness.[9]

Among those that have raised the matter were Gittelman and Dunning who posed the issue as follows: 'Can Japan continue to upgrade its industrial infrastructure if many of the necessary instruments of that upgrading (specialized R&D assets, technical and managerial personnel, inter-firm supplier networks) are geographically dispersed outside of Japan?' [Gittelman and Dunning 1992:266].

Historically, much of Japanese foreign investment has been induced by the need to avert potential market losses emanating from host country protectionist policies or by attempts to secure overseas raw material supplies. Such investments could not be deemed as having harmful economic effects. Had Japan not invested in import substituting countries, its firms would have automatically been precluded from those markets. As it happens, by setting up overseas assembly plants, Japanese firms were able to retain much of their exports, albeit in a different guise (parts instead of completed products). Investments undertaken in cheap labour countries to retain general export competitiveness are not in themselves the cause of local industrial problems. Here too, had such investments not occurred, local producers would sooner or later have lost overseas sales to foreign rivals and barring increases in local protectionism, they would have also been hard pressed on their home turfs. It is far better for Japan that its own companies continue to thrive, even at the cost of some international relocation. Positive spin-offs may include enhanced corporate financial viability on account of profits acquired abroad and a local concentration on more intricate and capital intensive production processes, stimulated in part by orders from foreign subsidiaries.

Economies in the Asian region have been and are continuing to experience major changes and rapid economic growth rates. While Japanese FDI has been of assistance to many of them, there is little doubt that they would have recorded substantial progress even without such investments. In short, the need for Japan to adjust to changing global conditions would have arisen one way or another.

Japan has generally faced the ongoing challenge of structural transformation by discarding declining industries. To no small extent direct foreign investment has been a vehicle for reducing the burden of carrying increasingly uncompetitive deadwood. When increased labour costs reduced the comparative advantage of certain industries, Japan 'engaged in exporting part of the low-productivity sector of her "dual economy"' [Allen 1981:175]. Such a process served the country well, for resources were released for use in more dynamic areas. When faced with similar circumstances, some other industrial countries by contrast, have erred in striving to preserve sunset industries by absorbing a large number of lowly paid 'guest workers'. Today, since Japan can capitalize on a large home market, it can easily 'shed low-end manufacturing through direct overseas operations without worrying about a possible hollowing-out of its home industrial base. FDI is thus undertaken basically as a by-product of the Schumpeterian process of "creative destruction"' [Ozawa 1991:47].

That Ozawa's views probably provide a suitable retort to those of Gittelman and Dunning is reinforced by figures revealing that in 1989 the ratio of Japanese overseas to home manufactured production hovered around 6 per cent compared with 17 per cent for the US and 20 per cent for Germany [Julius 1991a:8]. Lest there be fears for the future, especially in light of Asia's booming economies, Balassa and Noland remind us that 'the absorptive capacity of the NICs are too small to accommodate a mass exodus of manufacturing from Japan: The combined GNPs of Korea and Taiwan are only seven per cent of Japan's' [Balassa and Noland 1988:123].

Of course, one cannot rule out the possibility that in certain industries, FDI might displace local employment. For in taking the ratio of subsidiary output not to an industry's total Japanese production but to the amount produced by parent corporations, the 1989 ratios for electronics, transport and textiles were 19.9, 13.8 and 14.6 per cent respectively [MITI figures as reported by Komiya and Wakasugi 1991:58.]. With respect to Sharp's electronics products, it is believed that 85 per cent of its overall output is produced abroad [*Tokyo Business* 1993:44]. However, even if workers in specific fields are actually displaced, global unemployment need not increase. Asia's general economic progress may translate into more Japanese exports and hence jobs. For in the latter half of the 1980s when FDIs accelerated, Goto estimated that the resultant job loss would probably have tallied up to 330 000. Workers in the electronics and transport equipment industries in particular could be expected to feel the pinch. However, as against this, 'it should be borne in mind that 3 to 4 million jobs were created in the Japanese economy in the last few years. . . . Thus by our estimate, the recent fears of a possible deindustrialisation of the Japanese economy are not substantiated' [Goto 1990:181].

Much of the 'hollowing out' fears emanate from Asia's economic insurgency and a growing concentration there of household electronic firms. But as yet, Japan still maintains a healthy trade surplus with Asia and even in electronics, as more foreign plants are established, more technologically demanding tasks are found for the Japanese work force. For example, between 1991 and 1992 as Chinon began producing compact cameras in Taiwan, at home it shifted to floppy disk drives and printers. When Hitachi expanded its washing machine output in Thailand, it concentrated on fully automatic machines in Japan. Similarly, while Victor enlarged its compact TV capacity in Thailand, in Japan it turned to wide screen and BS tuner equipped large-screen TVs. Much the same sort of process has been reported for Canon, Kita-Nippon and TDK [JETRO 1993:20]. Had the Japanese economy been at a loss for creative initiative and adaptability, then the 'hollowing out' spectre might have become a reality but even then, the problem would have resided in internal circumstances and not in outward investment flows.

## 3   FDI INTO JAPAN

No discussion of Japan's FDIs would be complete without at least a brief mention of FDIs into Japan. FDI inflows are considerably more downbeat than outflows. On the basis of Bank of Japan data, in 1991 the value of cumulative inflows amounted to $12.3 billion ($231.8 billion for outflows). As a ratio of 1991 GNP, cumulative investment inflows were only 0.4 per cent. Elsewhere, as in the US and UK, the respective proportions were 11.5 and 23.3 per cent. The matter is not simply one of an imbalance of accumulated stocks; what rankles foreigners, and the US and Europe in particular, is that current movements are still very much skewed against them. In 1989, for instance, while Japan's FDI in the US amounted to $17.3 billion, US FDIs in Japan totalled $1.2 billion. Similarly, Japan's FDI to Europe equalled $9.7 billion against a counter inflow of $0.3 billion [JETRO 1991:5].

   Does investment asymmetry matter? Encarnation certainly thinks so. In a recent treatise, he has argued that 'the Japanese sell more in the United States than the Americans sell in Japan', not because of differences in competitiveness, exchange rate movements or trade policies but because of 'differences in the strategic *investment*[10] policies pursued by business and government in the two countries' [Encarnation 1992:212]. Similarly, Zysman contends that Japanese firms have been able 'to consolidate advantages from production or production technology in the United States while US firms were not able to do so in Japan' [Zysman 1989:109]. If these writers have judged the situation correctly, then the asymmetrical facility to invest abroad has enhanced Japan's economic standing, a consideration not without relevance for the 'hollowing-out' controversy.

Historically, Japan's relatively limited capital inflows can largely be attributed to the strict implementation of investment regulations. Even after most import quotas and tariffs were removed, the inflow of foreign investment 'was allowed only when the government was satisfied that it would meet an important need, and would not threaten established domestic interests' [Horsley and Buckley 1990:64]. In 1967, when an era of capital liberalization was officially inaugurated by the announcement of an immediate opening of some 50 industries, this proved to be merely 'a purely cosmetic public relations gesture'. All the industries in question 'were ones in which a Japanese enterprise controlled more than 50 per cent of the market, or in which most of the products were sold exclusively to the Japanese government (railroad cars), or for which no Japanese market existed (corn flakes)' [Johnson 1982:279].

One hundred per cent foreign ownership was only countenanced 'in industries in which foreign competition was unlikely (sake brewing, motorcycles, and the manufacture of geat (Japanese wooden clogs), are the famous examples)' [278]. Eventually in 1973, the Japanese accepted, in principle, the right of foreign companies to hold 100 per cent of equity in new or existing companies.

Before then, companies that managed to slip through the official net were constantly bullied through the use of various regulatory devices. For example, IBM failed to secure permission to manufacture computers in Japan until it agreed to license its basic patents to fifteen Japanese competitors [Prestowitz 1989:131]. Similarly, for Texas Instruments to obtain the go ahead to manufacture semiconductors, it had to license its patents to Japanese firms and agree to limit its supply to no more than 10 per cent of the Japanese market [131].

The widespread notion that the paucity of foreign firms operating in Japan can largely be traced to Japanese officialdom and institutions is dismissed by Abegglen and Stalk. While acknowledging that in the past, government restrictions have inhibited foreign investment, they insist that after 1973, FDI has been hampered by 'the indifference and ignorance of possible foreign investors regarding Japan, and their unwillingness in many cases to pay the price in effort and patience to make the investment' [Abegglen and Stalk 1985:217].

What Abegglen and Stalk seem to have overlooked is the force of social and institutional factors in impeding foreign direct investment inflows. Outsiders complain of excessive government regulations, high land costs and other problems associated with operating in the Japanese economy. The latter may include difficulties in recruiting professional staff, given lifetime employment practices, coping with the distribution system and restrictive practices engaged in by keiretsu. Instead of devoting excess attention to the accomplishments of a few American corporations, one might well ponder why their success has 'been marred by clashes with Japanese bureaucracy and dominated by Japanese oligopolists enforcing their country's strategic investment policy. (And why) by contrast, few such controversies can be found to characterize Japanese "success stories" in America' [Encarnation 1992:213].

## SUMMARY

- After the Second World War, Japan re-entered the foreign investment arena with a zero portfolio. Since then, it has experienced three large investment bouts, in 1968–73, 1978–81 and 1986–9. By 1989, it was the world's largest foreign investor.
- In Asia, industries favoured progressed from textiles to steel, non-ferrous metals, chemicals and eventually to transport and electrical equipment. Most projects are of a small size and many are involved in joint ownership ties with native entrepreneurs.
- FDI into Asia has been stimulated by host country import restrictions, cheap Asian labour, US import quotas on goods coming directly from Japan and by a range of government provided investment incentives.
- FDI in the US is largely in the field of finance. The manufacturing component arose mainly as a result of trade restrictions imposed in the late 1970s and 1980s and partly to secure access to US technology. Returns on FDI are smaller than in Asia.
- Similarly, in Europe FDI in manufacturing has only recently occurred and for much the same reasons as in the US.
- The general effects of Japan's FDI on host countries are difficult to determine.
- In Asia there seems to be some impact on capital formation in Singapore, Malaysia and Thailand. Local input procurement has been increasing, foreign trade has been boosted and while technological

transfers have usually been confined to low level ones, a certain amount of technical training has been imparted.

- Japanese FDI effects in both the US and Europe have been minimal on account of the small amount of investments relative to host country economies. In the US Japanese firms have influenced the behaviour of local automobile producers and in the UK they have made a large contribution in both automobile and television output.
- FDIs have been helpful to Japan itself in retaining foreign markets and in the restructuring of segments of Japan's industry. The threat of 'hollowing-out' seems unlikely to eventuate because as certain production activities are transferred abroad, at home others (which are more technologically demanding) are extended.
- FDIs into Japan are still rather limited. This reflects both past regulations and a current environment which still discourages the entry of foreign capital. Since this serves Japanese firms' interests while penalizing foreign ones, more external pressures are likely to be brought to bear to eliminate remaining inward investment obstacles.

# Part IV

# The Primary and Tertiary Sector

# 12 Agriculture

## INTRODUCTION

Agriculture has played an extremely critical role in Japan's transition to a leading industrial power. As mentioned in Chapter 1, it not only provided the country with food and export goods (such as silk) but in the early Meiji period (around 1880) it furnished the state with 91 per cent of its direct tax revenues.

Until fairly recently, the Japanese economy was essentially rural based. In 1885 agriculture provided employment for 73 per cent of Japan's work force and yielded 45 per cent of its GDP. Even by 1955 the figures were 39 and 21 per cent respectively. However, as postwar economic growth gathered momentum, the agricultural sector's relative importance rapidly diminished. By 1990 the proportion of people employed in farming was merely 6 per cent and agriculture's share of GDP was no more than 2.6 per cent.

Although now relatively small in terms of total labour usage and output produced, the agricultural sector still occupies centre stage in contemporary Japanese economic and political affairs. Thanks to a powerful and effective lobby, accommodating politicians and passive public support, the agricultural sector has been the recipient of an extraordinary amount of official protection and finance. This has resulted in a gross misallocation of the country's economic resources, in needlessly high consumer prices, inflated government outlays and growing friction with foreign trading partners.

Within this chapter these issues will constitute the focus of our attention. However, we commence by outlining the hallmarks of the 1946 land reform and the cooperative movement, both of which provide the institutional setting in which Japanese agriculture functions. From there we examine agricultural protection in some detail, paying special attention to the rice issue, and finally we turn to the problem of relatively low farm labour productivity.

258 The Japanese Economy

## INSTITUTIONAL BACKGROUND

### Land Reforms

As part of its programme to democratize Japanese society, the US occupying authorities pressurized the Cabinet to pass legislation instituting extensive land reforms. After an initial difference of opinion between the parties concerned, a bill was agreed upon in August 1946. It contained the following provisions:

(a) The government was authorized to purchase all land owned by absentee landlords.
(b) Resident landlords could hire out land only up to limited amounts ranging in the main islands from 0.6 hectares in Hiroshima Prefecture to 1.5 hectares in Aomori Prefecture. In Hokkaido, the limit was set at 4 hectares.
(c) The maximum holding for the landlords' own use was generally set at two hectares, except for Hokkaido where eight hectares were permitted.
(d) Amounts of land possessed by resident landlords above their legal entitlements were to be sold to tenants within two years of the bill becoming law.
(e) Prices paid for land transfers were set at 40 times the annual rent for lowland paddy fields and 48 times for upland ones.
(f) Farmlands acquired were not permitted to be resold within the first 30 years.
(g) To facilitate land transfers, a land committee was to be formed in each village comprising five tenants, three landlords and three owner-farmers.
(h) A national land committee was to oversee the entire process.

The land reform measures ushered in sweeping social changes throughout the entire Japanese countryside. By 1950, some 1.9 million hectares, about one third of Japan's arable land, passed into the hands of former tenants and landless farmers, benefiting close to four million families. With land prices having been fixed in terms of 1945 values, subsequent high inflationary rounds enabled the new owners to acquire their property at very little real cost. As if to add insult to injury to the remaining landlords, the 1952 Agricultural Land Law introduced rent controls at very low ceilings. All these changes radically transformed landholding arrangements, for whereas in 1945, 46 per cent of cultivated land was tenanted, by 1965 the ratio had plummeted to 5 per cent.

Without question, the reforms eliminated large inter-personal economic inequalities. In the prewar period, tenants were hard done by. They paid high rents (on average two fifths the value of their output), they supplied their own inputs and even their own farmhouses and had little security of tenure. Today's farmers are almost all land owners. As to be expected, they are also very conservative and are great supporters of the status quo. To that extent, the reforms have engendered rural harmony and social stability.

Where the reforms have not been helpful has been in the sphere of farm unit sizes. They simply reinforced the tendency for average farm units to be small. In 1946, before land was redistributed, 71 per cent of holdings were less than one hectare, by 1950, 87 per cent were [Rothacher 1989:18]. Such a situation has hindered subsequent attempts to improve productivity levels by increasing the scale of farm operations (more on this later).

**Cooperatives**

Effectively, the organizational structure of Japanese agriculture is characterized by a proliferation of small farms plus a widespread existence of rural cooperatives with which farmers are inextricably linked. At both the political and economic level, the agricultural cooperative movement is a major player not only in terms of the rural sector but also in relation to Japanese society at large.

At the ground root village level the agricultural cooperatives (known as Nokyo) rest on two separate pillars. First of all, there are general cooperatives (Sogo Nokyo) which market farm output and supply members with their inputs and consumer goods, as well as providing financial, insurance and welfare services. Then there are single purpose or specialized cooperatives (Senmonren Nokyo) which concentrate on specific products like citrus fruits, vegetables, dairy foods, beef and poultry. Both types of village cooperatives are federated at the prefectural and national level. The national bodies include the Central Cooperative Bank, the National Mutual Insurance Federation, the National Welfare Federation and the National Federation (Zenno) which coordinates the Nokyo's overall economic operations (warehousing, importation, processing, marketing, industrial participation, and so on). Overseeing the entire cooperative movement is the Central Union (Zenchu) which also assumes responsibility for representing the interests of all farmers. Its president is regarded as the agricultural sector's top leader, spokesman and negotiator.

On the basis of almost any criterion, Nokyo is a very powerful force. It had, at one time, exclusive rights to deliver almost all crucial food products to the Food Agency of the Ministry of Agriculture Forestry and Fisheries (MAFF). In addition, various government functions were assigned to it, such as the distribution of premium and deficiency payments, the administration of public extension services, the farm modernization programme, production adjustment schemes and the diversion of land from rice farming. Its economic activities are wide ranging (it is even involved in the food processing industry) and many of its component bodies are wealthy entities. For example, the financial reserves of its National Mutual Insurance Federation 'far exceed the largest insurance companies in both the life and non-life sector' [Rothacher 1989:50]. Aside from supplying farmers with their inputs, marketing their output and providing financial and insurance services, Nokyo is also active in health-care and cultural matters which cover agricultural training, publishing and the running of a daily newspaper.

Given Nokyo's towering status, farmers 'have little choice except to avail themselves of its services' [Van Wolferen 1989:60]. As a result, its farm household membership is in excess of five million. Furthermore, over two million rural based non-farm households attracted by Nokyo's credit facilities, are also incorporated. Nokyo has traditionally been a vigorous supporter of the LDP and during elections it has consistently mobilized its entire rank and file on the party's behalf. It has at times also amassed large campaign funds simply by deducting contributions from member savings accounts.

To fully appreciate the politics of the Japanese rural lobby it ought to be realized that unlike most Western countries where farm interests are clearly articulated by agriculturists themselves, in Japan farmers are represented (and manipulated) by Nokyo. Under the terms of the 1947 Agricultural Cooperatives Union Law, which formally established it, Nokyo has officially been accorded the right to present farmers' views within government forums. Since then, its involvement in agricultural policy formulations has been ubiquitous with no significant farm sector decision having been taken without its prior consent.

However, with nearly 300 000 on its payroll, Nokyo is also wont to feather its own nest. It extracts rents from farmers by the fulfilment of various semi-government functions and by using its monopolistic powers to impose unnecessarily high farm input prices. With this in mind, its efforts to maintain the size of the farming community by supporting agricultural protection are partially motivated by a desire to conserve its client base.

## AGRICULTURAL PROTECTION

As Japan's rapid postwar economic growth picked up steam, labour productivity steadily improved. However, progress achieved in industry consistently superseded advances in agriculture. Over the period 1960–80, the respective annual growth rates were 6.7 and 5.3 per cent [Hayami 1988:11]. This meant that incomes derived from industrial employment began to exceed those obtained by farming, even though in the early 1950s, the ratio of farm to non-farm incomes was greater than one. Not only did the Japanese industrial sector outpace agriculture in terms of labour productivity growth but its performance also topped that of all its foreign rivals. As a result, Japan's comparative trade advantages rested more firmly in manufacturing. Conversely, the agricultural sector began to be increasingly comparatively disadvantaged. (Although, over the period 1960–80, Japanese rural labour productivity recorded steady progress, its track record was no match for American, German or French farmers, to cite but a few.)

The corollary of all these noted trends is that the Japanese farming community began to be relatively impoverished. Over time, the situation would have righted itself by appropriate inter-sectoral resource flows but if left to their own devices, rural dwellers would perforce have shouldered all of the adjustment costs. Considering the short time frame in which changes were rapidly occurring, it would have been socially untenable to have allowed events simply to have taken their own course. Not surprisingly, the farmers were quick off the mark in canvassing for protection, and as their luck would have it, they met with a resonant public response.

Many Japanese citizens naturally empathize with their country's agriculturists since an extremely high proportion are only one or two generations removed from the land. In 1975, 20 per cent of the total population were members of farm households. Even by 1991, the proportion was 14 per cent, a factor which partly explains the strength of the non-urban electorate (apart from an ongoing rural gerrymander). Such people are well disposed to the agricultural sector and readily endorse government support for it, especially if it has the effect of enhancing employment and income generating facilities for the aged. It is quite possible, that in the absence of agricultural protection, Japan's unemployment rate would be higher.[1] Viable rural communities are also credited with maintaining good environmental conditions.

The farming community while welcoming expressions of sympathy also plays on Japan's fears for its general food security. Memories of serious shortages in the immediate postwar period endure. Added to this, the shock in 1973 of a temporary US trade embargo of soybeans (in response to local supply deficiencies) and the establishment of 200 nautical mile fishing exclusionary zones, are etched in the nation's consciousness. These factors have combined to produce a universal consensus, subscribed to by political parties of all persuasions, that by fostering food self-sufficiency, agricultural protection serves the national interest.

To outsiders, the Japanese defend their policies by noting that agricultural protection is also upheld in Europe and America and that as it happens Japan is one of the largest food importers. In 1990, for instance, it purchased 8 per cent of the world's agricultural exports. It has also been the world's single largest importer of feed grains, soybeans, pork and poultry, second to the US in beef import volumes and first in terms of beef values [Oga 1993:396].

Finally, the declining Engel coefficient (which relates the proportion of consumer budgets allocated to food expenditures to various per capita income levels) has had an important bearing in weakening any resistance to the price increase effects of protection. As Japanese real salaries have risen, the share of agricultural products in total consumer outlays has fallen. Hence, the impact of rising food bills on living costs has steadily declined.

Interestingly, in the pre-World War II period, there was also a discrepancy between labour productivity growth rates in agriculture and industry, with agricultural incomes being in a state of decline. Yet, unlike in the postwar years, the rural community was not protected. A higher Engel coefficient then prevailed, which meant that dearer food prices would have been relatively more onerous. Since Japan's industries were at the time predominantly labour intensive, increases in the basic cost of living would have caused an upward shift in wages, which in turn would have cut into profits. Accordingly, attempts to coddle farmers in the way they are pampered today, would have endangered the industrial process and would have met with strong urban opposition.

## The Nature and Extent of Agricultural Protection

The Japanese government has assisted its farming community by maintaining various forms of trade barriers, by favourably manipulating producer prices and by directly issuing monetary subsidies.

Table 12.1 gives an indication of the growth of import protection between 1955 and 1984, using nominal rates of protection (NRP) measure-

*Table* 12.1   Nominal Rates of Protection

|  | 1955 | 1960 | 1965 | 1970 | 1975 | 1980 | 1984 |
|---|---|---|---|---|---|---|---|
| Japan | 18 | 41 | 69 | 74 | 76 | 85 | 102 |
| EC Average | 35 | 37 | 45 | 52 | 29 | 38 | 22 |
| Switzerland | 60 | 64 | 73 | 96 | 96 | 126 | 153 |

*Source*: Hayami 1988:6

ments. The NRP is computed as the value of agricultural output in domestic prices minus its value at international ones, expressed as a percentage of the latter. As the table shows, Japan's protective levels were at first rather low, both in absolute and relative terms. But within a single decade, they experienced a near fourfold increase, becoming distinctly higher than average European ones. Thereafter, they continued to race upwards, albeit at a lower rate. Data relating to Switzerland demonstrate that though being exceedingly large, Japanese NRPs have by no means been unique.

On an individual crop basis, import protection has been particularly high for food grains such as rice, wheat and barley but low for feed grains used as fodder for the cattle industry.

In general, Japan's high import protective structure has rested less on tariffs and more on a strong battery of quantitative restraints. Compared with some other countries, import duties on agricultural products have been fairly modest. At the conclusion of the GATT Tokyo Trade Round, Japan's average agricultural tariff rates were set to be at the order of 8.6 per cent, appreciably less than the 12.6 per cent determination for the European Community.

A large number of import quotas were in place in the late 1950s. But the amounts steadily decreased from 102 separate quotas in 1958, to 58 in 1960, and then to 22 in 1974. In 1988 Japan agreed to relinquish (by 1991) import quotas for beef and fresh oranges and (by 1992) controls on orange juice. In the case of beef, the quotas were to be replaced by tariffs. As for the remaining items that were listed in 1974, in December 1993, the government agreed to substitute tariffs for quotas on all of them bar rice. This did not imply an immediate drop in protection rates, for while zero or low tariff rates were to be applied to import quantities that were previously allocated, beyond such amounts fairly steep tariff rates were imposed. For example, the 1995 tariff rates for 'excess' wheat, starch and peanuts were set at 556 480 and 516 per cent respectively [*Nikkei Weekly* 20 Dec. 1993]. The government has now committed itself to a lowering, over time, of agricultural tariff rates not only in relation to the above mentioned items but also with regard to others such as beef, oranges and dairy products.

The liberalization of agricultural trade has thus far had little impact on domestic output. Even though more beef has been imported, the domestic product, which is marbled and chilled fresh, commands a price premium over foreign products which are leaner and frozen. Generally speaking, imported beef is mainly used for processing for ground beef and is sold in fast food chains and cheap family restaurants, whereas domestic beef is consumed at home and at upmarket restaurants [Oga 1993:397].

Besides the overt limitations to agricultural trade that quotas impose, imports have also been constrained by official or quasi-official bodies such as the Food Agency, the Livestock Industry Promotion Corporation and the Japan Tobacco Corporation, all of which have enjoyed varying degrees of exclusive product purchasing rights. Since these trading bodies do not explicitly violate GATT rules, they have been subject to little international outcry or criticism.

Mention should also be made of the operation of additional non-tariff trade barriers such as health and other regulations and of public attitudes. To give some examples: at one stage, the limited amounts of imported orange juice allowable had to be blended with no less than 40 per cent of local tangerine juice. Restrictions on the numbers and types of synthetic food additives that could be marketed in Japan hindered processed food exports from Europe and the USA. In the US, unlike in Japan, extensive use is made of post-harvest agrochemicals which prevent crops from perishing and which preserve their appearance [Vogel 1992:131]. Notwithstanding the fact that in Japan more pesticides and chemical fertilizers are deployed per acre than in most other countries, Japanese consumer organizations have exclusively focused their attention on post-harvest pesticides found on imported agricultural commodities [147].

The producer prices of various products had been artificially maintained at high levels. Apart from rice (which is discussed separately below) wheat and barley had been purchased by the Ministry of Agriculture's Food Agency whenever prices dropped below predetermined ones. Similarly, state funded buffer stock price stabilization schemes set the prices for meat, dairy products and silk above market equilibrium ones. Lastly, producers of soya bean, rapeseed and milk (for processing) receive government deficiency payments amounting to the differences between targeted and marketed prices.

Japanese farmers have been lavishly bestowed with direct subsidy payments, which among other things, have financed a large share of agricultural capital formation. (In 1984, government grants met 40 per cent of the costs of fixed farm investments [Hayami 1988:58].) The ratio of general subsidies to agricultural output has been nearly three times higher in Japan than in Europe. The nominal rates of protection (NRP) estimates shown in Table 12.1 do not capture non-price income support. To include that category, producer subsidy equivalents (PSE) are relied upon.

Essentially, a PSE is the sum of money needed to compensate producers for removing all forms of government support, expressed as a percentage of total producer income. Calculations for 1987, spanning a number of countries, clearly identify Japan as being in the forefront of farm subsidy provisions. See Table 12.2.

There is yet one more dimension to the support that the agricultural sector receives, and that is in the domain of taxation. Imposts on land used for farming are negligible and generous concessions also apply to land inheritance taxes. Finally, although not officially sanctioned, it is widely believed that reported to actual taxable incomes are far lower in rural areas than in urban ones.

**The Protection of Rice**

By almost all accounts, whether it be in terms of its share of total agricultural output, its proportion of land under cultivation or the extent to which it is protected, rice is Japan's premier crop. As seen in Table 12.3, in 1990 rice was the farm sector's largest single income generator. In that year, it utilized 40 per cent of Japan's cultivated land. No other single crop commands anywhere near the same land area that rice does.

Farmers are attracted to rice cultivation because it requires relatively little effort (except when planting and harvesting), its yield is normally rather stable and above all, it is readily marketable at high prices, being Japan's most protected crop.

For many decades, rice sales have been subject to state supervision. The legal basis for this rests on the 1942 Food Control Law enacted to ensure equitable food rationing in the face of widespread scarcities and which placed the allocation of all food staples under the Ministry of Agriculture's Food Agency. As farm output improved, various food items were released from state managed distribution and by 1952, only rice sales continued to be publicly controlled. At first, the Food Agency

*The Japanese Economy*

Table 12.2   1987 Producer Subsidy Equivalents

| | |
|---|---|
| Japan | 76 |
| Australia | 11 |
| Austria | 51 |
| Canada | 48 |
| EC | 48 |
| USA | 40 |

*Source*: Citrin 1990:60

Table 12.3   1990 Share of Agricultural Income Derived from Various Farm Products

| Item | Percentage |
|---|---|
| Crops | 76 |
| Rice | 29 |
| Wheat and Barley | 2 |
| Other Cereals and Pulses | 1 |
| Potatoes | 2 |
| Vegetables | 24 |
| Fruit and Nuts | 7 |
| Crops for industry | 5 |
| Others | 6 |
| Sericulture | 1 |
| Livestock | 22 |
| Miscellaneous | 1 |

*Source*: MAFF 1991:12

determined rice prices from the farm gate all the way to the retail level. Later, in 1972, the link from wholesalers to retailers was liberalized allowing some give in the determination of final consumer prices.

Although the government's involvement in the rice industry was first motivated by a desire to protect consumers, it soon became exclusively beholden to producer interests. This is clearly manifested in the extraordinary high prices which Japanese rice growers command. In 1991 for example, Japanese producer prices were 6.6 times higher than those obtained by US farmers. Fortunately for Japanese consumers, retail costs generally exceed foreign ones by somewhat lesser margins but even so, the Japanese public currently face rice charges which are nearly threefold greater than those listed in US stores.

Price determination had been guided by the 1960 'Production Cost and Income Compensation Formula', which allowed producer prices to be set on the basis of production costs, general commodity prices and economic conditions. Within the production cost category, farm labour had been valued according to wages in manufacturing (where labour productivity is higher), imputed rent was factored in for land costs and average overall expenses have been based on data pertaining to marginal rice growers. Inevitably, such criteria guaranteed inordinately high producer prices. In an attempt to moderate the formula's upward price bias, computations from 1990 have been based on production expenses encountered in larger and more efficient farms. Still, a number of undesirable features persist. One of which lies in the estimation of imputed rent. As is well known, rental costs are associated with land values, which are partly determined by the value of output that the land yields. Inherent in the use of the formula is an interactive process whereby high rice prices cause land rents to rise, which in turn are taken into account in determining subsequent rice prices.

Guidelines for establishing wholesale prices took into consideration household expenditure levels, inflation rates and the state of the economy. Until 1967, wholesale prices consistently fell short of producer ones. While this deterred rice growers from attempting to bypass the Food Agency when selling their crops, the Food Agency itself incurred constant deficits which sapped the agricultural ministry's finances. In 1969, to alleviate the problem, a 'voluntary-rice' distribution channel was permitted to operate in tandem with the 'government-rice' one. Cooperatives could either dispose of their rice, at set prices, to the Food Agency or to wholesalers, at negotiated rates. To some extent, shipments to the voluntary channel were publicly subsidized but considering that this channel attracted rice of the highest quality, it readily commanded higher prices in its own right. (As of late, the premium over government rice has been of the order of 35 per cent.) Since the two-track distribution system was inaugurated, there has been a clear tendency to shift from the government to the voluntary network. The latter channel now handles more than 60 per cent of all Japanese marketed rice.

Having effectively closed the Japanese rice market to outsiders and having driven the internal price above the point which would equate domestic supply to demand, Food Agency warehouses were in the 1960s inundated with surplus rice stocks. Faced with this unwelcome protection by-product, a rice acreage control programme was launched in 1969. This entailed limits to the amount of land that could be devoted to rice. Farmers were induced by subsidies either to withhold rice land from cultivation or to put it to alternative uses. Regrettably, with the

advent of improvements in rice production technology, combined with a lessening of rice demand (per capita rice consumption fell from 118 kilograms in 1962 to 72 in 1987), the acreage control programme over time had to be more stringently applied. By the mid 1980s, nearly a quarter of Japan's paddy fields were not producing rice.

The entire process of providing rice protection has been costly, wasteful, and contradictory. First of all, the government has stimulated rice output by raising prices. Then it moved to subsidize farmers to limit supply, not discriminating between progressive farmers striving to obtain scale economies and run of the mill part-time cultivators operating on sub-optimal sized plots. The sums of money that this has involved have been enormous. In 1985, for example, food control outlays amounted to $4 billion. Added to this are the unnecessarily high imposts borne by consumers. In all probability, well over half of rice farmers' earnings are simply income transfers from Japanese consumers and tax payers [Hayami 1988:67].

From 1955 rice imports (save for insignificant quantities of glutinous varieties used in the food processing industry) had been virtually non-existent. One occasion when Japan received a foreign consignment was in 1984, when 150 000 tons were brought in from South Korea on a one-off basis. In 1993, due to unfavourable weather conditions, the country's rice harvest was the worst in postwar history, falling short of consumption by two million tons. This prompted the government to permit the importation of at least one million tons, temporarily making Japan the world's largest rice importing country. Fearing that this might be a prelude to a permanent change in policy, Nokyo called upon the government to raise its rice inventory to two million tons. The Ministry of Agriculture responded by considering shifting back some of the land previously withheld from rice production.

However, by mid-December 1993, despite vociferous internal opposition, the government finally bowed to international pressures and in the framework of the completion of the GATT Uruguay trade talks, Japan lifted its long-standing ban on rice imports. Under the terms of the GATT accord, it agreed to import 4 per cent of its total rice consumption in 1995 (approximately 400 000 tons) with the proportion gradually to be raised to 8 per cent by 2000. Thereafter, quantitative restrictions are expected to be removed, with tariffs replacing rice import quotas.

It had been anticipated that rice imports would not result in lower consumer prices, for the government originally intended to retain controls over rice purchases and distribution and was set on pricing foreign rice on a par with domestic rice [*Nikkei Weekly* 20 Dec. 1993]. Nevertheless, only ten months later (in August 1994) the Ministry of Agriculture decided to lay the Staple Food Control Act to rest, thus liberating rice from distributional and production restrictions. From the consumers' point of view rice prices should ultimately fall [*Economist* 20 Aug. 1994].

## Some General Issues Relating to Agricultural Protection

Japan's agricultural protective structure can be rated a success in terms of the alleviation of farmers from the burden of rapid agricultural adjustments and the safeguarding of their incomes. With regard to the latter, despite the fact that relative to manufacturing, agricultural labour productivity had continually declined, the ratio of farm to non-farm household income rose from 77 per cent in 1955 to 115 per cent in 1980.

Although an acute and probably painful agricultural adjustment process had been averted, protection simply provided the country with another serious long-term problem, namely the ossification of agriculture. Far too many inefficient part-time operators have been locked into farming and an optimal redeployment of resources across the sector has been stifled. For instance, Japan's interests would have been better served if its rural community had concentrated more on livestock and dairy farming.

In overall economic terms, agricultural protection has served the nation poorly. It has presented consumers with high food bills and has been a drain on the public purse. According to Van der Meer and Yamada's calculations, there have even been occasions (in 1980 and 1984) when the net value added of Japanese agriculture (valued at US and Dutch prices) has been negative [Van der Meer and Yamada 1990:131]. Essentially, this means that in terms of foreign prices, the value of farm inputs exceeds the value of farm output and that agricultural activity has diminished Japan's real income.

Paradoxically, Japan's food self-sufficiency rate has declined from 90 per cent in 1960 to 67 per cent in 1990. With respect to soybeans, the crop which in 1973 was momentarily not forthcoming from the USA (a situation which supposedly sent chills down Japanese consumers' spines), the 1990 self-sufficiency rate was just 5 per cent. It has even been argued that Japan is not self-sufficient in rice, in the sense that it is dependent on the importation of crude oil for the production of fertilizers, chemicals and fuels which are so heavily used in rice cultivation [Wailes, Young and Cramer 1993:382].

The steady rise in agricultural imports largely reflects a big influx of maize and sorghum used as feedgrains in the domestic livestock industry. Of late, some inroads have also been made in meat, fruit, vegetables, sugar and tobacco imports.

Opponents of agricultural protection have first and foremost been Japan's trading partners. They have been joined by Japanese manufacturers anxious for their country to offer food trade concessions, so as to forestall potential restraints on their access to Western markets. However, Japanese manufacturers are sometimes browbeaten by the rural lobby. Not too long ago, a Keidanren subcommittee castigated farmers for resisting agricultural trade liberalization. This drew the ire of Nokyo, which organized a boycott of corporations with which members of the subcommittee were associated. The dispute terminated with the subcommittee's chairperson apologizing and resigning [Okimoto 1989:172].


AGRICULTURAL PRODUCTIVITY

Japanese agriculture has, to its credit, made great strides in increasing farm output. Between 1960 and 1985, aggregate agricultural production rose by 43 per cent. Over the same period, the number of people engaged in farming fell from 14.5 to 6.4 million (that is by 56 per cent) so that undoubtedly, labour productivity vastly improved. Such progress has in no small measure resulted from the government's sponsorship of agricultural research and of course from the vast amount of general support that has been forthcoming.

Farmers have invested heavily in plant and equipment. In 1985, gross fixed capital formation as a percentage of rural output stood at 28.4 per cent in Japan, whereas in the EC and the USA the figures were 11.4 and 9.2 per cent respectively [Van der Meer 1990:147]. Almost all farms are highly mechanized and horticulturists liberally douse their soil with chemical fertilizers. Taking nitrogen as a case in point, the annual Japanese usage, amounting to 138 kilograms per hectare, far exceeds the 33 kilogram per hectare world average.

On the basis of output per hectare, Japanese agriculture is a front runner, certainly topping the EC average by a very wide margin. Confronted with a shortage of arable land, the Japanese successfully adopted a policy of maximizing yields per hectare. Unfortunately, when it comes to labour productivity, Japan's relative achievements are abysmal. For example, in 1985, output per farmer in Japan amounted to $1590 as opposed to $15 193 in the Netherlands or $14 265 in Denmark [Van der Meer 1990:45].

There is general agreement that small farm landholdings are the major stumbling block in raising labour productivity. The average farm is no more than a little over a hectare in size and many include separate parcels of land which are not contiguous to one another. This problem has long been acknowledged, and as far back as 1961 when the Agricultural Basic Law was promulgated, the government would have liked to have remedied the situation. It envisaged that within a decade, at least a quarter of farm households would have withdrawn from agriculture and would have relinquished their land to more enterprising agronomists. To expedite this process, legal restraints setting limits to farm sizes were relaxed. Most of the remaining farm units were to have been 'viable' ones in the sense that they were to have been large enough to require the full-time attention of all farm household members and at the same time would have yielded incomes that were equivalent to urban ones.

Contrary to expectations, the actual number of 'viable' farm units declined. There were two reasons for this. First, in the 1960s, when the economy was experiencing rapid growth, the average income of non-farm households was constantly rising, which necessitated ever increasing farm unit sizes to enable agricultural earnings to keep abreast. It has been estimated that in 1960 for a rice farm to be 'viable' at least 2.3 hectares were needed. Ten years later, the threshold rose to 3.5 hectares [Hayami 1988:80]. (In the mid-1980s, it reached 5.8 hectares.) Second, the number of people permanently leaving rural areas turned out to be smaller than was both expected and required for sufficient farm unit consolidations to be realized. Although more and more members of farm households sought and obtained employment in non-agricultural sectors, the family farm tended to be retained. The bulk of its cultivation is usually left to the elderly or womenfolk with the rest being undertaken by other family members on a part-time basis.

The existence of large numbers of part-time farmers is a distinguishing feature of Japanese agriculture. This has been the case throughout most of the postwar period with the dominance of part-timers strengthening as the years go by. See Table 12.4.

As Table 12.4 indicates, the overwhelming majority of Japanese farmers are not full-timers. Of the relatively few that are, many earn incomes that fall short of urban ones, for the average land area worked by these stalwarts (2.2 hectares) nowhere near meets current 'viable' farming requirements. It is ironic that though Japan's agricultural sector is so

*The Japanese Economy*

*Table* 12.4   Percentage Distribution of Japanese Farm Households

|  | Full-Time | Part-Time (Class 1) | Part-Time (Class 2) |
|---|---|---|---|
| 1960 | 34 | 34 | 32 |
| 1991 | 12 | 13 | 75 |

*Source*: MAFF

*Note*: Part-time Class 1 earned income mainly from farming, Part-time Class 2 earned income mainly from non-farm sources

extravagantly pampered, the small core of farmers completely dedicated to their land, are generally economically disadvantaged.

Part-time farming is currently well entrenched and is likely to remain so in the immediate future. Many rural folk live within easy commuting distances from non-farm employment centres. With the widespread diffusion of labour saving equipment, such as small hand tractors, their farms can readily be left in the care of elderly or female family members. No matter to what limited extent these farmers may depend on the soil, the majority would rather not entertain notions of either leasing or selling their land. In this respect, they may be motivated, among other things, by an ancestral identification with their property, by a need to retain it as a post-retirement benefit, by the tax breaks associated with farming and by the fact that land is a good capital appreciating asset. Reinforcing the status quo, the previous LDP government and Nokyo both felt that a large farming community well served their interests. The LDP from the point of view of electoral support and Nokyo in terms of prospective membership numbers and clients.[2]

Given the minority status of Japan's full-time farmers and the power of the vested interests that support the part-timers, the restructuring of the agricultural sector towards larger scale more efficient units, is turning out to be an uphill struggle. One ray of hope lies in the ageing of farm workers. Whereas in 1960, the proportion of active men and women over the age of 60 were 23 and 14 per cent respectively, by 1985 the corresponding ratios were 51 and 39 per cent [Hayami 1988:85]. Although this trend is cited by the Ministry of Agriculture as adversely affecting farm productivity, in the long run, as the number of farm households dwindle, it may help to pave the way towards land consolidation and thus more efficient farming.

## SUMMARY

- Extensive land reforms undertaken in 1946 radically transformed landholding arrangements, bringing a fair measure of equality and security of tenure to the countryside.
- Two types of agricultural cooperative societies exist, a general one and one specializing in a particular crop or product. They are both federated at the local and national level. The agricultural cooperative movement, which has seven million members, represents farmers' interests and provides them with various marketing, financial and other services.
- The rationale for agricultural protection has been based on labour productivity (and hence income) growth rates being lower in agriculture than in the rest of the economy.
- Agricultural protection has been provided by means of trade barriers (mainly in the form of import quotas), price maintenance schemes, direct subsidies and special taxation benefits.
- Rice is Japan's premier crop and has received very high degrees of protection. In 1991, producer prices were over six times those of American rice growers.
- In 1969 in response to a very large increase in rice output induced by high rice prices, a rice acreage control programme was introduced.
- Following the poor rice crop of 1993, a limited amount of rice imports was permitted and eventually the government agreed to a phased increase of rice imports for future years.
- Although protection has raised rural incomes, it has hindered the rationalization of the agricultural sector, has been excessively costly, has penalized consumers and has not enhanced Japan's food self-sufficiency.
- Land productivity in Japan is better than in most other industrial countries but the converse is the case for rural labour productivity. The latter has suffered from a surfeit of part-time farmers made possible by close commuting distances to non-farm employment, tax breaks, family ties to the land and the fact that land is a good appreciating asset.
- The government is seeking to improve rural labour productivity by increasing the size of the average farm. With at least 40 per cent of farmers being over the age of 60, future prospects for some form of farmstead enlargements are reasonably bright.

# 13 Some Service Industries

## INTRODUCTION

Within most industrial countries the tertiary or service sector over-shadows, by a very wide margin, the combined contribution of primary and secondary industries to both national output and employment. In this respect, Japan is no exception (see Table 13.1). Its service sector does, however, manifest certain traits which are more or less unique to Japan, some of which are beneficial, whilst others are rather problematic. Instead of reviewing the sector as a whole, we have decided to survey a few of the country's leading tertiary industries. Those selected include distribution, education and health.

The sectors in question have deliberately been chosen because collectively they employ an overwhelming majority of the tertiary labour force and, apart from financial institutions, they are the three most important service sectors from the general public's point of view. (While banking and financial institutions also merit special attention, we believe that the reader ought to have gained sufficient insights into their activities from the various references to them in preceding chapters.)

In looking at the distribution sector we have tried to emphasize its economic performance. However, on turning to education and health the economic purist might not take kindly to the fact that our treatment is largely descriptive. This follows from a dearth (in English) of analytical economic studies relating to Japan and in part from our own lack of confidence in the application of the economics of education. Be that as it may, considering that there is a strong consumption element in both education and health, an understanding of the way the two systems function would at the very least assist in evaluating the quality of their services.

## DISTRIBUTION

The distribution of goods that leave local farm or factory gates or which arrive at a country's port of entry are usually first handled by

Some Service Industries                                    275

Table 13.1   The Relative Role of the Service Sector in Various Countries,
1987

| Country | Percentage of GNP | Percentage of Employment |
|---------|-------------------|--------------------------|
| Japan | 63.2 | 58.5 |
| USA | 71.3 | 71.2 |
| UK | 64.2 | 69.4 |
| West Germany | 57.1 | 54.4 |
| France | 65.6 | 63.6 |
| Italy | 61.6 | 57.7 |

Source: Bank of Japan

wholesalers and then by retailers. In Japan, there are distinctly more
of both types of establishments per 1000 residents than is the case
in the USA. As Table 13.2 shows, in 1982 there were twice as
many wholesalers per person in Japan and nearly twice as many
retailers.

On the other side of the coin, Japanese companies, whether they be
retailers or wholesalers, tend on average to employ far less workers
than American ones. See Table 13.3.

The picture that emerges is that relative to a country like the USA,
Japan is encumbered with numerous and meagrely staffed distribution
channels.

Among wholesalers, activities are broadly structured within a three
tiered system (whereby some firms specialize in one type of good or
in a specific brand). First of all, there are primary wholesalers (either
a manufacturer's subsidiary or an independent company) through which
all of a producer's goods initially pass. Then there are regional outlets
which in turn service local ones. The result is that there is a high
wholesale to retail sales ratio. In 1982, for example, the ratio was 3.53
for Japan compared with 1.09 for the USA [Ito and Maruyama 1991:155].
Retailers are very much dependent on wholesalers and until fairly recently, even supermarkets and discount stores had no direct access to
manufacturers.

The retail section comprises a limited number of departmental stores,
a reasonable quantity of supermarkets, some keiretsu or manufacturer's
speciality shops and numerous 'mom-and-pop' stores, staffed in the
main by only one or two senior citizens. More than half of Japan's
retailers fall into the latter category.

*Table* 13.2   Number of Establishments per 1000 Residents, 1982

|  | Japan | USA |
|---|---|---|
| Wholesale | 3.3 | 1.5 |
| Retail | 14.5 | 8.3 |

*Source*: Ito and Maruyama 1991:152

*Table* 13.3   Employees per Establishment, 1982

|  | Japan | USA |
|---|---|---|
| Wholesale | 9.3 | 12.6 |
| Retail | 3.7 | 8.1 |

*Source*: As in Table 13.2

## The Distribution Sector and Welfare

Considering that mom-and-pop stores are primarily managed by workers with few, if any, alternative employment prospects, many observers subscribe to the view that 'the distribution system in Japan serves as a vast sponge for the unemployed or underemployed' [Johnson 1982:13].[1] However, the evidence for this is inconclusive; merely because the distributive trades happen to engage individuals who would in all probability be in want of a job elsewhere, does not in itself constitute proof that the distribution sector needlessly mops up surplus labour. More relevantly, it is necessary to establish whether or not that sector holds an unduly large share of Japan's work force.

Data from the Bank of Japan indicate that in 1987, the proportion of Japanese employees in wholesale and retail firms was significantly greater than in the UK, Germany and France but not much above the ratios that were recorded for the USA and Italy (see Table 13.4). Contrasting Japan with the USA, it would seem (from computations of the information supplied in Tables 13.2 and 13.3) that in 1982, there were 84.37 distributive workers per 1000 residents in Japan compared with 86.1 in the USA. Focusing only on retail workers, the respective figures were 53.6 for Japan and 67.2 for the USA. In other words, although Japan may have a relatively bountiful supply of retail establishments, it does not necessarily follow (bearing in mind their small average staff size) that it has a relatively higher proportion of retail

Table 13.4 Proportion of Workers Employed in Wholesale and Retail Firms, 1987

| Japan | USA | UK | Germany | France | Italy |
|-------|------|------|---------|--------|-------|
| 23.1 | 20.8 | 15.4 | 12.2 | 16.6 | 21.3 |

Source: Bank of Japan:143

employees. Whatever may have been the situation in the early postwar years, the importance of the retail industry as an employment haven for the elderly is now on the wane. Between 1982 and 1985, the number of retail stores operated by one to two persons fell by 9.3 per cent. From 1985 to 1988, they declined by a further 7.0 per cent. These setbacks were attributed by MITI to the demise of ageing shopkeepers combined with a lack of sufficient more youthful successors [Kuribayashi 1991:48].

**The Profusion of Small Stores**

Japan's relative abundance of small stores may largely be attributed to three factors. First, there have been a multitude of immobile and or elderly workers who have eagerly taken to retailing, notwithstanding the sparse returns that have typically been realized. To some extent, this has been made somewhat bearable by virtue of rental expenses having being minimized through the common practice of placing stores in the front section of proprietors' residences.

Second, it would appear that Japanese housewives have a need, and indeed a preference, to shop at least once a day. This partly arises from limited general household storage space and the small sized refrigerators that are widely owned, and partly from the necessity to acquire highly perishable items, such as raw fish, on a daily basis. Shopping also provides housekeepers with a temporary respite from cramped living quarters and with an opportunity to engage shop attendants in some general conversation. Given the congestion of many urban road networks plus the fact that high land costs limit the amount of parking facilities, consumers tend to patronize stores accessible to them on foot. In the early 1980s, at least one food shop was within ten minutes walking distance of the homes of 58 per cent of the population. Alternatively, 84 per cent could make it within 20 minutes [Rothacher 1989:99].

Third, the encroachment of departmental stores on the turf of the smaller stores has been constrained by legislation. Large stores have had to run an awesome gauntlet of bureaucratic obstructionism to become licensed and those that have seen the light of day have been subject to more restrictive regulations, relating to opening hours and so on, than have small stores.

## Legislation Limiting Large Stores

In the early postwar period, legal barriers against large stores were suspended and in a climate of general economic recovery, departmental stores began to make steady headway. Alarmed small retailers soon began to petition for a renewal of governmental protection, and in response, the 1956 Department Stores Law was enacted. The law required that applications for the construction or enlarging of departmental stores be lodged with MITI. MITI referred all such requests to an advisory council, which in turn consulted with a regional council that in large part was composed of members of local Chambers of Commerce. 'As these Chambers had the interests of small retailers at heart, the applications were often given short shrift.' [Allen 1981:135]

The 1956 Law did not apply to supermarkets and chain stores which began to compete both with existing departmental stores (whose freedom of action was limited) and with the small retailers. The aggrieved firms made their complaints abundantly clear, and to their satisfaction, the 1956 Department Stores Law was superseded in 1974 by the Large Retail Store Law, or Dai-ten Ho. In 1979, the Dai-ten Ho was revised and made even more stringent.

Dai-ten Ho, which explicitly purported to protect local retailers, covered two store categories, those with floor space in excess of 1500 square metres (3000 in large cities), and those with 500–1500 square metres (500–3000 in large cities). From an administrative point of view, prospective proprietors were expected to post notifications to MITI if their businesses were likely to fall in the first category and to a prefectural governor where the second category was likely to apply. Two notifications were required, an article 3 notification to be submitted by the builder and an article 5 notification to be submitted by the future retailer. In processing an article 5 notification, MITI was authorized to consult with the Large Stores Council which forwarded the documentation to the relevant local Chamber of Commerce. The latter body then established a Council to Recommend Commercial Activities (CRCA) which had a three week deadline to conclude its deliberations. The CRCA usually proposed recommended changes (to hours of business operations, floor space and so on) which would have very likely re-assured existing traders.

Strictly speaking, all the necessary paper work should have taken no longer than seven months but MITI adopted the procedure of in-sisting on an advance opinion from the CRCA before an article 5 notification could even be filed. No time limit was imposed in acquir-ing this opinion and in practice, it has taken some stores ages to ob-tain all the necessary clearances. Okuno-Fujiwara refers to two cases where one store's application was held up for eight and a half years and the other for more than ten [Okuno-Fujiwara 1991:293].

In May 1990, MITI altered its process to make it feasible for a store to open its doors within 18 months of it initially expressing its desire to do so. A year later, an amendment of the Dai-ten Ho abolished the CRCA and required the Large Stores Council to examine all applica-tions, on the basis of a common national standard. Then in 1994, the Large Retail Store Law was revised allowing retailers 'to open a store of up to 1000 square metres anywhere in Japan unless local govern-ments or chambers of commerce initiate objections on reasonable grounds' [*Nikkei Weekly* 2 Feb. 1994]. This led to the approval of thousands of large store openings, including more than 15 branches of the American chain 'Toys are Us'. Not surprisingly, many well estab-lished retailers did not take kindly to the changes, for the old system had clearly favoured insiders, regardless of size.

Of the three general factors which have tended to promote a pro-liferation of small stores in Japan, the Large Retail Stores Law (Dai-ten Ho) is commonly regarded as the most decisive. Although Flath does not totally dismiss the law's importance, for his investigations do provide a statistical confirmation that regulations are a positive deter-minant of small store numbers, he does part company with others in maintaining that that regulation had not been the most critical factor [Flath 1990:378]. According to Flath, the relative Japanese endowment of a multitude of small stores is economically desirable considering that consumer storage costs are high relative to those of retailers [367]. Since the abundance of small stores 'represents an efficient adaptation to the conditions of the country' [368], the situation would not be appreciably different had the law not existed. In fact, Flath maintains that 'the law itself is a reflection of the distribution system' [383]. We remain somewhat sceptical and wonder why if numerous small stores ideally suit the Japanese, small retailers felt an urgent need to canvass for legislative protection?

**The Relative Efficiency of the Japanese Distribution System**

The Japanese distribution system is generally perceived as being inefficient. Various reasons may be advanced in support of this view. For one, the fact that Japan has more stores per thousand people than other industrial countries and that they are, on average, staffed by fewer employees, seems to indicate that scale economies are yet to be realized. However, as Itoh reminds us, 'small or medium scale firms do not dominate only the distribution market; they also dominate the manufacturing sector and are usually said to be the source of competitiveness for the Japanese economy' [Itoh 1991:177].

Alternatively, it is often alleged that 'the productivity of the distributive trades relative to average productivity of the economy is lower in Japan than in other major developed countries' [Kuribayashi 1991:44]. For example, in 1985, the ratio of labour productivity in distribution to labour productivity in manufacturing was 59.4 per cent in Japan, 67.8 per cent in the USA, 71 per cent in France and 78.4 per cent in Germany [Montgomery 1991:71]. While information of this kind is indeed suggestive of a relative weakness of Japanese distribution, it is by no means conclusive. Aside from anything else, the relatively low degree of labour productivity recorded in that sector, may in part be attributed to above average industrial productivity levels in Japanese manufacturing.

The multi-layered structure of Japanese wholesaling, whereby goods pass through more channels en route to the retailer than is the case in the USA, is considered to be an important source of inefficiency or, what amounts to the same thing, a source of Japan's high consumer price levels. As if to confirm this, commentators are wont to point out that certain goods, such as cameras and video recorders, are cheaper abroad than in Japan.

Even if Japanese consumers face higher prices than are objectively warranted, it does not automatically follow that the fault lies with the country's distribution system. On analyzing gross profit (or mark-up) ratios, that is, the differences between selling and acquisition prices divided by selling prices, Ito and Maruyama discovered that irrespective of whether one considers the wholesale or retail sector, profit margins are lower in Japan than in either the USA or Germany [Ito and Maruyama 1991:163]. High Japanese consumer prices are, in their opinion, explained solely by strategies adopted by Japanese producers, for once the distribution system receives, as an input to the 'pipeline', goods from manufacturers, it 'is as efficient as its US counterpart' [171].

Ito and Maruyama's assertions have been challenged by Nishimura, who questions whether one can legitimately define efficiency in terms of distribution mark-ups. After all, as Nishimura argues, low services costs could theoretically be compatible with a willingness on the part of service workers to accept low incomes [Nishimura 1993:271]. However, if such incomes are no lower than the recipients' alternative opportunities, Nishimura may be confusing technical with economic efficiency.

Nishimura also faults previous studies (including Ito and Maruyama's) for not incorporating transport expenses in distribution costs. Notwithstanding his own reservations about the usefulness of mark-up ratios as a relative efficiency indicator, he in turn proceeds, with the use of input-output tables, to calculate them.

Essentially, Nishimura's results confirm that in considering distribution within a broader framework than had hitherto been done, it still holds true that 'the Japanese ratio of the cost of distribution services to the final price is comparable to the US ratio or lower than that' [276]. Nevertheless, the data reveal a disturbing trend. Over the period 1965–85, retail mark-up ratios rose from 15.2 per cent to 26.8 per cent. (Fortunately wholesale margins more or less remained constant.) Nishimura holds 'sluggish labour productivity growth' within retailing as a primary cause for observed increases in distribution costs [284]. In that sense, the current Japanese distribution system is a legitimate cause for concern.

Finally, statistics purporting to compare the relative efficiency of distribution in Japan *vis-à-vis* say the United States are likely to be problematic. No allowance is made for differences in quality. Many, particularly Japanese scholars, are of the view that standards are higher in Japan but this of course is debatable. Of more moment, certain data sources on which some researchers have relied, such as the Japanese Census of Commerce, exclude much of the distribution activities of agricultural cooperatives and of government agencies. Furthermore, in Japan, repair services are included in manufacturing as are wholesale branches of producers, whereas in the US both are classified as being in distribution. Another noted difference lies in eating houses. In the US they are included in distribution figures but usually not so in Japan. Although such discrepancies throw spokes into the wheel, judgements on the findings of the major works done to date, need not necessarily be suspended. What the situation does demand, is an open mind and a readiness to reconsider additional evidence as it emerges.

## Current Developments in Retailing

A number of Japanese retail firms have either concentrated on commodities originating from associated keiretsu organizations, as has been the case with certain departmental stores, or else (in such fields as cars, household electric appliances and cosmetics), have exclusively carried the products of a specific manufacturer. For example, some 25 000 cosmetic stores sell only Shizeido brands, or alternatively, some 18 000 electrical retailers are entirely beholden to Matsushita. In most instances, the stores are nominally under independent management, apart from a few 'antenna shops' used for market research. Nevertheless, manufacturers have exerted a large measure of control, specifying final selling prices, determining stock compositions and promotional strategies, and not infrequently, even dispatching some of their own personnel to assist with sales. This phenomenon of vertical distributive restraints, is referred to as 'keiretsuka'.

Keiretsuka yields certain advantages. It reduces transaction costs in that relations between parties are built on a basis of long standing trust and mutual confidence. Japanese retailers can often return unsold stock and producers are prepared to repair or exchange defective merchandise. Department stores which have lacked skilled and experienced apparel buyers have frequently resorted to the consignment system. This arrangement virtually provides manufacturers or wholesalers with the go-ahead to stock a store's clothing department with whatever selection of items is seen fit, on the understanding that retailing risks are borne by the supplier. Such a procedure has in the past worked to the mutual satisfaction of both parties.

Staunch critics of keiretsuka have not unexpectedly been outsiders, particularly potential overseas exporters, who have argued that in practice, it constitutes a formidable 'structural impediment' to the penetration of the Japanese market. Vertical restraints raise entry costs and in many instances, foreigners find difficulties in matching the services provided by insiders, particularly with respect to the returning of stock and the provision of generous terms of credit.

Fortunately, recent innovations and events suggest that the Japanese distribution system is neither immutable nor impermeable. Independent discount stores, partly buoyed by the nominal abolition of resale price maintenance in April 1992, have began to strike out fairly aggressively. In the past they had encountered strong resistance on the part of manufacturers, who denied them deliveries so as to protect the traditional dealers. This meant that stocks had to be obtained circuitously, through the intermediation of friendly, yet shadowy third parties. With the Japanese economy slipping into a recession in 1992–3, suppliers began to be encumbered with large volumes of unsold inventories. Since their conventional outlets have not been able to meet their needs, the *Economist* believes that 'desperate manufacturers will let upstarts sell their products instead' [*Economist* 6 Feb. 1993:67]. Big Mac, one of the fastest growing discounters, claims that at least one manufacturer which previously refused to do business with it, now openly does so [67]. Moreover, 'electronic companies including Sony and Matsushita Electric Industrial [sic], and leading breweries, have been warned by the Fair Trade Commission to allow retailers to discount their products without fear of losing contracts' [*Financial Times* 6 Dec. 1994].

Some stores, particularly certain chain ones, are now utilizing point-of-sale computers that track each product's turnover. 'Slow sellers are quickly cleared off the shelves, no matter how powerful the firm which made them. By the same token, less influential manufacturers (often foreign ones) can win shelf space if their products win approval from customers' [*Economist* 24 April 1993:70].

As for imported products, they are beginning to be more readily available but the inward flux is by no means dramatic. Until fairly recently, imports were conducted by agencies which had exclusive distribution rights. Currently, this monopolistic practice is being breached by 'parallel importing', which legally provides for other distributors to secure, through alternative channels, the same goods for which a sole agent had originally contracted. By 1987, about 51 per cent of department stores were selling some parallel import goods, chief among these have been tennis rackets, skis and jogging shoes [Kuribayashi 1991:50]. Some US companies, such as Shop America, have devised ways of by-passing the multi-layered Japanese distribution system by grafting on to existing outlets, in this case the 7-Eleven stores, which distribute Shop America's catalogues and accept orders on its behalf. Shop America has aimed 'to deliver US made products such as audio cassettes, compact disks, golf and tennis balls and cigarette lighters via air freight from New Jersey within five to twelve days' [Montgomery 1991:72].

Enterprising and tenacious foreign firms can certainly wend their way through the labyrinthine Japanese distribution system if they are prepared to expend time, effort and fairly high entry costs. There undoubtedly are some challenging 'structural impediments' that the distribution system poses but such problems are almost certainly compounded by mountains of governmental red tape. Just to shift merchandise from the docks is in itself a herculean task. In the case of importing say grapefruit, it is necessary to acquire separate permits from the Ministry of Agriculture and the Ministry of Health. Then inspectors from both Ministries have to clear the cargo which then has to be checked by yet another official for any illicit drugs. The zest for regulation does not only inconvenience importers, it also bears down heavily on local Japanese companies wishing to enter retailing. 'According to research carried out by major supermarket chain Daiei, setting up one large supermarket entails the acquisition of no less than 40 licenses in accordance with 19 different laws' (not counting the Large Retail Store Law) [*Tokyo Business* Dec 1993:7]. The financial costs of negotiating all the required licences and other bureaucratic hurdles has been estimated to be of the order of $1.6 million [9]. Excessive regulation has clearly hindered the streamlining of the Japanese distribution sector.

## SOGO SHOSHA – THE LARGE JAPANESE TRADING COMPANY

A significant share of Japan's external trade is coordinated by large trading companies, known as sogo shosha. These companies play a key role in the economy. In 1990, their gross revenue totalled 127 000 billion yen, an amount equal to 30 per cent of the country's GDP.

### The Nature of the Sogo Shosha

Other trading companies exist besides the sogo shosha but the differences between them are immense. Ordinary trading companies are typically subsidiaries of manufacturing corporations. They tend to concentrate on certain commodity lines and their exposure to foreign trade is more limited. Usually, they engage in some exporting or importing, seldom in both. For the sogo shosha, widespread foreign trade involving numerous commodities is their trademark. During the 1980s, about 60 per cent of Japan's total exports and 70 per cent of its imports passed through their hands.

The sogo shosha are not simply trade intermediaries. Other activities of theirs include the provision of finance, the gathering and dispensing of vital foreign economic data (most sogo shosha maintain at least 100 offices scattered across the globe), warehousing, transport, construction, overseas resource development and manufacturing. In almost all instances, these non-trading ventures had been initiated in response to trading imperatives. Occasionally, they even fortify the sogo shosha's trading bias. For example, their acquisition of fleets (which currently include large liquefied natural gas container vessels) provides the sogo shosha with an incentive to ensure that their ships are always laden with cargo irrespective of the direction in which they sail.

## Postwar Developments

In the early postwar period, the large trading houses (some of which had their origins in the late 19th century) experienced serious setbacks. Much of their overseas assets were confiscated by unsympathetic occupation authorities. Two companies in particular, Mitsubishi Shoji and Mitsui Bussan, were treated harshly. During 1947 Mitsui was compelled to split into at least 180 separate entities, Mitsubishi into around 140. (Perceived collaboration with the Japanese military appears to have been a major motive in the dismantling of these firms.) The vacuum created by the weakening of the traditional Sogo Shosha was, to a great extent, filled by leading cotton merchants and numerous other textile traders.

Shortly after regaining independence (in 1952), the Japanese government implemented a set of measures to help reconstitute and strengthen the traditional large trading companies. Tax write-offs against the costs of establishing foreign branches and against the formation of contingency funds in the event of losses resulting from unpaid trade transactions, were authorized.

Mergers were openly encouraged. With this in mind, financial assistance from the Bank of Japan was forthcoming, which included preferential treatment to large trading companies in the allocation of foreign exchange [Kunio 1982:163]. Not before long, both Mitsubishi and Mitsui reconstructed themselves, the former in 1954 and the latter in 1959. Their reconsolidation was fostered by MITI which strove to reduce the number of the trading companies from about 2800 'that existed after the occupation down to around 20 big ones' [Johnson 1982:206]. At the close of the 1950s, 14 firms led the pack. By the end of the 1960s, their number had fallen to ten. Then in the mid 1970s, Ataka and Itoh merged reducing the number still further.

The remaining nine now constitute the sogo shosha as opposed to the ordinary trading companies referred to above. They are listed, with the value (in billion yen) of their 1990 assets in brackets, as follows: Mitsubishi (8864.4), Mitsui (7944.1), C. Itoh (5777.7), Marubeni (5244.2), Sumitomo (4825.9), Nissho Iwai (3581.6), Tomen (2067.0), Nichimen (1668.1) and Kanematsu (1395.4) [*Tokyo Business* Jan. 1992:56].

All but one are members of a leading keiretsu, an outcome which sits well with MITI's prior drive for the 'keiretsurization' of trading companies and manufacturers.[2]

## The Sogo Shosha in the Japanese Economy

The sogo shosha have been very resilient. A good deal of their success can be attributed to the sheer magnitude of their trading operations which cover a large quantity and variety of products and which span the entire globe. Their vast overheads, which include a succession of overseas offices, sophisticated information gathering and processing systems and highly professional and well trained staff, are, because of the scope of their activities, more economically sustainable than the fixed costs of smaller and more specialized traders. Frequently it is to the advantage of manufacturers, especially when foreign transactions are involved, to commission the services of the sogo shosha, rather than to form their own trading subsidiaries. Only in areas where direct producer servicing is crucial, such as in electrical machinery, has it clearly been in the manufacturer's interest not to delegate distribution activities to outsiders.

The sogo shosha have, by virtue of their extraordinary data intelligence and network of contacts, been invaluable agents in transferring modern technology to Japan. Their large economic clout has also been instrumental in ensuring that foreign capital goods are obtained at competitive prices. In order to secure critical raw materials on a regular basis and at low costs, the trading companies have considerably involved themselves in overseas resource development projects. Where they really excel is in the exportation of manufacturing, power or telecommunications plants. In contrast to conventional exports, this category requires a number of different manufacturers in supplying the plant equipment. Furthermore, on site supervision and coordination needs to be administered by a single management body with a good understanding of local conditions, mores and so on. With their proven ability to activate and orchestrate complex activities across international frontiers, the sogo shosha have helped make plant exports a relatively large foreign exchange earner [Kunio 1982:225].

Thanks to the large trading companies, many small and medium sized firms have been able to obtain loan finance in securing necessary inputs or in disposing of their output. In the past, major banks preferred to deal with big corporations. Smaller ones were often shunned or subject to strict collateral guarantees. The sogo shosha, which maintained very close ties with their own keiretsu's leading bank, have been able to borrow fairly freely. They in turn, have been willing to re-lend to the smaller companies with which they deal. The arrangement works well. The sogo shosha are suitably placed to evaluate the loan risks of firms with which they have long had business relations, while the firms in question not only secure finance but also the good advice and sound intermediary services of the trading companies. On occasion, where the sogo shosha may perceive promising export potential, it may itself approach an eminently suitable manufacturer with offers of credits and loans to encourage it to capitalize on the trade opportunity.

The sogo shosha have survived partly because of their adaptability to changing conditions. They have kept abreast of modern events and have not been averse to moving into hitherto uncharted waters. Today, their distribution services are not confined to wholesaling. Mitsubishi for instance, has the Kentucky Fried Chicken franchise from which it has amply profited. They have now reached out into satellite communication and the aircraft industry, and in Eastern Europe they are setting a good pace in plant exports. Their resounding success testifies to the fact that the Japanese distribution sector is by no means an unqualified failure.

## EDUCATION

The Japanese have long placed much store in knowledge and learning. Teachers have traditionally been held in high regard and even presently, when educators in the West tend to be denigrated,[3] their counterparts in Japan continue to be venerated. Not only do Japanese pedagogues proudly bear the title 'sensei' (teacher), they also maintain a relatively high professional standing and are comparatively well remunerated. All this reflects the importance that is attributed to education.

### Attendance Rates

Currently, Japan ranks as a world leader in the dissemination of education. Not only is school attendance up to the completion of junior high school universally required but 94 per cent of students proceed to obtain a senior high school diploma. Rivalling the US, some 46 per cent of high school graduates enrol in tertiary educational institutions.

Mass participation in education reached international levels well before the introduction in 1872 of compulsory schooling. In the mid-nineteenth century, approximately 40–50 per cent of the male population and 15 per cent of females, were recipients of at least some degree of formal education. Such proportions were high, compared with those then prevailing in Europe and America [Allen 1981:5].

## Foreign Influences

The Japanese have readily incorporated foreign ingredients into their educational system without allowing them to overwhelm the essence of its distinctive features. Prior to 1870, the Chinese Confucian system of schooling was the sole foreign model to be emulated. Thereafter, the Japanese borrowed selectively from the leading industrial powers of the day. From France, they seized on the notion of a centralized national authority, from Germany they were inspired by a system of higher education revolving around a small number of elite universities, not to mention their seemingly everlasting infatuation with German school uniforms. The English impressed them with their emphasis on moral education (a practice that was central to Japanese culture) and from the Americans they acquired various teaching techniques and an interest in vocational training [Rohlen 1983:55].

In the period preceding the Second World War, the Japanese educational system was infused with ultra-nationalistic sentiments, stressing devotion to the Emperor, obedience and self-sacrifice. Effectively, the military had fully coopted it. However, when the country was defeated and occupied, the Americans set about reforming education, hoping that it would play a key role in democratizing Japan. Strenuous efforts were made to replicate the American approach. A corresponding structure embodying the 6-3-3-4 system (six elementary, three middle, three senior high and four university years) is now in place but the system is still manifestly Japanese.

## Kindergarten

At the age of four, at least 80 per cent of Japanese infants commence their formal education by entering kindergarten. By the age of five, almost all are involved. Emphasis is placed on helping children to integrate and interact with their peer groups. In the process, duties and privileges are shared on an equal basis and pupils are induced to conform to kindergarten norms by being ostracized and mocked when and if they fail to comply. Reading of phonetic scripts is taught and by the time they enter primary school, most youngsters can handle basic texts (without Chinese characters), making them functionally literate.

## Primary School

Progression to primary school takes place each April for all those who have already celebrated their sixth birthday. Conditions and educational contents are fairly standardized, as is the cross-sectional composition of the students. Most schools draw pupils from a reservoir of diverse natural aptitudes and socio-economic backgrounds. This means that the bulk of Japanese children experience similar primary school environments and standards.

The primary school curriculum provides for a wide and varied collection of subjects, which from the pupil's point of view, are personally enriching. Topics covered include Japanese language, Social studies (History, Geography and so on), Arithmetic, Science, Music, Drawing and Craft, Domestic science, Physical education, Moral education and Special activities. In terms of music, all students eventually learn two instruments, one wind and one keyboard.

## Junior High School

At the age of 12, children proceed to a junior high school. There, school hours are somewhat extended but a similar range of subjects is taught. From year one, a foreign language is introduced and time spent on Japanese as such is reduced. Similarly, period allocations to art and music are halved. On the other hand, increasing attention is given to science and mathematics. One's stay in a middle school culminates in sitting for entry examinations for high school and the passage from the junior to senior high school represents a watershed in the life of the student.

## High School

Pupils may opt to undertake the entrance examinations of any of the numerous public high schools which fall within their residential zones. These schools exhibit marked variations in academic standards and reputations, and are judged on the basis of their success rate in facilitating student access to prestigious universities. The pecking order of the schools available is both finely tuned and is well known to the public at large. Naturally, the order of difficulty in meeting a school's entrance examination requirements varies directly with its reputation.

## Private Schools

With at least 30 per cent of high schools being in the private domain, high schools are obviously not exclusively state run. The private ones, which receive government subsidies to offset teacher costs, usually accept students regardless of their residential locations. Like public schools, they vary in standards. The top ones now rank among the country's best and acceptance is strictly conditional on passing imposing entry examinations. The less eminent ones serve to provide an academic education to students not gaining access to respectable public schools.

## Vocational Schools

In addition to the high schools which are exclusively academically orientated (comprising just over 50 per cent of the total), there are also vocational high schools which focus on training in commercial and technical skills, music, domestic science, nursing, agriculture and fishing. For students entering the work force, night high schools may be accessible, though these are limited in scope.

Within the vocational high schools, the range of technical skills imparted is quite impressive. It includes knowledge of machinery, electricity, electronics, architecture, civil engineering, automobile repair, metalwork, textiles, interior furnishing, printing, radio communication, welding and information technology [Dore and Sako 1989:34].

A small number of vocational schools, representing no more than 15 per cent of all high schools, offer nothing but vocational courses. The others provide a broad range of subjects which includes Japanese, English, Mathematics, Physical and Social sciences.

In the early postwar years when entry into high school was much less commonplace and skilled labour was in short supply, attendance at a vocational school held out the promise of good career prospects. However, with a sharp rise in average educational attainments, the premium attached to a vocational education, as opposed to a university one, has depreciated considerably. This has led to an adverse change in the public's perception of vocational schools and as a result, they now attract relatively low calibre students. To their credit, they have at least two redeeming features. The technical training they provide is still appreciated by many small scale firms and for the more ambitious, if not particularly able students, assistance is provided in having them placed in certain low rung universities which pay heed to teacher recommendations.

## School Hours, Class Sizes and Discipline

More time is devoted to formal school work than in Western countries. The length of the academic school year exceeds the US one by four weeks and a five and a half day weekly cycle is in operation. (Since 1992, Japanese public school children have been granted one Saturday off per month.) Class sizes are large, averaging 44 students. On the whole, schools are well ordered and disciplinary problems are relatively minor. They are more likely to erupt in high schools at the lower end of the pecking order, where less gifted students from disadvantaged homes may vent their frustrations with their ultimately poor employment futures and their inability to cope with nationally determined academic standards. Reports of bullying and school violence, in some cases aided and abetted by teachers (in pre-high schools), have come to light. However, the actual number of such incidents has turned 'out to be minute compared with the size of the system' [Dore and Sako 1989:6].

## Examination Hell

For those wishing to secure both permanent tenure in a prestigious corporation or in a respected branch of the civil service *and* who wish to maximize their chances of rising to an organization's upper ranks, entry into a leading university is an absolute necessity. There is a general and almost precise awareness regarding the ratings of each university from the point of view of prospective employers. Streets ahead of all others, stands Tokyo (Todai) University. Not only are the largest single number of company presidents Todai graduates but so are the majority of senior government officials. (Among other elite universities are Keio, Kyoto and Waseda.)

Since Japanese employers primarily focus on job applicants' university affiliations and show limited, if any, interest in a student's undergraduate performance, and since it is well nigh impossible to switch from one university to another, the likely career path of aspiring high school students critically hinges on the outcome of university entrance examinations.

The examinations in question have two components. First, there is a universal test in Japanese, English, mathematics, social and natural sciences which serves as a prelude to examinations determined separately by each university. Both sets of examinations are based on nationally standardized high school curriculums. Eligibility for acceptance depends on a weighted score average, with weights varying according to university and faculty.

Almost all examination questions are either multiple choice or require very short answers. They are fitting in assessing mathematical and scientific knowledge and understanding but not so in relation to English, where composition and oral skills are not tested and not in the social sciences, where emphasis is given to the retention of miscellaneous facts, rather than to critical analysis. In no small way, success depends on tenacity and the possession of a good memory.

It is obvious that not everyone is accepted into a university or college of their choice. To make matters worse, the total number of students seeking admission exceeds the total number of places available. In 1989, of 1 100 000 student hopefuls, only 702 000 were accommodated, 477 000 in four year universities and 225 000 in two year colleges. That is, nearly one in three missed out entirely [Blumenthal 1992:457]. These unfortunates tend to join the ranks of the 'ronin' (masterless samurai), who reattempt the examinations after a period of individual preparation. (Repetition of the final high school year is not feasible.)

The above described situation certainly concentrates the minds of all those high school students with even a modicum of ambition. Preparation starts in earnest from the beginning of high school and even before, taking into account the need to get into a good school in the first place. The impending examinations set the tone for all formal activity. Previous papers are thoroughly scrutinized and mock tests are periodically administered. The expected level of knowledge is so expansive, that seldom, if ever, can a teacher digress or dwell 'needlessly' on a topic. At home, students habitually scan texts until late at night.

So frantic are large sections of the student body (or more realistically their mothers) that in the evenings, many attend special cramming colleges or engage private tutors. A booming examination coaching industry has emerged. It has two segments, Juko, which specializes in helping students to prepare for the entry examinations of top high schools and Yobiko, which concentrates on university admissions. Ironically, some select Juko levy their own entry tests since their reputation and fees depend on the success rate of their students. In 1985, 47.3 per cent of final year junior high school students went to Juko. Juko patronage extends down to primary school kids, where in the same year, 29.6 per cent of six graders were enrolled [Blumenthal 1992:450]. As for Yobiko, it usually draws in no less than 10 per cent of the high school body.

Blumenthal believes that an unfortunate by-product of the chronic examination frenzy is that as contestants improve on their skills and performance, the most sought after universities have felt a need to increase the level of difficulty of their tests [459]. If this is indeed the case, then assiduous high school students, whose lot is already generally perceived as an unenviable one, can look forward to yet greater sacrifices of their now limited leisure time.

**Education and Equality**

Japan has often prided itself on being a meritocracy. Certainly in the postwar era, leading positions in both the private and public sector have primarily been awarded on the basis of individual merit. As has already been made clear, high school examination performance is used as a screening device by universities and employers alike. All intelligent and industrious youth, regardless of their social origins (with the exception of barukumins (members of a uniquely low caste), Koreans or women) could, in theory, equally entertain notions of working towards high office. After all, the selection process, which sharply distinguishes student aptitudes, operates impersonally.

Equality of educational opportunity seems to be well entrenched in public elementary and junior high schools, where every child has an automatic right of entry. The resources of the Ministry of Education are fairly evenly disbursed throughout the country at large, with the result that general facilities are much the same comparing one school with another.

After junior high, teenagers are placed into specific high schools according to their test ratings. This seems to ensure that each high school has a student body with a given and clearly acknowledged range of intellectual capabilities, and that significant differences exist in standards between one high school and another.

Theoretically, students with comparable innate abilities, compete on an equal footing. However, in practice 'the high school academic ladder reflects household socioeconomic stratification' [Rohlen 1983:130]. That is, students from richer homes, whose mothers do not work and who receive extra tuition, are much more likely to proceed to a top ranking high school than others. The importance of a wealthy background is indicated by the fact that while in the 1950s, the top ten high schools from which Tokyo University drew its students were mostly public ones, by the 1970s, they were all superseded by private ones [21]. Needless to say, fees charged by elite private schools are well beyond the means of modest income families.

## Education of Females

Within the general confines of the education system, females are not discriminated against. The proportion of girls enrolled in academic high schools matches that of boys, and women face the same set of university entrance hurdles as do men. Nonetheless, the pattern of tertiary institute attendance differs across the sexual divide. Although over 90 per cent of male students enter into a four year undergraduate university programme, only one third of females do. The remaining two thirds proceed to two-year colleges where men are few and far between (less than 10 per cent of the total). Within the standard four year universities, female representation weakens as one considers institutions higher and higher up the academic ladder. In the early 1980s, women constituted less than 10 per cent of Tokyo University's first year intake.

Such patterns reflect the social pressures to which Japanese women are subjected. Girls are encouraged to set their sights at a good marriage and to lead (where feasible) a domesticated life. Ideally, a young woman should not become more educated than her prospective spouse and in any event, most large corporations are little inclined to consider women applicants for managerial track positions. On the other hand, to secure a post at a prestigious organization, where good matches could be made, graduation from a posh private two-year college carries some weight. Here, as before, money talks.

## University Education

After having been allocated to specific universities, which in turn implies that the basic course of their professional future has already been determined, Japanese undergraduates lead a somewhat relaxed and carefree lifestyle. What with relatively non-stressful continuous assessment procedures and with small weights attached to final examinations, their successful progression through university is virtually assured. Studies in the first two years are rather general. Only in the latter half of their university career, do students specialize.

Overall standards fall short of Western ones. Analytical rigour leaves much to be desired and class attendance is often sporadic. In general, the freedom afforded by active university affiliation is relished and the time spent on campus is regarded as a restful interlude between prior hectic studies at high school and exacting work schedules that lie ahead. Given that most students exert as little effort as possible, it would seem that the elite universities maintain their status more by the quality of their (student) inputs and less by the quality of their products.

Postgraduate programmes are not generally in high demand and of those seeking doctoral training, many prefer Western institutions. In a similar vein, 'Japanese corporations commission more research from universities in the US and Europe than from universities in Japan' [Dore and Sako 1989:53]. There are a number of indicators that suggest that Japan lags behind other industrial countries in basic research. For instance, up to 1988, it had secured only five Nobel laureates in the natural sciences, compared with 145 for the US, 64 for Britain, 57 for Germany, 23 for France, 15 for Sweden and 13 for Switzerland [Sawa 1992:46]. Even small countries like Denmark, Austria and the Netherlands had more. Turning to the social sciences and looking to output in economic research as a pointer (measured in terms of the number of papers faculty members publish in leading journals) as of 1984, Japan's then leading economics department, located at Kyoto University, had a world ranking of 111 [45].

An excessive amount of red tape and rigid hierarchical procedures, which inhibit the creativity of promising junior faculty members, as well as an incestuous tendency to favour graduates from one's own university, are among some of the factors that contribute to the lacklustre research effort of Japanese universities. In stark contrast to the US, where outstanding scholars have long been drawn from the world at large, it was not until 1982 that Japan finally opened its doors to foreign academics. Even so, the few universities that have availed themselves of overseas talent, have generally restricted their offers to a three year stay. Had the Japanese education system excelled in stimulating student curiosity, analytical thinking and originality, the dearth of faculty heterogeneity may not have been of much consequence.

Japanese postgraduate schools do at least hold their own in the fields of science and engineering, where masters programmes maintain standards on a par with those of Western universities. Atypically, the acquisition of additional training and qualifications in engineering does in fact enhance a person's labour marketability. As a result, engineering undergraduates realizing that access into postgraduate courses is fairly vigorously contested, apply themselves more conscientiously than do other students.

There is a widespread perception that Japan, compared with the West, generates a disproportionately large number of engineering graduates. Although estimates of Japan's alleged capacity to produce engineers are fairly numerous, they are not consistent. Porter cites data which indicate that 'in 1978 nearly 80 000 persons graduated in engineering at Japanese universities and colleges, compared with 9000 in Britain' [Porter 1990:95]. Rohlen asserts that 'Japan produces more than twice as many engineers per capita as the United States' [Rohlen 1983:324], while Mosk and Nakata produce statistics which indicate that 'the flows of new engineers per capita are *somewhat* higher in Japan than in the United States'[4] [Mosk and Nakata 1992:57]. Such claims are challenged by Kinmouth who believes that in 1976, the US had surpassed Japan in the per capita generation of engineers and that since then, the US advantage had steadily been increasing [Kinmouth 1991:331]. It would seem that there is some incompatibility in defining an 'engineer'. In the US, computer specialists are excluded but not so in Japan. Also, engineering categories used in Japanese statistics include a 'range of occupations that would be labelled "technician" by US standards' [333].

Finally, in considering the utility of university education from the point of view of professional training, the preference of Japanese corporations to recruit generalists rather than specialists, should be borne in mind. Japanese companies are inclined to select personnel who primarily commit themselves to their firm rather than to a specific vocation. Required skills are largely taught by the firm itself and even in relation to engineers, studies show 'that within two to three years of hiring, more than 40 per cent will be following a technical specialty substantially different from that which they studied in college' [Kinmouth 1986:411].

## The Quality of Japanese Education

The Japanese education system has been widely disparaged for stifling self-expression and critical thought. Students who become adept in memorizing miscellaneous information, are provided with limited scope for structuring and analyzing facts. Although the study of English is compulsory at junior and high school, the general level of spoken English is abysmal. Apart from mathematics, practically everything is rote learnt. In short, critics maintain that far from enriching students intellectually, the system primarily serves to function as a clearing house for future employers and to ensure that it generates a population capable of yielding sustained and efficient work efforts.

While there is certainly a grain of truth in all this, such a description is much too lopsided. In reality, taking all its flaws and defects into consideration, one cannot but conclude that in overall terms, the achievements of Japan's education system are quite startling. Comparative international tests invariably rate Japanese school pupils as the best in mathematics and science. Not only is the average high but the dispersion around the average is low.

The general standard of literacy is excellent, enabling newspapers to assume a well educated readership, and unlike in the US, production managers are not obsessed with making their equipment and procedures 'idiot proof' [Kinmouth 1991:346]. Despite tight study schedules, nearly half of high school students participate in cultural and sporting clubs. Their high school subject fields may be fairly narrowly focused but this is partly compensated for by a broad exposure in primary and junior high schools. All told, 'the average Japanese high school graduate has the equivalent basic knowledge of the average American college graduate' [Abegglen and Stalk 1985:133].

At around 6 per cent of national income (slightly less than the proportions expended in the UK, France and Germany, and about the same as the US), the government's expenditure on education yields a good social return.[5] Few doubt whether Japan's economic 'miracle' would have eventuated had the country's general educational achievements not have been so impressive. All this notwithstanding, there are many impairments which need to be redressed. Prime among these is the need to play down the central role of university entrance examinations so that high school education could be conducted in a more relaxed manner paying heed to students' personal and cultural needs. As a corollary, the Ministry of Education's tight control over the system should be lessened, allowing for the transference of more autonomy and decision making to individual teachers.

HEALTH CARE

During the early postwar period, the average life expectancy of a Japanese citizen was comparatively low. Data in 1947 indicated that men and women could typically anticipate a lifespan of not more than 50 and 53 years respectively. To a very large extent, death was the consequence of diseases such as tuberculosis, pneumonia, bronchitis, and gastro-enteritis. By the 1970s, thanks to a concerted effort in screening the entire population for TB, the establishment of numerous TB sanatoria and improvements in public health administration, TB, other chest and stomach ailments as well as contagious diseases were no longer the country's leading killers. Their place is now taken by stomach and lung cancer followed by cerebro-vascular disorders.[6]

Currently, Japan lays claim to the world's longest average life expectancy, 76 years for men, 81 years for women. Similarly, its infant mortality rate, at five deaths per 1000, is the world's lowest. Factors including high per capita incomes, low unemployment levels, excellent standards of education and of hygiene and cleanliness, plus low fat diets go a long way in accounting for Japan's enviable position. Still, the country's health care system, universally available to all citizens on an equal basis, must be given due credit for Japan's exemplary health record.

## Low Cost of Health Care

Japan's expenditure on health is relatively low. By the beginning of the 1990s, it amounted to 6.6 per cent of GDP compared with over 10 per cent in the USA. It has consistently fallen below the OECD average and in the 1980s, only seven of that organization's 23 member countries allocated an equal or smaller proportion.[7]

Official Japanese health statistics do not include items which are usually incorporated abroad. Among these are expenses for normal child deliveries (considered to be natural as opposed to pathological processes), medical education and research, preventive health measures, grants to public hospitals and private room charges [Ikegami 1991:93]. Also, in contrast to the USA, Japan's health system is less burdened by problems associated with drug abuse, criminal assaults and the widespread prevalence of AIDS. (In 1990, there were only 195 AIDS patients (mostly haemophiliacs) compared with approximately 180 000 in the USA.) However, even upon adjusting for all these differences, it would still be true that overall medical outlays are proportionally smaller in Japan than in most Western countries.

Where Japan's experience is in tandem with others, is that its health bill has risen over time. (In 1960, it had represented only 3 per cent of GDP.) Causes of the secular increase in costs are to be found in: One, a growing demand for medical services contingent on universal health insurance coverage and rising expectations (associated with better education). Two, demographic changes whereby the elderly, who call upon medical services more readily than do younger people, are constituting a growing proportion of the total population. Three, changes in the relative prevalence of medical disorders in which chronic ailments are becoming more pronounced and finally, a marked capital intensity bias in the development of medical technology.

Since the early 1980s, the government has striven to curtail rising costs. It met with some success in that the Central Social Medical Care Council of the Ministry of Health determined that between 1981 and 1990, fee schedules, which are legally binding on all medical care providers, were not to increase in net terms by more than 2.4 per cent. As it happened, the general price level went up by 15 per cent [Ikegami 1991:96].

**Health Insurance**

All citizens are required to be covered for medical insurance by one of a large number of officially recognized funds, each of which is authorized to operate on a non-profit basis only. Individuals have no discretion as to which fund they may join. They have to subscribe to the one provided by their company or tailored to their specific circumstances. Two broad fund categories exist, one group catering for employees and the other for the self-employed and pensioners. The first group embraces just over 60 per cent of the population, the second just under 40 per cent. In both cases, fund members' dependants are included.

There are four sub-divisions of employee based funds. They are:

(1) Government managed funds for workers in small enterprises.
(2) Insurance societies for workers in large corporations.
(3) The Seamen's Insurance Fund (which includes day labourers).
(4) Mutual Aid Societies for public sector employees and teachers.

The insurance societies for workers in large corporations are jointly administered by management and labour. Although each has a distinct corporate identity, they are legally independent bodies whose assets cannot be used for anything other than health insurance purposes. Currently, there are approximately 1800 of such societies.

For the self-employed and pensioners, two sub-divisions exist:

(1) Community based National Health Insurance Funds underwritten by municipal authorities.
(2) National Health Insurance Fund Associations which have occupation specific members (such as carpenters, barbers and so on).

In addition to all of the above mentioned schemes, an Elderly Pooling Fund, based on the 1983 Geriatric Health Act, finances all health costs incurred by senior citizens over 70 years of age (over 65 years for those who are bedridden) regardless of the fund to which such people are attached. The Elderly Pooling Fund derives its revenue from the central government and from all the other funds whose contributions are determined 'on a basis that is similar to the national ratio of elderly citizens in society' [Ikegami 1991:92].

Government assistance is also available to funds handling the self-employed and pensioners as well as to those concerned with small enterprise employees. With regard to all of the employee based funds, contributions are exacted from both management and labour. Deductions are income based and the average premium rate is around 8 per cent. The ratio of premiums paid by employers (to that of employees) in insurance societies varies between 50 and 80 per cent, while in government managed schemes it is uniformly 50 per cent. For the self-employed and pensioners, premiums are based on income, assets and number of dependants.

Essentially, all schemes provide a similar range of benefits which include consultations, medications, long-term care and dental treatment. As official fee schedules are legally binding, market forces are of no consequence in patient costing. Apart from a small co-payment made when a medical service is provided, the funds pick up the rest of the tab. For employee based funds, the co-payment has amounted to 10 per cent for members and 20 per cent for their dependants when seeking inpatient care. For outpatient care, the rate has been 30 per cent jointly. The self-employed and pensioners have met with a 30 per cent co-payment for either in or outpatient care. Moves are now afoot to standardize co-payments across the board at 20 per cent. Individual co-payments are capped at 57 000 yen per month for most of the population, 30 000 yen for people on very low incomes, and for the elderly, they are set at 900 yen per month for outpatient visits and at 600 yen per day for hospitalization. Between 1973 and 1983, the elderly incurred no out of pocket expenses whatsoever. However, considering that the 1986 monthly income of households consisting only of elderly members was 200 000 yen, the co-payments now required of them are of a small order of magnitude [Nishimura 1993:116].

Admirers of the Japanese Health System like to describe it as being an outstanding example of an equitable, single tiered system in which neither utilization rates nor unit costs are influenced by a patient's income. Although this is broadly true, it is not quite so idyllic. As already mentioned, there is some variation in premium rates and in practice, contributions are borne disproportionately by members of funds employed in declining industries which pay lower wages and carry an older work force [Ikegami 1991:101].

## Aged Patients and General Costs

In common with almost all industrial societies, Japan's population is ageing. Unfortunately, in Japan's case, the process is proceeding with startling rapidity. Between 1950 and 1990, the proportion of the country's inhabitants over 65 years of age jumped from 5 to 12 per cent. (Within the next 20 years, this group's representation is projected to reach 21 per cent [Ogawa 1993:144].) Because elderly people generally require more medical attention than do younger folk, their increasing numbers lead to an escalation of health care costs. Not only do per capita health expenditures for the elderly exceed the national average but since the 1970s, they have been rising at a faster rate. In 1987 they exceeded the national average by a factor of six, compared with the situation that existed in 1972 when they were then three and a half times as great [Nishimura 1993:108]. Alternatively, in 1974 the ratio of medical outlays on behalf of the elderly to total medical expenses was 12.4 per cent. Ten years later, it almost doubled to reach 23.9 per cent [Powell and Anesaki 1990:97].

By Western standards, there is a pronounced tendency for frail and elderly parents to be cared for by their children with whom more than half reside. It has been thought that the prevalence in Japan of three generation households, in which grandparents, children and grandchildren all cohabit, is a factor in lessening the fiscal impact of its greying community. Unfortunately, this does not seem to be substantiated. For one thing, traditional living patterns are slowing changing and for another, the rate of institutionalization for the over 65 year olds, which stands at 6.2 per cent, is comparable to that of USA where nuclear family households are the norm [Ikegami 1989:193].

As a way of partly stemming a health care cost blowout associated with ageing, the government, in keeping with the Ministry of Health's 1990 'Golden Plan', is aiming to reduce inpatients in geriatric hospitals by, among other things, providing more resources for home visits and by increasing the number of adult day centres [Rodwin 1993:130].

**Hospitals and Clinics**

Japan is well endowed with hospitals and clinics, of which just over 80 per cent are privately owned. They are all strictly non-profit making bodies in the sense that investment by non-participating shareholders is disallowed. Furthermore, the law requires that every chief executive be a qualified doctor.

Clinics are analogous to the consulting suites of Western physicians, except that some are equipped with beds (up to a legal maximum of 19), basic laboratory facilities, X-ray equipment and certain other state-of-the-art diagnostic devices. Under normal circumstances, clinics are not permitted to accommodate inpatients beyond a 48 hour period.

To be designated as a hospital, an institute must have at least 20 beds, stipulated treatment facilities and a designated number and range of medical personnel. To acquire the appellation 'General Hospital' (Sōgō Byōin), over 100 beds are needed and internal medicine, general surgery (including ear nose and throat), obstetrics and gynaecology, ophthalmology, laboratory and pathology services must be provided [Powell and Anesaki 1990:149]. Most of the larger hospitals are in the public domain and many are affiliated with one of the country's 80 or so medical schools.

For a country so renowned for its central guidance and direction, the Japanese Medical System lacks planning. No allowance is made for referral procedures and clinic doctors have no access to hospitals. By recommending patients for secondary care, doctors not only forego any role in the management of a patient's current ailment but they also run the risk of permanently losing that person. That the latter is likely to occur results from the fact that large hospitals are not only more prestigious and popular (they certainly have been expanding at a faster rate than either smaller ones or clinics) but because they also energetically vie for outpatients. With this in mind, it is barely surprising that clinic doctors do all in their power to replicate the services that hospitals provide and to avoid, wherever possible, forwarding their patients to them. This has resulted in a certain amount of excess capacity, particularly in relation to beds.

In 1983, mindful of the need to conserve medical resources, the Ministry of Health activated legislation providing for the limitation of hospital bed numbers. Noting that controls were not in fact being strictly enforced and fearing additional constraints in the future, private hospitals rushed to increase their stock of beds. As a result, within just five years the total quantity rose by 13 per cent, reaching an absolute figure of 1.7 million [Nishimura 1993:111]. Japan now has the world's largest number of hospital beds per 1000 people. Data for 1988 report 15.6 hospital beds per 1000 in Japan compared with 5.1 in the USA. Strikingly, Japan's hospital admission rate (as a proportion of the population) is nearly half the US one. The respective figures are 7.8 per cent for Japan and 13.8 per cent for the US [Rodwin 1993:124]. This large variance is partly explained by the reluctance of Japanese doctors to undertake invasive surgical and other procedures, unless they are highly indicated, and by a general proclivity for ambulatory attention.

For instance, in 1984 22 operations were performed per 1000 people in Japan as opposed to 91 per 1000 in the US. Alternatively, in 1987 the number of outpatient visits per person in Japan stood at 12.8, more than twice the US rate of 5.3 [Ikegami 1991:99].

In considering the issue of low Japanese hospital admission rates, cognisance must be taken of the long average duration of inpatient stays. In 1988, hospital confinements averaged 52.1 days in Japan against 9.3 days in the US [Rodwin 1993:124]. A failure on the part of the Japanese to differentiate clearly between hospital and nursing home services has some bearing on the data but intrinsic cultural and other differences also come into play. The tradition of emphasizing 'ansei' (peace and quiet or bed rest) and the pampering of the sick as the central way of handling disorders, still lingers. That hospitalization is readily affordable, given universal insurance coverage and that the real social cost is ameliorated by family members partially tending to kinsfolk's nursing needs, are additional factors [Iglehart 1988:1171]. Finally, the virtual absence of referrals and of any liaison with non-hospital doctors, places the onus on hospital staff to ensure that patients are fully recovered before being discharged.

**The Position and Role of Doctors**

Although Japan does not have a critical undersupply of physicians, it has relatively fewer medical personnel than all Western countries save Switzerland and Ireland. In 1988, there were 1.6 doctors per 1000 people in Japan compared with 2.3 per 1000 in the USA [Rodwin 1993:124]. As is the situation in the world at large, the ratio of doctors per population varies spatially, being above average in large urban centres and below average in rural areas. Previously, the country as a whole had even comparatively less doctors but since the 1960s, their numbers had steadily increased thanks to a government sponsored expansion of medical training facilities. The drive for a larger number of doctors is now over and currently the Ministry of Health is attempting to limit the annual growth in the supply of medical graduates to no more than 10 per cent, at least until the end of 1995.

To train as a doctor, students pursue two years of pre-medical courses followed by four years of clinical studies. On graduating and in order to practise, they must all pass a national medical examination set by the Ministry of Health. Until 1968, the examination could only be taken after serving a one year internship. Presently, the internship requirement is not in force. Instead, a two year hospital residency period is recommended to all successful examination candidates and some 80 per cent take up that advice.

Around 36 per cent of doctors practise general medicine within their own clinics, 56 per cent work as hospital employees and the rest are engaged in other spheres. During the last decade, despite the fact that private practice is much more financially rewarding, doctors have become increasingly interested in securing hospital appointments. Such an inclination reflects the prohibitively expensive capitalization costs in establishing modern clinics, the greater prestige associated with being on the staff of a large hospital and the prospect of working within a teaching environment.

As already alluded to, mean earnings are highest among doctors who run clinics with beds. They tend to make 7.3 times the average wage. Those with bedless clinics come out on 6.5 times standard incomes, while salaried physicians are only 3.4 times better off [Iglehart 1988:1170]. Since all of the latter are on an experience-based salary system which does not differentiate between areas of specialization, they have little personal scope for boosting their incomes. To some extent, private practitioners also face income constraints in that fees are officially regulated. Their bills are computed on the basis of predetermined skill and material provision points. Skill points are invariant with regard to experience and qualification but the practice of Japanese doctors directly selling drugs, has provided them with a lucrative source of revenue.

Some time ago, it was intended that the prescribing and dispensing of drugs was to be undertaken by completely separate entities. In 1951, legislation was enacted to this effect. Unfortunately, powerful lobbying by the Japanese Medical Association resulted in amendments to the law in 1951, which effectively and thoroughly emasculated it. From then onwards, doctors continued to sell drugs, at (scheduled) prices which exceeded acquisition costs. Not surprisingly, the Japanese consumption of drugs reached world record levels. In stark contrast to the other developed countries, where drug usage averages 5–8 per cent of total medical expenditures, in Japan it represents 30 per cent. All this has enabled the run of the mill Japanese bed-clinic physician to earn $327 000 per year, an amount clearly in excess of the $210 000 annual income accruing to a general US practitioner [*Economist* 27 March 1993:75]. Partly to rectify this anomaly, the Ministry of Health has been taking steps to lower the scheduled drug rates so that they edge closer to the wholesale ones. This attempt has partly been thwarted by drug companies offering higher discounts, a countermeasure which of course cannot permanently be sustained.

**Doctors' Services**

Given that the Japanese are three times more prone to seek medical advice than North Americans[8] and that Japan has a smaller ratio of doctors per 1000 people, Japanese physicians carry higher case loads. Access to them is usually on a first come first served basis (rarely by appointment), and typically patients wait two to three hours for a consultation which is often of only a few minutes duration. 'The so-called "Kamikaze" doctor who sees as many as one hundred patients per day is not an uncommon phenomenon.' [Powell and Anesaki 1990:128] It appears that considerably fewer Japanese wholeheartedly endorse their health care system than do Americans theirs. According to a 1990 survey, full approval rates were 12 and 55 per cent respectively [*Time* 9 Dec. 1991:29]. One major source of dissatisfaction is that Japanese doctors seldom divulge and explain the nature of a patient's illness. They take the view that they ought to command complete trust and respect and that questions by patients impugn their professional competence. This has reached ridiculous levels, in that according to a recent survey, only 43 per cent of medical institutions polled indicate that they inform all patients who are HIV positive, of their condition [*Japan Times* 11 Nov. 1994]. Such a situation had been shored up by the judiciary when in 1990, in response to a complaint by a deceased woman's relatives that the woman (in this case a nurse) was not apprised of the fact that she had cancer, a judge ruled that doctors were under no obligation to communicate with their patients [*The Lancet* 24 Nov. 1990:1309].

**Some Ongoing Problems**

There are many aspects of the Japanese Health System that are laudatory. Above all, it provides universal coverage at relatively low overall costs. It avoids unnecessary invasive therapies and it has unquestionably contributed to the general health well-being of the Japanese people. One the other hand, it is beset by a number of weaknesses.

Starting with its financing, there is general agreement that there are far too many separate insurance funds and that some rationalization in this area is well overdue. Considering the health system as a whole, it is characterized as being too loosely structured, lacking central direction and planning and not being sufficiently coordinated. On occasion, little provision is made to ensure that basic services are available after hours and on weekends and from an elderly person's perspective, there are not enough nursing homes. The system is biased towards an excess use of drugs and doctor payment arrangements inhibit professional qualitative improvements. Specialist training is not standardized and no mechanism is in place for ensuring that self-declared specialists have at least a minimum level of competence. The country does not have specialist colleges or associations similar to those in North America, the UK, Australia and so on. Instead, specialist training is loosely acquired through an apprenticeship type process within large hospitals.

In short, as Iglehart has noted, compared with the situation in industry, the Japanese Medical System 'operates without a similar emphasis on management, quality control and consumer sovereignty' [Iglehart 1988:1172].

SUMMARY

**Distribution**

- Japan has more retailers and wholesalers per person than does the US but they tend to employ fewer staff.
- The wholesale sector is tri-tiered having primary, regional and local establishments.
- Although the retail sector is represented by departmental stores, supermarkets and discount houses, most units are small 'mom-and-pop' stores. However, the number of retail stores managed by only one or two people is on the decline.

- The large number of small stores in Japan reflects a reservoir of 'retirees' willing to work for low returns, a general desire to shop daily at a store accessible by foot and legislation that curbed large store expansions. The legislation in question is the 1956 Department Store Law and the 1974 Large Retail Store Law (Dai-ten ho) amended in 1991 and revised in 1994.
- A large number of stores *per se* does not necessarily imply social economic inefficiencies, for price mark-ups are no higher than in the US.
- Many stores are subservient to manufacturers (keiretsuka) but independent ones have of late been growing rapidly.

**Large Trading Companies**

- The sogo shosha (large trading companies), which now number nine firms, have in the early 1980s handled 60 per cent of Japan's exports and 70 per cent of her imports. They also engage in finance, warehousing, transport, construction, information gathering and in overseas projects.
- They have contributed to the Japanese economy by (among other things) arranging for technological transfers, by obtaining foreign products at reduced prices, by assisting small firms to invest abroad and by sponsoring the construction of overseas production plants.

**Education**

- Education is compulsory up to the end of junior high school. High school and university enrolments are higher than in most other advanced countries.
- Schools are more or less standardized at the primary and junior high levels but high schools (of which 30 per cent are private) vary in quality and reputation. Vocational high schools are also well represented.
- The school system is geared towards the university entrance examinations. Competition to gain entry to university is very intense, with one in three students not succeeding. Many anxious students wishing to obtain supplementary examination preparation attend one of many cram colleges.
- Although public resources are fairly evenly distributed, as in all other countries, students from wealthier homes perform better.
- Girls have equal access to all educational institutions but 90 per

cent of them pursuing tertiary studies opt for a two year college course.

- The general standard of university education falls short of Western ones and very few students progress to postgraduate studies.
- The quality of school education is very high in that the country has an above average literacy and numeracy rate and high school students are equipped with a stock of knowledge that average US college graduates acquire.
- Unfortunately, the education system places too much weight on rote learning and does not sufficiently emphasize the development of analytical skills. It is also very rigidly controlled and does not allow for experimentation and personal initiatives on the part of teachers.

**Health**

- Thanks in part to its health system, Japan has the world's highest life expectancy.
- National health costs which are fairly low at 6 per cent of GDP (compared with 10 per cent for the US), are rising due to the ageing of the population, a general growth in demand for medical services and the increasing capital intensity of such services.
- A universal health insurance programme exists but it is made up of a large collection of separately administered funds catering for specific population sub-groups. Benefits are more or less the same and a small co-payment is attached to every service (capped at a certain cumulative outlay).
- Eighty per cent of hospitals are privately owned but most of the large ones are in the public domain.
- There is no system of referral procedures and clinics vie with hospitals for patients. An excess of beds exists, hospital admission rates are low and hospital stays are long.
- Doctors tend to large numbers of patients. Their fees are government controlled yet they supplement their income by selling drugs to patients. As a result, medical drug usage is higher in Japan than in other OECD countries.
- In overall terms, the system is too loosely structured and lacks a central direction. Furthermore, specialist training is not standardized.

# Part V

# Living Standards

# 14 Welfare and the General Quality of Life

## INTRODUCTION

In this chapter we turn our attention to the contemporary living standards of the Japanese. This necessitates consideration of their income levels, their physical and sociological environmental conditions and the range and nature of welfare provisions available to them. We shall commence with welfare issues and then move on to the other topics.

## THE JAPANESE WELFARE STATE

A striking feature of social security expenditures in Japan is that throughout most of the postwar era, they have been of a rather low order of magnitude. Having constituted less than 1 per cent of the national income in 1965, they rose rapidly from the mid 1970s onwards, reaching a share of close to 14 per cent by 1990 (see Table 14.1).

Despite their growing prominence, relative Japanese social security outlays still lag behind Western ones (see Figure 14.1). This may imply that Japanese officials have been less inclined to promote welfare spending than their foreign counterparts. In support of this view, it could be argued that in the early postwar years, government authorities decreed economic recovery and growth to be their overriding objectives. Implicit in their belief was a conviction that an upswing in economic activity would generate jobs and real wage increases, both of which would be welfare enhancing. Those who did not benefit directly or who had fallen on hard times, would, it was assumed, be taken care of by their families.

### Reasons for Low Welfare Outlays

Whether or not such considerations had any bearing on Japan's welfare outlays, there are more relevant and objective factors which place the country's social security commitments into perspective. Of these

311

Table 14.1    Ratio of Social Security Expenditures to National Income

| 1965 | less than 1.0% |
|------|----------------|
| 1975 | 3.0% |
| 1985 | 9.0% |
| 1990 | 13.7% |

Source: Foreign Press Center 1993, p. 74.[1]

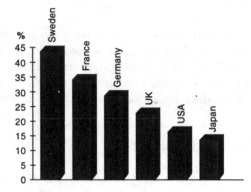

Figure 14.1    1989 Ratios of Social Security Expenditures to National
Income

Source: Foreign Press Center 1993:76

factors, five readily come to mind. First, for a long period of time, Japan had a relatively youthful population. During the 1950s, only 5 per cent were over the age of 65. Thereafter, the proportion of elderly rose to 7 per cent in 1970, 10 per cent in 1985 and 12 per cent in 1990. Throughout the 1980s, in many Western countries the elderly constituted around 15 per cent of the total population [Campbell 1992:6]. With comparatively fewer senior citizens, Japan could more readily sustain lower overall health expenses, as well as other social expenditure outlays which are particularly associated with the aged. (For instance, the country's various pension schemes presently carry a relatively low ratio of beneficiaries to contributors.) Second, incomes are more equally distributed in Japan than in most other industrial countries and partly as a result, Japan experiences less abject poverty. This brings us to the third factor, which clearly relates to the second. Japan has been remarkably successful in sustaining very low unemployment rates. Not only has this enabled virtually all able bodied workers to earn an acceptable livelihood but it has also contained unemployment insurance payments to relatively small aggregate amounts. Fourth, (as discussed in the previous chapter) Japan provides its citizens with universal health care which effectively meets patients' essential requirements at lower overall costs than in most other OECD countries. Fifth, due to relatively lower divorce rates and to more stable family structures, the incidence of single parent households is far lower in Japan than in say the USA.

Bearing in mind Japan's special circumstances, it would be foolhardy to conclude, solely on the basis of the sort of data shown in Figure 14.1, that Japan's welfare provisions are relatively meagre. As it happened, 'Japan in the early 1980s devoted nearly double the proportion of GNP to welfare than the United States did in 1965, when it had a comparable proportion of elderly' [Calder 1988:350]. Where Japan does seem to be out on a limb is in its current concentration on pensions and medical services, which collectively absorb over 80 per cent of its welfare budget.

**General Welfare Benefits**

Japan's welfare system does make some provision for the destitute, the physically and mentally handicapped and for single mothers. Child allowances are available to families with three or more children and whose incomes fall short of a prescribed level. However, aid is rather minimal and is only yielded after careful scrutiny and screening. In any event, given the general view that state welfare is not an automatic entitlement, many are loath to solicit public assistance. For those in certain critical situations, such as the small but growing number of homeless individuals, there is barely any mechanism in place to address their needs.

The unemployed are treated differentially. Applicants under the age of 30 or with less than one year's employment are only granted cover for a 90 day period, whereas those over 55 years may lodge claims for 300 days. Benefits are fairly generous, being set at 60 per cent of the worker's previous salary and capped at a going rate, which in the early 1980s stood at 200 000 yen per month. Discrimination in favour of the more elderly unemployed is warranted on the basis of their more limited job prospects, considering the recruitment policies of large Japanese corporations as well as the general problems (like retraining, relocating and so on) that such workers encounter.

Unquestionably, Japan's senior citizens appropriate the lion's share of welfare expenditures, both by drawing upon a large amount of health care resources and of course by virtue of being the exclusive beneficiaries of post retirement pensions. Let us look into the lot of the elderly a little more closely.

## The Aged and Japanese Pension Schemes

The Japanese are very respectful to their elderly and filial piety is commonly elicited and usually bestowed. By tradition, an eldest son's wife is duty bound to administer to her husband's ageing and ailing parents. Seemingly, this obligation is widely fulfilled, for most Japanese senior citizens dwell with their grown up children. While this practice has generally withstood the onslaughts of urbanization and modernization well, it has been subject to stresses and strains, and as a result, it has been slowly eroding. In 1980, 69 per cent of those over age 65 lived with their children but by 1990, the ratio dropped to 59.7 per cent [Anderson 1993:27]. Of course the proportion is still way above the 10 per cent USA figure but the trend has induced Yamanoi to exclaim that 'Japan's increasing affluence is prompting young people to abandon the Asian custom of caring for one's parents' [Yamanoi 1993:33].

Although Yamanoi might be somewhat alarmist (in Tokyo in 1989, some 73 per cent of the elderly either lived with their children, adjacent to them or in a nearby locality) [Miyajima 1993 (b):40], the plight of large segments of the elderly has been a growing cause of concern. Partly under the assumption that the elderly would mainly be taken care of by their children, Japan has devoted comparatively few resources in establishing nursing homes and other geriatric facilities.[2] That many senior citizens are desperately unhappy, is testified by the fact that the incidence of suicide is higher among their ranks than for any other age grouping whose members are less than 65 years old. In 1991, the national suicide rate stood at 17 per 100 000, whereas the rate for those 65 years and over was 37.4 per 100 000 [Foreign Press Center 1993:16]. Interestingly, 63 per cent of all elderly suicides occur in three generation households [Yamanoi 1993:33].

On the other hand, Japan does make reasonable provisions for post retirement pensions. What has happened is that in the course of time, a variety of independent schemes came into operation which have catered for distinctly separate constituencies. Then in 1985, the government reformed the system. The pivotal change involved the modification of the National Pension System (originally adopted in 1959) to provide universal coverage. Up to then, only the self-employed were included. Furthermore, all workers' spouses as well as divorced women who were often previously uninsured, can now claim entitlements in their own right. Benefits are all standardized at a flat rate depending on the period of an individual's membership standing. Ongoing payments are adjusted in light of cost of living increases. Claims may be lodged for full pensions at age 65 and for lower scale (58 per cent of the full amount) early retirement pensions at age 60 [Clark 1990:233].

Virtually all employees, whether in the public or private sector, belong to additional schemes which top up on the National Pension System's benefits (known as basic benefits). These supplementary schemes serve as agencies for the National Pension System, that is, they collect contributions on its behalf and distribute its benefits. Formally speaking, only those who are entirely beholden to the National Pension System are listed as its members. Essentially they include the self-employed, employees in firms with a paid staff of less than five, the unemployed, the disabled and all their spouses. Everyone in this category pays in a fixed monthly contribution (which in 1990 was about Y9000) to an approved financial institution for ultimate transfer to the government.

Among the supplementary employee schemes is the Employee Pension System (which covers all private commercial company personnel), national and local government employee Mutual Aid Associations, the Private School Teachers' Mutual Aid Association and the Mutual Aid Association of employees in agriculture, forestry and fishing. Effectively this gives rise to six different pension funds (counting the National Pension System as a separate entity). Of these six, two are dominant, the Employee Pension System which in 1991 was responsible for 47 per cent of all insured members and the National Pension System which carried 45 per cent of the total. (Table 14.2 provides an overall membership breakdown.)

Taking the administrative arrangements of the Employee Pension System as an example, 14.5 per cent (in 1991) of a worker's covered income is set aside, half of which is provided by the employee and the other half by the employer. This sum goes towards financing the worker's basic benefit, his or her earnings related one and the basic benefit for a dependent spouse.

All pension systems enjoy government funding equivalent to one third of the contributions of insured members as they relate to the basic benefit.

Benefits that pensioners throughout Japan actually receive depend of course on the fund to which they are attached and their contributory period. In 1990, those solely reliant on the National Pension System and who retired after reaching 65 years of age, obtained on average Y30 000 per month. The model basic pension amounted to Y55 000, which means that a couple on Y111 000 would have acquired less than 40 per cent of average wages [Campbell 1992:12]. This partly explains why more of the Japanese elderly continue working compared with their Western counterparts. In the 1980s over 35 per cent of those over 65 in Japan were still actively in the work force, while in the USA, West Germany and France, the respective magnitudes were around 15, 6 and 4 per cent [7].

The model pension for a member of the Employee Pension System, who receives benefits from the age of 60 approximates 69 per cent of previous earnings, not counting bonuses.[3] When bonuses are included, the income replacement ratio turns out to be close to 50 per cent or 'slightly below that for the average married retiree in the United States' [Clark 1990:237]. For a small number of workers, certain firms also offer (as an addition) lump-sum retirement allowances which commonly exceed 30 months' pay.

During the 1980s, Pension Fund revenues exceeded payments, giving rise to a healthy build up of financial reserves. However, the pension schemes are in a bind in that Japan's population, thanks to world record life expectancies and low birth rates, is rapidly ageing. By 2020, people over 65 are expected to represent around 24 per cent of the country's inhabitants. With this forecast in mind, it has become patently clear that current contribution rates would not cover actuarially determined future liabilities. An actuarial review conducted in 1989 indicated that Employee Pension Scheme contributions would have to be set at 31.5 per cent of covered wages compared with the 14.5 per cent 1991 rate. This has grave budgetary implications which are liable to impact negatively on labour costs and on the size of future benefits. Grappling with these problems is not going to be easy. No doubt partial solutions will be found which may include the raising of the mandatory retirement age and a longer retention of able older workers within the work force.

Taking everything into account, it can at least be stated that thanks to the revamping of the pension system in 1985, the 'economic woes of older people have declined significantly', and that 'the gap in levels of living between the elderly and the rest of the population has narrowed' [Campbell 1992:13 and 14].

Table 14.2   Pension Systems and Eligible Members

| System | No. of Members (in Thousands) | Percentage of Total Members |
|---|---|---|
| Employee Pension System | 30 997 | 46.8 |
| National System | 29 535 | 44.5 |
| Government Mutual Aid (National) | 1 622 | 2.4 |
| Government Mutual Aid (Local) | 3 266 | 4.9 |
| Private Teachers' Mutual Aid | 377 | 0.6 |
| Agricultural Mutual Aid | 493 | 0.8 |

*Source*: Derived from Foreign Press Center 1993:76

## ECONOMIC AND SOCIAL WELFARE INDICATORS

### National Income Figures

There is little doubt that Japan's per capita income is currently among the world's highest. (In terms of aggregate gross domestic product, it is surpassed only by the USA.) According to World Bank sources, in 1988, income per head in Japan was second only to Switzerland [World Bank 1990:179]. Alternatively, the OECD reports that in 1990, Japan was rated as having the sixth highest per capita income, following on Finland, Denmark, Norway, Sweden and Switzerland [OECD 1992: *Basic Statistics*].

It is well known that national income data are not 100 per cent reliable. Ostensibly, for a given period, usually one year, they record all market transactions relating to final expenditures on consumer and investment goods that originate in a specific country. Alternatively, they record all incomes generated in that economy, which conceptually ought to equal the measurement derived from the first procedure. In actual fact many market transactions are not adequately reported, and in relation to non-market activities (like self-help house repairs) values are imputed, or to use a more appropriate term 'guessed'.

## Selecting the Appropriate Exchange Rate

To make matters worse, each country's national income is first calculated in terms of its local currency and then, for the sake of international comparability, it is converted, at the current exchange rate, into US dollar terms. That would not be problematic if currency rates of exchange mirrored relative price levels, so that the cost of a commodity would more or less be the same irrespective of whether it is acquired in one country or another. For example, if it costs 200 yen to buy an apple (taken to symbolize goods in general) in Japan and one dollar to buy the same apple in the United States, an exchange rate of 200 yen to the dollar would reflect relative prices and would be regarded as the purchasing power parity exchange rate. Unfortunately, for various reasons, actual exchange rates frequently diverge from purchasing power parity ones. Assuming that in practice, one US dollar exchanges for only 100 yen, then in terms of our above example, the yen is overvalued, for it would now cost an American two dollars to acquire an apple in Japan, or twice as much as would be required in America itself.

If we utilize overvalued exchange rates to convert a country's gross domestic product (GDP) into dollar values, this would tend to exaggerate the extent to which a country fares *vis-à-vis* the rest of the world. For the sake of absolute simplicity, let us pretend that total incomes in Japan amount to 2000 yen and that the only products produced and consumed are apples. Let the above stated prices of apples in Japan and the USA apply and assume that total incomes in the USA amount to ten dollars. This means that Japan and America both have the same national income, each producing ten apples. But if the overvalued Japanese exchange rate of 100 yen to the dollar is employed, this would erroneously suggest that when one converts the yen value of Japan's national product into dollars, Japan's income is equivalent to 20 dollars or twice the actual US output.

To allow for over or under valued market exchange rates, the OECD has computed 1990 national incomes in terms of purchasing power parity exchange rates. What emerges is that although Japan still had the sixth highest per capita income, it was surpassed by a different constellation of countries, namely Canada, Germany, Luxembourg, Switzerland and the United States.[4]

Comparisons with the United States are fairly instructive. Based on market exchange rates, it would seem that the ratio of Japanese to American per capita GDPs rose from 67.2 per cent in 1985 to 121.1 per cent merely three years later [Horioka 1994:295]. Needless to say, it would have been nothing short of miraculous for Japan's incomes to have risen so incredibly steeply. However, bearing in mind that the yen sharply appreciated from 238 yen to the dollar in 1985 to 128 yen to the dollar in 1988, one is then able to grasp what actually occurred. As Horioka demonstrated, if purchasing power parity exchange rates had been applied, then between 1985 and 1988, Japan's per capita income as a ratio of America's per capita income would only seem to have risen marginally from 67.1 to 69.6 per cent [295].

## Rising Consumption Levels

While Japan still lags behind the United States as far as per capita incomes are concerned, the Japanese can derive great satisfaction from the fact that between 1960 and 1990, their real consumption levels have risen just over four-fold. Based on 1985 US dollar values, the 1960 and 1990 figures were $2156 and $8824 respectively [300]. Corroborating evidence that Japanese consumption standards improved remarkably is found in a drop of the Engel coefficient from 43.9 per cent in 1960 to 19.9 per cent in 1989 [303].[5] That Japan's Engel coefficient is still significantly higher than the US one (of about 12 per cent) is not only due to differences in income levels but also due to the fact that food prices in Japan are very much more expensive. In 1991, for example, food prices in New York were on average 74 per cent of those in Tokyo [Takahashi 1994:12].

Essentially, our interest lies in gauging contemporary Japanese living standards. Income data provide very good clues but in themselves, they are rather incomplete indicators. To really come to grips with the issue, we need a variety of other measures which may assist in our evaluation of the quality of life that the Japanese enjoy. Admittedly, we are incapable of arriving at a perfectly objective assessment but the more information we consider, the more likely it would be that we reach a reasonably balanced conclusion. As our first point of departure from the pure income approach, we turn to Japanese leisure opportunities.

## Work Hours and Leisure

The duration and quality of leisure is obviously an important ingredient as far as living standards are concerned. Without the incorporation of the sum of non-working hours available to the economically active population, international income comparisons are not sufficiently meaningful. Take the hypothetical case of two countries with equal monetary per capita incomes. If it transpires that in country 'A' people work twice as long as in country 'B', there would be no disputing the fact that in reality country 'B' is better off. For the same average work effort as country 'A' it could have attained even higher per capita incomes yet seemingly it chose instead per capita levels equal to that of 'A' in order to enjoy more free time.

It is well known that the Japanese work longer hours than do most others in the industrial world. In 1982, Japanese employees in the manufacturing sector worked, on average, 2136 hours compared with 1888 hours in Britain, 1851 in the USA, 1707 in France and 1682 in Germany [Bronfenbrenner and Yasuba 1987:116]. Even by 1990, Japanese workers were clocking in a yearly average of 2044 hours compared with around 1900 hours in countries like Australia and the USA.

The figures thus far quoted include paid overtime. Many Japanese workers, particularly those on the factory floor, are, as a matter of course, expected to prepare their work stations ahead of officially scheduled times and to tidy up loose ends after their shifts are formally over [see Woronoff 1990:228]. When unpaid overtime is also included, the average Japanese in 1990 probably worked around 2400 hours [*The Australian* 23 March 1992].

That the Japanese have less leisure time than Westerners, is also indicated by the overall number of work free days allotted to them per year. As is shown in Table 14.3, they clearly trail behind the US, UK, Germany and France. The problem seems to lie with weekend work. Westerners obtain two full days off, whereas most Japanese do a half day stint on Saturdays. There is, however, a definite tendency for Japanese workers to take a full two-day weekend and in the not too distant future, Japan will fully emulate its Western rivals.

Even if and when the Japanese do find themselves with more time on their hands, the recreational and cultural options available to them are quite limited. This unfortunate situation is largely the outcome of poorly planned and poorly structured metropolitan centres.

*Table* 14.3   Annual Holidays Around the Late 1980s, Early 1990s

|  | Japan | USA | UK | Germany | France |
|---|---|---|---|---|---|
| Paid holidays | 9 | 19 | 24 | 29 | 26 |
| Paid national and co. holidays | 21 | 9 | 8 | 12 | 8 |
| Weekend days off | 85 | 104 | 104 | 104 | 104 |
| Total | 115 | 132 | 136 | 145 | 138 |

*Source*: Ministry of Labour as reported in Iwata 1992:11

## Housing Costs and Conditions

Beginning with the home where most of one's non-working hours are generally spent, the most startling fact about Japanese housing is that it is exorbitantly expensive. This reflects extremely high land costs. An average urban unit of land fetches more than 60 times as much in Japan as in the US. As a result, in 1990, a standard Japanese home was equivalent in value to 6.7 times the average annual salary (8.5 times for the Tokyo area). This compares with ratios of 4.4 for the UK, 4.6 for Germany and 3.4 for the US [Iwata 1992:10]. Consequently, 'the average family frequently uses more than a third of its monthly income paying for housing' [Watanabe 1992:32]. (There are, as it happens, certain government and large corporation employees who are favoured with access to subsidized accommodation and in their case, rental charges are rather nominal.)

Even though homes are very costly, most are owner occupied. In 1983, 62.4 per cent of Japanese households lived in their own dwellings. This ratio compared favourably with the 64.7 percentage that was then attained in the US [Ito 1992:409]. According to the Ministry of Construction, Japan's stock of housing exceeds the number of its households, which suggests a more than adequate supply of real estate. But as Ito has pointed out, the decision of either adult children or elderly parents to form separate households is partly dependent on relative accommodation expenses [409]. In a previous section, we had mentioned that Japan was more prone than most other industrial nations to maintain multiple generation households. Such an assertion is partly confirmed by the fact that, in 1983, while the ratio of occupied home units to the population in the US stood at 36.0 per cent, in Japan it was only 28.7 per cent [409]. The extent to which this discrepancy is due to cultural or economic factors has not at this stage been unravelled. With this in mind, it is difficult to determine whether or not Japan suffers from an absolute housing shortage. What can in fact be unequivocally stated, is that in terms of quality, Japanese home units compare poorly with Western ones.

First of all, Japanese homes are fairly small. On average, they contain 81 square metres of floor space, which contrasts with average floor areas of 94 and 135 square metres in Germany and the US respectively [Woronoff 1990:244]. In terms of floor space per person, the divergence between say Japan and the US, is even greater. In the late 1980s, floor space per person in Japan stood at 25 square metres while in the US the average individual enjoyed 61.8 square metres [Foreign Press Center 1993:82].[6] Access to individual privacy in the more limited internal space of Japanese homes is exacerbated by the thinness of widely used sliding paper walls. Added to this, most 'homes and buildings are surrounded by small bits of land, hardly what one would call a lawn and perhaps only a metre or so from the road' [Woronoff 1990:245]. A large number of old houses, made of wood, tend to be draughty in winter and hot and stuffy in summer [Mills and Ohta 1976:708]. Not very much more than half of all houses have flush toilets and just over a third are connected to the sewerage system [Calder 1988:384]. Finally, inadequate zoning provisions have given rise to a situation whereby it is not uncommon for private residences, stores and factories to be lumped together in the same locality.

**High Land Prices**

One might well assume that the high cost of property and the more diminutive specifications of Japanese homes reflect objective resource scarcities. Japan is a very densely populated country, carrying in the late 1980s, 318 people per square kilometre. Of all the Western countries, only Belgium (with 324 per sq. km.) and the Netherlands (with 353 per sq. km.) are more densely populated [Calder 1988:381]. Because of Japan's mountainous terrain, only 21 per cent of the country's surface is suitable for housing. To make matters worse, the population is highly concentrated in a narrow coastal plain within close proximity to either Tokyo, Osaka or Nagoya. Approximately 32 per cent of the population live in this part of Japan which covers little more than 1 per cent of the country's total land area [Johnson 1982:293].

Surprisingly, prime responsibility for Japan's land and housing problems does not lie with the above mentioned factors. Instead, its current legal and institutional arrangements play a more decisive role. That this may be so, is suggested by the fact that even in the metropolitan regions, a fair quantity of land is potentially available for building purposes. The Ministry of Construction has estimated that about 650 square kilometres in the Tokyo area can be so used. Half can be derived from vacant lots (some of which were previously owned by the former National Railways and other defunct bodies) and the other half can be derived from urban farmlands [Noguchi 1992:53].[7] In 1983, urban farmlands constituted 12.6 per cent of the Tokyo Metropolitan area. Had these farms been converted to housing, residential accommodation could have been provided for at least another million inhabitants [Calder 1988:409].

The taxation structure fosters the practice of holding land as an asset. This practice is more widespread in Japan than in other industrial societies. Property is taxed at a standard rate of 1.4 per cent but the effective rate is far less because assessed values fall way below market ones. For Japan as a whole, the effective rate is merely 0.13 per cent, 'a fraction of that in American cities' [Iwata 1992:10], whereas in 1987 in Tokyo, it fell to 0.065 per cent [Noguchi 1992:55]. Capital gains taxation rates are higher for properties held for less than five years than for those held longer. These two fiscal imposts simply facilitate land hoarding in anticipation of land value appreciations.

In bequeathing one's wealth, it is prudent to maximize land holdings at the time of death. This is so, for like property taxes, the assessment of real estate for the purposes of calculating inheritance taxes is based on sub-market values, currently less than half. By contrast, bonds and other securities are assessed at full market rates.

Not only do taxes pertaining to land make it an attractive asset but the system also lends itself to the socially sub-optimal use of property. Two instances come to mind. First, the lower tax rates that fall on agricultural as opposed to residential or commercial land, have encouraged the continuation of farming pursuits within urban boundaries. Very often, these 'farms' are at best nothing but token ones. Second, lower property tax rates on holdings of less than 200 square metres needlessly sponsor land fragmentation.

### The Bias Against Property Renting

Apart from the stimulation of land hoarding that the taxation structure affords, legislation relating to rental agreements positively discourages landlords from leasing their property. In so doing, highly valued real estate is either partially or inadequately utilized. The problem lies in the fact that tenant rights seem to take priority over landlord ones. Leasing arrangements are automatically extended beyond a year of the original period and the landlord cannot waiver this extension unless he or she personally intends to take up occupancy. Furthermore, rents are not easily raised. In other words, renting one's property diminishes its value as a readily disposable wealth holding asset. Consequently, for those that actually do rent out home units, preferences are clearly shown for young single people who are more likely to be short-term tenants.

### Impediments to High Rise Construction

Faced with high land costs, a more intensive use of land sites would seem to be the obvious response. This would imply a widespread construction of high rise buildings. Considering that Japan is earthquake prone, its previous hesitation in embarking on such a course was then understandable but with subsequent progress in the engineering capabilities of its construction industry, it is less so today (the Kobe earthquake notwithstanding). The stumbling block consists of social obstacles, of which there are two main components. First, local 'ward councils have vigorously opposed metropolitan government plans to build multistoried housing in their midst because they believe that a new influx of residents would only add to the existing overload on public facilities' [Huddle and Reich 1987:201]. Second, the Japanese are generally adamant in having direct access to sunlight and whenever their homes are overshadowed by taller buildings, their market values erode. In the beginning of the 1970s, resident groups were formed in the Tokyo region expressly to protect themselves from potential sunlight deprivation. Their efforts climaxed in 1972 with the Supreme Court ruling that 'a home's sunlight and ventilation are essential living requirements for a comfortable and healthy life' [202]. In keeping with this pronouncement, 19 of the 26 cities within the Greater Tokyo Metropolitan Region issued ordinances limiting building heights. Subsequently (in the mid 1980s), the central government deregulated rights of access to sunlight [Watanabe 1992:42].

### Commuting Hassles

Due to outlandish home prices close to central Tokyo, millions of those that work in the city have had no choice but to seek accommodation further afield. For most, the advantage of acquiring cheaper property is largely offset by long commuting times, which in 1990 averaged one hour 31 minutes for a one directional trip [Foreign Press Center 1993:79].[8] Most travel by train, for the roads are heavily congested. Japan has been spending large amounts (2 per cent of GNP) on roads but as yet, road-building has not kept pace with automobile usage. In the early 1980s, the country had only 76 metres of highway per 1000 vehicles compared with 148 metres per 1000 vehicles in the UK [Mutoh 1988:320]. City streets are far narrower than those of the UK, the average widths for Tokyo and London being 13.6 and 16.6 metres respectively [Calder 1988:384]. Furthermore, many Japanese roads are bereft of sidewalks. Where this occurs, pedestrians have to trust in painted lines that supposedly separate them from motorists.

**Recreational Facilities**

Japanese urbanites have limited access to recreational, sporting and cultural amenities. As is shown in Figure 14.2 there is far less park space per capita in Tokyo than in other major world cities. Similarly, facilities for enjoying activities like golf or tennis are in short supply. The country has only about 500 tennis courts and 1500 golf ranges. A round of golf could well cost something in excess of $200 while the average club membership entry fee is in the region of five million yen, an amount which is above the average white collar worker's annual salary [Woronoff 1990:236.] Small amounts of land are devoted to schools, libraries, hospitals and other institutions. Japan has less than one quarter the number of public libraries than has the USA. It is also less well catered for in terms of concert halls, theatres or cinemas. The Japanese take in a movie less frequently than do people in North America and Europe. Seeking relaxation beyond city limits, as on beaches or at general holiday resorts, is not always a rewarding process. Typically, one would have to crawl through traffic snarls to arrive eventually at a site cluttered with hoards of other vacationers.

In brief, the quality of Japanese urban life is partly eroded by poor land use for both private and public purposes. That is not to say that Japanese cities are completely blighted. They offer a profusion of stores, restaurants and pubs which (especially in the case of the latter two) enhance the population's well-being. Japanese cities are basically spared the widespread defacement and degradation caused by graffiti artists and vandals that plague the USA. There are few outright slums and no-go areas but nonetheless, Japan's cities (and even its rural areas) have had their share of environmental problems.

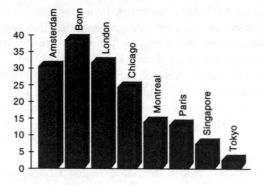

*Figure* 14.2    Park Space per capita in the 1980s (in Square Metres)

*Source*: Calder 1998:381, Watanabe 1992:60, Foreign Press Center 1993:82

## Pollution

In setting out to rebuild its postwar economy, Japan paid scant regard to environmental issues. Factories were located in and around major cities without any consideration of their possible unfavourable environmental impacts and 'by the late 1960s Japan was probably the most polluted country in the world' [Horsley and Buckley 1990:87]. The atmosphere became so contaminated that periodically in the Tokyo area smog alerts were issued cautioning children and the elderly to remain indoors.

Four landmark disasters and the subsequent litigation that ensued from them, generated public pressure for environmental safeguards. After much prevarication, politicians and businessmen eventually acknowledged their culpability.

Of all Japan's modern environmental misfortunes, that of Minamata, a fishing village on the south island of Kyushu, was the country's most serious and most dramatic. The first signs of any mishap manifested themselves in 1953, when birds lost their sense of coordination and cats acted strangely. Not too long thereafter, people were struck with numbness in the mouth, slurred speech, violent muscular spasms, loss of vision and control of bodily movements. Forty per cent of those stricken died after writhing continuously in agony.

A team of researchers from a local university medical school, suspected that the source of the problem lay in the Chisso company's aluminium plant. Far from cooperating with the investigators, the company, with MITI's connivance, thwarted all efforts to get to the root of the problem. Chisso even hired 'general meeting men' thugs to intimidate questioning shareholders [Clark 1979:231].

By 1959, there was clear evidence that Chisso was depositing methyl mercury into Minamata Bay. Water in the bay contained .0001 parts per million (ppm) of methyl mercury but the concentration at the firm's drainage outlet was 2000 ppm [Powell and Anesaki 1990:79]. The contaminant was ingested by fish and then by humans, with the result that mercury in patients' hair reached measurements of 281–760 ppm compared with a normal reading of 6 ppm.

Only in 1968, when it instituted stringent controls on mercury discharges, did the government officially concede that organic mercury was the cause of what became known as 'Minamata disease'. This preceded a court ruling in 1973 (20 years after the disease's outbreak) that ordered Chisso to pay victims full compensation. Fishing in Minamata Bay is now prohibited.

A carbon copy of events in Minamata was repeated in Niigata. There too, people were afflicted with methyl mercury poisoning resulting from the effluence of the Showa Denko company. This catastrophe, with a death toll of at least 70, began in 1964. When it did, the Ministry of Health and Welfare commissioned the Niigata University Medical School to determine its ultimate cause. An interim report identifying Showa Denko's waste materials as the most likely determinant, was first opposed and then suppressed by MITI [Huddle and Reich 1987:122]. Fortunately, it saw the light of day in April 1967 due to the pressures of socially aware and responsible citizens. Encouraged by the report's authoritative findings, Minamata disease sufferers at Niigata filed for damages.

In the Jinzu River Basin, residents in 1959 began to experience an awful disorder which was labelled itai-itai (ouch-ouch) disease due to the unbearable pain and weakness of bones associated with it. The malady's origin was traced to cadmium poisoning resulting from the activities of a local mining and smelting company. In 1968, nine years later, national controls on cadmium discharges were enforced.

Citizens of Yokkaichi (the fourth locality to encounter a pollution induced health crisis) were, in 1972, the first to win a group action against wayward companies. Their victory marked a turning point in the struggle for a clean environment. In brief, the petrochemical plants in their neighbourhood were judged to be collectively derelict for failing to undertake joint appraisals of the combined effects of their operations on the local environment.

Yokkaichi was singled out by MITI as a growth centre for the petrochemical industry. Sulphur oxides that were released into the atmosphere generated an increased incidence of respiratory complaints ranging from chronic coughs, asthmatic attacks, bronchitis and pulmonary emphysema [Powell and Anesaki 1990:78]. To counteract such tendencies, various measures have been taken to curtail sulphur oxide emissions. Through government support and subsidies, importers switched to lower sulphur content fuel, while producers created petroleum desulphurization devices and stack gas desulphurization equipment. They were rewarded for their efforts by a fall in annual average sulphur concentration from .059 ppm in 1967 to .013 ppm in 1982 [Huddle and Reich 1987:3].

As already noted, the Japanese government was at first a slow and reluctant convert to environmental conservation. In 1967 the Basic Law For Environmental Pollution Control was enacted but it lacked teeth in not *obliging* either the state or industry to combat pollution. Then in 1970, environmental quality standards were set in relation to air, water, soil and noise. (Later some 23 specific areas were designated to be monitored for air contaminants.) An Environmental Agency was established in 1971. It is charged with issuing an annual report detailing the country's environmental condition. However, the responsibility for implementing and enforcing most environmental policies falls on the shoulders of local authorities.

Thanks to a radical change in attitude on the part of both the government and industry, Japan has come a long way in tackling pollution. Its automobile emission control standards are now probably the world's strictest (see Table 14.4). Ironically, European automobile manufacturers have complained that Japan's high standards effectively constitute a non-tariff trade barrier hindering their access into the Japanese market [Mutoh 1988:322]. Seventy per cent of firms recently surveyed in Japan reported that they had established a division concerned specifically with environmental matters [*Economist* 11 Dec. 1993] and Japan is now a world leader in manufacturing pollution control equipment.

Improved environmental conditions have not only resulted from a more positive approach on the part of government and industry but are also a by-product of changing economic circumstances. In response to the 1973 oil shock, Japan was forced to conserve energy and to wind back some of its pollution prone activities, especially those concentrated in the metal and chemical industries. (The near complete demise of the aluminium smelting industry is an outstanding case in point.) The economy's transition from an era of high growth to a much more

*Table* 14.4   Passenger-Car Exhaust Controls by Country, 1992 (g/km)

|  | Carbon Monoxide | Hydrocarbon | Nitrogen Oxide |
|---|---|---|---|
| Australia | 9.3 | 0.93 | 1.93 |
| Japan | 2.1 | 0.25 | 0.25 |
| Sweden | 2.1 | 0.25 | 0.62 |
| Switzerland | 2.1 | 0.25 | 0.62 |
| USA | 2.1 | 0.25 | 0.62 |

*Source*: Nissan's Auto Handbook 1992 as reported by Foreign Press Center 1993, p. 65.

restrained one, as well as a gradual shift to service oriented activities, were additional contributory factors.

However, no matter what the ultimate causes were, most observers would concur that by the beginning of the 1980s, pollution was no longer a *major* social problem [see Bronfenbrenner and Yasuba 1987:122]. That is not to say that environmental issues are now a thing of the past. Despite stringent emission controls, there has been a steady rise in the atmospheric concentration of nitrogen oxide due to a growing volume of traffic and to a greater use of diesel driven vehicles [Shinohara 1992:31]. Linked to this, are perpetual complaints relating to noise. Nevertheless, Japan's environmental hazards are not as grave today as they were in the first three postwar decades.

**Consumer Interests**

The Japanese political establishment has consistently provided priority to producer interests whenever they have been in conflict with consumer ones. As the discussion relating to pollution indicates, it had been government practice to stand by manufacturers even while they were wrecking havoc on entire communities. Only when the anti-pollution movement became highly vocal did things change. Unfortunately, examples highlighting the government's indifference to or lack of sympathy with consumers are bountiful. The few that we cite below, ought to be sufficiently illuminating. It is well known and we have already mentioned it ourselves, that Japanese mainstream financial organizations have provided totally inadequate consumer loan facilities. As a result, in the late 1970s, loan sharks, known as 'sarakin', entered the arena. Hapless borrowers were soon saddled with usurious interest rates. Although the racketeers were publicly and regularly exposed by the press, corrupt LDP politicians blocked legislative measures for six years.

When a law was eventually enacted, it legitimized the sarakin and allowed them to charge interest rates of up to 73 per cent at the very time 'that there was a competing law on the books limiting interest rates to 20 per cent!' [Van Wolferen 1989:100].

One might well suppose that the government would act as a consumer watchdog when it comes to medical care. Yet, this is not so in Japan. Instead of being subject to the control and supervision of the Ministry of Health and Welfare, the Japan Medical Association levers the Ministry to adopt measures that conflict with patient interests. One flagrant instance is provided by the Association's successful efforts to ban the use of oral contraceptives, so as to shore up lucrative abortion clinics.

On another plane, the government instituted a two year delay in authorizing the marketing of a blood product which was sterilized against the AIDS virus, so that 'all five companies manufacturing the coagulants in Japan could market their products in unison' [Vogel 1992:141]. Had permission been granted to import the product in the interim, 20 per cent of the country's AIDS affected haemophiliacs would not have contracted the virus [141].

With regard to cigarette smoking, there are no controls over tar contents and consumers are not adequately warned about the ill effects of smoking. Japanese governments have a hand in tobacco merchandising.

Finally, the legal system had (until legislative changes in 1994) provided limited consumer protection. While in the West, firms have been liable for any damages sustained by the use of their products, in Japan an injured consumer had to prove that the firm behaved negligently.

Part of the problem is that the consumers' movement has effectively been coopted by the producers. On the rare occasion that the movement's representatives have spoken out, they have generally railed against moves afoot to increase imports of food and other consumer goods.

**Crime in Japan**

Japan is the world's most law abiding industrial country. As Table 14.5 indicates, murder and rape rates in Japan are a mere fraction of those in the USA. Although the total number of crimes per 100 000 people has risen from 1160 in 1980 to 1377 in 1991, the incidence of violent offences has continued to fall. Murder rates have steadily declined from 3.4 per 100 000 in 1955 to 1.1 per 100 000 in 1989. This is all the more remarkable considering the rapid rate of urbanization that had occurred during the period in question. Japan has also largely been

*Table* 14.5   Crimes by Country, 1989 (per 100 000 People)

|  | Homicide | Rape | Robbery | Theft |
|---|---|---|---|---|
| Japan | 1.1 | 1.3 | 1.3 | 1203 |
| Germany | 3.9 | 8.0 | 48.6 | 4147 |
| France | 4.6 | 7.8 | 94.6 | 3650 |
| USA | 8.7 | 38.1 | 233.0 | 5544 |

*Source*: Foreign Press Center 1993:83

spared widespread drug abuse. 'In 1991 a mere 60 people were arrested for offences relating to cocaine and 110 for ones relating to heroin' [*Economist* 16 April 1994:32].

A number of factors operate to curb Japanese criminal activity, and although they are readily identifiable, their relative significance and the extent to which they interact with other factors, is still not known with any degree of precision. Major ones, which are not necessarily listed in order of importance, are noted below.

Japan maintains a very high degree of income equality, with relatively small dispersions between society's richest and poorest. With very low unemployment rates, very few people are absolutely destitute. The family structure in Japan is much more stable than in other Western countries and contrasts starkly with the family situation in the USA. In 1990 divorce rates per 1000 population were 1.3 for Japan and 4.7 for the USA. Consequently, Japan has far fewer single parent households. In Japan, family ties are strong and meaningful and a potential offender would think twice before embarking on a course of action likely to bring the family into disrepute. In Japan, the individual is taught to subordinate his or her aspirations to a group, family, firm or society in general. To the extent that this is adhered to, Japanese workers, for example, would be less inclined to pilfer their firms' merchandise than would their Western counterparts. The Japanese education system inspires self discipline and respect for other people and public property. For instance, pupils undertake responsibility for cleaning and maintaining their schools and partly as a result, vandalism and mindless acts of destruction are rather rare. Japan's population is more or less homogeneous with fewer minority or migrant groups than in Europe or North America. Accordingly, Japan has less alienated and disgruntled outsiders. The police maintain very good relations with the community. They are well acquainted with the inhabitants of each small sub-division and have been able to sustain very high arrest rates. The judicial system welcomes genuine acts of contrition and is generally lenient towards first time petty offenders. Finally, strict controls are enforced regarding the possession of firearms and swords.

The low crime rate has been a boon to Japanese society. The country experiences less human injury and misery, less property losses, less insurance costs and it can afford to maintain the industrial world's lowest ratio of police officer per 1000 population. People can venture throughout the streets of Tokyo at all times during the day and night free of the fear that permeates cities like New York and London.

CONCLUDING COMMENTS

We have attempted in this chapter to assess the general economic fortunes of the average Japanese. What we have noted is that although we cannot take Japan's per capita income at face value, it certainly is enviably high. The country's citizens are endowed with a good health system and they can, on average, confidently anticipate a long lifespan. Their retirement pensions allow for reasonable living standards, unemployment is very low and their overall environment is moderately safe and relatively crime free.

On the debit side, Japanese housing conditions leave much room for improvement. More time could be set aside for leisure and more recreational facilities ought to be available. The cities are crowded and frequently congested. Commuting is rather tedious and uncomfortable and consumer protection is found wanting.

Every country has its pluses and minuses. The trick is to allot relevant weights to them. *The Economist*, on 24 December 1983 and 25 December 1993, published tables setting out its valuations of various social, cultural, political and economic variables for a number of different countries. After duly weighting and aggregating all these variables, *The Economist* in 1983 ranked Japan in fourth place. By 1993 it was demoted to the sixth position. Our confidence in *The Economist*'s judgement is marred by its consistent placement of Australia well ahead of Canada. Being intimately familiar with both of these countries, we would have been inclined to rank them on a par. What all this boils down to is that when it comes to relative economic well-being, the assignment of ordinal numbers to countries is an arbitrary process. The most that we are prepared to assert is that if the quality of the average citizen's living standard and lifestyle are the major criteria, Japan should certainly be included among the world's top ten countries.

SUMMARY

- Welfare spending in Japan has been comparatively low because of a previous relatively youthful population, income equality, full employment, an economical health service and stable families.
- Assistance is provided for the destitute, handicapped and single mothers. Unemployment benefits fall into two categories depending on age.
- The pension system was reformed in 1985 when the national pension was made universal. In addition, other schemes serve to supplement the national pension. All told, six large schemes are in existence.
- In terms of current exchange rates, Japan has a higher per capita income than the US. The situation is otherwise when purchasing power parity rates are utilized.
- Real consumption rose fourfold from 1960–90 but the Japanese still work longer hours than do people in other industrial countries.
- Although housing prices are exceedingly high, most homes are owner occupied. The houses are generally fairly small and only a third are connected to the sewerage system.
- Land prices are high in part because of low land taxes making land a desirable asset.
- Most metropolitan inhabitants commute long distances to work and have access to a comparatively small range of recreational amenities (such as parks, tennis courts and so on).
- Japan was plagued by industrial pollution in the period of high economic growth (1955–70) and while MITI then tried to gloss over the problem, the government subsequently adopted a series of anti-pollution measures which has rid Japan of major environmental degradation.
- Consumer interests have not been well served either by the government or official consumer bodies.
- Japan has a very low crime rate, probably on account of reasonable income equality, full employment, low divorce rates, the education system and a fairly homogeneous population. The low crime rate has been an economic boon in that there are less personal injuries and losses, less insurance costs and less policing expenses.

# Part VI

# Conclusion

# 15 Conclusion

Throughout this book we have attempted to paint a broad picture of the major features of the Japanese economy in the postwar era. As mentioned in the preface, we did not wish to dwell on the immediate present and for that reason, we have liberally resorted to statistical data spanning the entire period. What we have hoped to impart to the reader is an appreciation of the fact that although Japan is essentially a very conservative society, its economy has been in a constant state of flux. By that we are not referring to the obvious, such as the series of economic restructurings in which the composition of Japan's leading industries have periodically been rearranged. Rather, we have in mind the manifold institutional and behavioural changes, which cumulatively have engendered radical transformations. Change, of course has not been evenly distributed across all sectors, for in some, the forces of inertia have proved to be stronger than in others. Nor is it true that the Japanese economy is converging in character to that of a Western one. After all which country best typifies a Western one? The US or say Germany and Sweden? Finally, we can never be sure precisely how the Japanese economy is likely to continue evolving, for postwar literature is rife with forecasts indicating how this or that aspect is ripe for change and in many, if not most, instances prophecies have not materialized. Before singling out what we regard as likely future scenarios, we have summarized in point form, some of the numerous changes that have actually been in the making. The chapter in which they are discussed in this book is indicated in brackets.

## Some Changes that have Occurred in the Postwar Era

- Extensive financial deregulation has taken place in terms of both the workings of internal financial institutions and of Japan's financial relations with foreign countries. (2)
- Japan's taxation system was reformed in 1988. (2)
- Formal import controls were relaxed in the 1960s. (5)
- Industrial policy has new objectives and employs a different set of devices. (5)
- Large corporations have become less dependent on bank finance and the keiretsu associations appear to have been weakened. (6)

337

- Firms now tend more actively to diversify their product range. (6)
- More emphasis is now being placed on basic research and development. (8)
- The large volume of foreign direct investment has led to increased off-shore production setting off a new round of structural adjustments. (11)
- Restrictions on agricultural imports (including rice) have been lifted or eased. (12)
- Restraints on the expansion of large stores have largely fallen away. There is now greater scope for competition in the distributive sector and more and more foreign made goods are appearing on store shelves. (13)
- The work week is gradually being shortened as Saturday work is being phased out. (15)
- Pollution is no longer one of the country's biggest scourges. (15)

**Some Probable and some Possible Changes within the Japanese Economy**

Of all possible future scenarios relating to the Japanese economy, those involving the implications of the ageing population are among the most credible. By around 2020, close to 24 per cent of the population are likely to be over the age of 65, 'the highest proportion of elderly population projected for all OECD countries. In the United States, by comparison, the elderly population is estimated to reach 17.3 per cent in 2020' [Rodwin 1993:128]. With the rapid ageing of the Japanese population, national savings are slated to fall both because the elderly tend to be dissavers and because social security outlays would have to rise to keep pace with the growing needs of the aged, especially in the realm of medical services. With the concomitant fall in national savings, the country's current account surplus would be reduced. A favourable by-product would be the weakening of the yen.

Profound effects are likely to occur within labour markets. For one thing, the slowdown in the growth of population (which is one factor besides growing longevity, responsible for the emergence of a higher proportion of senior citizens) is likely to result in labour shortages. Nikkeiren has estimated that even by the year 2000, Japan could face a shortfall of five million workers [*Guardian Weekly* 9 May 1993]. Such a situation would most probably give rise to significant social developments. For women many new career paths may be opened and their working conditions and status are likely to be drastically improved. Even in the sphere of education important changes may be in the offing, for with prestigious universities encountering a shrinking student body, the examination hurdles may become less awesome. This may ultimately loosen the rigid high school teaching system, giving rise to less emphasis to rote learning and more to critical thinking.

The ageing population may well contribute towards a substantial weakening of the lifetime employment system. This system is already being threatened by a gathering momentum of technological change which either renders many corporations' stock of human capital obsolete or necessitates huge efforts to ensure that their work forces keep abreast with ongoing developments. Where younger workers, who are more flexible in tackling new assignments and who are easier to train and are paid less, outnumber older workers, then a firm is better placed in maintaining the lifetime employment system intact. But when their relative numbers fall, the lifetime system is accordingly subject to more stress.

There are also some signs that the seniority payment system is slowly being challenged. The supermarket giant Daiei Inc recently decided to adopt an annual pay system covering its entire work force which places more emphasis on job functions and individual worker performance levels than on seniority. Some other companies have at this stage introduced similar measures for their managerial staff [*Japan Times* 10 Jan. 1995].

One large obstacle that needs to be overcome is the perpetuation of widespread regulatory devices, which effectively ossify certain procedures. Without their removal, further speculation relating to future events in Japan becomes increasingly murky. For that reason, we would rather now turn our attention to the deregulation issue.

**Deregulation**

As has been made clear, the Japanese economy has been highly regulated. Even after the dismantling of many formal trade and investment obstacles from the early 1960s onwards, by March 1989, 'the percentage of industries covered by government regulations weighted by value added, amounted to 41 per cent of GNP' [OECD 1990/91:100]. Government regulations 'relate both to operational restraints, including price and quantity restrictions and bans on advertising, and entry barriers such as licences and permits' [98].

It is well known that excessive regulations are hampering progress, particularly in Japan's lagging service sector. Two simple examples ought to suffice. Consumer gasoline prices in Japan are higher than in other countries. One reason for this relates to the high wages of service station attendants. In most Western countries, service station proprietors economize on labour by adopting a self-service format but in Japan this option is not available because the Fire Defence Law prohibits self-service operations [Yutaka 1995:44]. This example might seem to be fairly trivial but magnify it by hundreds or even thousands of comparable regulations throughout the distribution, transport and building sectors and the value of total inefficiencies soon mounts up. Our second case lies in the telecommunications industry. Thanks to a highly regulated structure, telephone calls are very expensive in Japan. Unless this is rectified, extensive use of multimedia technology, in which terminals are connected to the phone system, is likely to be stifled in Japan and the country stands to fall behind in information technology.

Research conducted in 1994 by the keidanren (Japan's leading business lobby) indicated that a full-scale deregulation of the Japanese economy would by the year 2000 lead to an increase in 740 000 jobs and to a 5 per cent rise in GNP. This would follow from widespread falls in consumer goods prices, producing a rise in real incomes and demand, which would in turn stimulate output. The service sector is slated to be the largest beneficiary. Individual industries likely to benefit include those engaged in finance, sport, transport, telecommunications, multimedia and environmental pursuits. For example, the 'deregulation of the telecommunication business will help the market, whose size is presently 1.4 per cent of gross domestic product, to grow to 2.7 per cent – the equivalent of that in the US – by the year 2000' [*Financial Times* 6 Dec. 1994].

Unfortunately, opposition to deregulation is well entrenched by a coalition deriving rents from the system and from the bureaucracies that oversee it. Even the keidanren recognizes that the sudden elimination of most regulations would have undesirable short-term effects by way of a fall in output emanating from the collapse of inefficient businesses and a large (albeit temporary) increase in unemployment. Public officials would of course resent their loss of control over a large segment of economic activity. For these reasons, government efforts to remove controls have by and large been thwarted. In September 1993, when the then prime minister, Mr Hosokawa, asked the bureaucrats who implemented the thousands of regulations that then applied to private business to suggest some that might be lifted, they came up with only 94! [*Economist* 20 Nov. 1993]. In fact, between March 1992 and March 1993, the number of regulations in force increased from

10 942 to 11 402. The ministries with the most regulations are in decreasing order of magnitude: MITI, Transport. Agriculture, Finance and Health [*Nikkei Weekly* 27 Dec. 1993].

Notwithstanding the resistance to deregulation, there is a widespread understanding that unless the strangulating effects of regulation are largely removed, Japan would encounter no end of problems in furthering its economic restructuring (necessitated by numerous changes in the international arena) and in coping with ongoing trade friction with the US and with Europe. Recognizing this, in April 1995 the government ushered in a five year deregulation programme. If the past is any pointer to the future, the government's objectives cannot be expected to be realized in full. However, given the seriousness of the issue, some progress ought inevitably to be made.

## The Japanese Economy as a Model to other Countries

In our parting comments, we wish to briefly dwell on the appropriateness of the Japanese experience as an exemplar to other countries, particularly Third World ones. Considering that in the postwar period Japan had attained such a remarkable growth record and that within less than a lifetime, it raised itself from a penurious state, in the wake of its defeat, to the status of a leading industrial power, it is hardly surprising that many others have thought of Japan as a country worth emulating. This partly explains why Japan is the subject of such worldwide interest.

A common mistake among would-be Japanese imitators is to seize on specific aspects of the Japanese economy, whether it be the kanban system, lifetime employment, government industrial involvement and so on, and to then try and assimilate them within their own societies. Sometimes, they are partially successful (such as in the case of US automakers adapting Japanese production systems) but as often as not, the adaptations turn out to be failures. What is not generally appreciated is that the seemingly separate characteristics of the Japanese economy (and of Japanese society too) are in fact components of a complex system, in which each segment is highly dependent on and interactive with many others. Take lifetime employment as a case in point. For it to function smoothly, large Japanese corporations need to be fairly viable over a long time frame. To help ensure that, many firms adhere to keiretsu associations (for mutual support) and for reliance on a main bank, which to some extent underwrites their performance. The lifetime system is also based on the premise that workers would be loyal to their firms. This loyalty is forthcoming (among other reasons) by the prevalence in Japan of a version of Confucianism which emphasizes and instils obedience and respect. In addition, company unions rather than industry ones provide extra props. They facilitate payments on the basis of seniority ranking rather than on specific tasks, thus enabling the firm to reallocate jobs whenever the need arises. The company unions also endorse a promotion system largely based on age which allows for relatively low wages to be paid to young employees in whose human capital the firm may be intensively investing. The subcontracting system and the existence of a large number of part-time employees also allow for permanent staff to be retained in times of general economic slowdowns. One could go further by citing the low influence of shareholders, which enables boards of management to give certain priorities to their tenured workers, the bonus system which provides for wage flexibility and less employment fluctuation as additional factors that strengthen the lifetime employment system but by now it should be clear that lifetime employment does not exist as an independent force in its own right. The same is true for countless other phenomena.

What we are essentially asserting is that Third World countries, particularly those in Africa, cannot hope to recreate the Japanese experience. Not only do they lack the totality of ingredients that made Japan what it is but they are also operating in a different time frame and in different economic circumstances.

Does that mean that there is nothing that can be learnt from Japan? Certainly not. There are some important conclusions that can be drawn from the Japanese (though not of course exclusively from them). In our view, the workings of the Japanese economy highlight the importance of at least the following: A good and solid universal education system which is merit based. The need for an efficient bureaucracy staffed with officials dedicated to their country's advancement. A government which is development oriented, unafraid to tamper with the market mechanism when it malfunctions and which supports rather than stifles free enterprise and competition. A basic reservoir of entrepreneurial talent which takes a long-term view and which ploughs back profits. A general willingness to save. A strong work ethic. The rule of law and a stable and secure social environment.

Third World countries cannot simply will into existence the qualities that make or break economic development but at least they are able to discern from Japan many of the qualities that are worth pursuing.

Finally, for much the same set of reasons, industrial countries would have little to gain from an indiscriminate transfer of Japanese ways. As Morishima has so aptly put it, 'a policy which has been proved to be successful for Japan may turn out to be unworkable in Britain and vice versa, because of the differences in ethos, in the ways of behaviour of their peoples and in all other cultural characteristics which they have inherited from their respective pasts' [Morishima 1982:201]. In any case, Japan itself is unlikely to be a trail blazer in the immediate future. It is at its own crossroads where it faces an overvalued currency, potential paralysis caused by over regulation, an investment confidence crisis, a shaky banking structure (inherited from the 'bubble') and much trepidation resulting from an exodus of firms to Asia and elsewhere. With Japanese ingenuity, most of these problems will surely be solved but here again, most of the problems listed are fairly Japan specific, so that their solutions would not be more than of academic interest to others. If anything, Japan might look abroad for *some* of the answers but then that is what Japan has so successfully done in the past. By that we do not mean to imply that Japan is simply a great imitator, we would rather it be considered a great adaptor. Therein lies a lesson for us all.

# Notes

## 1 MACRO FOUNDATIONS OF THE JAPANESE ECONOMY

1. Factors that favoured the emergence and rapid growth of Japan's textile industry included a large internal market, a reservoir of pertinent handicraft skills, an abundance of cheap labour, an availability of cheap raw cotton, the low capital intensity of the textile industry and a climate sufficiently humid for spinning [Lockwood 1954:28].
2. Formally speaking, the allied powers consisted of the US, the UK, France and Russia but in practice the allied occupation was strictly an American affair in which the US dictated all the terms and had the last word.
3. Legend has it that the rate of 360 yen to the dollar was determined after the Americans learnt that the word 'yen' meant 'complete roundness'.

## 2 THE MACRO INSTITUTIONAL FRAMEWORK

1. Information in this section is largely derived from Suzuki 1987.
2. Calculated from Tables R 15 and R 16 of the OECD Economic Outlook, OECD, Paris, December 1992.
3. As calculated from Table 5, p. 26 of Sakakibara [1991].

## 3 THE MACROECONOMY

1. The basic balance is the current account balance adjusted for *long-term* capital flows.

## 4 JAPAN'S HIGH SAVINGS RATE

1. Interest and dividends are still taxed at a rate lower than the top marginal rate.

## 5 INDUSTRIAL POLICY

1. The notion that the postwar Japanese body politic was always united on the issue of industrial growth has been questioned by Muramatsu and Krauss [1986]. Basically, they argue that instead of a national consensus preceding industrial growth, it is more likely to have arisen in response to the success of the government's economic strategy.
2. In contrast to most other industrial countries, organized labour has exerted next to no clout. Labour-based parties have failed to capture political power

and except for a short period in the late 1940s, they had not, until the
early 1990s, even enjoyed government participation.
3. Information in this paragraph is derived by Johnson 1982, pp. 286–7.
4. The companies in question were all in the petroleum industry.
5. See Comment by Tyson in Krugman 1991, p. 299.
6. Kosai and Ogino 1984, p. 120. (Italics added). See also page IX.
7. See Eads and Yamamura 1986, pp. 434–5, and Okimoto 1989, p. 54.

## 6 BUSINESS ENTERPRISE

1. The figure for Ford relates to the year 1979.
2. Italics in the original.
3. Italics added.
4. Officially small-sized firms are defined as those that employ less than 20
workers while medium-sized firms are firms with a work force of less than
300. In this chapter, we make no distinction between these two categories
and we refer to them both as small firms.

## 7 LABOUR MANAGEMENT AND INDUSTRIAL RELATIONS

1. This and the following section draw heavily on Van Wolferen 1990:160–70.
2. For much the same reason, the rate of worker absenteeism in Japan is far
lower than in other industrialized countries.

## 8 PRODUCTIVITY, TECHNOLOGY AND STRUCTURAL CHANGE

1. In any case, Japan's markets were highly protected.
2. Horsley and Buckley [1990] p. 54 claim that between 1950 and 1980,
Japan acquired all the foreign technology it needed for about $10 billion.
However on p. 144, it is clear that they are referring only to transfers from
the US electronics industry.
3. Unlike Chapter 3, the approach to structural adjustment issues is largely
from a microeconomic point of view.

## 9 TRADE AND THE BALANCE OF PAYMENTS

1. In 1992 manufactures constituted 95 per cent of Hong Kong's exports, 90
per cent of Israel's, 78 per cent of Singapore's, 89 per cent of Italy's, 94
per cent of Switzerland's, 90 per cent of Austria's and Germany's and 80
per cent of the USA's exports.
2. This seems to be particularly so since at least the early 1980s.
3. In Japan, not only were interest rates low but so was the cost of physical
capital inputs, such as steel.
4. For example, given a trade deficit, a devaluation immediately worsens the
trade balance (in local currency) since faced with sudden price increases

for both imports and exports and being initially incapable of adjusting trade volumes (because of short-term demand inelasticities) the absolute rise in import bills exceeds the absolute rise in export proceeds, generating an even greater deficit. The situation improves once export volumes expand and import volumes contract.

5. Without using these simplifications, that is without discarding foreign remittances, etc, we would still arrive at the same results but the process would be a little more complicated or congested.

## 10  TRADE CONFLICT

1. Other countries, such as Australia, have also insisted on doing their own drug testing.
2. It was privatized in 1985.
3. At the time, Japanese-made TVs were selling in Japan at retail prices 50 per cent higher than those exported to the United States [Cohen 1991:30].

## 11  JAPAN'S FOREIGN DIRECT INVESTMENT

1. These include: the 1966 Korean Foreign Capital Inducement Act, the 1967 Singaporean Economic Expansion Incentives Act, the 1967 Indonesian Foreign Capital Investment Act and the 1968 Malaysian Investment Incentives Act.
2. In the short run at least, the yen appreciation can also be troublesome. It could lead to capital losses for firms which had previously made foreign investments and to the extent that subsidiaries are dependent on Japanese inputs, their production costs could rise.
3. All unreferenced data in the main body of the text are derived from the Ministry of Finance.
4. In 1984 the VER ceiling was raised to 1 850 000 vehicles and then to 2 300 000 for 1985 and 1986.
5. Such a preference also worked in Holland's favour, where most people know English as a second language.
6. In 1984 for instance, the ratio of exports to North America over Europe was three to one, whereas the corresponding ratio of manufacturing FDIs was 3.6 to one.
7. Calculated on the basis of data contained in Fig. B-4, p. 282 of Chen 1992.
8. To qualify for duty free passage among the three NAFTA members, cars must now have at least 50 per cent North American content. This ratio will shortly rise to 57 per cent and then to 62.5 per cent by 2001.
9. For example, *The Financial Times* (11 Nov. 1994) states that 'the shift of manufacturing production offshore in response to the high yen and the need for businesses to trim costs to remain competitive will weaken demand for labour.'
10. Italics in the original.

## 12 AGRICULTURE

1. While this does not constitute an argument for protection, the implicit social security benefits of agricultural protection are often overlooked in efforts to compute its social costs.
2. Although the LDP recognized the need for large farming units as an economic imperative, it ultimately deferred to political expediencies.

## 13 SOME SERVICE INDUSTRIES

1. See also Kuribayashi 1991:42.
2. During the 1950s, 'MITI would assign an enterprise to a trading company if it did not already have an affiliation.' [Johnson 1982:206]
3. The epigram 'those that can do and those that can't teach', is well beloved by Western philistines and materialists.
4. Italics added.
5. Private households also of course contribute to education. Expenses commonly amount to a fifth of the family budget.
6. It seems that the traditional Japanese diet, high in the concentration of pickled, cured and fermented ingredients, increases the risk of stomach cancer. As for lung cancer, at least 60 per cent of Japanese men smoke (one of the highest rates among industrial countries) and very little is done to curtail tobacco consumption. Large concentrations of salt in Japanese food exacerbate cerebro-vascular problems.
7. The countries in question were: Spain, Greece, Luxembourg, New Zealand, Portugal, Belgium and the UK.
8. On average, each Japanese undergoes at least one medical screening per annum.

## 14 WELFARE AND THE GENERAL QUALITY OF LIFE

1. A rather different set of data is provided by Campbell 1992, pp. 8 and 9, where the 1965 ratio is shown as 6.1 per cent and the 1983–5 ratio as 14 per cent but the Foreign Press data is based on a 1993 Ministry of Health White Paper.
2. This observation could be added to the list accounting for Japan's low social security expenditure ratio.
3. The pension includes the worker and his wife's basic benefits plus an earnings related benefit.
4. Apparently, Scandinavian exchange rates were at that time more overvalued than the yen.
5. The Engel coefficient measures the proportion of disposable income that is devoted to food, beverages and tobacco. As people (or countries) become richer, expenditures on food account for a relatively smaller share of their budget.
6. The current situation in Japan is distinctly better than it was earlier. In

1968, floor space per person amounted to 18.6 square metres [Mills and Ohta:1976:706].

7. The term 'urban farmlands' depicts pockets of land within an urban region used for food production.

8. Employees can take some solace in the fact that their employers reimburse their travel expenses.

# Bibliography

Abe, M.A., 'Japan's clinic physicians and their behaviour', *Social Science Medicine*, 20, 4, 1985.

Abegglen, J.C. and Stalk Jr, G., *Kaisha, The Japanese Corporation*, New York, Basic Books, 1985.

Allen, G.C., *The Japanese Economy*, London, Weidenfeld and Nicolson, 1981.

Anderson, K. and Hayami, Y., *The Political Economy of Agricultural Protection*, Sydney, Allen and Unwin, 1986.

Anderson, S.J., *Welfare Policy and Politics in Japan: Beyond the Developmental State*, New York, Paragon House, 1993.

Ando, A. and Auerbach, A., *The Cost of Capital in Japan*, National Bureau of Economic Research, Working Paper No. 3371, Washington, DC, 1988.

Ando, A., and Auerbach, A., 'The cost of capital in the US and Japan', NBER Working Paper No. 3371, Washington 1990.

Aoki, M., 'Aspects of the Japanese firm', in M. Aoki, *The Economic Analysis of the Japanese Firm*, Amsterdam, North Holland, 1984.

Aoki, M., 'The Japanese firm in transition', in K. Yamamura and Y. Yasuba (eds), *The Political Economy of Japan, Vol. 1, The Domestic Transformation*, Stanford, Stanford University Press, 1987.

Aoki, M., 'The nature of the Japanese firm as a means of employment and financial contracts: an overview', *Journal of the Japanese and International Economies* 3, 345–66, 1989.

Aoki, M., 'Toward an economic model of the Japanese firm', *Journal of Economic Literature*, March 1990.

Aoki, M. and Dore, R., *The Japanese firm*, Oxford, Oxford University Press, 1994.

Aoki, T., 'Japanese FDI and the forming of networks in the Asian-Pacific region: experience in Malaysia and its implications', in S. Tokunaga, 1992.

Argy, V., 'Exchange rate management in theory and practice', *Princeton Studies in International Finance*, 50, New Jersey, Princeton University, October 1982.

Argy, V., 'International financial liberalisation – the Australian and Japanese experience compared' *Bank of Japan Monetary and Economic Studies*, May 1987.

Argy, V., *International Macroeconomics: Theory and Policy*, London, Routledge, 1994.

Asanuma, B, 'The contractual framework for parts supply in the Japanese automotive industry', *Japanese Economic Studies*, XIII, 4, Summer, 1985.

Asanuma, B., 'The organization of parts purchases in the Japanese automotive industry', *Japanese Economic Studies*, XIII, 4, Summer, 1985.

Asanuma, B., 'Manufacturer–supplies relationships in Japan and the concept of relation-specific skill', *Journal of the Japanese and International Economics*, 3, 1, March 1989.

Asanuma, B. and Kikutani, T., 'Risk absorption in Japanese subcontracting: a microeconomic study on the automobile industry', *Centre for Economic Policy Research*, Stanford University, Publication No. 218, October 1994.

Baba, M., *et al.*, 'Conclusion', in R. Komiya, R. Okuno, M. and Suzumura, K. (eds), *Industrial Policy of Japan*, Tokyo, Academic Press, 1988.

Balassa, B. and Noland, M., *Japan in the World Economy*, Washington DC: Institute for International Economics, 1988.

Balasubramanyam, V.N. and Greenaway, D., 'Economic integration and foreign direct investment: Japanese investment in the E.C.', *Journal of Common Market Studies*, XXX, 2, June 1992.

Baldwin, C., 'The capital factor' in M. Porter, *Competition in global industries*, Boston, Harvard Business School Press, 1986.

Baldwin, R.E., 'The impact of the 1986 US-Japan semiconductor agreement', *Japan and the World Economy*, 6, 129–52, 1994.

Bank of Japan, 'Structural adjustments and problems of the Japanese economy after the second oil shock', Special Paper No. 108, July 1983.

Bank of Japan, *Comparative Economic and Financial Statistics*, Research and Statistics Department, Bank of Japan, Tokyo, 1990.

Bank of Japan, 'Recent balance of payments developments in Japan', Special Paper No. 208, November 1991.

Bank of Japan, 'Economic growth in East Asia and the role of foreign direct investment', *Bank of Japan Quarterly Bulletin*, February 1994.

Barro, R., 'Are Government Bonds Net Wealth?', *Journal of Political Economy*, Vol. 82, 1974.

Bayard, T. and Elliott, K., 'Aggressive unilaterism and Section 301: market opening or market closing?', *World Economy*, November 1992.

Bergsten, C.F., 'Pacific dynamism and the international economic system', Institute for International Economics, Washington, 1993.

Bergsten, C.F. and Cline, W.R., *The United States–Japan Economic Problem*, Washington, Institute for International Economics, January 1987.

Bergsten, C.F. and Noland, M., *Reconcilable Differences*, Washington, Institute for International Economics, 1993.

Bernard, M. and Ravenhill, J., 'New hierarchies in East Asia: the post Plaza division of labour', *Department of International Relations Working Paper*, Australian National University, Canberra, June 1992.

Blumenthal, T., 'Japan's Juken industry', *Asian Survey*, XXXII, 5, May 1992.

Boltho, A., 'Was Japan's industrial policy successful?', *Cambridge Journal of Economics*, June 1985.

Borner, S., *International Finance and Trade in a Polycentric World*, London, Macmillan, 1988.

Bovard, J., *The Fair Trade Fraud*, New York, St. Martin's Press, 1991.

Bronfenbrenner, M. and Yasuba, Y., 'Economic welfare', in K. Yamamura and Y. Yasuba, 1987.

Butler, A., 'Trade imbalances and economic theory: the case for a US–Japan trade deficit', *Federal Reserve Bank of St. Louis Review*, March/April 1991.

Butler, R., 'Japan and US health policies for the 21st century', *Japan and the World Economy*, 5, 157–72, 1993.

Calder, K.E., *Crisis and Compensation: Public Policy and Political Stability in Japan*, Princeton, Princeton University Press, 1988.

Calmfors, L. and Forslund, A., 'Wage setting in Sweden', *Institute for International Economic Studies*, Seminar Paper No. 430, Stockholm, January 1989.

Campbell, J.C., *How Policies Change: The Japanese Government and the Aging Society*, New Jersey, Princeton University Press, 1992.

Caves, R.E., 'Japanese investment in the United States: lessons for the economic analysis of foreign investment', *The World Economy*, May 1993.

Chalmers, N.J., *Industrial Relations in Japan*, London, Routledge, 1989.

Chen, J.A., 'Japanese firms with direct investments in China and their local management', in S. Tokunaga, 1992.

Chew, S.B., Chew, R., and Chan, F.K., 'Technology transfer from Japan to ASEAN: trends and prospects', in S. Tokunaga, 1992.

Chinwanno, C. and Tambunlertchai, S., 'Japanese investment in Thailand and its prospects in the 1980s', in S. Sekiguchi, 1983.

Christelow, D., 'Japan's intangible barriers to trade in manufacture', *Federal Reserve Bank of New York Quarterly Review*, Winter, 1985/6.

Christopher, R.C., *The Japanese Mind: the Goliath Explained*, Tokyo, Charles Tuttle, 1983.

Citrin, D., 'Agricultural studies in Japan and their economic consequences', *Staff Studies IMF*, Washington, September 1990.

Clark, R., *The Japanese Company*, New Haven, Yale University Press, 1979.

Clark, R.L., 'Social security systems in Japan', *Journal of Economic Committee*, Congress of the US, 1990.

Cohen, S.D., *Cowboys and Samurai*, New York, Harper, 1991.

Crocker, R., 'The changing nature of Japanese trade', *Finance and Development*, June 1991.

Cusumano, M.A., *The Japanese Automobile Industry*, Cambridge, Harvard University Press, 1985.

Czinkota, M.R. and Kotabe, M., *The Japanese Distribution System*, Chicago, Probus, 1993.

De Gregorio, J. 'Savings, growth and capital markets imperfections: the case of borrowing constraints', *IMF Working Paper*, 31, March 1993.

Dean, A., *et al.*, 'Savings trends and behaviour in OECD countries', *OECD Working Papers*, 67, June 1989.

Dicken, P., 'The changing geography of Japanese foreign direct investment in manufacturing industry: a global perspective', *Environment and Planning*, 20, 633–53, 1988.

Dicken, P., 'The changing geography of Japanese foreign direct investment in manufacturing industry', in E.J. Morris, 1991.

Dobson, W., 'Japan in East Asia: trading and investment strategies', *Institute of Southeast Asian Studies*, Singapore, 1993.

Dore, R., *Flexible Rigidities: Industrial Policy and Structural Adjustment in the Japanese Economy, 1970–80*, Stanford, Stanford University Press, 1986.

Dore, R., 'Japanese capitalism, Anglo-Saxon capitalism; how will the Darwinian contest turn out?', *Occasional Paper* 4, Centre for Economic Performance, London School of Economics, London, October 1992.

Dore, R.P. and Sako, M., *How the Japanese Learn to Work*, London, Routledge, 1989.

Dosi, G., Tyson, L. and Zysman, J., 'Trade, technologies and development', in C. Johnson, L.D. Tyson and J. Zysman, 1989.

Drake, T.A., 'Changing determinants of Japanese foreign investment in the

United States', *Journal of the Japanese and International Economies*, 6, 3, September, 1992.

Dunning, J.H., 'Explaining changing patterns of international production: in defence of the eclectic theory', *Oxford Bulletin of Economics and Statistics*, 41, 4, 1979.

Durand, M., Simon, J., and Webb, C., 'OECD's indicators of international trade and competitiveness', Working Papers No. 120, OECD, Paris, 1992.

Eads, G.C. and Nelson, R.R., 'Japanese high technology', in H. Patrick, 1986.

Eads, Y.C. and Yamamura, K. 'The future of industrial policy' in K. Yamamura and Y. Yasuba, 1987.

Eltis, W. and Fraser, D., 'The contribution of Japanese industrial success to Britain and to Europe', *National Westminster Bank, Quarterly Review*, November 1992.

Emmott, B., *Japan's Global Reach*, London, Century, 1992.

Encarnation, D.J., *Rivals Beyond Trade*, Ithaca, Cornell University Press, 1992.

Ennis, P., 'Canada set for a bigger share of Japanese auto investment', *Tokyo Business Today*, February 1995.

Fischer, S., 'International macroeconomic policy coordination', National Bureau of Economic Research, Working Paper, Series 2244, Washington, 1987.

Flath, D., 'Why are there so many retail stores in Japan?', *Japan and the World Economy*, 2, 365–86, 1990.

Florida, R. and Kenney, M., 'Japanese foreign direct investment in the United States', in E.J. Morris 1991.

Flynn, D.M., 'Science policy in Japan and the United States as it affects scientific and economic development', in *Joint Economic Committee Congress of the US*, October 1990.

Fong, C-O., 'Foreign direct investment in Malaysia: technology transfer and linkages by Japan and Asian NICs', in S. Tokunaga, 1992.

Foreign Press Center, *Facts and Figures of Japan*, Tokyo, Foreign Press Centre, 1993.

Frankel, J., 'The evolving Japanese financial system and the cost of capital', Working Paper No. CP92002, *Centre for International and Development Economics Research*, Berkeley, University of California, 1992.

Frankel, J., 'Japanese financial system and the cost of capital' in S. Takagi, *Japanese Capital Markets*, Oxford, Blackwell, 1993.

Fukao, K., *et al.*, 'R&D investment and overseas production: an empirical analysis of Japan's electric machinery industry based on corporate data', *Monetary and Economic Studies*, 13, 1, 1994.

Fukao, M., 'Liberalization of Japan's foreign exchange controls and structural changes in the balance of payments' *Bank of Japan Monetary and Economic Studies*, September 1990.

Fuzimoto, T., 'Why do Japanese companies automate assembly operations?' Research Institute for the Japanese Economy, University of Tokyo, December, 1992.

George, A. and Saxon, E., 'The politics of agricultural protection in Japan', in K. Anderson and Y. Hayami, 1986.

Georgiou, C. and Weinhold, S., 'Japanese direct investment in the US', *The World Economy*, November 1992.

Gerlach, M., 'Business alliances and the strategy of the Japanese firm', *California Management Review* 30, 1, Fall, 1987.

Gerlach, M., 'Keiretsu organization in the Japanese economy', in C. Johnson *et al.*, 1989.

Gerlach, M.L., 'Twilight of the Keiretsu? A critical assessment', *Journal of Japanese Studies*, 18, 1, 1992(a).

Gerlach, M.L., *Alliance Capitalism*, Berkeley, University of Berkeley Press, 1992(b).

Gittelman, N. and Dunning, J.H., 'Japanese multinationals in Europe and the United States: some comparisons and contrasts', in Klein and Welfens, 1992.

Goto, A. and Wakasugi, R., 'Technology Policy,' in Komiya *et al.* 1988.

Goto, J., *Labor in International Trade Theory*, Baltimore, Johns Hopkins Press, 1990.

Goto, J. and Imamura, N., 'Japanese agriculture: characteristics, institutions and policies', in Tweeten *et al.*, 1993.

Gross, M., 'Foreign direct investment in ASEAN – its sources and structure', *Asian Economies*, June 1987.

Hadley, D., 'Counterpoint on business groupings and government–industry relations in automobiles', in M. Aoki (ed.), *The Economic Analysis of the Japanese Firm*, North Holland, Amsterdam, 1984.

Hadley, E., 'Counterpoint in business groupings and government–industry relations in automobiles', in M. Aoki, 1984.

Hagemann, R.P. and Nicoletti, G., 'Ageing populations: economic effects and implications for public finance', *OECD Working Papers*, 61, January 1989.

Haley, J.V., 'Weak law, strong competition and trade barriers', in K. Yamamura, 1990.

Hamada, K., 'Lessons from the macroeconomic performances of the Japanese economy', in V. Argy and J. Neville, *Inflation and Unemployment Theory Experience and Policy Making*, London, Allen and Unwin, 1985.

Hamada, K. and Kurosaka, Y., 'Trends in unemployment, wages and productivity: the case of Japan', in C. Bean, R. Layard and S. Nickell (ed.), *The Rise in Unemployment*, Oxford, Basil Blackwell, 1987.

Harada, M., 'Minamata disease: man-made tragedy', *Look Japan*, September 1992.

Harris, M.C., 'Asymmetries and potential complementarities: scientific and technological relations between Japan and the United States', in *Joint Economic Committee Congress of the US*, October 1990.

Hayami, Y., *Japanese Agriculture Under Siege*, New York, St. Martin's, 1988.

Hayashi, F., 'Why is Japan's saving rate so apparently high?' in S. Fischer (ed.), *NBER Macroeconomics Annual 1986*, Cambridge, The MIT Press, 1986.

Hayashi, F., 'Explaining Japan's saving: a review of recent literature', *Bank of Japan Monetary and Economic Studies*, 10, 2: 63–78, November 1992.

Hayden Lesbirel, S., 'Structural Adjustment in Japan', *Asian Survey*, XXXI, 11, November 1991.

Healey, D., *Japanese Capital Exports and Asian Economic Development*, Paris, OECD, 1991.

Heitger, B. and Stehn, J., 'Japanese direct investment in the EC – response to the internal market 1993?', *Journal of Common Market Studies*, XXX, 1, September 1990.

Hendry, J., *Understanding Japanese Society*, New York, Croom Helm, 1987.
Hickman, B.G., *International Productivity and Competitiveness*, Oxford, Oxford University Press, 1992.
Hickok, S., 'Japanese trade balance adjustment to yen appreciation', *Federal Reserve Bank of New York Quarterly Review*, 14, 3, Autumn, 1989.
Hiemenz, U., 'Foreign direct investment and industrialization in ASEAN countries', *Welwirtschaftliches Archiv*, 123, 1, 1987.
Holbrooke, R., 'Japan and the US: the unequal partnership', *Foreign Affairs*, Winter, 1991/92.
Horaguchi, H., 'Withdrawal of overseas Japanese firms from Asia: 1971-1988', *Japanese Economic Studies*, 21, 4, Summer 1993.
Horioka, C., 'Why is Japan's private savings rate so high?' *Finance and Development*, December 22–25, 1986.
Horioka, C., 'Why is Japan's household saving rate so high?' A literature survey', *Journal of the Japanese and International Economies*, 4: 49–92, 1990.
Horioka, C.Y., 'Japan's consumption and saving in international perspective', *Economic Development and Cultural Change*, 42, 2, January 1994.
Horiuchi, A., 'Financial structure and the managerial discretion in the Japanese firm', Working Paper No. 93–17, Centre for Japanese Economic Studies, Macquarie University, 1993.
Horiuchi, T., 'The effect of firm status on banking relationships and loan syndication', Economic Development Institute Working Paper No. 94–9, Washington, World Bank, 1994.
Horsley, W. and Buckley, R., *Nippon: New Superpower, Japan since 1945*, London, BBC Books, 1990.
Hoshi, T., 'Evolution of the main bank system in Japan', Centre for Japanese Economic Studies Working Paper No. 93–4, Macquarie University, 1993.
Hoshi, T., 'The economic role of corporate groupings and the main bank system', in M. Aoki and R. Dore, 1994.
Huddle, N. and Reich, M. with N. Stisken, *Island of Dreams: Environmental Crisis in Japan*, Cambridge, Schenkman Books, 1987.
Hutchinson, M., 'Aggregate Demand, Uncertainty and Oil Prices: The 1990 Oil Shock in Comparative Perspective', *Bank for International Settlements (BIS) Economic Papers*, 31, August 1991.
Hymer, S.H., *The International Operation of National Firms: A Study of Direct Foreign Investment*, Cambridge, Mass., MIT Press, 1976.
Iglehart, J.K., 'Japan's medical care system', *New England Journal of Medicine*, 319, 807–12 and 1166–72, 1988.
Ikeda, M., 'Trends of Japan's direct investment for Asia', *Exim Review*, 6, 2, 1985.
Ikegami, N., 'Best medical practice: the case of Japan', *International Journal of Health Planning and Management*, 4, 181–95, 1989.
Ikegami, N., 'Japanese Health Care: low cost through regulated fees', *Health Affairs*, 4, 2, Autumn, 1991.
Imai, K., 'Japan's industrial policy for high technology industry', in H. Patrick, 1986.
Imai, K., 'Industrial policy and technological innovation', in R. Komiya *et al.*, 1988.

Imai, K., 'Japanese business groups and the structural impediments initiative', in K. Yamamura, 1990.

Imai, K. and Komiya, R., *Business Enterprise in Japan*, Cambridge, MIT Press, 1994.

Institute of International Economics, *International Economic Insights*, Washington, DC, 1992.

Ishigami, E., 'Japanese business in ASEAN countries: new-industrialization or Japanization?', *IDS Bulletin*, 22, 2, 1991.

Ishikawa, T., and Ueda, K., 'The bonus payment system and Japanese personal savings', in M. Aoki (ed.), *The Economic Analysis of the Japanese Firm*, Amsterdam, Elsevier Science Publishers, 1984.

Ishizaki, Y., 'The automobile industries of Asian countries', *RIM*, 1, 23, 1994.

Itami, H., 'The "Human-Capital-ism" of the Japanese firm as an integrated system', in R. Imai and R. Komiya, 1994.

Ito, M., 'Interfirm relations and long-term continuous trading', in K. Imai and R. Komiya, 1994.

Ito, T., *The Japanese Economy*, Cambridge, MIT Press, 1992.

Ito, T. and Krueger, A.O., *Trade and Protectionism*, Chicago, University of Chicago Press, 1993.

Ito, T. and Maruyama, M., 'Is the Japanese distribution system really inefficient?' in P. Krugman (ed.), *Trade with Japan*, Chicago, University of Chicago Press, 1991.

Itoh, M., 'The Japanese distribution system and access to the Japanese market', in P. Krugman (ed.), as above.

Itoh, M. and Kiyono, K. 'Foreign trade and direct investment', in R. Komiya *et al.*, 1988.

Itoh, M. and Urata, S., 'Small and medium enterprise support policies in Japan', paper presented at the Australia-Japan Research Centre, Public Seminar, Canberra, 28 February 1990.

Itoh, M., *et al.*, 'Industry promotion and trade', in R. Komiya *et al.*, 1988(a).

Itoh, M., *et al.*, 'Industrial policy as a corrective to market failures', in R. Komiya *et al.*, 1988(b).

Iwasaki, A., 'Markets and mergers', in R. Komiya *et al.*, 1988.

Iwata, K., 'Relative Richness', *Look Japan*, October 1992.

JETRO, *White Paper on Direct Foreign Investment*, Tokyo, JETRO, 1991.

JETRO, *White Paper on International Trade*, Tokyo, JETRO, 1993.

JETRO, *White Paper on Foreign Direct Investment*, Tokyo, JETRO, 1994.

Johnson, C., *MITI and the Japanese Miracle*, Stanford, Stanford University Press, 1982.

Johnson, C., 'Trade, Revisionism and the factors of Japanese–American relations', in K. Yamamura, 1990.

Johnson, C., Tyson, L.D. and Zysman, J. (eds), *Politics and Productivity: The Real Story of Why Japan Works*, New York, Harper Business, 1989.

Joint Economic Committee Congress of the United States, *Japan's Economic Challenge*, US Govt Printing Office, October 1990.

Jorgenson, Dale W. and Kuroda, M., 'Productivity and international competitiveness in Japan and the United States 1960–85', in B. Hickman, 1992.

Julius, D., *Foreign direct investment: the neglected twins of trade*, Washington, Group of Thirty, 1991(a).

Julius, D., *Global Companies and Public Policy*, Washington, Group of Thirty, 1991(b).

Kada, R. and Goto, J., 'Present issues of sustainable land use systems and rural communities in Japan', in L. Tweeten *et al.*, 1993.

Kagono, T. and Kobayashi, T., 'The provision of resources and barriers to exit', in K. Imai and R. Komiya, 1994.

Kamata, S., *Japan in the Passing Lane*, New York, Pantheon Books, 1982.

Kasman, B., 'Japan's growth performance over the last decade '*Federal Reserve Bank of New York Quarterly Review*, Summer, 1987.

Kawasaki, K., 'The saving behaviour of Japanese households', *OECD Working Papers*, 73, January 1990.

Kester, W.C., and Luehrman, T., 'Real interest rates and the cost of capital', *Japan and the World Economy*, No. 1 pp. 199–232, 1989.

Kindleberger, C.P., *American Business Abroad: Six Lectures on Direct Investment*, New Haven, Yale University Press, 1969.

King, M., 'The ownership and financing of corporations', in Aoki, M. (ed.), *The Economic Analysis of the Japanese Firm*, North Holland, Amsterdam, 1984.

Kinmouth, E.H., 'Engineering education and its rewards', *Comparative Education Review*, 30, 3, August 1986.

Kinmonth, E.H., 'Japanese engineers and American myth makers', *Pacific Affairs*, 64, 3, Autumn, 1991.

Klein, W. and Welfens, P.J.J., *Multinationals in the New Europe and Global Trade*, Berlin, Springer-Verlag, 1992.

Kodama, F., *Analyzing Japanese High Technologies: The Techno-Paradigm Shift*, London, Pinter, 1991.

Kogat, B., and Chang, S.J., 'Technological capabilities and the Japanese foreign direct investment in the United States', *Review of Economics and Statistics*, 75, 401–13, 1991.

Koiki, K., 'Human resource development and labor-management relations', in K. Yamamura and Y. Yasuba, 1987.

Koiki, K., *Understanding Industrial Relations in Modern Japan*, New York, St. Martin's Press, 1988.

Kojima, K., 'Japanese-style direct foreign investment', *Japanese Economic Studies*, XIV, 3, Spring, 1984.

Kojima, K., *Japanese Direct Foreign Investment*, Tokyo, Bunshindo, 1985(a).

Kojima, K., 'Japanese and American direct investment in Asia: a comparative analysis', *Hitotsubashi Journal of Economics*, June 1985(b).

Komine, T., 'Structural change of Japanese firms', *Japanese Economic Studies*, Summer, 1991.

Komiya, R., 'Introduction', in Komiya, R., Okuno, M. and Suzumura, K. (eds), *Industrial Policy of Japan*, Tokyo, Academic Press, 1988.

Komiya, R., 'Japan's Foreign Direct Investment: facts and theoretical considerations', in S. Borner, 1988(b).

Komiya, R., *The Japanese Economy: Trade, Industry and Government*, Tokyo, University of Tokyo Press, 1990.

Komiya, R., Okuno, M. and Suzumura, K. (eds), *Industrial Policy of Japan*, Tokyo, Academic Press, 1988.

Komiya, R. and Irie, K., 'The US-Japan trade problem: an economic analysis from a Japanese viewpoint', in K. Yamamura, 1990.

Komiya, R., and Suda, M., *Japan's Foreign Exchange Policy 1971–82*, London, Allen and Unwin, 1991.

Komiya, R., and Wakasugi, R., 'Japan's foreign direct investment', *Annals*, AAPS (American Association for the Promotion of Social Science), January 1991.

Kon-ya, F., 'The rise and fall of the bubble economy', *Centre for Japanese Economic Studies*, 94–2, Sydney, Macquarie University, 1994.

Kosai, Y., *The Era of High Speed Growth*, Tokyo, University of Tokyo Press, 1986.

Kosai, Y., 'The Reconstruction period', in R. Komiya *et al.*, *Industrial Policy of Japan*, Tokyo, Academic Press, 1988.

Kosai, Y. and Ogino, Y. *The Contemporary Japanese Economy*, London, Macmillan, 1984.

Koshiro, K., 'The employment system and human resource management', in K. Imai and R. Komiya, 1994.

Kotlikoff, L.J., *What Determines Savings?* London, The MIT Press, 1989.

Krasner, S.D., 'Asymmetries in Japanese–American trade', *Institute of International Studies*, Berkeley, University of California, 1987.

Krause, L.B., 'Japanese investment in the United States', in K. Yamamura, 1989.

Kreinen, M.E., 'How closed is Japan's market? Additional evidence', *The World Economy*, 11, 4, December 1988.

Krugman, P. (ed.), *Trade with Japan*, Chicago, University of Chicago Press, 1991.

Kuen-Choi, K. and Ann, L.D., 'Japanese direct investment in Singapore manufacturing industry', in S. Sekiguchi, 1983.

Kumur, B.N., 'Japanese direct investments in West Germany', in E.J. Morris, 1991.

Kunio, Y., 'Sogo Shosha', Oxford University Press, Tokyo, 1982.

Kuntjoro-Jakti, D., Tjiptoherijanto, P. and Adji, S.S., 'Japanese investment in Indonesia', in S. Sekiguchi, 1983.

Kuribayashi, S., 'Present situation and future prospect of Japan's distribution system', *Japan and the World Economy*, 3, 39–60, 1991.

Lawrence, R.Z., 'An analysis of Japanese trade with developing countries', *Brookings Discussion Papers in International Economics*, 87, April 1991(a).

Lawrence, R.Z., 'Efficient or exclusionist? The import behavior of Japanese corporate groups', *Brookings Papers on Economic Activity*, 1, 1991(b).

Lawrence, R.Z., 'How open is Japan?', in P. Krugman, 1991(c).

Lebra, T.S., *Japanese Patterns of Behaviour*, Honolulu, University of Hawaii Press, 1976.

Lee, C.H. and Ramsletter, E.D., 'Direct investment and structural change in Korean manufacturing', in E.D. Ramstetter, 1991.

Lesbirel, S.H., 'Structural Adjustment in Japan', *Asian Survey*, Vol. XXXI, No. 11, November 1991.

Lim, C.P. and Ping, L.P., 'Japanese direct investment in Malaysia with special reference to Japanese joint ventures', in S. Sekiguchi, 1983.

Lincoln, E., *Japan: Facing Maturity*, Washington, Brookings Institution, 1988.

Lincoln, E.J., *Japan's New Global Role*, Washington, Brookings Institution, 1993.

Lincoln, E.J., *Japan's Unequal Trade*, Washington, The Brookings Institute, 1990.

Lockwood, W.M., *The Economic Development of Japan*, Princeton, Princeton University Press, 1954.

Maddison, A. *Economic Growth in Japan and the USSR*, London, Allen and Unwin, 1969.

Maki, O., 'Gender and the labour market', *Journal of Japanese Studies* 19, 1, Winter, 1993.

Makin, J.H., 'The effects of Japanese investment in the United States', in K. Yamamura, 1989.

Makino, N., 'The advantages of Japan's management strategy', *Economic Eye*, Autumn, 1992.

Marston, R.C., 'Price behavior in Japanese and US manufacturing', in P. Krugman, 1991.

Maruyami, M., 'A study of the distribution system in Japan', *Economics Department Working Papers*, 136, Paris, OECD, 1993.

Mason, T.D. and Turay, A.M., *US-Japan Trade Friction*, New York, St. Martin's Press, 1991.

Masson, P.R. and Tryon, R.W., 'Macroeconomic effects of projected population aging in industrial countries', *International Monetary Fund Staff Papers*, September, 27, 3: 453–79, 1990.

Mastanduno, M., 'Setting market access priorities: the use of super 301 in US trade with Japan', *The World Economy*, November 1992.

Meredith, G., 'Discretionary monetary policy versus rules: the Japanese experience during 1986–91', *IMF Working Paper*, August 1992.

Mills, E.S. and Ohta, K., 'Urbanization and urban problems', in H. Patrick and H. Rosorsky, 1976.

Minami, R., *The Economic Development of Japan*, London, Macmillan, 1986.

Ministry of Agriculture, Forestry and Fisheries, 'Abstract of statistics on agriculture, forestry and fisheries', 1991/92.

Ministry of International Trade and Industry, *White Paper on Small and Medium Enterprises in Japan*, Tokyo, 1988.

MITI, *Japan's overseas investments*, Tokyo, MITI, 1977.

MITI, *White Paper on Small and Medium Enterprises in Japan*, Tokyo, MITI, 1982.

MITI, *Japan Statistical Yearbook 1990*, Tokyo, MITI, 1990.

Miwa, Y., 'Coordination within industry', in R. Komiya *et al.*, 1988.

Miwa, Y., 'The subcontracting system in Japan: a critical survey', *Japanese Economic Studies*, Winter, 1991–2.

Miyajima, H., (a) 'Japan's aging society', *Japanese Economic Studies*, 21, 6, Winter, 1993–4.

Miyajima, H., (b) 'The family structure in contemporary Japan', *Japanese Economic Studies*, 21, 6, Winter, 1993–4.

Modigliani, F., 'The life cycle hypothesis of saving and intercountry differences in the saving ratio', in W.A. Eltis, M.F.G. Scott and J.N. Wolfe (eds), *Industry, Growth and Trade: Essays in Honour of Sir Roy Harrod*, Oxford, Clarendon Press, 1970.

Montgomery, D., 'Understanding the Japanese as customers, competitors and collaborators', *Japan and the World Economy*, 3, 61–91, 1991.

Morishima, M., *Why has Japan Succeeded?*, London, Cambridge University Press, 1982.

Morris, E.J., *Japan and the Global Economy*, London, Routledge, 1991.

Morris-Suzuki, T., 'Reshaping the international division of labour', in E.J. Morris, 1991.

Mosk, C. and Nakata, Y., 'Education and occupation: an enquiry into the relationship between college specialisation and the labour market in postwar Japan', *Pacific Affairs*, 65, 1, Spring, 1992.

Mukoyama, H., 'Active investment by Japanese parts and materials – process industries in Asia', *RIM*, II, 24, 1994.

Muramatsu, M. and Krauss, E.S., 'The conservative policy line and the development of patterned pluralism', in Kosai, Y., 'The politics of economic management', in K. Yamamura and Y. Yasuba, 1987.

Muraoka, T., 'Pursuing the new international economic order', in E.J. Morris, 1991.

Mutoh, H., 'The automotive industry', in R. Komiya *et al.*, 1988.

Nakamura, T. *Economic Development of Modern Japan*, Ministry for Foreign Affairs, Tokyo 1985.

Nakatani, I., 'The economic role of financial corporate grouping', in Aoki, M. (ed.), *The Economic Analysis of the Japanese Firm*, Amsterdam, North Holland, 1984.

Nakakita, T., 'The globalization of Japanese firms and its influence on Japan's trade with developing countries', *The Developing Economies*, December 1988.

Newhouse, J.P., 'How urgent is medical care cost containment', *Japan and the World Economy*, 5, 93–106, 1993.

Nicolaides, P. and Thomsen, S., 'Can protectionism explain direct investment?', *Journal of Common Market Studies*, XXXIX, 6, December 1991.

Nishimura, K.G., 'The distribution system of Japan and the United States: a comparative study from the viewpoint of final-goods buyers', *Japan and the World Economy*, 5, 3, 1993.

Nishimura, S., 'Financing of health care for the elderly in Japan', *Japan and the World Economy*, 5, 107–20, 1993.

Noguchi, Y., 'Japan's land problem', *Japanese Economic Studies*, Spring, 1992.

Noguchi, Y., 'The bubble and economic policies in the 1990s', *The Journal of Japanese Studies*, 20, 2, Summer, 1994.

Odagiri, H., *Growth Through Competition, Competition Through Growth: Strategic Management and the Economy in Japan*, Oxford, Clarendon Press, 1992.

OECD, *Economic Survey of Japan*, Paris, OECD, 1972.

OECD, *Economic Survey of Japan*, Paris, OECD, 1978.

OECD, *Economic Surveys Japan 1988/89*, Paris, OECD, 1989.

OECD, *Economic Surveys: Japan*, Paris, OECD, 1990/91.

OECD, *Economic Surveys: Japan*, Paris, OECD, 1991/2.

OECD, *Economic Survey of Japan*, Paris, OECD, 1992.

OECD, *Basic Statistics*, Paris, OECD, 1992.

OECD, *Economic Survey of Japan*, Paris, OECD, 1993.

Oga, K., 'Impacts of trade arrangements on farm structure and food demand', in L. Tweeten *et al.*, 1993.

Ogawa, N., 'Impact of changes in population and household structure upon the allocation of medical resources in Japan', *Japan and the World Economy*, 5, 137–56, 1993.

Ogura, S. and Yoshino, N., 'The tax system and the fiscal investment program', in Komiya *et al.*, 1988.

Ohashi, J., 'On the determinants of bonuses and basic wages in large Japanese firms', in K. Imai and R. Komiya, 1994.

Okabe, M., 'The Japanese firm (1): behavioural and structural characteristics', *Working Paper Series* No. 92–3, Centre for Japanese Economic Studies, Sydney, Macquarie University, September 1992.

Okabe, M., *The Structure of the Japanese Economy*, London, Macmillan, 1995.

Okimoto, D.J., 'Regime characteristics of Japanese industrial policy', in H. Patrick, 1986.

Okimoto, D.J., *Between MITI and the Market: Japanese Industrial Policy for High Technology*, Stanford, Stanford University Press, 1989.

Okimoto, D.J. and Saxonhouse, G.R., 'Technology and the future of the economy', in K. Yamamura and Y. Yasuba, 1987.

Okumura, H., 'Japan's corporate capitalism in peril', *Japanese Economic Studies* 21, 4, Summer, 1993.

Okuno-Fujiwara, M., 'Industrial policy in Japan: a political economy view', in P. Krugman, 1991.

Ono, S., 'Sino-Japanese economic relations', *World Bank Discussion Paper*, 146, Washington, 1992.

Organization for Economic Cooperation and Development (OECD), *Industrial Adjustment Policies*, Paris, 1978.

Osaki, A. and Fujiyasu, M., 'Open the Japanese Rice Markets', *Tokyo Business Today*, December 1992.

Ozawa, K., 'A new phase for rice in Japan: production, marketing and policy issues', in L. Tweeten *et al.*, 1993.

Ozawa, T., 'Japan's resource dependency and overseas investment', *Journal of World Trade Law*, January/February 1977.

Ozawa, T., *Multinationalism Japanese Style*, Princeton, Princeton University Press, 1979.

Ozawa, T., 'Japan in a new phase of multinationalism and industrial upgrading: functional integration of trade, growth and FDI', *Journal of World Trade*, 25, 1, February 1991.

Pangetsu, M., 'Foreign firms and structural change in the Indonesian manufacturing sector', in E.D. Ramstetter, 1991.

Panglaykim, I.J., *Japanese Direct Investment in ASEAN; the Indonesian Experience*, Singapore, Maruzen, 1983.

Park, Y.C. and Park, W.A., 'Changing Japanese trade patterns and the East Asian NICs', in P. Krugman, 1991.

Patrick, H., *Japan's High Technology Industries: Lessons and Limitations of Industrial Policy*, Seattle, University of Washington Press, 1986.

Patrick, H. and Rosovsky, H., *Asia's New Giant: How the Japanese Economy Works*, Washington, Brookings Institution, 1976.

Patrick, H.T. and Rohlen, J.P., 'Small-scale family enterprises', in K. Yamamura and Y. Yasuba, 1987.

Peck, M.J., Levin, R.C. and Goto, A., 'Picking losers: public policy towards

declining industries in Japan', *Journal of Japanese Studies*, 13, 1, 1987.
Petri, P.A., 'Market structure, comparative advantage, and Japanese trade under the strong yen', in P. Krugman, 1991.
Phongpaichit, P., 'The new wave of Japanese investment in ASEAN', *Institute of Southeast Asian Studies*, Singapore, 1992.
Plummer, M.G. and Ramstetter, E.D., 'Multinational affiliates and the changing division of labor in the Asia-Pacific region', in E.D. Ramstetter, 1991.
Porges, A., 'US–Japan trade negotiations: paradigms list', in P. Krugman, 1991.
Porter, M., *The Competitive Advantage of Nations*, London, Macmillan, 1990.
Powell, M. and Anesaki, M., *Health Care in Japan*, London, Routledge, 1990.
Prestowitz, C.V., *Trading Places*, New York, Basic Books, 1989.
Ramstetter, E.D., *Direct Foreign Investment in Asia's Developing Economies and Structural Change in the Asia-Pacific Region*, Boulder, Westview Press, 1991.
Reid, N., 'Japanese direct investment in the United States manufacturing sector', in E.J. Morris, 1991.
Rodwin, V.G., 'Health insurance and health policy, American and Japanese Style', *Japan and the World Economy*, 5, 121–36, 1993.
Rohlen, T.P., *Japan's High Schools*, Berkeley, University of California Press, 1983.
Rothacher, A., *Japan's agro-food Sector*, St. Martin's, New York, 1989.
Saito, M., 'Incentives to save: Japan and the United States', *Economic Eye*, September: 23–7, 1986.
Saito, T., 'The Road To Recovery', *Look Japan*, May 1995.
Sakakibara, E., 'The Japanese-style system of market economy', *Japanese Economic Studies*, 20, 1, Autumn, 1991.
Salvatore, D., *National Trade Policies*, North Holland, Amsterdam, 1992.
Samels, R. and Whipple, B., 'Defense production and industrial development', in C. Johnson, L.D. Tyson and J. Zysman.
Sasaki, N., *Management and Industrial Structure in Japan*, London, Pergamon Press, 1990.
Sato, K., 'Trade policies in Japan', in D. Salvatore, 1992.
Sawa, T., 'The growing service sector in the Japanese economy', *Japanese Economic Studies*, Spring, 1992.
Saxonhouse, G.R., 'Industrial restructuring in Japan', *Journal of Japanese Studies*, 5, 2, 1979.
Saxonhouse, G., 'Comments on Lawrence's Paper', *Brookings Papers on Economic Activity*, 1, 1991.
Saxonhouse, G. and Stern, R., 'An analytical survey of formal and informal barriers to international trade and investment in the US, Canada and Japan', in R. Stern, 1989.
Schive, C. and Tu, Jenn-Hiwa, 'Foreign firms and structural change in Taiwan', in E.D. Ramstetter, 1991.
Sekiguchi, S., 'ASEAN–Japan relations: investment', *Institute of Southeast Asian Studies*, Singapore, 1983.
Sekiguchi, S. and Horiuchi, T., 'Trade and adjustment assistance', in R. Komiya *et al.*, 1988.
Seth, R. and Quijano, A.M., 'Growth in Japanese lending and direct investment in the United States: are they related?' *Japan and the World Economy*, 5, 363–72, 1993.

Shafer, J.R., Elmeskov, J. and Tease, W. 'Saving trends and measurement issues', *Scandinavian Journal of Economics*, 94, 2: 155–75, 1990.

Sheard, P., 'Auto-production systems in Japan: organisational and location features', *Australian Geographical Studies*, April 1983.

Sheard, P., (a) 'The Economics of Japanese Corporate Organisation and the "Structural Impediments" Debate: A Critical Review', *Pacific Economic Papers*, Australia–Japan Research Centre, 205, March 1992.

Sheard, P., (b) *International Adjustment and the Japanese Firm*, Sydney, Allen and Unwin, 1992.

Sheard, P., 'Keiretsu and closedness of the Japanese market: an economic appraisal', Centre for Japanese Economic Studies Working Paper 93–5, Sydney, Macquarie University, 1993.

Sheard, P., 'Interlocking shareholders and corporate governance in Japan', in M. Aoki and R. Dore, 1994.

Sheridan, K., *Governing the Japanese Economy*, Cambridge, Polity Press, 1993.

Shibuya, H., 'Japan's household savings: a life-cycle model with implicit annuity contract and rational expectations', manuscript, International Monetary Fund, February 1988.

Shigehara, K. 'Some reflections on monetary policy issues in Japan' *Bank of Japan Monetary and Economic Studies*, September 1990.

Shimada, H., 'Japanese capitalism: the irony of success', *Japan Echo*, XIX, 2, Summer, 1992.

Shimokawa, K., 'Japan's Keiretsu system: the case of the automobile industry', *Japanese Economic Studies*, XIII, 4, Summer, 1985.

Shinjo, K., 'The computer industry', in R. Komiya *et al.*, 1988.

Shinohara, K., 'Don't look up, the sky's falling', *Look Japan*, November 1992.

Smith, R.S., 'Factors affecting saving, policy tools, and tax reform: a review', *IMF Staff Papers*, 37, 1: 1–43, March 1990.

Smitka, M.J., 'Business-business relations: auto parts sourcing in Japan', in Joint Economic Committee Congress of US, 1990.

Stein, L., *Trade and Structural Change*, London, Croom Helm, 1984.

Stern, R., *Trade and Investment Relations Among the US, Canada and Japan*, Chicago, University of Chicago Press, 1989.

Steven, R., 'Structural origins of Japan's direct foreign investment', in E.J. Morris, 1991.

Sturm, P., 'Determinants of saving: theory and evidence', *OECD Economic Studies*, Autumn, 1: 147–96, 1983.

Sullivan, J.J., *Invasion of the Salarymen: the Japanese Business Presence in America*, Westport, Praeger, 1992.

Suzuki, Y., 'Japan's monetary policy over the past ten years', *Bank of Japan Monetary and Economic Studies*, September 1985.

Suzuki, Y., *The Japanese Financial System*, Oxford, Clarendon Press, 1987.

Suzuki, Y., 'Prospects for the Japanese', unpublished paper, Tokyo, Nomura Research Institute, April 1995.

Suzumura, K. and Okuno-Fujiwara, M., 'Industrial Policy in Japan: Overview and Evaluation', *Pacific Economic Paper*, 146, Australia–Japan Research Centre, Canberra, April 1987.

Tachibanaki, T., 'Labour market flexibility in Japan in comparison with Europe and the US', *European Economic Review*, 31, 647–84, 1987.

Tachiki, D.S. and Aoki, A., 'The competitive status of Japanese subsidiaries', *RIM*, IV, 18, 1992.

Takahashi, E., 'Household daily life', *Japan Update,* April 1994.

Takaoka, H., 'Present status and impact of Japan's investment in manufacturing industries in the United States', *Exim Review*, 11, 1, 1991.

Takeda, M. and Turner, P., 'The Liberalisation of Japan's Financial Markets' *Economic Papers*, No. 34, November, Basle Bank For International Settlements, 1992.

Takeuchi, J., 'Foreign direct investment in ASEAN by small and medium-sized Japanese companies', *RIM*, IV, 22, 1993.

Takeuchi, K., 'Does Japanese direct foreign investment promote Japanese imports from developing countries?', Working Paper No. 458, International Economics Department, World Bank, Washington, June 1990.

Tambunlertchai, S. and Ramstetter, E.D., 'Foreign firms in promoted industries and structural change in Thailand', in E.D. Ramstetter, 1991.

Tanaka, H., 'Overseas direct investment and trade: investment by Japanese consumer electrical appliance industries in ASEAN and the import of such products into Japan', *Exim Review*, 13, 1, December 1993.

Tanaka, N., 'Aluminum refining industry', in R. Komiya *et al.*, 1988.

Taylor, J., 'Differences in economic fluctuations in Japan and the United States', *Journal of the Japanese and International Economies*, 3, 127–44, 1989.

Tejima, S., 'Japanese foreign direct investment in the 1980s and its prospects for the 1990s', *Exim Review*, 11, 2, July 1992.

Tejima, S., 'Future prospects of Japanese foreign direct investment in the 1990s', *Exim Review*, 13, 1, December 1993.

Tejima, S., *et al.*, 'The recent trends of Japanese foreign direct investment', *Exim Review*, 14, November 1994.

Tezuka, K., 'The foreign worker problem in Japan', *Japanese Economic Studies* 21, 1, Autumn, 1992.

Thomsen, S., 'Japanese direct investment in the European community: the product cycle revisited', *The World Economy*, 16, 3, May, 1993.

Tobin, J.T., *Re-made in Japan*, New Haven, Yale University, 1992.

Tokunaga, S. (a), 'Japan's FDI-promoting systems and intra-Asia networks: new investment and trade systems, created by the Borderless Economy', in S. Tokunaga, 1992.

Tokunaga, S. (b), *Japan's Foreign Investment and Asian Economic Interdependence*, Tokyo, University of Tokyo Press, 1992.

Toyota Motor Corporation, 'Production at Toyota', 1991.

Trezise, V.H. and Suzuki, Y., 'Politics, government and economic growth in Japan', in H. Patrick and H. Rosovsky (eds), *Asia's New Giant: How the Japanese Economy Works*, Washington, Brookings Institution, 1976.

Tsuru, S., *Japan's Capitalism: Creative Defeat and Beyond*, Cambridge, Cambridge University Press, 1993.

Tsuruta, T., 'The rapid growth ERA' in R. Komiya *et al.*, 1988.

Turner, P., 'Japan and Europe as trading partners: retrospect and prospect', Centre for Japanese Economic Studies, *Working Paper Series* 91/2, Sydney, Macquarie University, 1991.

Tweeten, L., *et al.*, *Japanese and American Agriculture*, Boulder, Westview Press, 1993.

364                                   *Bibliography*

Tyson, L.D., *Who's Bashing Whom? Trade Conflict in High-Technology Industries*, Washington, Institute for International Economics, 1992.
Tyson, L. and Zysman, J., 'Developmental strategy and production innovation in Japan', in C. Johnson, L.D. Tyson and J. Zysman, 1987.
Tyson, L.D. and Zysman, J., 'The argument outlined', in C. Johnson, L.D. Tyson and J. Zysman, 1989.
Uekusa, M. 'Industrial organisation: the 1970s to the present', in K. Yamamura and Y. Yasuba, *The Political Economy of Japan, Vol. 1, The Domestic Transformation*, Stanford, Stanford University Press, 1987.
Uekusa, M., 'The oil crisis and after' in R. Komiya *et al.*, 1988.
Uekusa, M., 'Government regulations in Japan', in K. Yamamura, 1990.
Uekusa, M., 'The privatization of public enterprises', in K. Imai and R. Komiya, 1994.
Ueno, H., 'Industrial policy: its role and limits', *Journal of Japanese Trade and Industry*, July–August 1983.
UNIDO (United Nations Industrial Development Organization), *Malaysia*, Geneva, 1994.
Urata, S., 'The rapid increase of direct investment abroad and structural change in Japan', in E.D. Ramstetter, 1991.
Urata, S., 'Japanese foreign direct investment and its effects on foreign trade in Asia', in Ito and Krueger, 1993.
Urata, S., 'Changing patterns of direct investment and the implications for trade and development', in Bergsten and Noland, Pacific, 1993.
Uyehara, C.H., 'Appraising Japanese science and technology', in Joint Economic Committee Congress of the US, October 1990.
Van der Meer, L.J. and Yamada, S., *Japanese Agriculture*, Routledge, London, 1990.
Van Wolferen, K., *The Enigma of Japanese Power: People and Power and Politics in a Stateless Nation*, London, Macmillan, 1990.
Vestal, J.E., *Planning for Change: Industrial Policy and Japanese Economic Development, 1945–1990*, Oxford, Clarendon Press, 1993.
Vogel, D., 'Consumer protection and protectionism in Japan', *Journal of Japanese Studies*, 18, 1, 1992.
Vogel, E.F., *Japan as Number One: Lessons for America*, Cambridge, Harvard University Press, 1979.
Wagner, H.M., 'Alternatives of disinflation and stability policy', *Bank of Japan Monetary and Economic Studies*, April 1989.
Wailes, E.J., Young, K.B. and Cramer, G.L., 'Rice and food security in Japan: an American perspective', in E.D. Tweeten *et al.*, 1993.
Wakasugi, R., 'Is Japanese foreign direct investment a substitute for international trade?', *Japan and the World Economy*, 6, 45–52, 1994.
Wassmann, W. and Yamamura, K., 'Do Japanese firms behave differently?' in Yamamura, 1989.
Watanabe, C., 'Japanese industrial development', *Australian Journal of Public Administration*, 49, 3, September 1990.
Watanabe, C. and Honda, Y., 'Japanese industrial science and technology policy in the 1990s', *Japan and the World Economy*, 4, 1, 1992.
Watanabe, S., 'Trends in Japan's manufacturing investment in the United States', *Exim Review*, 7, 2, 1987.

Watanabe, S., 'Restructuring of the Japanese National Railways: implications for Labour', *International Labour Review*, 133, 1, 1994.

Watanabe, T., 'National planning and economic development: a critical review of the Japanese experience', *Economics of Planning*, 10, 1–2, 1970.

Watanabe, Y., 'The new phase of Japan's land, housing and pollution problems', *Japanese Economic Studies*, 20, 4, Summer, 1992.

Weil, D.N., 'What determines savings? a review essay', *Journal of Monetary Economics*, North-Holland, 28: 161–70, 1991.

Wie, Thee Kian, 'Japanese direct investment in Indonesian manufacturing', *Bulletin of Indonesian Economic Studies*, August 1984.

Wolff, A.W., 'US–Japan relations and the rules of law', in K. Yamamura, 1990.

Wong, Kar-Yiu, 'The Japanese challenge: Japanese direct investment in the United States', in K. Yamamura, 1989.

Wood, C., *The Bubble Economy*, London, Sidgwick and Jackson, 1992.

World Bank, *World Development Report 1990*, Washington, World Bank, 1990.

World Bank, *World Development Report 1994*, Washington, DC, World Bank, 1994.

Woronoff, J., *World Trade War*, Tokyo, Lotus Press, 1983.

Woronoff, J., *Japan as Anything But Number One*, London, Macmillan, 1990.

Yagi, M., 'The political economy of Japan–US automobile friction', *Centre for Japanese Economic Studies*, Sydney, Macquarie University, September, 1992.

Yaginuma, H., 'The Keiretsu issue: a theoretical approach', *Japanese Economic Studies* 21, 3, Spring, 1993.

Yamada, T. *et al.*, 'Productivity of Japanese manufacturing industries and their market competition', in *Joint Economic Committee Congress of the US*, October 1990.

Yamamura, K., *Japanese Investment in the United States: Should We be Concerned?*, Seattle, Society for Japanese Studies, 1989.

Yamamura, K., *Japan's Economic Structure: Should it Change?*, Seattle, Society for Japanese Economic Studies, 1990.

Yamamura, K. and Yasuba, Y. *The Political Economy of Japan, Vol. 1, The Domestic Transformation*, Stanford, Stanford University Press, 1987.

Yamanoi, K., 'There's no place like home?' *Look Japan*, January 1993.

Yamamura, Y., 'The Japanese model of political economy' in K. Yamamura and Y. Yasuba, 1987.

Yamashita, S., *Transfer of Japanese Technology and Management to the Asian Countries*, Tokyo, University of Tokyo Press, 1991.

Yamawaki, H. 'The steel industry', in R. Komiya *et al.*, 1988.

Yamawaki, H., 'Exports and foreign distributional activities: evidence on Japanese firms in the United States', *Review of Economics and Statistics*, 73, 294–9, 1991.

Yamazawa, I., 'The textile industry', in R. Komiya *et al.*, 1988.

Yano, I., 'Nippon a charted survey of Japan', 1989/90, Tsuneta Yano Memorial Society, Tokyo, 1991.

Yokokura, T., 'Small and medium enterprises', in R. Komiya *et al.*, 1988.

Yonenezawa, Y., 'The shipbuilding industry', in R. Komiya *et al.*, 1988.

Yoshida, M., 'Characteristics of foreign direct investment in Thailand', in S. Tokunaga, 1992.
Yoshihara, K., *Japanese investment in Southeast Asia*, Honolulu, University Press of Hawaii, 1978.
Yoto, A. and Wakasugi, R., 'Technology policy' in R. Komiya *et al.*, 1988.
Yutaka, H., 'Deregulation and the price gap', *Japan Echo*, Spring 1995.
Zysman, J., 'Contribution or crisis: Japanese foreign direct investment in the United States', in K. Yamamura, 1989.


NEWSPAPERS AND PERIODICALS

*The Australian*
*The Economist*
*The Financial Times*
*The Guardian Weekly*
*The Japan Times*
*The Lancet*
*Nikkei Weekly Review*
*Sydney Morning Herald*
*Time*
*Tokyo Business Today*
*Tokyo Business Trading*

# Index

367